Aug. 2000

Michelle

THE
ONE YEAR®
BOOK OF
Devotions
for
Kids
#3

Tyndale House Publishers, Inc., Wheaton, Illinois

Visit Tyndale's exciting Web site at www.tyndale.com

Edited by Debbie Bible

Stories written by Katherine R. Adams, Susan S. Arcand, Elzena A. Arguello, Esther M. Bailey, Lisa A. Baird, Shari L. Barr, Michael R. Blackman, Ruth E. Blount, Judith K. Boogaart, Kathy A. Brand, Carol J. Brookman, Julie J. Brooks, Gail D. Brown, Wanda E. Brunstetter, Daniel A. Burns, Jane K. Chase, Karen E. Cogan, Mildred P. Colvin, Rosalie J. Currier, Mary L. De Mott, Carol A. DeCesare, Harriet A. Durrell, T. Suzanne Eller, Teresa J. Ellifrits, Bethany R. Elms, Helen C. Eshleman, Nancy J. Ferrier, Dean A. Fowler, Hope L. Funderberg, Cathy L. Garnaat, Dianne V. Godbold, Cynthia M. Graybill, Sheila M. Green, Jeane K. Greiser, Jonnye R. Griffin, Veronica R. Guerriero, Jan L. Hansen, Mary Kay Harllee, Nancy G. Hill, Christine P. Honey, Beth R. Hopper, Ed J. Horton, Vera M. Hutchcroft, Ruth I. Jay, Pam E. Jones, Christi B. Kehn, Nance E. Keyes, Emily C. King, Bonnie L. Kinne, Dell S. Klein, Phyllis I. Klomparens, Daryl B. Knauer, Manfred T. Koehler, Carolyn L. Kridiotis, Sherry L. Kuyt, Bertha E. Laird, Jacqueline J. Leacraft, Dolores A. Lemieux, Lynne M. Lepley, Karen R. Locklear, Myra J. Luetje, Richard S. Maffeo, Linda M. Magoon, Deborah S. Marett, Hazel W. Marett, Lorna B. Marlowe, Tanya K. Marshall, Elva M. Martin, Della D. May, Myrina D. McCullough, Ruth McQuilken, Valerae C. Murphy, Sarah L. Nelson, Bill K. O'Connor, Elaine M. Okupski, Linda J. Opp, Mary Rose Pearson, Raelene E. Phillips, Cynthia Y. Powell, Margaret M. Primrose, Mark L. Redmond, Victoria L. Reinhardt, Pat L. Rennie, Brenda M. Rice, Lucinda J. Rollings, Shelly L. Russworm, Marlo M. Schalesky, Doris J. Schuchard, A. J. Schut, Doris L. Seger, Patricia C. Singletary, Nita M. Smiley, Steven R. Smith, Winona W. Smith, Dorellen Smith-Belleau, Linda R. Stai, Irene C. Strobel, Sam L. Sullivan, Lois A. Teufel, Betty J. Thomas, Mary Ellen Uthlant, Charlie VanderMeer, Trudy VanderVeen, Sandy K. Vaughn, Rebecca L. Velez, Lyndel F. Walker, Linda M. Weddle, Barbara J. Westberg, Karen H. Whiting, Deborah L. Whitsitt, Bonnie L. Winters, Carolyn E. Yost, Letitia L. Zook.

Author's initials appear at the end of each story.

All stories are taken from issues of *Keys for Kids,* published bimonthly by the Children's Bible Hour, P. O. Box 1, Grand Rapids, Michigan 49501.

Library of Congress Cataloging-in-Publication Data

The One year book of devotions for kids.
    p. cm.
    Includes Indexes.
    Summary: A collection of devotions for each day of the calendar year, including readings, illustrative stories, memory verses, and questions to internalize the messages.
    ISBN 0-8423-5087-X (#1-pbk.)
    ISBN 0-8423-4592-2 (#2-pbk.)
    ISBN 0-8423-4662-7 (#3-pbk.)
    1. Devotional calendars—Juvenile literature. 2. Children—Prayer books and devotions—English. [1. Devotional calendars. 2. Prayer books and devotions. 3. Christian life.]
BV4870.064 1993
242'.682—dc20
                   93-15786

Printed in the United States of America

03 02 01 00
7   6   5

Table of Contents

D E C E M B E R

Introduction

For many years Children's Bible Hour has published *Keys for Kids*, a bimonthly devotional magazine for kids. Their fine ministry to parents and children has been appreciated over the years, and Tyndale House is proud to present this third collection of stories from *Keys for Kids*.

The One Year Book of Devotions for Kids #3 has a full year's worth of stories, each illustrating a Scripture reading for the day. Following each story is a "How about you?" section; this asks children to apply the story to their lives.

There is also a memory verse for each day, usually taken from the Scripture reading. Unless otherwise noted, memory verses are quoted from the New Living Translation. Verses marked NIV are from the New International Version, those marked NKJV are from the New King James Version, and verses marked KJV are from the King James Version. You may want to encourage your children to memorize the verses as they appear, or have them use the Bible translation your family prefers.

Each devotion ends with a "key." This two- to five-word phrase summarizes the lesson.

The stories in this devotional are geared toward children between the ages of eight and fourteen. Kids can enjoy these stories by themselves as they develop their own daily quiet time. (You can supervise that time as much or as little as you wish.) Or the stories can be used as part of your family devotions. Like stories from the Bible, the stories here speak not only to children but also to adults. They are simple, direct, and concrete; and they speak to everyone in understandable terms just as Jesus' parables do.

This book contains Scripture indexes of daily readings and of memory verses as well as a topical index. The Scripture indexes are helpful for locating a story or verse related to a passage that you want to discuss. The topical index is useful for dealing with concerns that arise in any family such as moving, illness, and the loss of a friend or family member.

We hope that you'll use this book every day, but don't feel locked into any one format. Please use any story any time you feel it relates to a special situation in your family.

I Resolve (Read Psalm 28:6-9)

"Russ," called Mother, "please go out and shovel the walk before Grandma and Grandpa come."

"Just a minute," replied Russ. He continued to read over his list of New Year's resolutions. *I resolve to do my chores without grumbling. I resolve to obey promptly. I resolve not to quarrel with . . .*

"Russ!" called Mother a second time. At the third call, he finally got to his feet, pulled on his coat, and went out to get the shovel.

1

JANUARY

"Don't see why I always get stuck with the shoveling," he muttered unhappily. He finished the job just as his sister came out to play. "Oh, now you come out, when the work is all done," he said. "You could've helped!"

"Why should I? It's your job," she retorted. She climbed the snowbank at the side of the walk and slid down.

"Hey!" shrieked Russ. "You're messing up the walk again!" He threatened to hit her with a snowball, but just then their grandparents arrived, and he greeted them with a big grin.

Later that day Russ brought out his list of resolutions. "Want to see my New Year's resolutions, Grandma?" he asked.

"So you've made resolutions, have you?" asked Grandma. She looked them over. "And how are you doing?" she wanted to know. "Have you kept them so far?"

Russ was startled. He knew he hadn't. He had grumbled about his chores, he hadn't obeyed promptly, and he had quarreled with his sister. *Oh, what's the use?* he thought as he admitted that already—before even one day of the new year had passed—he had broken his resolutions.

"Let's see now," said Grandma. "How does each of your resolutions begin?"

"Why," said Russ, "they say, 'I resolve . . .'"

"Whoa!" exclaimed Grandma. "There's your trouble. The big 'I.' You're trying to do these things in your own strength, and you can't. You need the strength of the Lord to help you. He'll help if you'll ask him." *HWM*

HOW ABOUT YOU?

Have you made resolutions? Wanting to improve is good, but resolving to do it is not always enough. If you are a Christian, you have a source of strength always available to you. Ask God to help you. He will.

MEMORIZE:

"Don't be afraid, for I am with you. Do not be dismayed, for I am your God. I will strengthen you. I will help you. I will uphold you with my victorious right hand." *Isaiah 41:10*

 **Use God's Strength**

God and Mountains (Read John 20:26-31)

2
JANUARY

Paul and his dad got up early to hike the valley below the Teton Mountains. As Paul looked at the glistening snow-capped mountains, his dad took pictures. "What a wonderful God we have to create this beauty!" exclaimed Dad.

Paul was quiet a moment. Then he said, "I wish my friend Ben was here. He says God doesn't exist since we can't see him. Maybe seeing these mountains would convince him."

"You could show him some pictures of the mountains," suggested Dad. "He won't be able to see the mountains—just the pictures. But I'm sure he'll understand that, even though we can't see the mountains from our house, it doesn't mean the mountains don't exist. And—"

"And it's the same with God, right?" interrupted Paul eagerly.

"Right," agreed Dad.

Paul continued, "But we'll have pictures to remind us of the mountains. We don't have real pictures of Jesus."

"No," agreed Dad. "But we do have the Bible, and we have faith in God. The Bible tells us about the life and teaching of Jesus—how he came in human form to the earth long ago and was crucified. He died and was buried, but he rose again. After he arose, his disciples saw him. Since he returned to heaven, those of us on earth can't physically see him anymore, but we have the true stories from those who did see him."

Paul nodded. "I know what I'll tell Ben when we get home," he said thoughtfully. "I'll tell him he can learn about our trip from looking at our pictures and listening to me. And he can learn about Jesus from looking at the Bible and listening to its stories. Even though we can't see Jesus, we know he still exists." *KEC*

HOW ABOUT YOU?

Do you remember that Jesus is just as alive today as he was when he walked the earth? Even though we cannot see him with human eyes, his teachings are just as real now as they were during the time of the disciples. He is the Author of life and Conqueror of death.

MEMORIZE:

"What is faith? It is the confident assurance that what we hope for is going to happen. It is the evidence of things we cannot yet see." *Hebrews 11:1*

 *Live by Faith*

Keep Knocking (Read Luke 18:1-8)

"Amen." As the Anderson family ended their devotions, Beth stretched. "Every night we pray for Mrs. Gerard, but she just gets meaner," she observed. "I'm tired of praying for her."

"Me too," agreed Zack. "Yesterday she yelled at me because my ball bounced into her yard."

"All the more reason to pray for her," said Dad. "God says we are to pray for those who are mean to us. Besides, Mrs. Gerard may be closer to becoming a Christian than you realize." He reached for his coat. "Who wants to go to the post office with me?"

3
JANUARY

"I do," Zack answered.

Mother replied, "I'll stay here and help Beth shampoo her hair."

"We won't be long," Dad promised.

Soon Beth's hair was a mountain of suds. She squeezed her eyes shut. "I think I hear the doorbell," she murmured.

Mother stopped the shampooing and listened. "Oh, dear," she said as she reached for a towel. She dried her hands. "I'm coming! I'm coming!" she called as the bell rang again.

Beth looked at her mother. Some sudsy water rolled into one eye. "Ohhh, I got soap in my eye."

Mother handed her the towel. "Just sit still," said Mother. "I'll be back in a minute."

Beth rubbed her eye gently as she waited. In a few seconds Mother returned. "Who was it?" Beth asked.

Mother shrugged as she turned on the faucet to rinse Beth's hair. "I don't know," she said. "They drove off just as I got to the door."

Beth wrapped a towel around her head. Her mother smiled. "This reminds me of our conversation about Mrs. Gerard."

"How?" asked Beth.

"Well, those people in the car gave up just before I answered the door and—"

"Maybe God is just about to answer our prayers for Mrs. Gerard!" finished Beth.

"Exactly," answered Mother. *BJW*

HOW ABOUT YOU?

Have you been praying for someone for a long time? Are you getting discouraged? Don't quit. Keep praying.

MEMORIZE:

"Men always ought to pray and not lose heart." *Luke 18:1,* NKJV

 *Keep Praying*

The Broken Cup (Read Romans 12:1-2, 9)

The cup slipped from Janice's hands and crashed to the floor. "Oh no!" she gasped. And then she said a swear word under her breath.

"Janice Richard!" exclaimed Grandma, who was washing dishes while Janice wiped them. "I've told you not to say words like that."

"Oh, Grandma, it's not a bad word," protested Janice, picking up pieces of the broken cup. "Everybody at school says it."

"I don't care who says it," answered Grandma. "It's still wrong to talk like that. Now, when you've picked up all the pieces, sit down at the table." Grandma left to get a tube of glue. "I want you to put those pieces together again," she said as she entered the kitchen.

Janice worked a long time. Finally she was finished, but the cup didn't look like it had before. There were small crack lines everywhere. "Grandma, is this good enough?" she asked. "I can't make it look any better."

"No, you can't, honey," agreed Grandma. "But after the glue hardens we'll be able to use it again. You know, to God our lives probably look a lot like this cup. We all do wrong things. And each time we do, there are consequences. The consequences are like the cracks in this cup. A consequence might be the sick feeling in your stomach when you know you've done something you shouldn't have."

"Or like the scar on my finger from when Mom told me not to touch the hot stove and I did anyway?" asked Janice.

"Yes," answered Grandma. "Even though God promises to forgive us for the wrong things we do, we have to live with the consequences."

Janice looked at the cup. "But it's so hard not to do what the other kids are doing."

Grandma nodded. "But Jesus can help you choose to do right."

"Grandma, may I take this cup to school to remind me to do what is right?" asked Janice.

"That's a great idea," Grandma replied. *BKO*

HOW ABOUT YOU?

Do you follow the example of your friends only when they're doing the right things? When what they're doing is wrong, ask Jesus to help you resist the temptation to join in. Trust him to help you do and say the right things.

MEMORIZE:

"Hate what is wrong. Stand on the side of the good." *Romans 12:9*

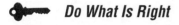 **Do What Is Right**

If Takes Two (Read Luke 6:27-35)

5

JANUARY

"That Keith Gordon really makes me mad!" said Joe as he sat in the living room with his mom. "He's always saying mean things to me."

Just then, four-year-old Ted came into the room. "Play catch with me, Joey," he begged.

"Not now," replied Joe.

"Catch this, Joey!" interrupted Ted as he threw a soft, foam ball into Joe's lap.

Joe looked at Ted angrily. "I told you I don't want to play right now," he said as he tossed the ball back. Undaunted, Ted threw it right back. Now Joe was really annoyed. "Cut it out!" he shouted, throwing the ball to the other side of the room. With a happy grin, Ted ran to retrieve it from under a table. He tossed it to Joe.

"Make him stop!" whined Joe in disgust. "He's driving me crazy!" He kicked the ball in Ted's direction.

"That's obvious," said Mother dryly. "But it's your fault, too, you know."

"My fault?" objected Joe. "He's the one who keeps throwing the ball!"

"But you're the one who keeps throwing it back," she said. "It takes two to keep the ball going. Next time he throws it," whispered Mother, "put the ball down on the floor."

Joe looked doubtful, but he followed his mother's suggestion. Sure enough, Ted soon grew tired of playing a one-person game and went off to do something else.

"Now, about your problem with Keith," she said. "I think you're part of the problem there, too. It sounds like Keith enjoys throwing mean words your way so you'll . . ."

"Throw angry ones back," finished Joe. "Maybe if I ignore him, he'll quit."

"Maybe," answered Mom. "That would certainly be a step in the right direction. And you could also try saying nice things to him occasionally. Who knows, maybe you and Keith will one day be friends." *SLK*

HOW ABOUT YOU?

Remember, it takes two to make a quarrel. When someone irritates you, why not try saying something nice instead of responding in anger? You'll be surprised at the difference it sometimes makes.

MEMORIZE:

"A gentle answer turns away wrath, but harsh words stir up anger."

Proverbs 15:1

 **Don't Return Insults**

True Strength (Read Mark 15:1-5)

6

Sarah listened with a sick feeling in her stomach as her friend Marie taunted her. "What a goody-goody you are. You think you're so much better than I am, now that you go to church all the time." Marie scowled and turned her back to Sarah.

Sarah started to say something mean to Marie. She knew this wasn't right. But Sarah wanted to hurt Marie for embarrassing her in front of their friends. She felt stupid just standing there quietly. Finally, Sarah just walked away.

That afternoon, Sarah talked with her mom about the problem with Marie. "I felt so stupid," Sarah said. "I looked like I was too dumb to think of anything to say."

Mom nodded. "It's hard to keep mean words back when you're hurt or embarrassed, isn't it?" she sympathized. After a moment she added, "I suppose Jesus felt that way when people told lies about him. He could have said mean things back, but he didn't. And I'm proud of you for doing the same. It took a lot of strength to do that."

Sarah thoughtfully twirled a strand of red hair around her finger. "I guess I never thought about how strong Jesus had to be to do nothing!" she said. "But, Mom, does that mean I shouldn't ever stand up for myself?"

"Oh no, Sarah," said Mom. "There are times when you will be angry and you will need to stand up. Being angry is not wrong. It's how you handle your anger that is important. Now let's think, what could you have said to Marie without being mean?"

"I could have said, 'I don't think I'm better than you, but I'm sorry you feel that way,'" suggested Sarah.

"That would have been a good thing to say, Sarah," said Mom. "I think you will do fine the next time something like this happens. God will help you know what to say. And remember, it takes more strength to speak gently than to yell in anger." *MLD*

HOW ABOUT YOU?

Do you think you're acting strong when you speak out in anger? Jesus demonstrated that true strength is shown by self-control. When someone hurts your feelings or embarrasses you, ask God to help you know how to answer. He will!

MEMORIZE:

"God blesses those who are gentle and lowly, for the whole earth will belong to them." *Matthew 5:5*

 Being Gentle Takes Strength

Heaping Coals (Read Romans 12:17-21)

Kevin entered the boys' locker room. He stopped in his tracks when Corey, one of his classmates, looked up. Quickly, Kevin retreated to his own locker. Corey slammed his locker shut. Then he banged Kevin's locker as he passed by on his way out.

Kevin sat on the bench a long time. *Corey doesn't have to be such a poor sport just because his team lost to mine in gym class,* he thought.

As Kevin walked home, a car pulled up beside him. "Need a ride?" called a voice. It was Mr. Williams, his Sunday school teacher. Kevin smiled and got in. He enjoyed talking with Mr. Williams. He told him about the way Corey had been treating him. "I want to get even with Corey," said Kevin. "But I know you think I shouldn't."

Mr. Williams was quiet for a moment. "I think," he said, "you should heap hot coals on his head." Kevin looked up in surprise. Mr. Williams grinned. "The Bible says to do that," he said. "In Bible times, people needed fires to cook food and to keep warm. Sometimes their fires would go out. There were no matches back then, so the easiest way to start a fire was to get hot coals from someone else. Historians tell us that a person needing to start a fire would place a container on his or her head and walk by everyone's windows. Some people would show kindness by placing a few hot coals from their own fires in the container. So when Jesus says we should 'heap coals of fire' on the heads of our enemies, he's telling us . . ."

"To be kind to them," Kevin answered as they pulled up in front of his house.

"That's it, Kevin," said Mr. Williams. "But being kind doesn't mean we let other people hurt us all the time. It can mean doing something nice for a person, walking away from a fight, or standing up for yourself in a way that doesn't hurt the other person."

"I'll think about what you said. And Mr. Williams, thanks a 'heap,'" Kevin said as he got out of the car. *CAD*

JANUARY 7

HOW ABOUT YOU?

Do you feel like being kind to people who mistreat you? Probably not . . . but the Bible tells us to be kind. Maybe a small note or a smile would help.

MEMORIZE:

"Don't let evil get the best of you, but conquer evil by doing good."

Romans 12:21

 Be Kind to Enemies

A Young Real Estate Agent

(Read Revelation 21:22-27)

8

JANUARY

By the time Steve learned that his school was called off for the day because of a furnace breakdown, his mother had already left for a long day of shopping. Steve's father, who was a real estate agent, looked thoughtful. "You can go to work with me, Steve," he said decidedly.

So Steve went to the office with his dad and met Mr. and Mrs. Harris, who were looking for a house. Dad explained why Steve was with him.

"No problem." Mrs. Harris smiled. "We have three sons—one is just about the same age as Steve," she said.

Steve did not like the first house they went to see. It was too fancy-looking for him. The second house looked dark, and the rooms were small.

"Now, this is my kind of house," Steve announced when they reached the third place. "Look at that creek and all those climbing trees!" Steve was excited about the inside of the house, too. "There are lots of hiding places here," he declared with shining eyes.

Mr. Harris laughed. "I think you made a sale, Steve. I imagine if you like this house, our boys will like it, too."

That evening Steve took his Sunday school workbook to his father. "You're not going to believe this, Dad," he said. "Look what we're supposed to do for part of our lesson—write a real estate ad for heaven! Wanna see what I wrote?"

Dad took the book. "Sure," he agreed. He smiled as he read aloud, "A mansion built for you on a golden street. No bedrooms, for there is no night. No hospitals nearby, because there is no sickness. The entire city is decorated with fabulous jewels. Cost: Nothing! It is a gift from the Lord Jesus Christ." Dad grinned as he returned the book. "Great!" he said. "But remember, your best ad for heaven is . . ."

"My actions!" finished Steve.   *LMW*

HOW ABOUT YOU?

Have you ever read a real estate ad? Ads can make things sound very attractive. The heavenly piece of real estate described in the Bible sounds the most attractive of all, but not everyone reads about it. How well do you advertise it by your actions?

MEMORIZE:

"The city does not need the sun or the moon to shine on it, for the glory of God gives it light, and the Lamb is its lamp." *Revelation 21:23,* NIV

 Advertise Heaven by Actions

Hidden Berries (Read Psalm 119:9-16)

9

John tried not to laugh, but when Joe made a funny face, he just couldn't hold it back. Mrs. Smith, the Sunday school teacher, gave them a stern look. The other kids in class grinned. No one was listening to the Bible story. They'd heard it before. Then Mrs. Smith said, "How many of you went berry picking last summer?" John, Joe, and several others raised their hands. "Do you like fresh berry pie?" asked Mrs. Smith. Even John and Joe were listening now.

"Well, one day last summer, I saw some blackberry bushes," she said. "There didn't seem to be many berries, but I got a container and began to pick them anyway. As I worked, I noticed a few berries hiding under some leaves," continued Mrs. Smith. "I picked those, and then I saw even more berries hiding under some other leaves. It seemed that the closer I looked at those bushes, the more berries I found. There were so many more than I had seen at first!"

Mrs. Smith paused and smiled. "Did you know that hearing stories from the Bible is sometimes like picking berries? How could that be?" she asked.

Joe answered, "At first when you listen to a Bible story, it seems like just a nice story. But maybe if you looked closer at the story and thought about it, you would find more interesting things there."

"That's right, Joe," Mrs. Smith agreed. "What kinds of things, John?"

"Well, things that will help you know God better and love him more."

"That's right," answered Mrs. Smith. "Now, let's go over today's Bible story again and see how many 'hidden berries,' or interesting things about God, we can find." This time as Mrs. Smith retold the story, John and Joe listened in a different way. They wanted to see what new things they could discover. *CEY*

HOW ABOUT YOU?

Do you get bored when you hear a Bible story you've heard often before? How could you listen differently? In this new year, see how many "hidden berries," or new things, you can find in your Sunday school lessons.

MEMORIZE:

"Open my eyes to see the wonderful truths in your law." *Psalm 119:18*

 Look Closely for God's Lessons

Best Friend (Read John 15:13-17)

10
JANUARY

"Mom, I don't think I want to be Amanda's best friend anymore!" Kristi announced as she came in from school. "In fact, I don't know if I want to be friends with her at all."

Mom looked up from the salad she was preparing for supper. "Really?" she asked. "When did you decide that, Kristi?"

"Today. You just won't believe how she acted!" Kristi helped herself to an apple from the fruit bowl and plopped down on a chair. "I wanted to tell Amanda about my weekend, but she hardly talked to me all day," she said. "During the first recess, she played baseball with some other kids. Then when we had free time in class, she worked on a special project all by herself. Usually we have lots of time to talk at lunch, but during lunch, she talked to the new girl in class the whole time. Then we sat together on the bus, but she read her book on the way home."

"Sounds like a rough day," observed Mom, "but I hope you won't let one day ruin your friendship."

That evening at family devotions, Kristi had a request. "May I be excused from our prayer time tonight?" she asked. "I'm really tired, and I just don't feel like praying right now. Besides, I have a test tomorrow, so I need to get my sleep."

"Hmmm," murmured Mom. "Remember what you told me about Amanda today?" Kristi looked puzzled as she nodded. "Well, if you skip prayer time, won't you be acting pretty much like she did?" asked Mother. "You didn't like it that Amanda didn't have time for you today—you were even considering not being her friend anymore, right?" Slowly, Kristi nodded. "Since you asked Jesus into your heart, *he* is your very best friend," continued Mother. "He likes to have you talk to him each day, and prayer is the way we talk with him. When you don't want to pray, he misses spending time with you the way you missed spending time with Amanda today."

"Hmmm," said Kristi. "I never thought of it that way before. I think I'll stay." *ICS*

HOW ABOUT YOU?

Do you have a good friend you like to talk to? If you've asked Jesus to be your Savior, he wants to be your best friend. Do you talk to him in prayer often?

MEMORIZE:

"Devote yourselves to prayer with an alert mind and a thankful heart."

Colossians 4:2

 Talk with Jesus Each Day

When Parents Say No (Read Hebrews 12:5-11)

"Is your dad going to let you go to Jenny's all-night party?" asked Leslie as she and her friend Sara walked home from the park.

"No," said Sara. "He didn't really say why not . . . just that he didn't want me to go."

"My parents said no at first, too," replied Leslie, "but I told them how unfair that was and that they never trust me! They gave in and said I could go. Why don't you tell your dad how unfair he's being? Maybe he'll change his mind, too!"

Sara shook her head. "You know, Leslie, I really trust my dad," she said. "I guess since my mom left, I've realized how hard he's trying to make the right decisions for me. I know he has to say no sometimes. Maybe *you* should trust *your* parents more. Did you ever think that when they tell you no it's because that's what's best for you?"

Leslie frowned. "Oh, that's what they always say! But I don't believe it. I think it's mean to boss kids around."

By now the girls were on the sidewalk across from Leslie's house, and they turned to cross the street. Her dog, Lady, came running out to meet them. "Stop, Lady! NO!" Leslie yelled. Lady stopped right away. "Good dog!" approved Leslie when she reached her pet.

"You're sure mean to Lady!" said Sara. "She just wanted to come meet you."

"Mean?" asked Leslie in surprise. "I'm not mean. If I just let her run across the street, she might get hurt."

"So saying no was really for her good?" asked Sara with a smile.

"Of course it . . ." Leslie stopped. "OK . . . OK. I see your point," she said. "Parents sometimes have to say no, too." *SKV*

HOW ABOUT YOU?

Do you get angry or upset when your parents say no? God has given them the responsibility of making decisions regarding you. Even though you don't understand their reasons, trust them.

MEMORIZE:

"No discipline is enjoyable while it is happening—it is painful! But afterward there will be a quiet harvest of right living for those who are trained in this way." *Hebrews 12:11*

 Accept Parents' Decisions

The Right Diet (Read Philippians 4:4-9)

12

JANUARY

When Susan got home from school, Mother was taking chocolate chip cookies from the oven while Susan's little brother, Joey, watched.

Mother smiled. "You may each have a glass of milk and two cookies for a snack," she said.

Joey got his milk and eagerly took two cookies, but Susan shook her head.

"I'm getting ready to run an important track race, so I'm going to have only healthy snacks for the next week," she declared. She chose a banana and took it into the living room where she turned on the television and settled down to relax.

After a few minutes, Mother came into the room. "What are you watching?" she asked.

Susan blushed. "It's just an afternoon talk show. I'm going to turn it off and start on my homework as soon as I finish my banana."

Mother frowned as she watched the program for a moment. "You know we don't like for you to watch most of these shows," she said. "They are not the kind of thing you should be feeding your mind."

"I'm watching it for only a few minutes," protested Susan. "I don't think it's going to hurt me."

"You were so careful to choose a healthy snack today, and that was smart," said Mother. "You should feed your mind healthy things, too. The Bible says that the things you listen to and think about will determine what you become."

"Well, I don't want to become like the people on this program," agreed Susan. She turned off the television. "From now on, I'll try to be more careful about what I watch." *KEC*

HOW ABOUT YOU?

Are you careful about what you feed your mind? It's good to take care of your body and keep it healthy. It's important to take care of your mind, too. The television programs and music that you "feed" your mind can change the way you live and think.

MEMORIZE:

"Let heaven fill your thoughts. Do not think only about things down here on earth." *Colossians 3:2*

 "Feed" Your Mind Good Things

Go Down Deep (Read Proverbs 2:1-5)

13

JANUARY

Joshua was sprawled on his bed examining a stack of photographs when Dad looked into the room. Joshua glanced up. "Hey, Dad! Look at these pictures!" he exclaimed. "They're the ones Aunt Jenny took when she was deep-sea diving."

Dad peered over Joshua's shoulder. "What unusual plants and animals!" he exclaimed. "They're fascinating. And what vivid colors!" Together they examined the pictures. "God must have a wonderful imagination to create such a variety of life forms," added Dad.

Joshua nodded. "Aunt Jenny says the farther down in the ocean you go, the more beautiful it gets," he said. He paused and turned to his dad. "Why do you suppose God made such interesting creatures and then hid them down deep in the ocean where most people don't ever see them?"

Dad thought a moment. "I'm not sure," he said, "but when I see these pictures, it reminds me of what a great God we have. And somehow it also reminds me of the riches to be found in the Bible."

"The Bible!" exclaimed Joshua. "Why do these remind you of the Bible?"

"Well," said Dad, "when I was younger, I used to think personal devotions were rather unnecessary. I figured I'd already heard all those Bible stories."

"You probably had," said Joshua. "I have, too."

"Well, I'm sure we haven't actually heard them all," said Dad, "though we have heard a lot of them. But Aunt Jenny has seen the ocean many times, and yet she decided she wanted to go down deep to see what she could discover. Do you think she was rewarded for her efforts?"

"She sure was!" said Joshua as he looked at the pictures once more.

Dad nodded. "The point is if you and I go deep into God's Word and study it, God will reward us, too. He will reveal hidden knowledge, insights, and wisdom to those who are willing to dig deep into his Word." *LRS*

HOW ABOUT YOU?

Do you ever think that you know all you need to know about the Bible? If you spend more time reading and studying his Word, God will give you more knowledge about him and a greater understanding about life.

MEMORIZE:

"Work hard so God can approve you. Be a good worker, one who does not need to be ashamed and who correctly explains the word of truth."

2 Timothy 2:15

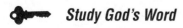 *Study God's Word*

Why, Dad? (Read Proverbs 4:1-11)

14

"Why can't I go sledding on Hill Street with the other kids?" Ken begged at supper one night. "Everybody else is allowed to go sledding there. I know you think it's dangerous, but I don't see why! There are hardly any cars on that street. Besides, the drivers usually go real slow. Matt's dad says they know kids like to play there."

Dad leaned back in his chair. "Well, Ken, that may be true," he said. "But when I was a boy, I had a bad experience on one of the hilly streets in our town. Didn't I ever tell you about that?"

Ken shook his head.

"We all would go sledding there," continued Dad. "Halfway between the top and bottom of the hill was a cross street, and we always had someone watching there to tell us whether or not the coast was clear. One day as I was going down the hill on my sled, the lookout told me no cars were coming. But just as I reached that intersection, a truck reached it, too. I was going fast, and there was no way I could stop. There was no way that truck could stop either because the streets were slippery. I slipped right under him, missing the tires by inches. Even now I can remember the fear, knowing how close I was to being killed—or at least seriously injured. That's why I don't want you sledding on the street. There may not be many cars, but it takes only one for a serious accident to happen."

"Wow, Dad, I never heard that story!" Ken exclaimed. "I can see now why you made that rule for me."

Dad smiled. "Parents usually have good reasons for the rules they make," he told Ken. "Sometimes you can understand them and sometimes you can't. The real test, Ken, is when you don't understand my reason but are still willing to obey me." *LMW*

HOW ABOUT YOU?

If you don't understand why your dad and mom made a certain rule, ask them to explain it to you. If you don't agree, remember that God says it's your responsibility to respect and obey those rules.

MEMORIZE:

"Listen, my child, to what your father teaches you. Don't neglect your mother's teaching." *Proverbs 1:8*

 Obey Your Parents

Dusty Gears (Read Psalm 51:1-12)

Jeremy stopped in at the jewelry repair shop where his Uncle Dick was just lifting a large metal clock down from a shelf. "Hello, there," called Uncle Dick. "Did you come to help me fix the chimes on this old clock?"

Jeremy grinned at his uncle. "I'll just watch," he said.

Uncle Dick opened the back of the clock, and in a few minutes he had found the problem. "Look here, Jeremy," he said. "These gears are the ones that control the chimes. They have little cogs that interlock so that as they turn, each gear turns the next gear. Then these tiny hammers can strike to sound the chimes. Can you see what the problem is here—why this old clock can't chime?"

15
JANUARY

Jeremy leaned closer. He liked to see all the little wheels and gears that moved in the old clocks. "Looks like there's dirt inside there," he said.

Uncle Dick nodded. "That's right. And all the dirt prevents the cogs from fitting together properly."

"That sounds simple to fix," remarked Jeremy.

"Shouldn't take too long," agreed Uncle Dick. Jeremy watched his uncle clean each cog. He talked as he worked. "Got any dust in your gears, Jeremy?"

"Huh?" Jeremy asked. "What do you mean?"

"Well, these clock gears are a lot like people," stated Uncle Dick. "Those who read their Bibles and put God first keep 'dust' from gathering in their 'cogs.' What do you suppose that 'dust' is?"

Jeremy thought about it. "I guess it must be sin."

"Right." Uncle Dick nodded. "When we let sin build up in our lives, it keeps us from functioning properly and from fulfilling God's purpose for us." He smiled at Jeremy. "Well, that should do it. Let's check the chimes of this clock." Uncle Dick adjusted the hands, and Jeremy waited. Then the clock began to chime. *DAF*

HOW ABOUT YOU?

Is there anything keeping you from living for Jesus? Perhaps there's unconfessed sin—a lie, a nasty remark you made, or a person you need to forgive. Keep your life running smoothly by confessing the things you do wrong and seeking God's help.

MEMORIZE:

"Wash me clean from my guilt. Purify me from my sin." *Psalm 51:2*

 *Let Jesus Make You Clean*

Lost and Found (Read Luke 15:4-7)

16

JANUARY

As Rachel stood by the heavy door, looking out into the parking lot at the mall, she cried as if her heart would break. "Are you lost?" someone asked her.

"Y-yes." Rachel sobbed as she nodded her head. She knew the man was a security guard—her mother had pointed him out to her.

"Come with me, and I'll help you find your mother," said the guard, holding out his hand.

"Will you take me to the lost and found?" asked Rachel through her tears.

"Something like that," said the guard with a smile.

Rachel bravely brushed at the tears running down her freckled cheeks. Then she clung tightly to the man's hand as they walked together down the wide hall. When they reached the information center, Rachel's description was given over the loudspeaker.

Very soon a woman came hurrying out of the crowd, tears in her eyes. "Oh, Rachel," said the mother as she knelt down to hug her daughter, "I've been looking everywhere for you!"

That evening at bedtime, Mother read the story of the lost sheep from Rachel's Bible storybook. After she finished, Mother said, "The lost sheep reminds me of you, lost in the mall this morning. You hoped I would find you, didn't you?"

Rachel nodded. "I was so scared all by myself, Mommy," she said.

Mother nodded. "I know, but it's even worse to be lost from God," she replied.

Rachel settled her head on her pillow and listened as her mother continued. "Just as the sheep went astray and got lost, boys and girls go astray. They do wrong things. But just as the shepherd went to search for the lost sheep, Jesus came to earth to seek and to save lost boys and girls and men and women. We can ask him to forgive the wrong things we've done and to be our Savior." *CEY*

HOW ABOUT YOU?

Are you still "lost"? Jesus will save you if you will believe on him. Ask him to forgive your sins. Then you will be "found forever," and God will never leave you. You'll never be truly lost no matter where you are.

MEMORIZE:

"And I, the Son of Man, have come to seek and save those like him who are lost." *Luke 19:10*

 **Be Found Forever**

Fame and Fortune (Read Colossians 3:1-3, 16-17)

17

JANUARY

"Someday you're going to walk through that place and see *my* helmet and number all over the place," said Ryan as he and his Sunday school class left the Football Hall of Fame.

Jamie laughed aloud. "Fat chance," he responded.

Ryan was not ready to dismiss the subject. "You just wait—you'll see! I'm going to be just as well known as the guys whose stuff is in there now. Everybody will recognize me when I walk down the street, and I'm going to make a whole bunch of money."

"Sounds impressive," said Mr. Bradley, their teacher. "But don't forget that for a Christian, the important thing is to be willing to do whatever God wants you to do. God will take care of the details—such as whether you're famous or not and whether you make lots of money or only a little. Those things alone can't make you happy."

"Yeah," agreed Jamie. "I think I'm going to be a missionary." He looked at Ryan. "You better just forget those silly ideas you have," he added smugly.

"Whoa! Wait a minute!" exclaimed Mr. Bradley. "If the Lord wants you on the mission field, Jamie, that will be wonderful. But if the Lord wants Ryan to be a rich and famous football player with a testimony for him, that will be great, too. What I'm saying is that whether you become a football player, an engineer, a missionary, a schoolteacher, or whatever, be sure to keep the goal of serving the Lord and bringing glory to him." *SLK*

HOW ABOUT YOU?

If God wants you to be a football player, be a good one—with a witness for Christ rather than a desire for popularity. If God calls you to be a missionary, be the best missionary you can be. Ask God to help you honor him in whatever you do.

MEMORIZE:

"Whatever you eat or drink or whatever you do, you must do all for the glory of God." *1 Corinthians 10:31*

 Serve God in Whatever You Do

A House or a Home (Read Colossians 3:17-25)

18

JANUARY

The large house down the block was a model home, open for inspection. Some of the neighborhood girls decided to take the tour. Back home, Sabrina told her mother all about it. "You ought to see the place!" she began excitedly. "It's got four bedrooms and four baths. And you should see the living room! There's a huge fireplace!" Sabrina paused. "It sure makes our house look like a dump."

Mother looked up from her work. "A dump?" she repeated. "Well, then it's a beautiful dump, as far as I'm concerned." She smiled. "I think the place you just toured is even more different from ours than you realize. It's a house, but our place is a home."

"What's the difference?" Sabrina asked.

"A house is a building," explained Mother. "Maybe it has a lot of things people will need; perhaps it has almost everything. But—"

"Oh, this one does," Sabrina broke in. "It has everything!"

"No, I don't think so," her mother continued. "It doesn't have a family where the people love each other. It's an empty building, needing to be filled with people who want the best for each other. That's what we have here."

Sabrina thought about what her mother was saying. In their home, her folks showed lots of love and affection. Suddenly Sabrina began to realize how fortunate she was to live in a home—a Christian home. Maybe it wasn't as big as the house down the block, but it was filled with love. That was much more important.

"OK, you win," agreed Sabrina. Then she grinned at her mother. "But see . . . if *we* lived in that big house, *it* would be a home, too." She smiled as she headed for her room. Yes, a "home" was a whole lot better than any "house." *RIJ*

HOW ABOUT YOU?

Do you sometimes compare what you have with what other people have? Does it make you feel dissatisfied? jealous? unhappy? critical? Stop and thank God for your home, your parents, your family. Ask him to help you do your part to make your house a home!

MEMORIZE:

"There is treasure in the house of the godly." Proverbs 15:6

 Be Thankful for Your Home

Hungry People (Read Hebrews 5:12-14)

"The Church of the Open Bible," read Cody as Dad pulled up to the curb. The Davis family was on a skiing trip to Colorado. They had decided to visit this church because of its name. When they went inside, however, they discovered they were the only ones who even had their Bibles with them—and there were none in the church pews, either. The message was more about voting for a new mayor than it was about the Lord. They were disappointed.

19

JANUARY

As they drove along the highway the next day, they became very hungry and thirsty around noon, but all they saw were snowy, white hills—and no places to eat. Cheri looked at the map. "There's a town up the road," she reported. "They must have a restaurant there."

"How far away is it?" Cody asked.

"About fifteen miles, I think," said Cheri. Together they counted off the miles. Finally they could see a sign in the distance—the kind that told whether gas, food, and lodging would be available.

"Oh no," Mother groaned as they drove closer. "That sign says No Services. This town must be made up of just a few houses."

Cheri and Cody groaned, too. A few minutes later, Cheri began singing a silly little song they had learned at camp, and Cody joined in. "Here we sit like birds in the wilderness . . . waiting to be fed," they sang.

Dad grinned. "We're not doing so well lately, are we?" he asked. "Yesterday we sat in a church like 'birds in the wilderness' waiting to be fed spiritual food, but we weren't given any. Now we've come to a town with no place for us to eat."

As they were thinking about what to do next, Cody sat straight up and pointed out the window. "Hey, look!" he said. "I see a bunch of signs up ahead advertising restaurants in the next town!"

LMW

HOW ABOUT YOU?

Have you ever had to skip a meal? Did you feel hungry? How about your spiritual food? Do you often think of other things to do when it's time to go to church or to study your Bible? It's important to get spiritual food, just as it's important to get physical food.

MEMORIZE:

"You must crave pure spiritual milk so that you can grow into the fullness of your salvation. Cry out for this nourishment as a baby cries for milk." *1 Peter 2:2*

 Seek Spiritual Food

Their Own Bibles (based on a true story) (Read Psalm 119:9-16)

20
JANUARY

Prema and Jaya sat under a big tree and watched the other children at play. Prema (whose name means "love") and her brother, Jaya ("victory"), were orphan children who lived at a mission boarding school in southern India. "Prema, don't you wish you had a Bible?" asked Jaya. "I do. Since I received Jesus as my Savior, I want to read God's Word every day. But it's hard to borrow a Bible all the time."

"Yes," replied Prema. "I want my own Bible. But we are too poor to buy one."

Just then a boy walked by carrying a basket. He was headed for the bungalow where the missionary, Miss Ruth, lived. "That's it!" exclaimed Jaya. "Why didn't I think of it before? Miss Ruth will give us Bibles for bringing her baskets of buffalo chips. They're used for fertilizer."

"That's a good idea," said Prema, her eyes sparkling. "Let's do it."

Prema and Jaya began at once to hunt for their chips. At last each had a basket filled to the top, and they lined up at the missionary's door behind other children with baskets. "Prema and Jaya, do you want to earn Bibles, too?" asked Miss Ruth.

"Yes, Miss Ruth," they replied.

"You have nineteen more baskets to go, then," said the missionary as she recorded their names and the amount they brought.

Day by day, the children filled their baskets with chips. At last they heard the glad good news—they had only one more basket to fill! As soon as possible they filled that last basket. Proudly they lined up with the other children, and eagerly they held out their hands to receive their new Telugu Bibles. (Telugu is the language they spoke.)

"Oh, I can hardly believe it—my very own Bible!" cried Prema.

"Yes," said Jaya with a big smile. "Now we can read God's Word every day!" *MRP*

HOW ABOUT YOU?

Do you have a Bible? What did you have to do to get it? The story you just read is a true one. Do you think Prema and Jaya neglected their daily reading after working so hard to get their Bibles? We need to love and cherish God's Word, reading and studying it.

MEMORIZE:

"Your law is more valuable to me than millions in gold and silver!"

Psalm 119:72

 *Appreciate Your Bible*

Childproof Caps (Read John 15:4-8)

"I don't think I'll ever get Grandpa Evans to go to church with us," said Craig, plopping the receiver down on the phone. "He says he's gotta fix his truck, so he's too busy. I just have to get him to come—I'm sure he'd like it," he said with a sigh. "It's hopeless."

"Oh, now don't say that," said his mother, who was up on a chair cleaning kitchen cupboards. She took two bottles from the top shelf and handed them to Craig. "There are only a few pills in each of these," she said. "You can put all of them into one bottle and throw the other away."

21
JANUARY

Craig struggled to open the bottles. He twisted and turned them and even tried opening them with his teeth! "I can't do it," he complained, handing them back.

Mother took them and opened them quite easily. "I forgot that they have childproof caps," she said. "You're not supposed to be able to open them." She looked thoughtfully at the bottles. "You know, as I listened to you talk about your grandfather, I heard you say that you had to get him to church. But Grandpa is like these bottles with the childproof caps. It will take Someone stronger than you or me to cause him to be open to what God has for him. You can't change Grandpa! Only God can change a person."

Craig thought about it for a moment. Then he nodded. "If I can't open a little bottle, I sure can't change anyone's life!" he agreed. Suddenly he smiled. "But you know what? It feels good knowing that I'm doing my part and that I can leave the rest to God." *SLN*

HOW ABOUT YOU?

Have you been trying to change people? You can't do it. Pray for them and ask God what you could say to them. After you've done your part, leave the rest to God. Only he can change a person's heart.

MEMORIZE:

"Yes, I am the vine; you are the branches. Those who remain in me, and I in them, will produce much fruit. For apart from me you can do nothing." *John 15:5*

 Only God Can Change People

The Dead Battery (Read 1 Thessalonians 5:11-18)

22

JANUARY

"I get so tired of Jim Simons! He's supposed to be a Christian, but he sure doesn't act like one," grumbled Tony one evening. "He never buys a lunch, so he's always begging stuff from me. And besides that," added Tony, "he's so rough when we're playing. Then if he gets bumped a little, he tattles. We're not going to hang around with him anymore."

"Jim's father is an alcoholic, isn't he?" asked Dad.

Tony nodded, and Dad continued, "And I believe his mother has to work long hours. Things must be pretty tough around his house."

"And Jim's a brand-new Christian," added Mother.

The doorbell interrupted their discussion. It was their neighbor, Mr. Crane. "Hey, I'm sorry to bother you, but my car won't start," he said. "The battery isn't strong enough to start the engine. Could you give me a jump?"

Tony watched as his dad first attached cables under the hood of his own car and then stretched them to reach Mr. Crane's car. Mr. Crane tried to start his car again, and they all applauded when the dead engine jumped to life.

Dad put his hand on Tony's shoulder as they walked back to the house. "Son, Jim is like Mr. Crane's battery," he said. "He's a Christian, but he gets drained emotionally and spiritually by his home situation. He needs someone stronger to give him a boost—he's too weak to function on his own."

Mother overheard the conversation. "Christians are supposed to help their weaker brothers," she added. "The Bible tells us to bear the burdens of the weak and to encourage them."

Tony understood what his parents were saying. He knew it wasn't going to be as easy as jump-starting a car, but maybe he and the guys could get together and think of some ways to be friends to Jim. *NGH*

HOW ABOUT YOU?

Are you irritated by some Christians you know? Maybe they need a helpful hand, a listening ear, or a friendly smile to help "jump-start" their spiritual "batteries." Perhaps you can think of other ways to offer encouragement.

MEMORIZE:

"Share each other's troubles and problems, and in this way obey the law of Christ." *Galatians 6:2*

 *Help the Weak*

Explosion (Read Ephesians 4:26-32)

23
JANUARY

Ann Marie stomped into the house, slamming the door behind her. "Elaine bugged me all day yesterday, and now she's wearing my very best shirt!" she said. Tears streamed down her face as she kicked a nearby chair. She had been angry at her sister Elaine all week until there finally was a blowup.

"Pick up that chair, sit down, and cool your temper," Mother said. "I'll be right back." Soon Mother returned, carrying a photo album. She pulled up a chair, opened the book, and began flipping the pages. "One summer my friend Carolee and I rented a place for a week," Mother said, pointing to a picture of a small red cottage. "It was great, until we decided to bake stuffed pasta shells." She wrapped her arm around Ann Marie. "I opened the oven while Carolee lit the match. At first nothing happened. Then . . . *BANG! Whoosh!* A bright yellow flash smacked our faces."

"Were you hurt?" Ann Marie asked.

"We both had deep burns," Mother said. "And the kitchen was a mess."

"Why did it happen?" Ann Marie asked.

"It was the first time the oven was lit that season, and dirt had clogged the gas line," Mother explained. "When the gas forced its way through, it came with a rush and caused an explosion. Do you know why I told you that story?"

Ann Marie looked at the floor. "Because my temper exploded?" she guessed.

Mother nodded. "If the oven had been cleaned and the dirt hadn't been allowed to build up, the explosion would have been prevented," she said.

"I guess I should have talked to Elaine about what was making me angry rather than letting it build up, huh," said Ann Marie.

"That's right," said Mom. "Let's pray first; then we'll talk with Elaine and get this whole thing straightened out." *NEK*

HOW ABOUT YOU?

Do you let bad feelings build until you're out of control? When you feel upset with someone, ask God to help you deal with both the situation and your feelings. Then work out the conflict in a loving manner before the day ends.

MEMORIZE:

"And 'don't sin by letting anger gain control over you.' Don't let the sun go down while you are still angry."

Ephesians 4:26

 Settle Angry Feelings

Things That Go Together (Read James 2:14-18)

24

JANUARY

Kimberly was playing Things That Go Together with her little sister, Bonita. "What goes with this?" asked Kimberly, pressing a felt shoe onto the felt board. As Bonita picked up felt socks to put them next to the shoe, their brother, Steve, came barging into the room. "Get out of here!" Kimberly ordered. "This is our game." But Steve didn't leave. He stayed and teased and made a nuisance of himself. "I said get out of here!" repeated Kimberly. She felt her temper swell. He continued to tease her. Finally Kimberly hit her brother.

"Mom!" Steve called. "Kimberly hit me!" When Mother appeared, both children bombarded her with complaints. A few minutes later, both were sent to their rooms.

It seemed like forever before Mother called Kimberly and Steve back to the playroom. She had set up the felt board, and on it she had placed some paper figures. "This Things That Go Together game is good to use in teaching Bonita how to match things," Mother began, "and it can be good for big kids, too." She pointed to some pictures on the board—a Bible, a person praying, a cross, and a church. "All of these items represent our faith in God or our belief in him," she said. Then Mother pointed to some words—*love, faith, worship, anger, teasing.* "Which of these go with the pictures?" she asked.

As Kimberly looked at the board, her lip quivered. Even though Steve had teased her, she knew that hitting him did not go together with her Christian faith. And Steve knew that pestering his sister did not belong there, either.

"When we say we believe in God, our behavior should . . . ," started Mother.

"Go together . . . ," continued Kimberly.

"With our faith," finished Steve. *NEK*

HOW ABOUT YOU?

How do you treat the kids at school whom you don't particularly like? Are you patient and kind with your brothers and sisters? If you believe in Jesus, you need to do things that match your faith.

MEMORIZE:

"Now someone may argue, 'Some people have faith; others have good deeds.' I say, 'I can't see your faith if you don't have good deeds, but I will show you my faith through my good deeds.'" *James 2:18*

 Faith and Good Works Go Together

Foolish Choices (Read Acts 24:24-27)

25

JANUARY

"Come on, Dan," Uncle Pete called, "let's take a ride."

"OK," agreed Dan. He enjoyed his uncle's company. Uncle Pete was Dad's brother, but they certainly were not alike. For one thing, Dan's dad was a Christian, while Uncle Pete seemed to have no interest at all in the things of the Lord. But Dan wasn't a Christian either. Maybe that was why he enjoyed Uncle Pete so much.

As Dan reached for the seat belt, Uncle Pete turned to him. "You don't need to fasten that thing," he said with a laugh. "We're just going a short distance."

But Dan buckled up just the same. "In school we were taught that seat belts save lives," he said. As he spoke, he noticed his uncle pulling out a cigarette.

"I suppose now you'll tell me that smoking is bad, too," said Uncle Pete.

Dan grinned. "As they say, If the shoe fits, wear it. It makes sense."

Uncle Pete turned and glanced at the boy. "You're getting to sound more and more like your dad," he snapped.

"Well, Uncle Pete, you know you should use seat belts, and you know smoking is dangerous," retorted Dan. "So how come you ignore all the statistics?"

Dan's uncle took a firmer grip on the steering wheel. He was quiet for a long time. "The truth is," he said at last, "I don't really know. If your dad were here, he'd also want to know why I haven't become a Christian." He turned and looked at Dan. "And," he added, "he'd ask the same question of you!"

Dan had no answer to that, but he thought about his uncle's words long after they returned home. Later that night Dan thought, *I'm going to do it! I'm not going to be like Uncle Pete anymore! At least not in this.* He jumped up and went to find his dad. He knew Dad would explain to him again what it meant to trust in Jesus. *RIJ*

HOW ABOUT YOU?

Do you ignore warnings concerning your physical welfare? That can be dangerous. It's even more dangerous to neglect your spiritual welfare. Why not talk to a trusted adult soon about becoming a Christian?

MEMORIZE:

"For God says, 'At just the right time, I heard you. On the day of salvation, I helped you.' Indeed, God is ready to help you right now. Today is the day of salvation." *2 Corinthians 6:2*

 ***Don't Put Off Salvation***

Jenny Serves Jesus (Read 1 Samuel 1:20, 24-28; 2:11)

26

JANUARY

Jenny listened attentively as her Sunday school teacher told how the boy Samuel served the Lord. "Remember," finished Mrs. Jones, "you're never too young to serve God."

Jenny looked down at the floor. *What could a little girl like me do for Jesus?* she wondered. *I can't preach or teach or even sing very well.*

When Sunday school was over, several children pushed hard to get out the door first. Jenny waited until the crowding was over and then walked out. "Thanks for the good story today," she called with a smile as she left the room. Then she went to her younger sister's classroom.

"Change your clothes, Jenny," said Mother when they got home. "Dinner is ready."

The next week Jenny's friend Lisa agreed to go along to church and Sunday school. The lesson was about Paul, who traveled all over the world serving Jesus by preaching. Jenny's heart felt heavier and heavier. After class she asked Lisa to go after her sister while she stayed to talk to her teacher. "Mrs. Jones, I can't find any way to serve Jesus," said Jenny.

The teacher looked surprised. "But, Jenny, I see you serving Jesus in many ways," she said. "Today you brought your friend so that she could hear about Jesus. You're kind and thoughtful to your little sister and to me. And when you obey your mother, you're serving Jesus, too."

Jenny's face brightened. "Is that really serving Jesus?" she asked. "Wow! I bet I can find more ways to serve him." *CEY*

HOW ABOUT YOU?

Jesus doesn't expect you to go out and preach or teach like an adult, but you can serve him by obeying your parents, helping others, being kind, and inviting friends to Sunday school or Bible club. Begin serving Jesus today.

MEMORIZE:

"All of us must quickly carry out the tasks assigned us by the one who sent me, because there is little time left before the night falls and all work comes to an end." *John 9:4*

 You Can Serve Jesus

Grandfather's Will (Read Hebrews 9:13-22, 28)

27
JANUARY

Mr. Dutton, the lawyer, opened a folder and cleared his throat. "The last will and testament of Andrew Phillip Blackburn," he read. "I, Andrew Phillip Blackburn, being of sound mind . . ."

What a strange thing for Grandpa to say, Andrea thought. She glanced around the lawyer's office. Everyone looked very solemn.

". . . to each of my grandchildren I leave five thousand dollars to be used for their education," read the lawyer. Andrea's eyes widened. *Wow! Five thousand dollars for me?* She could hardly believe it.

Grandfather had remembered everyone—and all the children had received something special to help them remember their grandfather.

"May we go to the farm, Dad?" Andrea asked as they got into the car. "I want to see Princess!" Grandfather had left his horse to her.

Dad nodded. "We'll do that," he agreed. "I want to pick up Dad's Bible, too."

When they were home later, Andrea leafed carefully through the pages of the old Bible. "The New Testament of our Lord and Savior Jesus Christ," she read aloud. She looked up. "That's almost the same as what the lawyer said this morning," she told her mother. "He called Grandfather's will a testament."

Mother nodded. "That's right. The will is an important document telling what your grandfather left to us when he died. The New Testament is an important document, too. From it we learn that, because Jesus died for us, there's a valuable inheritance—everlasting life in heaven—available to everyone. But not everyone will receive it because a condition must be met. To receive it, it's necessary to accept Jesus as Savior."

Andrea raised her eyebrows. "I'm excited about the inheritance Grandfather left me," she said, "but the inheritance God has for me is even better!" *BJW*

HOW ABOUT YOU?

Have you met the condition that makes you a child of God and assures you of an inheritance? Just think—you can be an heir of God! If you'd like to find out more, talk to a trusted Christian friend or adult.

MEMORIZE:

"For it is my Father's will that all who see his Son and believe in him should have eternal life—that I should raise them at the last day."

John 6:40

 Claim Your Inheritance

It Won't Work (Read Ephesians 2:1-10)

28 JANUARY

Maria and her mother were chatting about their purchases as they walked through the parking lot. When they reached the car, they got in, and Mother placed the key into the ignition. "Something's wrong," she said with a puzzled look. "I just had this new key made a few days ago, and it has worked up till now. But I can't get it to go all the way into the keyhole." She pushed and wiggled and wiggled and pushed the key, but it just would not go in! "It won't work," she said finally. "Let's get some help."

Soon they were back with a man from a nearby service station. As they approached the car, Mother stopped. "Oh no!" she said, blushing. "It isn't my car that I was trying to start. I parked next to this brown truck, but my car is there on the other side of it. This one is the same color and style as mine, but I have a luggage rack on my trunk."

"I can't believe we both climbed into this car and never noticed that it wasn't ours," said Maria. "I guess we were too busy thinking about the things we bought."

Mom took her keys and started her own car with ease. "I'm sorry to have taken your time," she said, apologizing to the serviceman.

Maria and her mother laughed and laughed when they arrived home and told their story to Dad. He laughed with them. Then he became serious. "You know," he said, "some people are a lot like you. You tried to get home in the wrong car. Many people try to get to heaven in the 'car' of good works, but that's the wrong vehicle, too. Only Jesus can get them to heaven. If you don't mind, I'd like to use your experience to illustrate my sermon tomorrow."

Maria and her mother gladly gave their consent. *CLG*

HOW ABOUT YOU?

Are you trying to get to heaven by being good? Attending church, praying, and doing good things for others are good, but they are not the right vehicles to get you to heaven. Only through Jesus can you be saved from your sins and receive eternal life.

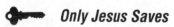 *Only Jesus Saves*

MEMORIZE:

"God saved you by his special favor when you believed. And you can't take credit for this; it is a gift from God. Salvation is not a reward for the good things we have done, so none of us can boast about it."

Ephesians 2:8-9

Fast Sunday (Read 1 John 3:16-18)

"This is 'fast' Sunday at our church," said Aunt Louise as she set orange juice and cereal on the table.

"Fast Sunday?" Alex repeated. "Oh . . . I remember my mom saying something about that. What is it you do?"

His cousin Vic laughed. "It's what we *don't* do," he said. "To 'fast' means to go without food. This is the Sunday we don't eat at noon."

29
JANUARY

Alex's eyes widened. "You don't eat lunch? Why not?"

"On the first Sunday of every month, people in our church take the money they would normally spend for lunch and give it to buy food for those who are starving," explained Vic. "You've seen pictures of starving children, haven't you?"

"Sure," Alex said as he sipped his orange juice. "But there's not much I can do about it. Except I wish I could send them my peas and green beans," he said, smiling.

Vic laughed again. "You're gonna do something about it today," he said. "The money saved from the meal you miss will be put into the fund."

"It may not seem like much, but it would be if everyone would do it," said Aunt Louise. "Now, let's hurry, or we'll be late for Sunday school."

As the boys played games that afternoon, Alex rubbed his stomach. It was growling. "It would be awful to be hungry every day, wouldn't it?" said Alex thoughtfully.

Vic nodded. "My dad says some people never know what it's like to have enough to eat—not in their entire lifetime!"

That evening when Aunt Louise fixed a light snack, the boys came promptly to the table. "How did it go, Alex?" asked Aunt Louise.

"It wasn't so bad," Alex answered slowly, surprised at himself. "My stomach may be empty, but I feel good! I feel more thankful for the food I get every day—even the peas and green beans!"

BJW

HOW ABOUT YOU?
Could your family miss a meal to help starving people? Would you be willing to do without pop or candy and give the money to missions?

MEMORIZE:
"John replied, 'If you have two coats, give one to the poor. If you have food, share it with those who are hungry.'" *Luke 3:11*

 Share Your Blessings

The Fog Lights (Read John 1:1-12)

30

As Kyle and his family traveled home, Dad slowed down and even stopped a few times because of thick fog. "At this rate it will take a long time to get home," said Mother. She sighed heavily. "I still can't believe my little brother would do such a thing," she added. In his mind, Kyle could still hear the judge sentence his uncle Vernon to twenty years in prison.

Dad took Mother's hand in his. "One of life's greatest mysteries is how children raised in the same home can turn out so differently," he said. "You're a good homemaker and community worker; your older brother, Carl, is a respected doctor. . . ."

"And my baby brother, Vernon, is a convicted criminal," Mother said, brushing the tears from her cheeks. "Vernon never would listen to anyone," she said sadly. "He was always stubborn and determined to have his own way." She recounted time after time when Vernon had broken the rules. "He refused to obey God's laws, too," she said. "He rebelled against our parents, against the church, and against all authority."

Dad leaned forward and turned on the windshield wipers. "This fog is so thick I can barely see twenty feet in front of us," he said. At that moment a large semi passed them. "Good," said Dad, and he drove faster. "He has fog lights. We can safely follow him."

"You know," said Mom thoughtfully, "Vernon sure could have saved himself a lot of trouble if he had followed Jesus, the light of the world. Instead he's been stumbling around all these years in the fog of sin."

Kyle added, "Maybe now he'll see that he can't make it through this world on his own. Can we pray that he'll come to Jesus?"

BJW

HOW ABOUT YOU?

Are you stumbling around in the "fog" of sin? Obey the light of God's Word. It will lead you home to heaven.

MEMORIZE:

"Jesus said to the people, 'I am the light of the world. If you follow me, you won't be stumbling through the darkness, because you will have the light that leads to life.'" *John 8:12*

 *Follow Jesus*

It's a Problem (Read Ephesians 6:10-17)

31

JANUARY

Jimmie slouched through the kitchen door and dropped into a chair next to Mother. She was holding his baby sister, Amy. "I have a problem," he said with a sigh. "I'm always losing my temper. I know God doesn't want me to do that."

"No," agreed Mother as she stood Amy on her feet. "Guess what?" she added. "Amy took her first step today. And you took a first step, too. You admitted that you have a problem."

Together they watched Amy take a few wobbly steps. Then . . . *plop!* Down she went. Her face puckered, but she crawled to a chair and pulled herself up again. Jimmie watched as Amy walked a few more steps and then fell again. "She'll never learn to walk," he said grimly.

"You started the same way," said Mother, "and look how strong your legs are now. The Christian walk works that way, too."

Jimmie's face broke into a wide grin—he *was* a strong runner. "You mean if I keep trying to stop losing my temper, I'll get better at that, too?" he asked thoughtfully.

Mother smiled and nodded as she picked up Amy. "But you will need God's help, too."

"Yeah," Jimmie agreed soberly. "I already know I can't do it by myself." He got up and headed for his room. "I'm going to talk to God about it." *HAD*

HOW ABOUT YOU?

Have you admitted that you have a problem such as losing your temper, acting selfishly, or disliking others? That's the first step toward overcoming it. Then look to God for the strength to gain control over it. He wants you to have the victory, and he will help you.

MEMORIZE:

"For I can do everything with the help of Christ who gives me the strength I need." *Philippians 4:13*

 God Gives Strength

A Soft Answer (Read Proverbs 15:1-7)

1

FEBRUARY

"Last Sunday we agreed to try an experiment for one week," Mr. Bennett reminded his Sunday school class. "We were to try giving a soft answer when we were tempted to argue. Who wants to report on what happened?" Six hands shot up.

"You know how mad it makes me to be teased about my red hair," said Jill. Everyone nodded. "First thing Monday morning, some kids called me Carrottop. I just laughed and said, 'My hair sure gets me lots of attention.' You should have seen their faces."

Mr. Bennett laughed. "That's great!" he said.

Nathan was next. "I just moved into a new neighborhood," he began. "The other day I was playing ball and got on my neighbor's vacant lot. Well, he came out of his house and ordered me off his property. It made me mad at first, but then I remembered what we had talked about, so I apologized. Just then his dog ran down the street and wouldn't come when it was called. Mr. Black, my neighbor, is too old to run, so I went after it. When I carried it back, Mr. Black mumbled, 'Thanks, boy.' The next day he told my dad I could play on his vacant lot."

"All right!" Mr. Bennett nodded. "Who's next?"

"My problem is my brother," said Stephanie. "The other day I borrowed one of his books. When I came home, he grabbed it and yelled, 'I didn't say you could read that!' I wanted to hit him over the head. Then I remembered—'a soft answer.' So I said, 'Oh, I'm sorry. I didn't think you'd care if I read it!' He was so shocked he said, 'Aw . . . that's OK, but next time ask.' And he gave the book back to me."

After hearing the reports, Mr. Bennett said, "When we turn away wrath with soft answers, we are pleasing the Lord and making the world a better place. Let's continue to do this even though our experiment has ended. OK?" *BJW*

HOW ABOUT YOU?

Do you generally give a soft answer to stop a quarrel? How much better it is to please the Lord in this way instead of giving a sharp reply that stirs up an argument! The real winner is the one who stops the fuss, so be a winner. Give soft answers today, tomorrow, and the next day.

MEMORIZE:

"A gentle answer turns away wrath, but harsh words stir up anger." *Proverbs 15:1*

 *Don't Speak Angrily*

Splash! Splash! (Read Psalm 1:1-6)

"Mom, Kyle has ruined my favorite outfit!" complained Christa, coming in the door. "He splashed mud all over me."

"That's too bad," said Mom. "It will wash out. I'm sure he didn't mean to get mud on you."

"Maybe not, but he didn't have to laugh about it," grumbled Christa. "And he said it was my fault—that I shouldn't have been standing so close to him." Turning, Christa went to change clothes.

2
FEBRUARY

Several days later, Christa came home from school looking upset. Without saying a word, she handed her mother a note from Mrs. Kirby, her teacher. Opening the note, Mother read aloud, "Christa was causing a disturbance in the lunchroom today. Since this has happened more than once, I am asking her and the others involved to stay after school tomorrow."

Mother frowned. "Well, what's this about?" she asked.

"Mom, I didn't do anything," whined Christa. "It's the girls I sit with. They're always goofing off. Sometimes I can't help myself and I have to laugh, but I don't start anything. Can't you write a note to Mrs. Kirby and explain?"

Mother thought a moment before replying. "Christa, do you remember when Kyle splashed mud on you the other day?" she asked. Christa nodded. "Well, just like the mud splashed on you because you were too close to Kyle, the wrong actions of your friends have 'splashed' on you, too. By staying with them while they were doing wrong, you became as guilty as they are."

"So I have to stay after school tomorrow?" asked Christa.

Mother nodded. "But can you think of some things you can do so this doesn't happen again?"

"Well," Christa said thoughtfully, "I could ask them to stop, or I could move to a different seat." *CPH*

HOW ABOUT YOU?

Have you ever let your friends talk you into doing something you knew was wrong? Why do you think you did that? What can you do the next time someone tries to get you to do wrong? Remember, try to choose friends who will help you live as God would want you to.

MEMORIZE:

"Oh, the joys of those who do not follow the advice of the wicked." *Psalm 1:1*

 *Choose Friends with Care*

Best Birthday Ever (Read Philippians 2:3-8)

3

FEBRUARY

Keesha was gazing dreamily out the window. "What are you thinking about?" asked Mom.

"Oh . . . about the big birthday party I had last year—and how different things are going to be this year," replied Keesha sadly. Since her last birthday, she had moved to a new country with her parents. They lived in a small village far away from her friends.

"Well, different isn't always bad," said Mom. "In fact, maybe you'll find that God has something special planned for you. And we can still have a birthday party, too." Keesha rolled her eyes. "Maybe Cita would like to come," suggested Mom. "I doubt she's ever had a birthday party. Many of the people here don't think about time the way we do. Some of them have no idea what day—or even what year—they were born."

Keesha thought this was interesting. She'd never had a friend who didn't know when his or her birthday was. Over the next couple of days Keesha thought about Cita a lot. Then one afternoon she had an idea. "Mom, can I ask Cita if she wants to share my birthday and my party?" Keesha asked.

"Of course!" agreed Mom. "That would be fun."

When the big day finally arrived, Cita's family came over for dinner. For dessert, Mom brought out two birthday cakes with eight candles on each. Cita beamed as she followed Keesha's example and blew out the candles on her cake. Then she laughed and laughed!

It was so much fun watching Cita and her reaction to everything that Keesha forgot all about her own cake. As she shared her birthday with Cita, she suddenly understood what her dad meant when he talked about the joy of showing the love of Christ to people who had never known of it before.

As Keesha posed with Cita for a picture, she grinned at her mom. "Thanks for the party, Mom!" she said. "Sharing is fun. This was my best birthday ever!" *SMG*

HOW ABOUT YOU?

Do you sometimes feel sorry for yourself when things don't go exactly the way you want them to? When that happens, look for ways to help someone else. You'll be surprised at what happens!

MEMORIZE:

"Don't think only about your own affairs, but be interested in others, too, and what they are doing." *Philippians 2:4*

 Put Others Ahead of Yourself

What's Wrong with Wendy?

(Read Proverbs 17:27-28; 18:13)

4

"Come on, Wendy!" Jill begged her friend. "Don't quit yet!" But Wendy sat down and began unlacing her skates, saying that she was cold. "It's not *that* cold!" grumbled Jill. Wendy didn't answer, and Jill went back to the pond.

"Hey, Jill," called Cindy as she skated by, "you and Wendy want to go to Angelo's Café?"

"I'll check," Jill yelled back. She spun around and turned to the bench where Wendy was still sitting. Wendy had her head in her hands and wasn't even watching the skaters. "Are you sick?" Jill asked. Wendy shook her head. "You want to go to Angelo's Café with Cindy?" asked Jill.

"No," murmured Wendy. "I don't feel like it." Jill sighed. Wendy sure wasn't being any fun! Jill felt angry.

Back home, Jill told her mother about it. "Wendy just moped around all day. She probably just wanted some attention," she complained, watching as Mother stirred a cheesecake. "Mmmm, my favorite." Jill picked up a spoon her mother had been using and took a lick. "Yuck!" she exclaimed. "What is this? I thought it was cheesecake." She hurried to the garbage and spit it out.

Mother laughed. "It's shortening, Jill," she said. "How many times have I told you not to jump to conclusions?" She paused, then added, "Are you sure you haven't jumped to a wrong conclusion about Wendy, too? Maybe there's a good reason for the way she acted."

That evening Jill's mother came to her room. "Honey," she said, "Wendy's mother just called. Wendy's dad has been gone since yesterday. And they don't know where he is."

"I guess that's why Wendy wasn't acting like herself today," said Jill. "I jumped to conclusions again, didn't I?"

"It seems so," agreed Mother. "I think we should pray for Wendy and her family, don't you?"

Jill nodded. "I'll call her, too," she replied, "and let her know I'm here if she needs to talk." *HWM*

HOW ABOUT YOU?

Do you jump to conclusions like Jill when your friends aren't acting like themselves? Do you always know when a friend is feeling sad? The next time you start to get angry with a friend who is moping around, what can you do instead?

MEMORIZE:

"Those who control their anger have great understanding; those with a hasty temper will make mistakes." *Proverbs 14:29*

 Be an Understanding Friend

Homesick for Heaven (Read Philippians 1:20-27)

5

FEBRUARY

Clop, clop, clop. Bartholomew, the farm horse, plodded slowly along. Donald pressed his heel lightly into the side of the old animal, but Bartholomew refused to walk faster. Donald didn't really mind, though—he had a lot to think about. *Why is it taking Dad so long to get here?* he wondered. *I've been here at Uncle George's dairy farm for two weeks, and it's time to go home. Or is it? I can't wait to get home again, but I hate to leave here, too.*

Donald had felt sad that morning feeding the chickens for the last time, pitching hay to the cows, and now, one last ride on old Bartholomew. Donald fingered the cap Uncle George had given him. He wore it proudly, for on it were the words *George's Dairy*. He did like being here. Still, at breakfast this morning, the thought of Mom and Dad at home had made Aunt Millie's pancakes stick in his throat.

Just then Bartholomew turned down the farm lane. Donald tried to turn him back. "Bartholomew!" said Donald, tugging at the reins. "I'm not ready to go to the barn yet." But old Bartholomew tossed his head and plodded on. Suddenly Donald was glad he had, for there at the barn was Dad!

All the way home, Donald talked about the farm. "It's so neat there," he said, "but I missed you and Mom . . . a lot!"

Dad smiled. "I think that's the way Grandma Morly often feels," he said. "Remember how she says she's eager to get to heaven and live with Jesus and enjoy everything he's preparing for her? But she hates to think of leaving us. Sometimes I feel that way, too. Like Grandma, I want to see others who have already gone to heaven. At the same time, I want to stay with you and Mom."

Donald nodded. He knew that kind of feeling, too. *CJB*

HOW ABOUT YOU?

Do you know someone who longs for heaven? Perhaps heaven seems a bit unreal and far away to you. Learn more about Jesus and the wonderful home he is preparing for those who love him. Enjoy life now, but look forward with joy to your life in heaven as well.

MEMORIZE:

"For to me, living is for Christ, and dying is even better."

Philippians 1:21

 Look Forward to Heaven

Rich Indeed! (Read John 14:1-6)

6

Todd and Stan whistled as they walked home from school. Occasionally they were in tune with one another, but not often. Their duet may not have been harmonious, but it was loud. That was the important thing to them. Suddenly Todd stopped whistling and sniffed the air.

"Chocolate chips," he said.

Stan understood immediately. They were nearing Mrs. Simmons's house, and she often baked cookies for the neighborhood children. Even when she didn't have cookies, they would sometimes stop to help her in the garden or visit with her. It was fun to listen as she talked about the things she had done when she was a girl.

"Come in, boys," Mrs. Simmons said as she set a plate of cookies on the table.

"We shouldn't come here so often," Stan said. "My mother says cookies cost money, and we shouldn't be eating up your food."

"Don't worry about that," said Mrs. Simmons. "Eat all you want." She smiled at the boys. "Did you know that I am actually very rich?"

"Really?" asked Todd. "Then why do you live in such a little house?"

"Oh, this is just a place where I'm staying for a while," Mrs. Simmons answered. "I have a mansion that I'm going to move into some day."

"Really?" Todd asked again. "Where is it?"

Mrs. Simmons chuckled. "It's in heaven, of course," she said. "A lot of people think money is what makes you rich, but money won't get anyone into heaven."

"I guess not," acknowledged Todd.

Mrs. Simmons grinned at the boys. "I think love is what makes you rich," she said. "I have the love of all my friends, my children and grandchildren, and all the boys and girls who stop to visit me. Best of all, I have the love of Jesus. He loved me so much he gave his life to pay the penalty for my sins. I love him, too, and he's preparing a place for me in heaven. Yes, I am very rich indeed." *MRB*

HOW ABOUT YOU?

God's love is more valuable than any treasure earth has to offer. All the money in the world is of no value if you don't have a place in heaven. Jesus is preparing a place for you if you've trusted him as Savior. If you haven't done that, talk to someone about how to do that.

MEMORIZE:

"And how do you benefit if you gain the whole world but lose your own soul in the process?"

Matthew 16:26

 Be Rich in God's Love

Really Winning (Read Psalm 119:11-16)

7

FEBRUARY

"I do, too!" exclaimed Toby.

"No, you don't," declared Megan. "I do."

Dad came into the room. "What's all this about?" he asked.

Megan balanced on one foot. "I know more Bible verses by heart than Toby does."

Dad put up his hands. "Wait a minute. Are you in some kind of contest?" he asked.

"I wish we were!" said Megan. "I'd win all the prizes!"

"I'd win more than you," boasted Toby.

"No, you wouldn't," answered Megan. "I'd win more."

"Hold it!" said Dad. "I'm glad you have both learned a lot of verses. But let's think about what the verses mean. For example, Psalm 133:1. Can you quote it?"

Toby and Megan hesitated. Then together they blurted out, "How wonderful it is, how pleasant, when brothers live together in harmony." Each tried to finish ahead of the other.

Dad nodded. "Now think about those words," he said. "There doesn't seem to be much harmony here this afternoon. I'm wondering if you've 'won' anything by learning that verse." Megan blushed, and Toby looked at the floor. "You really win when the verses you memorize help you act the way God wants you to," said Dad.

"Like not stealing things?" asked Toby.

"And to be honest?" asked Megan.

Dad nodded. "Those are good illustrations," he agreed. "What are some of the other verses that can help you?"

"When I was scared during the bad storm the other night, I remembered that Jesus is with me always," said Megan.

Toby looked at Dad. "When we do something wrong, we should remember that the Bible says to confess it and ask God to forgive us."

Dad nodded. "Good examples! Perhaps you've won something important by memorizing verses after all," he said. "If you practice what you memorize, then you'll be living the way God wants you to live. And that's how to be real winners!" *HAD*

HOW ABOUT YOU?

Do you learn Bible verses just so you'll know the most or win a prize? Or do you memorize them to learn how to live a life that will please God? Which do you think is the most important? Why?

MEMORIZE:

"That you may live a life worthy of the Lord and may please him in every way: bearing fruit in every good work, growing in the knowledge of God."

Colossians 1:10, NIV

 Use the Verses You Memorize

Small Things Count (Read John 21:3-13)

Cathy watched anxiously as her family sat down to a supper of meat loaf, mashed potatoes, carrots, and salad. She had made it all by herself.

"You did a good job," said Mother a little later. "Everything tastes wonderful."

Cathy's brother, John, made a face. "Yeah, it's great—if you like tough vegetables and mushy meat loaf, that is."

"All right, smarty," said Cathy with a frown. "I'd like to see you try to cook."

8
FEBRUARY

"Not me!" replied her brother. "Men don't do that!"

Dad shook his head. "I disagree with you, Son," he said. "After all, a lot of the world's great chefs are men. And do you know who I think was the greatest cook of all?" he asked.

"Who, Dad?" asked Cathy.

"Jesus!" replied her father.

"Jesus? I didn't know he ever cooked!" exclaimed John.

Dad smiled. "Remember the story about the disciples who went fishing?" he asked. "They caught nothing all night. Then Jesus called from the shore and told them to throw out their nets on the other side of the boat."

"I remember the story," said John, "but what's this about Jesus cooking?"

"Well," answered Dad, "when the hungry fishermen reached shore, they found Jesus cooking breakfast."

"I didn't remember that part," said John. "I wonder why he bothered with cooking. Why didn't he just do a miracle and make the food suddenly appear, already cooked?"

"Maybe he wanted to teach us a lesson about serving others," suggested Dad. "If Jesus didn't feel that he was too important to do a task like cooking, we shouldn't think any job is too small or unimportant for us, either. We should be glad to serve others any way we can."

"That makes sense," said John, as he took the last bite on his plate. "Perhaps I could learn to cook something after all. Pizza!"

SLK

HOW ABOUT YOU?

Do you want to do some important work for the Lord someday? That's good, but don't forget about the small jobs you can do today. Helping with the dishes, cleaning house, reading to a brother or sister, writing a note to someone—all of these are good ways to show your love for others and the Lord!

MEMORIZE:

"I have given you an example to follow. Do as I have done to you." *John 13:15*

 *Be Faithful in Small Jobs*

The Least of These (Read Matthew 25:34-40)

Eric and Evan got off the bus at their grandparents' farm. As they walked up the driveway, they talked about a new boy at their school. "Did you ever see such a sissy?" sneered Evan.

9

FEBRUARY

"Wait till Buddy and the guys get through with him tomorrow," said Eric with a grin. Buddy had planned a practical joke for the newcomer.

"Hi, boys." Grandma greeted them with a smile as they came into the kitchen. "What's so funny?"

"Oh, just a trick Buddy's going to play tomorrow on the new kid at school," Eric answered. "It'll probably scare him half to death."

Grandma frowned. "I hope you boys aren't in on it," she said.

"Well . . . not really," said Evan. "It wasn't our idea." Then he quickly changed the subject. "Did your chicks come in?"

Grandma nodded. "They're in the garage," she said.

"Come on, Eric. Let's go see them."

Soon the boys burst back into the kitchen. "Grandma, come quick!" they urged. "There's one poor little chick about to die!"

"The others are pecking it to death!" exclaimed Evan. He was horrified. "It has blood all over it."

In the garage, Grandma gently picked up the half-dead chick. She doctored its wounds while the boys watched.

"Mean old chicks!" raged Eric. "Picking on a little one!"

His grandmother looked him straight in the eye. "Chicks are not the only creatures who can be cruel," she told him.

Evan looked puzzled. "What do you mean?" he asked.

"I know what she means," Eric said slowly. "She's talking about us picking on the new boy in school."

"Oh . . . but we weren't going to hurt him," protested Evan.

"There are other wounds besides those that leave bruises, and other cuts besides those that bleed," Grandma reminded them.

As the boys followed their grandmother into the house, Eric whispered, "About tomorrow, Evan. Let's see if we can get Buddy to change his mind." *BJW*

HOW ABOUT YOU?

Do you know someone the other kids are always picking on? Have you joined them? Or do you stand up for the one being picked on? What do you think Jesus would do?

MEMORIZE:

"And the King will tell them, 'I assure you, when you did it to one of the least of these my brothers and sisters, you were doing it to me!'" *Matthew 25:40*

 *Don't Hurt Others*

Bad Company (Read Proverbs 1:10-15)

Matt was in a bad mood. He had just listened to another lecture from his dad about his friends. *So what if my friends aren't all goody-goodies? We have such fun together! Good thing Dad doesn't know about the fun we had throwing stones at old Mr. Foley's chickens. When Mr. Foley called the police, we almost got caught.* Matt's thoughts were interrupted as he saw his dad approaching.

"Come with me, Matt," Dad called. Matt followed as Dad led the way across the open field toward the river. The hot Florida sun beat down on them. Dad seemed to be searching for something. Finally he spoke. "Here it is! Be very quiet."

Matt crept closer. *Oh, it's nothing but an old alligator!* he thought. *I've seen them hundreds of times.* He was about to speak when Dad put up a finger to keep him quiet. In a whisper that could hardly be heard, Dad said, "Do you know why that alligator is lying there in the sun?"

Matt shrugged. "Sure!" he whispered. "He's taking an afternoon nap with his mouth open."

Dad smiled. "To a lot of insects it looks like a good place to sunbathe," he said. "Notice the beetles and the flies in the alligator's mouth?"

Matt nodded. "Look! A frog hopped up there and a small lizard. They'll enjoy eating the bugs!"

"Things may not turn out the way you expect," replied Dad.

All of a sudden the alligator closed his mouth, and down went his dinner. Then the big mouth opened again to wait for more visitors. Dad spoke as he and Matt turned to go home. "Son, sometimes we're like the lizard or the frog. We do things that we think are going to be fun even though they're wrong, not realizing that we're in danger. We need to ask God to help us run away from the wrong before it's too late."

Dad's talking about my friends again, Matt thought. But in his heart, Matt knew Dad was right. *HWM*

10

FEBRUARY

HOW ABOUT YOU?

Are you running around with the right kind of friends? Or do your friends coax you to go places and do things that are wrong? Like the frog and the lizard, you may not see the danger. Ask God to help you as you choose your friends.

MEMORIZE:

"My child, if sinners entice you, turn your back on them!"

Proverbs 1:10

 Choose Friends Carefully

The Tattletale List (Read Colossians 3:12-15)

11

Shawn and Keri were always arguing. They also were constantly interrupting their mother to tattle on one another. Often things they complained about were little annoyances. "Do you think your attitude pleases God?" Mother asked them. "Don't you think you need to work out those problems and forgive one another and get along together?" But the children kept on tattling.

One day Mother said, "I'm tired of all this! I'm going to give each of you a notebook. Write down anything the other one does that bothers you. Next Friday after supper, Dad and I will look at your lists and give out any punishments we feel are necessary."

Oh, boy! thought Shawn. *Is Keri ever going to get it!* He could hardly wait till she did something wrong . . . and he didn't have to wait very long before he saw his sister playing with his cars without asking. He ran to get his notebook! He watched all week, and by Friday, Shawn had written more than twenty things about Keri on his "tattletale list."

Just before supper, Keri came to him. "I'll show you my list if you'll show me yours," she said. Curious, Shawn agreed. He was surprised to see almost thirty things on Keri's list! "Shawn slammed the door in my face," it said. "Shawn messed up my dollhouse today." "Shawn called me names." And worst of all, "Shawn hit me when I wouldn't give him some of my candy."

"Oh no!" moaned Shawn. "If Mom and Dad see these things, I'll really get in trouble!"

Keri was busy reading Shawn's list. "Me too," she said. "Shawn, I'm sorry I did all these things. Will you forgive me?"

"I will, if you'll forgive *me,*" said Shawn. "Let's tear up these lists. Keeping a tattling list isn't as much fun as I thought it was going to be!" *SLK*

HOW ABOUT YOU?

Do you enjoy tattling on your brother or sister? When your complaints are about small things, wouldn't it be better to just forgive one another—and try harder to get along? Think of all the things God has forgiven *you* for. Then you'll be more likely to forgive others. Don't be a tattletale!

MEMORIZE:

"You must make allowance for each other's faults and forgive the person who offends you. Remember, the Lord forgave you, so you must forgive others." *Colossians 3:13*

 Don't Be a Tattletale

Myrtle the Turtle (Read 1 Corinthians 9:24-27)

Timmy had a pet turtle named Myrtle. He had decided to enter Myrtle in the annual turtle race. For several weeks Timmy worked with Myrtle. He coaxed her on by dangling food in front of her. The rules said you couldn't touch the turtle in any way during the race, but just about anything else to get the turtle to move was allowed.

The day of the race excitement ran high as each contestant placed his or her turtle at the starting line. With a loud *bang* from the starting gun, the turtles were off. All the turtle owners were jumping up and down and screaming. Some were even blowing on the turtles to make them go faster.

12
FEBRUARY

Timmy didn't try any of these methods. Instead, he dangled a spider, one of Myrtle's favorites, in front of her eyes. Myrtle moved faster and faster trying to get it. "Come on, ole girl," he quietly encouraged. "You can do it!" Myrtle was the first to cross the finish line! Timmy was given a blue ribbon, which he promptly taped to Myrtle's back.

"That was fun, wasn't it, Timmy," said Dad while they were driving home. "Your spider really did the trick."

"Yeah, it worked all right," Timmy replied. "I even have a couple of spiders left that I can give Myrtle for dessert!"

Dad laughed. "You know," he said, "strange as it may seem, the turtle race reminded me of the race we enter when we become Christians. Myrtle kept her eyes on that spider, and by following it, she won the race. The Bible tells us that we must keep our eyes on Jesus and follow him. Then we will win the race of life."

"Yeah." Timmy nodded. Then he grinned at Dad. "And just like Myrtle kept looking forward to getting the spider, we look forward to being in heaven with Jesus, right? Sure sounds better than eating a spider!" he said, then laughed. *CV*

HOW ABOUT YOU?

Have you "entered the race" by trusting Christ as Savior? Then keep looking to him—learning about him, talking to him, doing the things that please him.

MEMORIZE:

"All athletes practice strict self-control. They do it to win a prize that will fade away, but we do it for an eternal prize."

1 Corinthians 9:25

 *Follow Jesus*

The Snapping Turtle (Read Proverbs 18:6-8, 21, 24)

13
FEBRUARY

Suny lay on her bed sniffing. "Go away!" she snapped when her father tapped on her door.

"Don't you want to go fishing with me?" asked Dad.

Quickly Suny jumped to her feet. "Oh, I do! Wait for me!"

Later, as they sat on the riverbank waiting for the fish to bite, Dad asked, "Has something been bothering you? You spend a lot of time in your room alone."

"Oh, Daddy," said Suny, "nobody wants to be my friend."

"Do you have any idea why?" Dad asked.

"No!" snapped Suny. "They're all selfish and mean! I . . . Oh! Get away! Get away!" Suny yelled, jumping to her feet and dropping her reel.

"What is it?" Dad asked as he rushed to her side. A few feet away a turtle was glaring at her and snapping furiously. "Not a very friendly fellow, is he?" laughed Dad. "Leave him alone, Suny, and he won't hurt you."

Suny shuddered. "I don't like snapping turtles. Let's move. The fish aren't biting here anyway."

"Suny," said Dad when they were settled in a new spot, "could it be that everyone is leaving you alone because you've been acting like a snapping turtle, too? I've noticed that you've been snapping at people lately with your words. When that turtle started snapping at us, what did we do?" asked Dad.

"We got out of his way," Suny answered. "Maybe that's what my friends are doing—getting out of my way."

Dad replied. "The Bible says to have friends, you must be friendly. That snapping turtle wasn't very friendly. And you aren't very friendly, either, when you snap at people."

The next day when Suny came home from school, she was smiling. "You were right, Daddy," she said. "When I stopped snapping at my friends, they stopped getting out of my way." *BJW*

HOW ABOUT YOU?

Have people been avoiding you? Is it because you've been snapping at them? God's Word is filled with practical wisdom, and one thing it teaches is that your tongue can cause you all kinds of trouble. Check your attitude and your tongue. Ask God to help you use it to make friends instead of driving people away.

MEMORIZE:

"I said to myself, 'I will watch what I do and not sin in what I say. I will curb my tongue.'"

Psalm 39:1

 Speak Kindly to Others

Grandpa and God (Read Romans 8:35-39)

Bobby groaned as the bowling ball hooked slowly toward the left and bounced into the gutter. "I bet you wish you'd left me home," he said, slumping into the seat beside his grandpa. "I can't seem to do anything right."

Grandpa smiled and put his arm around Bobby's shoulders. "Some days are like that," he said. "And no . . . I don't wish I'd left you home." Grandpa looked at him, then pursed his lips like he always did when he was thinking about something important.

14

FEBRUARY

As they changed shoes a little later, Grandpa asked, "How would you like to stop for a hamburger and some fries?"

Bobby shrugged and looked at the floor. "I guess so," he answered softly.

They walked slowly across the parking lot. When they reached the car, Grandpa playfully ruffled Bobby's hair. "You know," he said, "I really had fun today. Do you know why?" Bobby looked up at him and shook his head. "I had fun because I was with you," said Grandpa. "I do wish you could have bowled a good game—just because you'd have enjoyed that more. But what's important to me is that I can just be with you because I love you." He smiled at Bobby, and Bobby grinned back.

"I want you to remember something else, Bobby," said Grandpa. "As you grow older, you may wonder from time to time if God really loves you, especially when you aren't the best student in class, or the fastest runner, or the most popular person in school." Grandpa unlocked the car door, and they got in. "I hope you'll remember that God's love for you isn't based on those things," Grandpa said. "In one way he's like me—he loves you for who you are, like I do." He fastened his seat belt. "Now," he said, "let's go get those hamburgers, OK?"

Bobby nodded. "OK," he said with a grin. *RSM*

HOW ABOUT YOU?

Do you sometimes think God doesn't love you? Don't let that thought stay in your mind. God's love for you never changes. He loves you very, very much even when you are having a hard time loving yourself.

MEMORIZE:

"Nothing in all creation will ever be able to separate us from the love of God that is revealed in Christ Jesus our Lord." *Romans 8:39*

 God Loves You Always

Outstanding (Part 1) (Read 1 Peter 3:10-12)

15

FEBRUARY

It was Friday, and the last bell had rung. Rick and Randy Thompson headed home, each carrying a letter from the principal. "Mother!" called Rick excitedly when he reached home. "Guess what! I was chosen to be student of the week!"

"That's wonderful!" exclaimed Mother, taking the letter Rick held out and opening it. "My! It says here that you've been an excellent example to the entire school. That's great. Congratulations!"

When Randy arrived home, he quietly laid his envelope on the table where Mother found it later. She looked concerned as she read that Randy and some other boys had been caught writing on the bathroom wall. They would be staying after school next week to help the janitor. She showed both letters to Dad when he arrived home.

At the dinner table, Dad congratulated Rick on his achievement. Nothing was said about Randy's problem until after dinner when Dad took him aside for a talk. "I see I have two outstanding sons this week," began Dad. "But they are outstanding for such different reasons."

Randy looked defiant. "The other guys started it," he said. "I don't see why Mr. Croswell had to get so upset about it." He stuck out his chin.

"Randy," Dad spoke sternly, "you will not speak of your principal in that way! As for whose fault it was . . . the other boys are responsible for what they did, but God made *you* responsible for what you did. It doesn't matter who started it. Now, I'm afraid I'm going to have to ground you next week. I want you to go to your room and think this over."

With a sigh Randy headed up the stairs. *HWM*

HOW ABOUT YOU?

Are you "outstanding"? In what way? The Bible says you should not behave in such a way that you'll have to suffer for doing wrong. If that does happen, admit that you did wrong. Then ask God to forgive you and to help you correct your behavior.

MEMORIZE:

"If you suffer, however, it must not be for murder, stealing, making trouble, or prying into other people's affairs."

1 Peter 4:15

 Don't Be a Wrongdoer

Outstanding (Part 2) (Read 1 Peter 4:14-16)

Deep down, Randy knew he deserved to be punished. Before he went to sleep, he asked both God and his parents to forgive him. He also wrote a letter to the school principal and apologized for his misbehavior. Having done that, he felt much better even though he knew that he would still have to be punished.

16

FEBRUARY

As Randy and the boys stayed after school each day and washed walls, the other boys grumbled about their punishment and tried to think up new ways to cause trouble. Randy quietly did his job, not joining in with the troublemakers. They soon noticed.

One day Joe, the biggest boy, challenged Randy with these words, "Hey, I heard you apologized to old man Croswell," he growled. "You nuts or something?"

The other boys stood around watching. "Well, we *were* wrong," offered Randy. "I don't want any more trouble."

"You got your choice—trouble with old Croswell or trouble with us," Joe told him. "Take your pick."

Randy stood his ground. "I'm not going to do anything else wrong." He hesitated, then added bravely, "I'm a Christian." How the boys hooted! The rest of the week they called him names and continually mocked and bullied him.

On Friday Randy again carried a letter from the principal to his folks. This time, when Dad read the letter, a smile spread across his face. "Mr. Croswell says you've done a fine job this week," he reported. "You've been an excellent worker and an outstanding example, even though there has been pressure from the other boys. Has it been pretty rough, Son?"

"Pretty rough," Randy admitted.

"I'm proud to have an outstanding son again this week," Dad said with a smile. "It's not easy to take the heat for what you believe." *HWM*

HOW ABOUT YOU?

Are you a Christian? If so, do you dare say no when someone wants you to do wrong? Will you behave as Jesus wants you to, even if others tease you and laugh? You'll be happy if you stand true to Jesus.

MEMORIZE:

"Be happy if you are insulted for being a Christian, for then the glorious Spirit of God will come upon you." *1 Peter 4:14*

 Be Willing to Suffer for Jesus

"I Want It!" (Read 1 Timothy 6:6-11)

17

FEBRUARY

"Let's look in the department store first," suggested Mother as she and Erin entered the shopping mall. They were looking for a birthday present for Erin's cousin, Heidi.

Erin followed her mother into the store. "Oh, Mom, look at that blue sweater with hearts! I want one of those!" she exclaimed.

Mother smiled and said, "We're looking for something for Heidi, remember?"

"Oh, but it's . . ." Erin's voice trailed off as she spotted the jewelry counter. "Oh! I want a bracelet like that one!"

"Come on, Erin. We don't have much time," said Mother as she looked at the rack of clothes. "I don't see anything here. Let's go to the toy store."

The toy store was also filled with a lot of nice things. Erin immediately spotted a doll that she wanted. But she forgot about it as she followed her mother to the game section. "Mom, there's that new game I want," Erin said, pointing.

Mother sighed. "Well, here's a game that Heidi might like. Let's buy it and get home before your 'I want it' develops into a serious disease."

"What do you mean?" asked Erin.

"Erin, you've seen all kinds of things this morning that you want," Mother answered. "The Bible tells us to be content with what we have. I want you to be a girl who is thankful for what you have instead of always wanting more."

Erin frowned for a moment. Then she suddenly laughed. "You know what? I can't even remember most of the things I told you I wanted. But I better keep my eyes straight ahead on the way out."

"Good thinking," said Mother. "I'll do that, too. Let's both ask the Lord to help us to be content with what we have." *LMW*

HOW ABOUT YOU?

When you go shopping, do you greedily ask for everything you see? Sure, it's nice to have toys and pretty clothes, but it's wrong to selfishly desire them. Thank the Lord for the many things you do have. Get out of the habit of constantly asking for more.

MEMORIZE:

"Stay away from the love of money; be satisfied with what you have. For God has said, 'I will never fail you. I will never forsake you.'" *Hebrews 13:5*

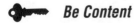 **Be Content**

Booster Shots (Read Mark 14:32-38)

18
FEBRUARY

Sarah was going with her mother to take her baby sister for an appointment at the doctor's office. "Does Becky have to have shots today?" asked Sarah.

Mother nodded. "A checkup and shots," she said.

"I don't think she's going to like those shots!" exclaimed Sarah, thinking of her own experience with shots.

"Maybe not," Mother agreed, "but it's for her protection—to keep her from getting sick. It's easier and safer to get a shot now than to suffer with a sickness later."

"I guess so, but I'll be glad when I outgrow shots," Sarah observed as they went out to the car.

"Well, even adults need shots sometimes," said Mother. After a moment, she added, "And as Christians we need booster shots regularly, too." She smiled at Sarah's startled expression.

"What do you mean, Mom?" Sarah wanted to know.

"To guard against temptation, we need to protect ourselves before it strikes—before our resistance is worn down and we give in to its ways," Mother explained. "Do you know how we can do that?"

Sarah thought for a moment. "We can read the Bible so we'll know if something is right or wrong," she suggested. "And we can memorize verses, too."

"Good," approved Mother. "And how about staying away from the people or places that could cause us to sin? That prevents us from getting into a situation we can't handle. Can you think of anything else?"

"Prayer!" exclaimed Sarah. "We can ask God to help us."

"Very good." Mother smiled. *JLH*

HOW ABOUT YOU?

Are you memorizing God's Word, staying away from sinful places, reading your Bible, and praying regularly? These are your spiritual "booster shots" to protect you from sin.

MEMORIZE:

"Keep alert and pray. Otherwise temptation will overpower you. For though the spirit is willing enough, the body is weak." *Mark 14:38*

 Guard against Sin

Quilting Steps (Read Psalm 37:23-31)

19
FEBRUARY

"Grandma, what's that song you're humming?" asked Nancy one day as she and Grandma worked together on a quilt for Nancy's bed.

"Oh, that's a chorus I learned years ago—about God leading us just one step at a time," replied Grandma with a smile.

Nancy picked up a quilt piece and gave it to her grandmother. "We're almost done, aren't we?" asked Nancy eagerly.

Grandma laughed as she put the last piece in place. "Well, the top of the quilt is all together now," she said, "but we've still got lots of work to do! Let's get the special pencils and start marking the lines where we'll do the actual quilting."

"What else do we have to do?" asked Nancy.

"Well, when you make a quilt you piece the top together first—we've got that done," said Grandma. "Then you mark the quilting lines. Next you baste the top of the batting and backing. Then it's ready to put on the frame to do the actual quilting stitches. Finally, you must bind the edges, and then it's all done!"

"Whew!" exclaimed Nancy. "We'll be at this forever!"

"Not quite," said Grandma. "You just have to be patient and do it one step at a time . . . just like life."

"Like life?" Nancy asked.

Grandma nodded. "When I was your age, I sometimes wanted so badly to know what my life would be like in the future. But my mother always told me to let the Lord lead me just one step at a time. I've found out that's the best way."

Nancy wondered where she would be in a few years and what she would do when she grew up.

Grandma began humming again. Then she grinned at Nancy. "I'll teach you this song," offered Grandma, "and then whenever you see this quilt, it will remind you to live your life one step at a time as the Lord leads you." *REP*

HOW ABOUT YOU?

Are you willing to let the Lord lead you each step of your life? Ask him each day to help you with the problems and opportunities of that day. Listen to Christian radio programs. Read good books. Learn about God through Sunday school and church. Study his Word to learn more of the way he wants you to live.

MEMORIZE:

"We can make our plans, but the Lord determines our steps."

Proverbs 16:9

 God Leads One Step at a Time

The Right Pattern (Read James 4:13-17)

"Let's go pick out the material for your new dress, Heather," said Mother. "It will do you good to get out." Heather sat up and blew her nose. She had just learned that her father was being transferred to a different city. She would have to say good-bye to her friends. Mother continued, "If this is God's will for our family, it's what we want because it's best for us."

20
FEBRUARY

When they entered the fabric shop, Heather almost immediately spied some material she liked. "Oh, Mom!" she exclaimed. "Can we get this material?"

Mother nodded. "It's your color," she agreed. "Let's find a pattern."

Seated at the counter, they flipped through the large pattern books. "Here's the pattern I want," Heather said after a bit. "All the girls are wearing this style."

Mother leaned over to see the pattern Heather had chosen. She shook her head. "That pattern isn't right for the fabric you've chosen," she said. "I don't think you'd be happy with the finished product."

Heather gritted her teeth and sighed loudly. "Then you'll have to choose the pattern!" she said.

Late one afternoon of the next week Mother called, "Heather, your dress is finished. Come and try it on."

Heather hated to admit that Mother's choice of a pattern was a good one, but she did like it. As she was modeling it, Dad came home. He whistled. "My, what a beautiful young lady I see." Heather beamed. But before she could reply, Dad continued, "I've got good news. The Farleys are being transferred to Houston, too."

"The Farleys!" Heather squealed. "My best friend, Dawn, is going to live in Houston, too?"

Mother smiled. "See, Heather, the pattern God has for our lives isn't always the one we want, but if we trust him, everything turns out beautifully in the end. I must admit, we're not always able to see it so quickly. In fact, sometimes he doesn't allow us to see it at all in this life. But we still need to trust him." *BJW*

HOW ABOUT YOU?

Are you having trouble understanding some things that are happening to you? Remember, God is cutting and piecing your life together. Trust him.

MEMORIZE:

"And we know that God causes everything to work together for the good of those who love God and are called according to his purpose for them." Romans 8:28

 *Trust God*

The Right Start (Read Proverbs 4:10-18)

21

FEBRUARY

"Look, Kurt, there's old Tony at his fruit stand," said Kyle. "You keep Tony's attention, and I'll get an apple for each of us." A few moments later, in an alley, each boy held a big, red apple. "Tony didn't even notice me!" exclaimed Kyle.

Kurt laughed. "Yeah. That was great fun!"

"Maybe you think prison will be fun, too," said a voice behind the boys. They whirled around to see a police officer standing there.

Since it was the boys' first run-in with the law, Tony agreed not to press charges. However, the boys were taken to the police station, and after a lecture, their parents were called. "I can't see why there should be such a fuss over snitching a couple of apples," complained Kyle when they were ready to go.

"Yeah," agreed Kurt. "It was such a little thing."

"But you stole something and thought it was fun," said Kyle's father. "That's serious—it's the way a life of crime often begins. You might go on to bigger things."

"Aw, Dad, you don't really believe we'd do that, do you?" objected Kyle.

"It could happen," replied Dad. He put on his overcoat. "I find this especially disappointing since both of you claim to be Christians. You do, don't you?"

"Well, sure," said Kurt, "but you can't expect kids to act like grown-ups. I'll settle down when I'm older."

"Me too," agreed Kyle. "We'll end up OK."

"You're old enough to know right from wrong," said Dad. "And God expects you to use that knowledge to live a life pleasing to him right now." He began to button his coat. When he finished, he said, "Would you look at that? Something's wrong with my new coat. It doesn't button the right way."

The boys looked at Dad and laughed. "You started out wrong," said Kyle. "If you want to finish right, you have to start out right."

"My point exactly," agreed Dad. *MRP*

HOW ABOUT YOU?

Do you think it doesn't matter what you do while you're young, as long as you end up OK later on? It does. The way you conduct yourself now may well be the way you'll end up, too. Choose the right way now.

MEMORIZE:

"For God made Christ, who never sinned, to be the offering for our sin, so that we could be made right with God through Christ." *2 Corinthians 5:21*

 Serve God While You're Young

Taking Care of the Important Things

(Read 2 Corinthians 5:20-21; 6:11-12)

22

FEBRUARY

Tim picked up something from his closet floor and waved it at Allan. "Remember the game piece we lost when we played Spider last time you were here?" he asked.

Allan nodded. "Did you find it?" he asked eagerly.

"Take a look," said Tim, offering the item to Allan.

Allan held out his hand and took the object. "Hey! You did find it!" he said. He looked at Tim's closet. "It's a wonder you ever found it in there," he said.

Tim set up the game board. "Let's have a game," he said.

"Don't you want to pick up this stuff first?" asked Allan.

"Naw. I'll do it later," replied Tim.

Allan grinned. "You're a great one for putting things off," he said. "Remember the mess we made in the backyard a while ago? I had to rush home, but you said you'd pick it all up. Only you didn't."

"I remember," said Tim. "Wow! Was my dad upset! We couldn't play together for a whole week." He grinned at Allan. "When we play at your house, you pick things up right away, don't you?"

Allan nodded. "I don't like to leave a mess like that."

Tim jumped up. "OK," he said. "Let's clean this up right now before my dad gets home. This time I'll surprise him."

Together they put games in place and sorted out sneakers, shoes, magazines, and even some dirty socks. "There," said Tim. "I took care of what I usually put off. Now how about taking care of what you keep putting off?"

Allan looked puzzled. "What would that be?" he asked.

"Becoming a Christian," replied Tim promptly. He had been witnessing to Allan and taking him along to church for some time. "You like things to be taken care of right away. And this is the most important thing you need to take care of."

"Tell me more about it," said Allan. *HAD*

HOW ABOUT YOU?

Have you put off receiving Jesus as Savior? Nothing is more important than that. If you haven't done so before, won't you trust him today?

MEMORIZE:

"Don't let the excitement of youth cause you to forget your Creator. Honor him in your youth before you grow old and no longer enjoy living."

Ecclesiastes 12:1

 Receive Jesus Today

Good Advice (Read Romans 13:8-10)

23
FEBRUARY

Kim walked home, her eyes brimming with tears. A cold ache filled her. *No one even sees me,* she thought as her schoolmates ran by, laughing. That night she cried herself to sleep.

"Daddy, let's move back to Miami. I hate it here!" she said the next morning.

"We can't," her father replied. "I'm sorry you're so unhappy."

Tears rolled down Kim's cheeks. "We've been here six weeks, and I still don't have one friend—not one!"

Mother looked up. "Kim, maybe this poem will help. Listen," she said. "'I went looking for a friend, but not one could be found; I went out to be a friend, and friends were all around.'"

Kim wiped her face with a napkin. "What does that mean?"

Mother explained gently. "It means that you shouldn't worry about finding a friend. Instead, look for someone who needs a friend."

Dad stood up. "The Bible gives the same advice in the book of Proverbs," he said. He squeezed her shoulder. "Now grab your books, and I'll give you a ride to school."

When they got to school, Kim jumped from the car. "Be friendly today," encouraged Dad.

As Dad drove away, Kim noticed a girl going up the walk. *That looks like the girl who sits across from me in homeroom,* Kim thought. *What's her name? Oh, yes—Nadine. I wonder where all her friends are. Maybe . . .*

"Nadine, wait up," Kim called. "Could I walk with you?"

Nadine looked up. A smile spread over her face. "You sure can. I'm new here and don't know many people yet."

A warm feeling filled Kim. Perhaps she and Nadine would become good friends. *BJW*

HOW ABOUT YOU?

Do you feel lonely? left out? Do you always wait for others to speak to you first? Start today to be a friend instead. You'll find friends everywhere.

MEMORIZE:

"A man that hath friends must shew himself friendly."

Proverbs 18:24, KJV

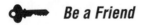 **Be a Friend**

Not Alone (Read Mark 10:13-16; Luke 17:11-19)

Jenny huddled under the ragged sheet on her bed. She didn't like being left home alone while her mother went out at night. And she was hungry as well as lonely. For her supper, she'd had to fend for herself, and she hadn't found much to eat. But at least she had gotten Ruffles, her teddy bear, back. Ruffles was very old and worn, and Mother had tossed him into the trash. Just in time, Jenny had seen him there, and she had rescued him.

24

FEBRUARY

As Jenny lay there, she began to think of Mr. and Mrs. Adamson. They came to the community center after school and taught a children's Bible club. Each Wednesday they were there with a new Bible story and friendly smiles.

Jenny loved to hear about Jesus because he cared about children. Although Jenny had been going to the Bible club only a few weeks, she had asked Jesus to be her Savior. It seemed Jenny could still hear Mrs. Adamson telling how Jesus loved children. And this week's Bible story had been about how he loved and healed some lepers. Mrs. Adamson had said, "Leprosy was a terrible disease. It often made people look ugly. Their disease was contagious, but Jesus didn't run away from them. He loved them and helped them. You, too, may have troubles in your life, but remember—Jesus cares. He's always with you. He cares for you and will help you, just as he helped those lepers."

As Jenny remembered those words, she thought about Ruffles, and it helped her understand what Mrs. Adamson meant. Jenny loved Ruffles, even though he was old and ragged and some of his stuffing was gone. If a girl could love an old teddy bear so much, she knew that Jesus could love a girl even more!

Jenny's lips curved up in a smile as she hugged Ruffles closer to her. She sighed a big sigh of relief, pulled the thin blanket up around her shoulders, and fell asleep. *CEY*

HOW ABOUT YOU?

Are there things in your life that make you unhappy? Do you feel alone and think that no one cares about you? Jesus cares. He's with you no matter where you are or what happens to you. He loves boys and girls. He loves you!

MEMORIZE:

"But when Jesus saw what was happening, he was very displeased with his disciples. He said to them, 'Let the children come to me. Don't stop them! For the Kingdom of God belongs to such as these.'"

Mark 10:14

 Jesus Loves Children

Bobby's Dinner (Read Psalm 37:3-9)

25

Bobby picked up a book and settled down into his favorite chair as smells from the kitchen drifted into the living room. A moment later, he called, "Is dinner ready yet, Mom?"

"By the time Dad gets home, it'll be ready," said Mother.

"I'm hungry," Bobby moaned as he turned back to his book. He read a page or two, then called out, "Do we have to wait for Dad? Why can't we eat now?"

A short time later Mother called him to the table. "Oh, yummy!" said Bobby as he sat down. "Pizza and hot chocolate! And caramel pudding for dessert!" But when he bit into the pizza, he was disappointed. "Yuk!" he said. "This is barely warm." He reached for the hot chocolate to wash the taste from his mouth. After a small sip, he set it back down. It wasn't hot, either. Discouraged, he tried the pudding. It was warm and quite runny.

Confused, Bobby turned to Mother. "I don't get it, Mom," he said. "Nothing tastes right. The pizza and chocolate aren't hot, and the pudding is warm."

Mother put her hand on his shoulder. "That's because I didn't give your food enough time to get done," she explained. "To make something right takes time and patience, but you wanted your dinner right away. I think you'll have to admit that you've been very impatient lately."

Bobby didn't know what to say. He knew she was right. Bobby looked at his meal. "If you'll finish cooking this for me, I promise I'll wait patiently," he said. And he did. *DAB*

HOW ABOUT YOU?

Are you impatient? Do you get upset when things don't happen as fast as you would like? Learn to be patient regarding the ordinary, everyday things of life. It's a characteristic of which God approves.

MEMORIZE:

"But when the Holy Spirit controls our lives, he will produce this kind of fruit in us: love, joy, peace, patience."

Galatians 5:22

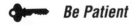 ***Be Patient***

Two Friends (Read Leviticus 26:3-6, 14-17)

"Tell me if you see a speed-limit sign," Mother told Richie as they approached Centerville.

"OK," agreed Richie. A few minutes later, he said, "There's one! It's forty-five miles per hour ahead."

"Thank you," said Mom, and she slowed down.

After driving a few miles farther, Richie looked out the back window. "Oh no, Mom!" he exclaimed. "There's a police car right behind us!"

26
FEBRUARY

"There's nothing to worry about," Mother answered.

Richie's eyes opened wide in surprise. "Why not?" he asked. "We might get a ticket."

Mother answered by asking Richie a question. "How can we get a ticket when we're going forty-five miles an hour?" She chuckled, and Richie began to smile, too, as he realized Mother was right. "Actually, that policeman is helping us," Mother added. "He sees to it that we drive at a safe speed and that others do, too."

"So we think the policeman is our friend when we're going the right speed," said Richie, "but if we're going faster than the speed limit, we're afraid of him."

"That's right," said Mom. She glanced in her rearview mirror. "In a way, God is like a policeman," she added. "See if you can think of some reasons why."

Richie thought about it. "I think I know," he said after a while. "Is this right? If we're doing something wrong, we feel afraid of God, like people who are speeding are afraid of the police."

"That's right," said Mother with a nod. "And . . ."

"And if we're doing right," Richie continued, "we can feel good that God is watching us because he'll be pleased. Besides, he protects us from those who might harm us while they are doing wrong." Mother nodded, and Richie looked out the back window once more. "The policeman and God," he said slowly. "They're both our friends." *CLG*

HOW ABOUT YOU?

Do you feel afraid of God? It's good to fear him in the sense that you respect him because he is holy. But if you're his child and you're trying your best to follow his commandments, you don't need to be afraid of him. He loves you.

MEMORIZE:

"I will honor only those who honor me." *1 Samuel 2:30*

 *God Is Your Friend*

Worth the Wait (Read Luke 8:4-8, 11-15)

27

FEBRUARY

John loved garden catalogs, especially when they came in winter. They reminded him that, even though their farm was still covered with snow, spring would soon arrive. He picked up a catalog and began making a long list of things he wanted to order. He looked at a section titled "Unusual Seeds." First on the list was ginseng. The catalog claimed it was so valuable that its dried roots would sell for a lot of money in health food stores. It also said that ginseng seeds took a year or more to sprout!

"Can I get some ginseng seeds, Dad?" asked John.

"I don't know," said Dad. "Those seeds take a long time to grow. Are you sure you want to wait that long before you see them come up?" he asked.

John shrugged. "Well, you always say that anything worth having is worth waiting for," he said. "If they grow, they could be worth a lot of money."

Dad was thoughtful. "Son, you've just reminded me of something important," he said. "I've been pastor at our church here for eight years now, and lately I've become a little discouraged. You've reminded me that every time I preach, I plant valuable seeds. Sometimes they may take a long time to grow or may never sprout at all. But if they do grow, it's well worth the effort because the fruit they produce will last forever. The same is true for you whenever you tell others about Jesus."

"So I may grow some ginseng?" asked John.

Dad nodded as he looked over the order form. "After you cut this list down just a wee bit, we can send it in," said Dad. "And after you plant the seeds, you and I can remind each other to have faith, follow the directions, and resist the temptation to keep digging them up to see how they're doing! OK?"

"Gotcha," said John with a grin. *LBM*

HOW ABOUT YOU?

Are you willing to wait for the things you want most? Do you get impatient with God, other people, or perhaps even yourself when things aren't happening as fast as you feel they should? Have faith; your prayers are always heard. Leave the timing to God, and you won't be disappointed!

MEMORIZE:

"But the good soil represents honest, good-hearted people who hear God's message, cling to it, and steadily produce a huge harvest." *Luke 8:15*

 Trust God's Timing

The Bride-to-Be (Read Revelation 19:7-8; 21:2, 9-10, 27)

28

"Brian! Look!" Julie said, pointing to their older sister, Kay. Brian looked up and watched as Kay picked up a dirty plate from the table and placed it in the refrigerator. "That's the second time she's done that," whispered Julie. Brian raised his eyebrows, and they both burst out laughing.

"Mom," Julie said later, "have you noticed Kay lately? All she thinks about is Chad! She can't concentrate on anything!"

Mom smiled. "That's pretty normal for a girl with only a few weeks left till her wedding."

Julie sighed. "But all she talks about is Chad."

Mom laughed. "You know, I think we should all be more like Kay," she said. "We're also waiting for our 'bridegroom' to come. The Bible calls Christians the 'bride of Christ.' When Jesus comes back, he'll take us—his bride—to heaven. We should be eagerly looking forward to that time."

"Well, I hope you don't mean we should put dirty dishes in the refrigerator like Kay did!" said Brian as he came into the room.

Mom smiled. "No, but maybe we should talk about Jesus more. Chad is constantly on Kay's mind because she loves him so much. That's why she thinks about him and talks about him all the time."

Julie was quiet. "I don't think about Jesus all the time. Does that mean I don't love him?" she asked.

"No," Mom said reassuringly, "but if your love for him doesn't grow, that would be a cause for concern. Keep following Jesus, and think about all he's done for you. Don't hesitate to talk about him, too." *KRL*

HOW ABOUT YOU?

Do you think about Jesus a lot? Did you know that he thinks about you all the time? And he loves you even more than people love one another. Think about the many blessings he provides for you. As you do that, your love for him will grow, and you'll want to talk about him often.

MEMORIZE:

"But we are citizens of heaven, where the Lord Jesus Christ lives. And we are eagerly waiting for him to return as our Savior." *Philippians 3:20*

 Talk about Jesus

The Water Hole (Read 1 Peter 3:8-12)

1

MARCH

Dad's van squealed to a halt. Everyone leaned forward. In front of them the entire road was flooded. "Wow!" exclaimed Jonathan. He smiled—this looked like fun! "Barrel through, Dad," he said. But six-year-old Annie looked scared.

Dad glanced over his shoulder. Behind him was the steep hill they had just come down. On either side were fences. Where could they turn around? "I don't know, Son. We're miles from a telephone, it's growing dark, and if we get stranded . . ." Dad hesitated. "No, I've got to find a place to turn around," he said. So very carefully Dad backed the van up the hill. Mother quieted Annie and then closed her eyes. Jonathan knew she was praying. Finally, they reached the top of the hill. Dad found a tiny space and turned around.

"Aw, we should have gone right through the water," said Jonathan. "It would have been fun."

"Son," said Dad, "sometimes you have to know when to turn around. We don't know how deep that water is. What *looks* like fun can sometimes lead you straight into trouble—in life as well as on the road."

"In life?" asked Jonathan. "What do you mean?"

"Well, sometimes sinful things look fun—like watching some TV shows or going to a wild party with friends—any number of things," replied Dad. "Just as I turned away from the flooded street . . ."

"God wants us to turn away from things that are bad for us," said Jonathan. Then he continued. "It's not so hard to turn away from things that you know for sure are wrong," he said. "But it *is* hard to turn from things that *could* be wrong but don't really seem so bad."

Dad nodded. "Backing up that hill was difficult, too," he said, "but we did it. When both you and Annie face tough choices, remember, God can help you." *CJB*

HOW ABOUT YOU?

Is there something you'd like to do, but you're not sure you should—something that seems like fun, but you think it might be wrong? Don't take a chance on it—it could get you into trouble. Talk to a trusted adult and ask God to help you know what to do.

MEMORIZE:

"The path of the upright leads away from evil; whoever follows that path is safe."

Proverbs 16:17

 *Turn from Evil*

Get Out of the Boat (Read Matthew 14:25-32)

Niki walked over to the edge of the school skating pond where some older girls were jeering and pointing at a classmate out on the ice. "Come on, Alex. Get up," called one girl. "We want to see you fall again!"

"He's so clumsy," observed another loudly. The group laughed and hooted.

Those girls are teasing Alex, thought Niki angrily. She had never spoken to him before because she was shy. But she had wanted to. Alex didn't seem to notice the teasing, though. "Why don't you all come skate?" he called with a smile.

2

MARCH

"And make fools of ourselves like you're doing?" asked one of the girls.

After school Niki told her older sister, Shannon, about it. "Those girls were so mean, but Alex didn't get mad," she said.

"You know," replied Shannon, "my Sunday school teacher talked about someone in the Bible kind of like Alex. It was Peter. Remember when he walked on the water?"

"Yeah," answered Niki. "He walked a little while, then sank. Jesus had to rescue him. I always felt embarrassed for Peter because he messed up."

"But at least he tried," answered Shannon with a twinkle in her eye. "Niki, who do you think Jesus was more pleased with—the disciples who stayed in the boat or Peter?"

"Peter, because he got out of the boat and tried," said Niki with a smile.

"My teacher said that it's especially important to 'get out of the boat' when it comes to trying new things and doing things we think God wants us to do."

Niki nodded. "I think I will try to talk to Alex tomorrow. I want to tell him how brave he was to try skating in front of all those other kids."

"Well," said Shannon, "I think you're brave for trying to make a new friend." *CBK*

HOW ABOUT YOU?

Do you feel scared to try something new? Are you shy when it comes to making new friends? Are you afraid someone will laugh at you? Often those who make fun of others are the most afraid of all. So go ahead. Get out of the boat!

MEMORIZE:

"Don't be afraid, for I am with you." *Isaiah 41:10*

 Dare to Try New Things

Cocoa on the Carpet (Read Psalm 51:1-12)

3

MARCH

Mark sat in the living room, stirring his cocoa. He wasn't supposed to bring drinks into this room because of the new carpet. But Mom wasn't home, and there was a program he wanted to watch. *I'll be careful,* he thought. He set the mug on the coffee table. Then he reached for the TV control and plopped his feet on the table. "Oh no!" he cried as his foot knocked the mug onto the floor. The chocolate drink made a huge stain on the new carpet.

Mark raced for a towel. He rubbed and dabbed, but he could not get the spot off the carpet. Hearing Mom's car, Mark covered the stained carpet with the coffee table.

Mark heard his mother putting the groceries away. He felt guilty. *If I tell her now, maybe she'll know a way to take it out,* he thought.

Slowly Mark headed for the kitchen. "Mom, I-I disobeyed you and took cocoa into the living room," he confessed. "I accidentally spilled it on the carpet, and I can't get it out."

"Oh, Mark! You didn't!" exclaimed Mom. "Not on the new carpet!" She hurried to survey the damage. "Where is it?" she asked. Slowly Mark pulled the table away. "It looks like you tried to cover it up," Mom said.

"I did," admitted Mark. "I know that was wrong. I'm sorry."

"Well, I've got some carpet cleaner that works well on fresh stains," said Mother. As she worked on the carpet, she added, "I'm glad you decided to tell me and not hide the stain, Mark. Hiding it won't fix it. It's like when we try to hide sin—the only way to fix sin is to bring it to Jesus and confess it. He can cleanse away our sin stains."

"Like that cleaner is taking the stain out of the rug, right?" asked Mark.

"Like that," said Mom, "but even better!" *KEC*

HOW ABOUT YOU?

Have you confessed your sins to Jesus and asked him to forgive you? You can't hide sins or fix them yourself, no matter how many good things you try to do. Only the blood of Jesus can wash your heart clean. If you want to know more about this, talk to a trusted adult.

MEMORIZE:

"And the blood of Jesus, his Son, cleanses us from every sin." *1 John 1:7*

 Jesus Can Cleanse You

Protective Gear (Read Ephesians 6:10-17)

"Brian, grab your catcher's equipment, and I'll help you practice a little," called Dad. Brian grabbed his gear and rushed out the door. His little sister, Megan, was close behind him.

Brian stopped on the patio and put his chest protector, shin guards, and face mask on. Then he grabbed his mitt.

4

MARCH

Megan giggled. "You look so funny!" she said. "What are you dressed like that for?"

"This stuff protects me when I'm catching the ball," Brian explained. "See how strong it is." He hit the padded chest protector with his fists before he ran out to the backyard.

Brian bent down and steadied himself on his feet in the "catcher's position." Megan ran to the picnic bench and watched Dad wind up and throw the ball forcefully to Brian. The ball bounced off the catcher's mitt, popped up, and struck the face mask hard.

Megan ran toward her brother. "Brian, are you hurt?" she asked.

"It's OK," he said. "See, the mask stopped the ball from hurting me."

For family devotions that evening, Dad read about the armor of God. "Today, you both saw how Brian's equipment kept him from getting hurt."

"And it helped me do my job well, too," added Brian.

"Well, God gives us special equipment for our spiritual lives, too. The armor of God protects us from Satan's evil tricks."

Megan's eyes grew big. "We don't have to be afraid of him?" she asked.

"That's right, honey," said Dad. "Just as Brian's equipment protected him from those hard-thrown balls, God's armor protects us from the tricks of the devil so that we can be strong Christians."

BMR

HOW ABOUT YOU?

Do you sometimes feel that you aren't strong enough to fight Satan? What types of things does Satan do to trick us? God provides his own armor to protect you: truth, goodness, readiness, faith, salvation, and his Word.

MEMORIZE:

"Put on all of God's armor so that you will be able to stand firm against all strategies and tricks of the Devil." *Ephesians 6:11*

 *Put on God's Armor*

Dirty Dishes (Read 2 Timothy 2:19-22)

5

MARCH

It was Wednesday evening, and Mom was running late.

"I'll set the table," Grandmother offered. Though nearly blind, she liked to help.

"Thanks," said Mom. "Use the dishes that are in the dishwasher."

When supper was ready, Mom called everyone to the table. Kelly was the first to notice that something was wrong. "Yuck!" she exclaimed. "These dishes are dirty. Why are they on the table?"

Mother looked at her plate. "Oh!" she gasped. "I must have forgotten to turn on the dishwasher last night!"

"And I couldn't see that they were dirty," said Grandma. After a good laugh, everyone helped remove the dirty dishes and replace them with clean ones.

At family devotions that night, Dad said, "In the verses we just read, our bodies are called 'vessels.' A vessel is like a dish. Tonight we saw how awful it would be to eat out of dirty dishes. God tells us to keep our bodies clean for him. Do you suppose he means we should take a bath?"

Kelly replied, "I don't think that is what God means. Does he, Dad?"

Dad laughed. "No, though we should keep our bodies clean, of course," he said. "But God is more concerned that we live a clean, pure life. That's what the apostle Paul is talking about here. He tells Timothy to do that by running away from wrong things. What are some wrong things that kids your age are tempted to do?"

Dana answered first. "Lie, cheat on tests at school, take things that don't belong to us . . ."

Kelly continued, "Say mean things to each other, watch things on TV that aren't good for us, and not obey you and Mom."

"Those are good examples, girls. I hope that when you are tempted to do those things, you will remember that God wants you to do what is right so you can be a clean vessel. You don't want to be like the dirty dishes, do you?" he asked.

"No way!" shouted Dana and Kelly. *MRP*

HOW ABOUT YOU?

Are you keeping your "vessel"—your body—clean and pure? Follow Paul's advice to Timothy, and then you'll be a vessel God can use.

MEMORIZE:

"Be a vessel for honor, sanctified and useful for the Master, prepared for every good work." *2 Timothy 2:21, NKJV*

 Keep Your Body Pure

Running the Race (Part 1)

(Read 1 Thessalonians 5:11-15)

6

MARCH

Merry looked back at her mom splashing through the puddles. Her mom's eyes were half shut against the drizzle. They were training for the Crawdaddy Days Fun Run. When Merry had won a ribbon in the race the year before, her mother had decided she would like to race next time, too. But her mom didn't look nearly as enthusiastic now, practicing in the cool soggy weather.

As her mom slowed to a walk, Merry dropped back. "Come on, Mom," she encouraged. "You can make it to the stop sign. It's not much farther." Mom smiled weakly and jogged to the sign. "Now, just once more around the block," Merry urged. "I'll be right beside you." As Mom frowned, Merry added, "It helps to think about something else while you run. Sometimes I recite Bible verses to myself."

A determined look crossed her Mom's face as they continued onward. Soon they were finished with the day's workout.

Back home Merry and her mom changed into dry clothes and crashed onto the couch together. "I wasn't sure you were going to make it this time," admitted Merry, "but you did just fine."

Mother rubbed her aching legs. "I don't know if I would have, sweetheart, without your encouragement," she said. "You've been a big help to me." Merry smiled, and her mother gave her a hug. "I appreciate your help with my training, especially when you encourage me to not quit. And thanks for that suggestion about reciting Bible verses. I think it will help me keep going when we hit the course again tomorrow. Merry, you are a treasure!" *SSA*

HOW ABOUT YOU?

Are you an encouragement to your parents and other family members? Can they count on you for a kind word or perhaps an uplifting Bible verse? You may be young, but that doesn't mean that you can't be a help to those around you.

MEMORIZE:

"Don't let anyone look down on you because you are young, but set an example for the believers." *1 Timothy 4:12,* NIV

 *Encourage Your Family*

Running the Race (Part 2) (Read Hebrews 12:1-3)

7

It was the day before the big race, and Merry was tearing everything out of her closet and drawers. "What did I do with them?" she moaned.

"What's going on?" asked her brother Jack, wide-eyed at the mess he saw.

"I can't find my favorite running shorts!" grumbled Merry, her head still in the closet. "Have you seen them?"

"Me?" asked Jack. "Not me!" He picked up a pair of jeans from the bed. "Here!" he said, tossing them at her. "Can't you just wear these?"

Merry peered around the closet door to see what he was offering. "Of course I can't wear those!" she said angrily. "What a dumb idea! They would be impossible to run in!"

"Not impossible," corrected Mother, entering the room with a pile of clean laundry, "but certainly uncomfortable and difficult. Were you looking for these, Merry?" Merry grinned sheepishly as she remembered having put the shorts in the laundry basket.

"It's important for Merry to have these tomorrow, Jack," Mother said as Merry picked up the shorts and put them in a drawer. "When we race, we don't want to carry any extra weight."

"So neither of you wants to carry my lucky horseshoe?" asked Jack with a grin.

"Pooh!" scoffed Merry. "You don't even have such a thing! And if you did, we wouldn't want it weighing us down. My coach at school says that on the day of the race we should put everything else out of our minds—and out of our pockets, too."

"The writer of Hebrews gives the same advice," Mother added.

"The Bible gives advice for racing?" asked Jack in surprise.

Mother smiled. "The apostle Paul refers to our Christian life as a race," she explained. "And the author of Hebrews urges us to put aside the sinful 'weights' in our lives and to run patiently. The weight of any sin—such as telling lies, making a hurtful remark, or carrying a grudge—will keep us from doing our best." *SSA*

HOW ABOUT YOU?

Are you running the Christian race? As all athletes know, to race successfully, you must be free of extra weight. If you're weighed down with unconfessed sin, confess those things to the Lord, and get back in the running!

MEMORIZE:

"Let us throw off everything that hinders and the sin that so easily entangles, and let us run with perseverance the race marked out for us."

Hebrews 12:1, NIV

 Get Rid of Sin

Running the Race (Part 3)

(Read Matthew 25:14-15, 19-23)

The day of the Crawdaddy Days Fun Run finally came. Dad and Jack were waiting at the finish line. They cheered for Merry when she crossed it—and, later, for Mother, too.

"I don't understand something, Mom," Jack said on the way home. "Why did you get a ribbon when so many people were ahead of you? I mean, Merry was the fifth to cross the line. But you were twenty-ninth!"

Mother smiled. "Well, Jack, I got my red ribbon because I came in second for my age-group," she explained. "Although I ran the race with everybody, I was competing only with other women my age."

"Oh, I get it! That's a good way to do it," mused Jack.

"Judging according to talent and ability is God's way, too," said Dad. "It would be discouraging if we had to be the best in the world to be recognized by him. But God made us. He knows our weaknesses and our strengths. He just expects us to do our best with the talents we have been given."

"Hmmm," said Jack. "I've got a talent I'd like to use today."

"What's that?" asked Merry.

"My talent for eating ice cream. Can we stop for some?" asked Jack with a grin. *SSA*

8

MARCH

HOW ABOUT YOU?

Do you feel down when it seems that you're behind in the Christian race? God knows when you're doing your best. Invest your time and talents wisely. You will be rewarded in the end.

MEMORIZE:

"See, I am coming soon, and my reward is with me, to repay all according to their deeds."

Revelation 22:12

 *Do Your Best*

Thirst Quencher (Read John 4:7-14)

9

MARCH

"It's hot today, and I'm so thirsty! May I have a glass of milk?" Becky asked her mother.

"You sure may," Mother answered. She got out a glass, went to the refrigerator, and poured some milk for Becky.

It wasn't long before Becky had another question. "May I have some soda pop?" she asked. "I'm still thirsty."

Mother frowned. "How about some juice instead?" she suggested.

"OK," agreed Becky, and Mother poured a small glass of juice for her.

Becky sipped the juice. Soon after it was gone, she rinsed her glass and filled it with cool water. Then she added two ice cubes. Becky took a long drink. "You know what, Mom?" she asked. "The milk was good, and the juice was, too. But this water works best to take away my thirst."

Mother smiled. "I agree," she said. "I always think nothing quenches thirst the way water does. I think I'll have some, too." As she got a glass, she added, "Did you know God gave us cool water to take away our physical thirst? And he gave us Living Water to take away our spiritual thirst."

"Living water?" repeated Becky.

"That's right," said Mother. "Jesus is referred to as Living Water. Just as your body gets thirsty, so does your spirit. Learning about Jesus through reading the Bible and going to church are ways to take away your spirit's thirstiness. Sometimes people try to take away their spirit's thirst by getting lots of things or trying to be the most popular. But only Jesus satisfies our spirit."

"Hmmm," said Becky. "Perhaps we should get a drink from the Bible, too. My spirit could sure use a story about Jesus."

"Good idea!" said Mother. *WEB*

HOW ABOUT YOU?

Do you think having lots of money or being popular will make you happy? While these things are not bad, only Jesus will bring you true happiness and satisfy your spirit. If you would like to ask him to be your Savior, talk to a trusted adult or a friend.

MEMORIZE:

"But the water I give them takes away thirst altogether."

John 4:14

 Jesus Can Satisfy Spiritual Thirst

Slow to Anger (Read Proverbs 14:14-18)

Philip and Ryan were playing tag. Suddenly Ryan tripped over Philip's foot and fell down, skinning a knee. "Ouch!" he cried. "You tripped me!" He held his sore knee and rocked back and forth.

"You fell over my foot," said Philip.

Ryan's face was angry, and he was trying not to cry. "You stuck your foot out on purpose because I was about to tag you," he accused his brother.

10

MARCH

"I did not. It was your fault!" replied Philip loudly. He was angry, too. Ryan stood up, doubled up his fists, and lunged toward Philip. Philip moved aside quickly, but not before Ryan managed to hit his arm hard.

Mr. Harmon, their neighbor, had been watching the boys from his yard. When he saw them fighting, he rushed over. "Boys!" he called. "Boys!" He was just about to pull them apart when some loud growling and barking began in the yard across the street. Philip and Ryan stopped fighting and turned their heads in the direction of the noise. Two dogs were snarling and snapping at each other.

"That little dog is gonna get hurt!" exclaimed Ryan, starting toward them. To his relief, their owner came out of the house and separated the dogs.

"I don't like it when dogs fight," Philip said. "It scares me."

Mr. Harmon nodded. "It probably started over a bone or something," he said. After a moment he added, "How do you think God feels when he sees people fighting like you boys were just doing?"

The boys looked at each other. "He probably doesn't like it," suggested Philip.

Mr. Harmon smiled. "No, he doesn't. I think it makes him sad to see people hurting one another," he said. "He tells us in the Bible to be slow to anger and quick to listen. Perhaps you boys need to practice that," Mr. Harmon added with a chuckle.

"I guess you're right," said Ryan.

"We'll give it a try," said Philip.

Ryan and Philip looked at each other. "I'm sorry," they blurted out together. *WEB*

HOW ABOUT YOU?

When you get angry, do you sometimes do foolish things like arguing or even fighting? Ask Jesus to help you be slow to become angry and to talk things out with your friends instead of fighting with them.

MEMORIZE:

"Dear friends, be quick to listen, slow to speak, and slow to get angry." *James 1:19*

 Talk, Don't Fight

A Good Guide (Read Proverbs 1:2-9)

11

MARCH

Janice sat with some other children near the front of the room and listened eagerly as Mr. Peters, the guest speaker in junior church, told of some of the experiences he had while visiting Egypt. "Who can tell me one of the most exciting tourist sights in Egypt?" the speaker asked.

Janice raised her hand. She was sure she knew the answer. "The pyramids," she said.

"That's right," said Mr. Peters, "and it was exciting to see them. In the area we visited, one of the most popular guides was a fourteen-year-old boy. He started his work as an official guide when he was only nine." Janice gasped as she thought about a nine-year-old boy being a guide.

Mr. Peters continued his story. He told how from early childhood, the boy, Noubi Aly, had learned everything there was to learn about the pyramids and other sights in Egypt. He had listened as others spoke and had watched as he visited the area. He had studied all the historical notes as well. By carefully following the instructions that his father and other older people gave him, he became one of the most sought-after guides.

Mr. Peters looked at the children. "Noubi Aly reminds me of you," he told them. "God has given many of you parents who teach you what is right. He has given you a pastor and Sunday school teachers. He has given you his Word so you may learn to live the way he wants you to. And now, you can be a 'guide' to others."

RIJ

HOW ABOUT YOU?

Do you think you're too young to be a spiritual guide? You're not. Listen carefully to teachers, pastors, parents, and God's Word. Then begin right now to share Christ and his love with people around you. Use the knowledge he has already given you to guide others to him.

MEMORIZE:

"A wise child accepts a parent's discipline; a young mocker refuses to listen."

Proverbs 13:1

 Learn to Guide People to Jesus

View from the Top (Read Proverbs 3:5-7)

12
MARCH

Bridget panted as she forced her tired legs up the last part of the rocky hill. Her cousin Amy pointed toward the valley below. "Look down there at Brett!" she said breathlessly. "He's almost got the cows into the corral."

Bridget watched her brother, Brett, dart around behind the cattle, herding them toward the gate. Everything looked so small from up on the hilltop. She could see almost the whole farm—the green fields of cotton, the winding river, even part of the neighbor's field. Then she gasped. Coco, their dog, had somehow gotten out of the fenced yard and was headed straight for the cows.

Bridget and Amy waved and shouted, trying to catch Brett's attention. But he couldn't see or hear them, nor could he see Coco yet. But sure enough, when Coco reached the cattle, she barked wildly and scattered the cows away from the gate. Brett had to round them up all over again.

That evening Brett complained to Dad. "If only I had seen Coco in time, it would have saved me a lot of work," he said.

"We saw her coming. We were on the top of the hill, and we could see the whole farm," said Bridget. "We were shouting and waving, but you didn't see us and couldn't hear us."

Dad smiled. "I'm sorry about your extra work, Son," he said. "But I think you just gave me an illustration I need to go along with the Sunday school lesson I'm teaching next week. What happened is a great example of how much more God sees than we do. He sees our whole life, just like Bridget and Amy could see the whole farm. That's a pretty good reason to let him lead us."

"I guess he could save us from a lot of trouble," Brett said thoughtfully.

"And make sure we don't miss anything good!" Bridget added.

KRL

HOW ABOUT YOU?

Do you trust God to lead you? He surrounds you with older and wiser Christians, and he gives you his Word, the Bible. All of these are provided to help you follow him. Trust him as he leads. He knows your life from beginning to end, and he knows what's best for you.

MEMORIZE:

"Seek his will in all you do, and he will direct your paths."

Proverbs 3:6

 *Let God Lead You*

Sometimes God Says No (Read Matthew 6:9-15)

13

MARCH

Sammy watched his little brother crawling all over the living room. Jimmy picked up a toy, chewed on it, and then threw it down. Next, he made his way to the television set and began pushing all of the buttons. "No," Mom said as she gently picked Jimmy up. Jimmy squirmed and fussed a little.

Sammy smiled as his little brother crinkled up his nose. "He sure is a busy baby!" he said.

"Yes, he is," Mom agreed.

Jimmy wriggled free from Mom's arms and threw himself onto the floor. He crawled to the television set again. "No, Jimmy!" repeated Mom. She picked Jimmy up and carried him toward his room. "I think it's time for a nap. You're a very tired little boy."

When she returned, Sammy was seated on the floor looking out the window. He didn't hear his mom quietly slip down beside him. "Penny for your thoughts," Mom teased.

Sammy grinned. "Do you think God gets tired of telling us no sometimes?" he asked.

"Well, we know that God wants the best for us," Mom said as she hugged Sammy. "He doesn't want us to be hurt by getting something that isn't good for us."

Sammy thought for a moment. "But sometimes we don't like the answers he gives us . . . like Jimmy," he said.

Mom nodded. "Yes, but as Jimmy grows older he'll learn to listen to what we say and accept our answers," she said. "And as we grow and learn more about God, we will learn to accept his answers, too, even when they're not what we want." *VRG*

HOW ABOUT YOU?

Do you sometimes ask God for something and then don't get the answer you want? Do you think God didn't hear you? He always hears when you talk to him, and he knows what is the right answer for each situation. Pray for his will to be done, and trust him to give you what is best!

MEMORIZE:

"And we can be confident that he will listen to us whenever we ask him for anything in line with his will." *1 John 5:14*

 Trust God to Give You the Best Answer

The Way to Give (Read 2 Corinthians 9:6-11)

14
MARCH

"Do you think she'll be OK?" Ryan asked, turning to his mom anxiously.

"I think so, but we'll just have to wait and see," Mom replied. Their dog, Bubba, had broken her leg, and the veterinarian was setting it.

"I'll help pay for the vet," offered Ryan. "You can use all the money I've saved." Things had been pretty tough on the farm lately. He knew this visit would be expensive.

Mom smiled and put her arm around Ryan's shoulders. "Thank you, Son, but don't worry. We can pay for it," she said. "I appreciate your willing heart, though." Mom was thoughtful. "Remember a few days ago when we were talking about tithing?"

"And I didn't want to?" Ryan asked.

"Yes." Mom nodded. "It was hard for you to be a cheerful giver right then. But today you didn't hesitate to offer your whole savings to help Bubba."

Ryan swallowed. "I'd give anything to make her all right, Mom."

"I know," Mom said. "When we really love someone, we give eagerly. That's how God wants us to give to him—because we love him so much."

"I really want to give to God like that," Ryan said wistfully, "but it's hard sometimes."

"That's true, but God will help you," Mom said. "Ask him to give you a willing heart."

The vet came into the waiting room. "Your dog will be fine," he said with a smile. "It was a clean break, and she'll heal in no time."

KRL

HOW ABOUT YOU?

Did you know that God wants you to give him part of your income? But he wants you to do it willingly. It's easy to say you love God, but it's harder to prove it by giving! If you know you haven't given cheerfully, but would like to, just ask God to help you.

MEMORIZE:

"You must each make up your own mind as to how much you should give. Don't give reluctantly or in response to pressure. For God loves the person who gives cheerfully."

2 Corinthians 9:7

 *Give Cheerfully*

A Fresh Start (Read Psalm 32:1-5)

15

MARCH

Evan looked at his little brother and burst out laughing. "Your shirt is buttoned wrong, Travis!" he said. "See how one side is longer than the other at the bottom? Here . . . I'll help you fix it."

"I can do it myself," insisted Travis. So Evan left him and went downstairs for breakfast.

The rest of the family was seated at the table when Travis arrived. "Having a little trouble with your shirt?" Dad asked.

"I told him it wasn't right!" Evan said. "I offered to help him, but he wouldn't let me."

As Travis's face puckered up to cry, Mother shushed Evan and called Travis to her. "It's not that serious," she said with a smile.

"I tried to fix it," Travis said, sniffing. "The bottom is straight now."

"Yeah, now it's sagging halfway down the front." Evan laughed, but a stern look from Dad quieted him.

"The problem is here," Mother said, pointing under Travis's chin. "You started out wrong. When that's the problem, the way to fix it is to go back and start over." Mother quickly unbuttoned the shirt and set it right.

"I don't like to start over," Travis muttered as Mother helped him into his chair.

"Nobody does," answered Mother, "but it's often the best way."

"Yes, it sure is," agreed Dad, "especially where God is concerned. The Bible tells us that if we confess our sins, God will forgive us and cleanse us. It's wonderful that we can put our mistakes behind us and start over."

"Hey, Mom," said Evan. He winked at Dad. "I'm sorry I ate my pancakes so fast! Can I start over with a new stack?" *SSA*

HOW ABOUT YOU?

Is there something that has happened—something you've done wrong—that you're truly sorry about? Tell God. He's ready to forgive and let you begin again, fresh and clean. God forgives and forgets.

MEMORIZE:

"Finally, I confessed all my sins to you. . . . And you forgave me! All my guilt is gone." *Psalm 32:5*

 Confess Sin and Start Over

The Clever Goat (Read Matthew 25:31-34, 41, 46)

16

MARCH

"Why does Chomper have to go?" Freddie asked his dad. "Why can't we save the money some other way?"

"I'm sorry about Chomper. I know you've enjoyed having a pet goat," said Dad. "But he's cost us quite a bundle with his mischievous ways."

Freddie knew that was true. Their two sheep ate only grass, but the goat preferred to snack on the neighbors' flowers and shrubs. Last week, Chomper had also eaten two apple tree saplings Dad had planted. They tried to keep him penned in, but sooner or later the clever animal always managed to get out.

"The worst was today," Dad went on. "Look at this." Freddie followed his father outside. He saw what Dad meant. Over a dozen wooden shingles had been pulled from the side of the house. Several chewed pieces lay scattered on the ground.

"Chomper may get into trouble sometimes, but he seems much smarter than the sheep," said Freddie. He shook his head.

Dad added, "Goats can be a lot of fun—and be useful, too—but they have a reputation for getting into trouble. Even in Bible times goats were known for their willfulness."

"Is that why Jesus compared people who don't follow him to goats?" asked Freddie.

"I don't know," said Dad with a smile, "but that's an interesting thought. It's certainly true that many people who don't know the Lord are beautiful, charming, and entertaining. Many are also very bright. But we need to be careful not to follow their lead." *LBM*

HOW ABOUT YOU?

Do you encourage the class clown to disrupt the class? Do you admire the daring of children who break the law or disobey their parents? Are you attracted by glamorous-looking boys and girls who do things you know are wrong? Be careful not to follow their example.

MEMORIZE:

"You will be accepted if you respond in the right way. But if you refuse to respond correctly, then watch out! Sin is waiting to attack and destroy you, and you must subdue it." *Genesis 4:7*

 Follow Jesus' Example

Teacher's Pet (Read James 3:13-18)

17

MARCH

"Are we going to invite Dee to our slumber party Friday night?" Nila asked.

Patti shook her head. "No way. We can do without the 'teacher's pet.'"

"But," Nila said, "she's the only one in the class not invited. If my folks find out, we'll have to invite her. Keep it quiet, will you?"

"Girls!" called Nila's father. "Come see what I've got."

Nila slipped the list into her desk drawer, and the girls went out to the porch. "Oooohhh!" they squealed when they saw the puppy in Mr. Hill's arms. "Can we keep him?" Nila asked. "What's his name?"

Dad laughed. "Butch—and yes, we'll keep him if Frisky will let us."

When they opened the patio door, a collie came bounding across the yard. Suddenly he stopped and growled deeply. "Frisky, don't act like that," coaxed Nila. "Butch wants to be your friend. Don't you, Butch?" The puppy whined, and the other dog growled once again. "Shame on you, Frisky!" scolded Nila. She turned to her father. "Why is he being so hateful, Dad?"

"Because he's jealous," Dad answered. "It'll take some time, but I think Frisky and Butch can learn to be friends," said Dad. "Bring the puppy in, girls. We'd better not leave him out here."

In the house, Patti carried the pup into Nila's room. Without a word, Nila pulled out the list and added "Dee." Patti nodded. "I guess Frisky taught us a lesson about jealousy," she said.

"Yeah," said Nila. "Imagine Frisky being a teacher!"

Both girls laughed. *BJW*

HOW ABOUT YOU?

Have you allowed jealousy to creep into your life? It can rob you of friends. If you're jealous of someone, ask God to forgive you. Then do something nice for that person.

MEMORIZE:

"**For wherever there is jealousy and selfish ambition, there you will find disorder and every kind of evil.**" *James 3:16*

 Get Rid of Jealousy

Your Father and You (Read 1 John 1:3-7)

18

"I don't care what you say, Mom!" grumbled Brad sullenly. "You can defend Dad all you want. He might be Mr. Wonderful to you, but he's not a good father."

Brad's mom sat down next to him. "Brad," she said softly, "what's bothering you? Why are you so angry with Dad?"

"He's never there for me!" declared Brad.

"When wasn't your father there for you?" asked Mom.

"Tuesday! He missed my football game!" Brad blurted out.

"True," agreed Mom, "but why didn't he go?"

"He went to the hospital with Grandma in the ambulance," mumbled Brad.

Mom nodded. "Next complaint?" she asked.

"Dad never listens when I talk to him," said Brad. "The other night I told him I was going to a party this weekend. He just said, 'No! End of discussion!'"

"But wasn't that *after* you told him who would be at the party?" asked Mom.

"Well . . . yes," admitted Brad.

"Dad tried to explain why going to that party wasn't a good idea, didn't he?" asked Mom. "Because he said no, you assumed your father wasn't listening, right?"

"Oh! Well . . . maybe," Brad stammered. "But I never get to see Dad!"

"Hmmm." This time Mom nodded in agreement. "I see where that may be true. He's at work all day. But then, you're at school all day!"

"But what about last night?" asked Brad. "Dad wasn't here, and I was bored, so I went out to find my friends!"

Mom began to laugh. "You sure do see only what you want to see!" she said. "Correct me if I'm wrong, but I believe it was *you* who breezed right past *him* on your way out!"

"I did?" Brad thought for a moment. "Wow, Mom," he said slowly, "I guess it's *me* who doesn't spend much time with my father, isn't it?" *MJL*

HOW ABOUT YOU?

Do you sometimes feel like your Father (that is, your heavenly Father) doesn't care about you? That he lets bad things happen to you? That he's far away, because you can't see him? God wants you to spend time with him. He loves you very much. He's available. Are you?

MEMORIZE:

"Draw close to God, and God will draw close to you." *James 4:8*

 Spend Time with God

Stuck in the Fireplace (Read Romans 8:1-6)

19

MARCH

"What's that noise?" asked Carlos as he and Greg played a game in Greg's living room.

Greg grinned. "Squirrels use our roof for a playground," he said. *Kerplunk!* Both boys jumped at the loud thump. "Something fell down the chimney!" shouted Greg. He ran to the fireplace and peered in. Jumping back, he gasped, "There's a squirrel sitting in there. He was staring at me."

The boys decided to make a path to the open front door so the squirrel could escape. But nothing happened. "He's just too scared," said Carlos. "We'll have to drag him out."

"Squirrels are mean when cornered," said Greg. He glanced down at his T-shirt and shorts. "Let's put on heavier clothes."

The boys ran to the hall closet and put on long coats, heavy mitts, and boots. Greg wore a ski mask and gave Carlos his catcher's mask. Then they tied a fishnet to the end of a broom handle. They edged to the fireplace where Greg raised the broomstick toward the squirrel. With a quick movement, he whipped the net over the little animal. The squirrel squirmed and scratched as Greg dragged him outside. Greg shook the net open and the squirrel escaped. Once free, the squirrel shot up the nearest tree. Safe on a limb, he made angry noises at the boys.

"The silly critter doesn't know what's good for him," said Carlos. "All we were doing was setting him free!"

"Yeah. He didn't even know he was in danger," said Greg. "He wanted to stay in that dirty, dark old fireplace."

"Well, even if the squirrel didn't say thanks . . . ," began Carlos.

"I'm glad we did it!" finished Greg. *LLZ*

HOW ABOUT YOU?

Are you afraid to follow Jesus? You may think that if you become a Christian, Jesus will make you give up everything that's fun. That's not true! He wants to rescue you from sin and its penalty. Following him is the greatest adventure in the world.

MEMORIZE:

"So if the Son sets you free, you will indeed be free."

John 8:36

 Jesus Can Set You Free

Fading Flowers (Read Isaiah 40:6-8; James 4:13-17)

20
MARCH

"Wheee!" cried Jan and Katy as they ran through an empty field near their house. The warm summer breeze rustled in the grass, and golden butterflies danced among the wild flowers. "I'm glad Mom's letting us have a picnic out here, aren't you?" asked Jan as she plopped down under a shady tree.

"Sure am," replied Katy. She sat down beside her sister and placed their picnic basket on the ground. "Oh, look!" She pointed to a clump of pink flowers. "Aren't those pretty? Pink is Mom's favorite color—let's pick some for her."

The girls quickly gathered the flowers and placed them in the shade under a big tree. They played happily all morning and then ate their picnic lunch. How good it tasted! They were hot and tired when it was time to go home. "Let's not forget Mom's flowers," said Katy. She ran over to the tree to pick them up. "Oh no!" she cried, holding them up. "Look! They're all wilted and ugly."

"We should have taken them to Mom right away," moaned her sister. "It's too late to pick more now."

When the disappointed girls told their mother about the flowers, she nodded. "I'm sorry they're wilted, too. But I think we can learn a lesson from these flowers," Mother added.

"What's that?" asked Katy.

"That there's a time to wait and a time not to wait. We should never wait to do what's good and right. And thinking to bring me flowers was a very good thing to do!" *SLK*

HOW ABOUT YOU?

When you see something nice you could do for someone, do you just think about it? And when you know what's right to do, do you hesitate because you're afraid of what others will think? Ask God to help you take advantage of the opportunities to do good and right today!

MEMORIZE:

"Teach us to make the most of our time, so that we may grow in wisdom." *Psalm 90:12*

 Don't Wait to Do What's Good and Right

The Potter and the Clay (Read Isaiah 64:6-9)

21

MARCH

Jessie worked the clay carefully with her fingers. Soon, what had begun as a brown glob was turning into a vase. When Mom came into the kitchen, Jessie held up the vase for her to see. "That's very pretty," said Mom.

"It's a present for Gran's birthday," said Jessie. "I'm going to keep working on it until I have it just right."

Jessie patiently worked on the vase until it was just the way she liked it. Then she put it on a shelf to dry.

That afternoon, Jessie was in the middle of an exciting book when Mom asked her to empty the trash. "Hurry," urged Mom. "I think I hear the truck."

"I don't see why I always have to stop what I'm doing to do my stupid chores," she grumbled as she got up to do what Mom had asked.

Later, Jessie's friend Karen came over. But after playing a little while, Jessie lost her temper. Karen got angry and went home.

Jessie thought about what had happened. She felt bad about having gotten angry. She also felt bad about her attitude when Mom had asked her to do her chores. Jessie went to talk with her mother. "Mom," she began hesitantly, "I . . . I'm sorry I was grouchy about my chores. I lost my temper with Karen, too," she added. "I guess I'm hopeless. I'll never be the kind of person I want to be."

Mom wiped her hands and pointed to the shelf holding the vase Jessie had made. "That vase started out as a lump of clay," she said. "It took a potter—you—to mold it into something lovely. And you worked at it until you had it just right, didn't you?" Jessie nodded. "Well, when you accepted Jesus, you agreed to let him mold your life," continued Mom. "It takes time and patience, but he can smooth out lumps that keep you from being who he wants you to be."

"Lumps like my bad temper?" asked Jessie.

"Exactly," said Mom. *KEC*

HOW ABOUT YOU?

Are you discouraged because you do and say things for which you are sorry? Do you sometimes feel hopeless? You're not! God won't give up on you!

MEMORIZE:

"And I am sure that God, who began the good work within you, will continue his work until it is finally finished on that day when Christ Jesus comes back again." *Philippians 1:6*

 God Is Still Working on You

Follow Directions (Read James 1:22-25)

22

MARCH

Troy struggled to unscrew the lid of a small bottle of paint. Dad had left to run an errand, and Troy wished he would hurry and return. He and Dad were going to use the paint to decorate the model airplane that Troy had gotten for his birthday.

Troy's face turned red as he tried to turn the lid. When he failed, he grew angry and impatient. He picked up one of Dad's screwdrivers and tried to pry off the lid. The screwdriver slipped and jabbed his finger. "Ouch!" Troy cried. He put the bottle down and went in for a bandage.

He met Dad coming in the front door. "What did you do to your finger?" Dad asked. Troy explained about the lid. "Did you read the directions?" Dad asked.

Troy shook his head. "Directions?" he asked. "To open a bottle? I didn't know there were any."

Dad helped Troy bandage his finger, then went with him to the garage. Dad picked up the paint and pointed to the writing on the top of the lid. "It says to push down and then turn."

Troy followed the directions, and the lid came off easily. "Guess I should have paid attention," he said. "I didn't even see those directions before."

"Remember our discussion last week when you asked why you should read the Bible and memorize your verses?" Dad asked thoughtfully.

Troy nodded. "You said the Bible gives directions for life," he replied. "And without those directions, we may do things that are wrong and then we're sure to get hurt. Like I hurt my finger when I ignored the directions on the bottle of paint, right?"

"Right," said Dad, "only you can get hurt a lot worse when you don't follow God's directions on how to live your life." *KEC*

HOW ABOUT YOU?

Do you read the Bible to learn God's directions for your life, or do you attempt to do things your own way? Read the Bible, and do what God says.

MEMORIZE:

"But if you keep looking steadily into God's perfect law—the law that sets you free—and if you do what it says and don't forget what you heard, then God will bless you for doing it." *James 1:25*

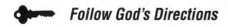 *Follow God's Directions*

The Password (Read John 14:1-6)

23

MARCH

"Hi, Mom," said Miguel as he tossed his book bag onto a chair and sat down at the kitchen table. Mom was pulling a pan of chocolate brownies from the oven.

"Hi, Miguel." Mom turned and smiled. "How was school today?"

"Great!" he answered. "May I have one of them?"

"One of those," Mom corrected. "Sure, but just one." She handed him a brownie and then asked, "So, what was so great at school?"

"We learned about passwords in our computer class," he answered. "Do you know what a password is, Mom? It's a special word you have to type into the computers. If you don't know the right word, the computers won't let you in to the programs," explained Miguel.

"Hmmm," Mother said as she smiled. "That sounds a lot like what I told our neighbor, Mrs. Goldman."

"You were telling Mrs. Goldman about computers?" asked Miguel.

Mom laughed. "No. But I was telling her about Jesus."

Miguel's forehead creased in confusion. "Huh?"

"Well," Mom said as she sat next to Miguel, "Mrs. Goldman believes that people who lead a good life will be in heaven, no matter what their beliefs. We talked about that for quite a while. Then I showed her John chapter 14 where Jesus said, 'I am the way, the truth and the life. No one can come to the Father except through me.' I told her that each of us will stand before God some day. And only those who have trusted Jesus as Lord and Savior will be able to enter his kingdom."

"Kinda like a password?" said Miguel with a smile.

"In a way, yes." Mom nodded. "Kind of like a password." *RSM*

HOW ABOUT YOU?

Is Jesus your Lord and Savior? Have you asked him to forgive you for the wrong things you have done? If not, talk to a trusted friend or adult to find out more.

MEMORIZE:

"There is salvation in no one else! There is no other name in all of heaven for people to call on to save them." Acts 4:12

 Jesus Is the Only Way to Heaven

Living Stones (Read 1 Peter 2:4-10)

The Wilsons were eager for their new house to be completed. They had watched the progress from the very beginning. The land had been cleared and leveled. The house had been framed, a roof put up, floors and Sheetrock added, and windows cut out. They had watched in amazement. "From a piece of wooded land, to our new home!" said Dad.

24
MARCH

"Yeah!" exclaimed Tom. "I can hardly wait!"

The day came for the bricklayers to cover the wooden walls, and Dad and Tom went to watch. "Tom, look how perfectly straight the men are laying those bricks," said Dad. The two had been watching for some time, and they had noticed that a string was stretched from one corner to another corner. The bricks were in line with the string.

"If the string were not there for the men to eyeball, the line of bricks could be crooked, right?" asked Tom.

"That's right," replied Dad. They sat and watched the bricklayers a while longer. "Tom, did you know this brick building can be compared to our lives as Christians?" asked Dad. "The Bible calls us 'living stones' built into a spiritual house. It says that Christ is the chief cornerstone."

"You mean . . . like that first stone where the string begins?" asked Tom.

"Yes, that stone is the guide, just as Christ is the guide in our lives," replied Dad. "He is perfect because he is God. Now . . . what would happen if some bricks were left out of the wall?"

Tom thought for a minute. "The wall would be weaker and could fall," he suggested.

"Right." Dad nodded. "Every brick is important. And in the spiritual realm, each Christian is important, too." *DLW*

HOW ABOUT YOU?
Do you feel that you are not important? You are important to God. Always remember that Jesus is the cornerstone. He is the guide for your life. And as a Christian, you are a "living stone."

You Are Important

MEMORIZE:
"And now God is building you, as living stones, into his spiritual temple. What's more, you are God's holy priests, who offer the spiritual sacrifices that please him because of Jesus Christ." *1 Peter 2:5*

Leftovers (Read Deuteronomy 16:1-2, 10-11)

25
MARCH

"May I have a kitten? Please? Please?" Jessica begged. A big sign in their neighbor's front yard said Free Kittens. Jessica persistently pleaded with her mother to let her have one. Finally, Mother reluctantly agreed, and Jessica hurried off to claim her prize.

When Jessica returned, she was carrying a very small kitten. "I took the littlest one," she informed her mother. "His name is Runt."

A few weeks later, Mom and Jessica took Runt for his first visit to the veterinarian. "Hmmm," murmured the vet, after checking Runt. "This kitten is a bit scrawny. What have you been feeding him?"

"Leftovers," said Jessica promptly.

"That may be the problem," said the vet. "Your leftovers don't have the right nutrients to help Runt grow properly. If you'll feed him food made especially for kittens, he should soon be healthy and strong." On the way home, Jessica and her mother stopped at a store to buy the special food the veterinarian had suggested.

"No more leftovers for Runt," Jessica told her dad that evening. "Only good, healthy food."

"All right!" exclaimed Dad with a grin. "I'm sure Runt will appreciate that." After a moment he added, "And do you know who else shouldn't get leftovers?"

"You?" asked Jessica.

"Well, I didn't mean me," said Dad. "I was thinking of God. We need to give our best to God instead of giving leftover time, love, or effort."

"Hmmm," Jessica said, "I never thought about that before."

LJR

HOW ABOUT YOU?

Do you give God only a little time at the end of the day for Bible reading and prayer? Do you just give him leftover change after you buy what *you* want? Do you run out of energy to help people because you're tired from doing what *you* want to do? Give God your best!

MEMORIZE:

"As you harvest each of your crops, bring me a choice sample of the first day's harvest. It must be offered to the Lord your God." *Exodus 23:19*

 Give God Your Best

Off the Hook (Read Psalm 119:9-12)

26 MARCH

"Jared, have you learned your memory verse for Sunday yet?" asked Mother.

Jared shook his head. "I got my lesson done. But it takes too long to learn the verse," he said as he held up the model plane he was putting together. "I want to finish this so I can take it to show-and-tell at school." He frowned. "My friend Ben was supposed to come over this morning to help me with it. He said he'd call if he couldn't come. It's almost noon, and he still hasn't come or called."

"Well, I want you to learn that verse before you finish your plane," said Mother. "You can work on that this afternoon. Maybe Ben can come then instead. Why don't you call him and see?"

"Yeah, I guess I'd better," Jared agreed. He put the model down and went to the telephone. "Oh no!" Jared exclaimed. "Now I know why Ben hasn't called. The phone's off the hook!"

"Someone must have bumped it," Mother said. "Ben's probably been trying to call, but you've been missing his message." She looked at Jared. "Christians sometimes miss the Lord's messages, too."

"What do you mean?" asked Jared.

"In a way, our receivers are off the hook, and he can't get in touch with us."

"Because we're too busy doing other things?" asked Jared.

"That's right," Mother answered. "Studying God's Word and memorizing Bible verses is one way we can stay in touch with him."

Jared sighed. He knew what Mother meant. "You're talking about my Sunday school verse again, aren't you?" he asked.

"Yes, I am," replied Mother.

Jared sighed. "OK," he agreed. "I'll call Ben and tell him to come over this afternoon. Then I'll get to work on my verse." *WEB*

HOW ABOUT YOU?

Is your "receiver" in place? God is eager to communicate with you through his Word. Read it, think about it, memorize it, and act on it.

MEMORIZE:

"I will study your commandments and reflect on your ways." *Psalm 119:15*

 Memorize Bible Verses

Life or Death (Read Deuteronomy 30:15-20)

27

MARCH

Carl was thoughtful as he helped Mrs. Brown straighten the room after Bible Club. The children took turns doing this, and as a reward, they got to finish whatever was left over from their snack time. However, Carl shook his head when Mrs. Brown offered a cookie. "No, thanks," he said. He was thinking of what his dad had asked him. "If God is really so kind and loving as Christians say, why wouldn't he take everyone to heaven?"

Mrs. Brown noticed that Carl was quieter than usual. "Is something bothering you?" she asked.

Carl hesitated. "Yeah," he said. "If God is so kind, why doesn't he take everyone to heaven?"

"Good question, Carl," answered Mrs. Brown. "Let's see—how can I help you understand?" She thought for a moment. "Tell me, are you angry with me for not giving you any more cookies today? When you get home, will you say, 'That mean Mrs. Brown sent me home without any more treats'?"

"Course not," said Carl in surprise. "You offered them, so why should I be mad? They sure are good, but I just didn't want any more."

Mrs. Brown nodded. "I offered them, but you chose not to accept," she said. "It's a little like that with God. He offers heaven to those who will accept Jesus as their Savior. Jesus died on the cross and paid the penalty for our sins, so no one needs to go to hell. But then he allows people to make the choice of believing in Jesus or not. However, some people refuse to accept what Jesus has done for them. Does that make sense to you?"

Slowly Carl nodded. He'd have to tell Dad what Mrs. Brown had told him. *CEY*

HOW ABOUT YOU?

Have you chosen to follow Jesus? He's calling you today to receive him into your life. Admit your need and ask him to forgive your sin. Then you'll have eternal life in heaven. Easter is a great time to find out more about becoming a Christian.

MEMORIZE:

"Today I have given you the choice between life and death. . . . Oh, that you would choose life, that you and your descendants might live!"

Deuteronomy 30:19

 Choose Jesus and Life

A New Life (Read John 3:14-18, 36)

Becky loved the deep, rich colors of African violets, and she often helped her mother take care of them. "Look, Mom, this big leaf broke off our purple African violet," she said sadly one day. Then she threw the leaf in the wastebasket.

Mom quickly took it back out. "Here . . . let me show you what we can do with that leaf," she said. She filled a glass with water and cut a thick paper to fit over the rim. Then she put a slit in the paper and inserted the leaf into the slit so the stem was in the water. "Now we have to wait for that to sprout roots," she said.

28

MARCH

Several days later Becky noticed that the end of the stem was getting fuzzy with tiny roots, and as more days passed the roots continued to grow. "Now," Mom said one day, "it's time to plant the stem in soil, Becky. It will have to be watered occasionally, and I'll leave that job to you."

Becky faithfully watered the little plant, and soon she was thrilled to see tiny leaves peeking up from the soil. But a few days later she was upset again. "Mom, look! The big stem is starting to die. What do we do now?" she wailed.

"There's nothing we can do, Becky. That's the way it's supposed to be. You see, the 'mother leaf' has finished its job," Mom explained. "It has given its life so there can be new plants."

That evening Becky told her dad what happened. "That's interesting," he said. "You know what it reminds me of, Becky? It reminds me of our Lord Jesus. He died that we might live. He gave his life so that we can have eternal life in heaven. Unlike the plant, however, Jesus didn't remain dead! He rose again, and right now he's in heaven preparing a place for all those who have received new life from him." *CV*

HOW ABOUT YOU?

Have you received new life in Jesus Christ? He died so that you can live forever. If you are interested in finding out more, talk to a trusted adult.

MEMORIZE:

"And all who believe in God's Son have eternal life. Those who don't obey the Son will never experience eternal life."

John 3:36

 Christ Gives New Life

A Box of Puppies (Read James 2:14-23)

"Mom! Come see what I found!" Andy said, tugging on his mother's hand. Taking her to the front porch, he pointed to a brown box.

Mom peeked inside. "Five puppies!" she exclaimed.

"Yeah. I found them in the ditch on the way home from school," Andy said.

29

MARCH

"They will need milk soon," Mom said, petting a fuzzy black puppy.

"I'll get some from the refrigerator," volunteered Andy.

"That milk might not be the best for puppies," said Mom. "I'll call the veterinarian to see what we should give them." She went to the phone to get the information.

After the puppies had been fed, Andy carefully placed the box in the garage. "Sleep tight," he whispered. Then he went back into the kitchen.

"I love dogs," he told his mother. "I like all animals."

"I know," said Mom. "Your actions show it." She smiled. "It reminds me of what Pastor said yesterday—about our actions showing others our faith. He said that when we truly believe in God, we will show our faith by the things we do."

"The things we do prove we love God?" Andy asked.

"That's right," agreed Mother. "You *say* you love animals, and you prove it by your deeds—by the way you treat them. You *say* you have faith in God, and you prove that with your deeds, too. You prove it by the way you obey him and by the way you treat others."

Just then Mom and Andy heard Dad's car door slam shut. "The strangest thing . . . ," said Dad, entering the room. "I thought I heard squeaking out in the garage."

"You did," said Andy. "Follow me. I'll explain everything." *JKG*

HOW ABOUT YOU?

Can people tell you believe in God by watching your actions? Do your friends know that you love God by what you say and do? Everything you do tells others about what you are thinking and what is important to you. What do your actions say?

MEMORIZE:

"**Now someone may argue, 'Some people have faith; others have good deeds.' I say, 'I can't see your faith if you don't have good deeds, but I will show you my faith through my good deeds.'**" *James 2:18*

⚷ Don't Just Talk; Do

Jesus Loves Me (Read Romans 8:35-39)

Today was the worst day of Dedra's life! Earlier that morning, her father and mother had sat on the couch and calmly spoke the words that tore her world apart. "We still love you. We just can't live together anymore," said Dad.

"You'll spend weekends with Daddy and weekdays with me," said Mother.

Dad nodded. "We'll go to special places every weekend. We'll have fun . . . you'll see," he added.

30

MARCH

As time went on, Dedra's life fell into a new pattern. After school on weekdays, she and her mother cooked dinner and spent the evenings together. On weekends her father picked her up after school on Friday.

One Friday her father did not show up. Instead, her mother was parked outside. After that, Dad sometimes came, but often he did not. One day he showed up, but the car was full—filled with his new family! The love she once had known was split into two, and now into five. She didn't know where she fit in.

One week Dedra's next-door neighbor invited her along to Sunday school, and Dedra decided to go. The Sunday school lesson was about the love of God. Dedra scoffed as the teacher talked. *One day you're a family, and the next day you can be lost somewhere in the middle,* thought Dedra. Tears began to well up, and she continued to sit in her seat, even after the other children left.

"Can I help?" asked Mrs. Mason as she knelt beside Dedra.

"I don't believe what you said. Love's not like that," said Dedra abruptly.

"Dedra, God's love is not like human love," Mrs. Mason told her. "Nothing can separate us from the love of God." Dedra listened intently as the teacher shared the good news of God's love with her. It felt wonderful to know of a love like that! *TSE*

HOW ABOUT YOU?

Have you been disappointed in friends or family or circumstances? Have they failed you? God cannot and will not fail you. He loves you so much. Remember that his Word says nothing can ever separate you from his love.

MEMORIZE:

"And I am convinced that nothing can ever separate us from his love. . . . Our fears for today, our worries about tomorrow, and even the powers of hell can't keep God's love away." *Romans 8:38*

 God's Love Doesn't Change

A Great Sacrifice (Read John 15:9-13)

Dan stared at the painting on the living-room wall. It was a picture of two hands clasped in prayer and was titled *Praying Hands.* "Mom, aren't those the hands of Jesus?" asked Dan.

31
MARCH

Mom shook her head. "No, the artist was Albrecht Dürer, and the hands are those of a very special friend of his," she said. "Albrecht Dürer was born in Germany more than five hundred years ago. He came from a very large family, and they were poor," said Mother. "Albrecht had to work hard, but he loved to paint, and he dreamed of becoming a great artist. Finally he left home to study art. Since he also had to work, he had little time to paint. One day he met an older man who also wanted to be an artist. They decided to room together, and then his friend had an idea. 'I'll work while you study, and when your paintings are selling, I'll study,' said Albrecht's friend. So the friend washed dishes and scrubbed floors while Albrecht studied. At last Albrecht sold his first paintings. Now his friend, eager to begin his studies, took his paints and brushes and began to do what he had wanted to do for so many years."

"Cool!" said Dan. "So did he get to be a good artist, too?"

Mother shook her head. "All that scrubbing had made his hands stiff and rough," she said. "He was unable to paint. But one day Albrecht saw his friend with his hands folded in prayer. So Albrecht painted them."

"So Albrecht's friend really sacrificed his dream," Dan said. "I'm sure Albrecht did all he could to help his friend after that."

"Probably," agreed Mother. After a moment she added, "I'm thinking of some other hands—hands of someone who made an even greater sacrifice."

"You mean Jesus, don't you?" asked Dan.

Mother nodded. "He gave his life for us. He actually became sin for us so that we could have our sins forgiven," she said. "His hands bear the print of the nails. Surely we should do all we can for him." *EAA*

HOW ABOUT YOU?

Easter is a good time to remember all Jesus has done for you. Are you willing to serve him?

MEMORIZE:

"Only fear the Lord, and serve Him in truth with all your heart." *1 Samuel 12:24,* NKJV

 *Serve God Gladly*

April Birthday! (Read Ephesians 5:1-2, 8-10)

1

APRIL

"Happy birthday to you," sang Jerry and Annie as their mother brought the dessert to the table. "Happy birthday, dear Daddy. Happy birthday to you." Dad beamed as Mother set the cake with several lit candles in front of him. "Blow out the candles," clamored the children, "and don't forget to make a wish."

Dad closed his eyes and thought for a minute. Then he took a deep breath, puffed out his cheeks, and blew! All around the cake the little lights went out. But one of them recovered and burned brightly again. "Oops," said Dad. He tried again. Again the candle flickered and appeared to go out, but when Dad stopped blowing, the flame came right back. Dad tried a third time with the same results. "Hey, wait a minute," said Dad, while the children roared with laughter. He looked at the still burning candle. "Whose idea was this?" he growled playfully.

"Jerry got that candle down at Frye's Magic Supplies," laughed Annie. "It's a special candle, and it won't blow out. You have to put it under water to put it out."

"That's what you get for having your birthday on April first," teased Jerry. "Happy birthday, and happy April Fool's Day!"

The children each took several turns to see if they could blow out the candle. Even Mother tried, but no one could do it. "That special candle reminds me of what God has done for us," said Dad finally. "He has given us the privilege of being lights in this world. There are many things and people who 'blow' against us, causing our lights to flicker. And when we do wrong things our light burns dim. But the Lord gives us the courage and the ability to keep shining for him." *HWM*

HOW ABOUT YOU?

Is your "light" burning brightly? Or is there a sin that is causing it to burn dimly? If there is, confess that sin, ask God's forgiveness, and shine for him.

MEMORIZE:

"For though your hearts were once full of darkness, now you are full of light from the Lord, and your behavior should show it!" *Ephesians 5:8*

 Sin Hinders Your Light

A Walk in the Woods (Read Colossians 1:15-18)

2

APRIL

"Would you like to come to Sunday school with me, Jill?" asked Angie as the two girls walked along. Everyone in their science class had to identify twenty-five different wildflowers. They had decided to go on a hike together and see how many they could find.

In answer to Angie's question, Jill shook her head. "My parents believe you can get closer to God walking in the woods than you can sitting in some boring, old building reading an out-of-date book," she said. "I think that's true."

"Well . . . that's interesting," admitted Angie. "But the Bible may not be as outdated as you think."

"My dad says it is," insisted Jill. She pointed. "Look at that field—it's practically covered with flowers!"

"Wow!" Angie exclaimed. "Get out that guidebook on wildflowers that we brought from school, Jill."

"I didn't bring the book," said Jill. "Didn't you bring it?" She groaned as Angie shook her head.

"Oh, well," said Angie after a moment, "I guess that's an awfully old book anyway, isn't it? It was probably written before we were even born. I bet looking at the flowers will do us a lot more good than the stuff we'd learn from such an out-of-date book."

"Wildflowers don't change!" protested Jill. "That book is still good!"

"So is the Bible," Angie said softly. "It's as important today as it was when it was first written. God doesn't change, either. And even though we appreciate his creation, we still need to learn about God through the Bible—just like we need to learn about the flowers from the book." *LMW*

HOW ABOUT YOU?

Do you think you can learn more about God by looking at his creation than you can by going to church? Do you ever use that as an excuse to skip church and go fishing or hiking? It's good to appreciate what God has created, but it's even more important to learn what he says in his Word.

MEMORIZE:

"He existed before everything else began, and he holds all creation together." *Colossians 1:17*

 Honor the Creator

Warning: Danger (Read Proverbs 4:13-21)

3

APRIL

Michael looked up at the bright red bird in the tree. The brilliant crest on top of the cardinal's head bobbed as the bird made nervous, short chirps. Nearby, another bird was making the same warning noise while jumping from branch to branch. This bird's feathers were not so bright, but on its head was the same crest. The baby cardinals were learning to fly, and they were perched on different branches. Their parents knew the babies couldn't fly well enough to escape danger, so they were warning them to stay in the tree.

Just then Michael felt something soft rubbing against his legs. He looked down and saw his cat, Fluffy, who had just walked out of the bushes. Michael hadn't seen her before, but the parent birds knew the cat was there. Now the babies were safely out of reach because they had obeyed their parents' warning.

Picking up Fluffy, Michael carried her into the house. "You can't have those pretty birds," he told her. "You'll have to stay inside until the baby birds learn to fly well."

When Dad came home from work, Michael told him all about the cardinals. Dad smiled and put his arm around Michael's shoulder as they walked in the yard. "That's a beautiful picture of how God helps us," Dad said. "Those baby birds probably didn't see Fluffy at all—or maybe they would have liked a closer look, but they were warned to stay away. God warns us of danger, too. Sometimes we don't see anything wrong with certain activities. We may even wish we could try them. But God has told us to stay away from things like lying, stealing, bad friends, and mean actions. God knows these things hurt us as well as others."

Michael looked up at his dad. "And the babies were safe because they listened to their parents and obeyed," he said.

"Right," said Dad. "And we'll be safe if we listen to God and obey him." CEY

HOW ABOUT YOU?

How does God warn us? Remember, when God tells us to avoid certain activities, it's because he knows they will harm us. Are you listening to God's warnings?

MEMORIZE:

"Keep my commands and you will live." *Proverbs 4:4,* NIV

 Obey God's Warnings

Pony Express Rider (Read Joshua 1:6-9)

4

APRIL

"Hey, Mom! Guess what?" Joel called, running into the house and flinging his schoolbooks on the table. "At Bible Club today, my teacher talked about the Pony Express. Did you know that a long time ago, mail was carried from Missouri to California by forty guys? Each one rode as hard as he could for fifty miles until they covered nineteen hundred miles. It took 'em ten days, nonstop! They couldn't wear heavy clothes, and the mail had to be really lightweight, too. It was pretty dangerous on the trail, but they couldn't even carry a gun because it might slow 'em down. . . ." Joe paused for breath.

"That's really interesting," said Mom. "But why was your Bible Club teacher giving you a history lesson?"

"It wasn't a history lesson," said Joel. "It was . . . ah . . . it was more like an object lesson, Mom. And guess what else?" Joel's eyes sparkled. "Every rider carried a full-sized Bible that he received when he was accepted into the Postal Service. Because of the possibility of bandits or even death on the way, the Service believed it was important for the men to carry a Bible . . . even though it was heavy."

"So . . . how is all that an object lesson?" asked Mother.

"Well, just like the Pony Express riders carried important messages, God gave us an important message to carry to the world," replied Joel. "He wants some people to carry it far away—like to other countries. Not everybody gets to go that far, but all of us do have to carry it—even if it's just to the people near us. And you know what else?"

"What else?" asked Mother.

"Just like the Pony Express riders had to go fast, we have to hurry, too, because time might run out," said Joel. "So I stopped on the way home and invited Greg to come over this week and watch my new Christian video with me. Is that OK?"

Mother smiled. "It sure is," she said. *PIK*

HOW ABOUT YOU?

Are you telling your friends about Jesus and what he has done for you and for them? Are you sometimes afraid? Ask God for courage. Remember, he will be with you all of the time.

MEMORIZE:

"Be strong and courageous! . . . For the Lord your God is with you wherever you go."

Joshua 1:9

 Carry God's Message

Peer Pressure (Read Daniel 1:8-15)

Michelle watched as her mother screwed lids on several jars of vegetables and placed them in a pressure cooker. Then Mother put the lid on the cooker and turned up the heat. "How does a pressure cooker work, Mom?" asked Michelle.

"Well, I'm not exactly sure," Mother said. "I just know that the heat causes pressure to build up inside the cooker. The force of the pressure will help to preserve the beans inside the jars. When they're done, we'll be able to store them for a year or more, and they won't spoil."

5
APRIL

When the gauge on the cooker reached ten pounds, Mother lowered the heat, and some time later, turned the burner off. "Now we have to wait till the pressure goes to zero before we open the cooker," she said. "Pressure is a powerful thing."

"Yeah," murmured Michelle. "I feel like I'm in a pressure cooker at school! The kids in my class are mad at me for not cheating on the last history test, 'cuz Mr. Wilson caught them. They want me to sign a petition asking for a different teacher. They want it to be signed by everybody, but I think he's OK. I don't want to sign. I wish they'd lay off." Just as she finished speaking there was a loud *crack!* Michelle jumped. "What was that?" she asked.

Mother frowned. "A jar inside the cooker has cracked," she said. "It must have had a weak spot and couldn't stand the pressure." After a moment she added, "Pressure in our lives can work two ways, too. It can cause us to give in to what's wrong because we're weak. Or it can cause us to let God be our strength when we feel weak. Each time we see how strong God is it helps us grow in our faith."

"Do you think he would help me in my situation?" asked Michelle.

"I know he will," answered Mother. "Even though it may be difficult, he will help you do the right thing." *BJW*

HOW ABOUT YOU?

Are you pressured by friends to do wrong things? Christians—especially young people—are always under peer pressure to be like everybody else. Stand firm for right. Purpose in your heart, as Daniel did, not to let the wrong actions of others influence you!

MEMORIZE:

"And the Lord will deliver me from every evil attack and will bring me safely to his heavenly Kingdom." *2 Timothy 4:18*

 *Grow under Pressure*

Salt and Such (Read Romans 15:4-6)

Colleen skipped into the kitchen. "Good morning! Breakfast is ready," said Mother. "It's already on the table."

"It's hot cereal, and *I* made it," added Colleen's sister, Sarah, as she got milk from the refrigerator.

6

APRIL

Colleen sat down, and after they gave thanks, she scooped some sugar onto her cereal and tasted it. She added a little more sugar and tried it again. Sarah stopped eating, looked at her cereal distastefully, and added more sugar. Colleen followed her example.

"You're using an awful lot of sugar, aren't you, girls?" asked Mother. "Is something wrong with the cereal?"

"It doesn't taste right," admitted Sarah. "What did I do wrong?"

Mother tasted the hot cereal. "It's just a little bland," she said. "Did you add the salt, Sarah?" Sarah shook her head, so Mother took a salt shaker and sprinkled a little salt on everyone's cereal.

"It's better now," declared Colleen after trying it.

Mother nodded. "The salt helps the flavor," she said. "It's good to be reminded of that now and then. The Bible says that we are to be like salt."

Colleen and Sarah looked at each other. "What are you talking about, Mom?" asked Sarah.

Mother smiled. "We are to sprinkle the earth with the joy of Jesus. How do we do that?"

"By doing nice things for people," said Colleen.

"That's one way," agreed Mother.

"I have a suggestion," said Sarah. "After breakfast Colleen and I could visit Maria. Her mother says she's been pretty lonely since she broke her leg."

"OK," agreed Colleen. "We'll go and sprinkle some joy on Maria today." The girls both giggled. *BRH*

HOW ABOUT YOU?

Are you "sprinkling" the lives of others with the joy of Jesus? Perhaps a friend's parents are getting a divorce; maybe you know someone who is disabled or sick or new in your school; or maybe someone needs help with homework. Be a friend and helper.

MEMORIZE:

"You are the salt of the earth."

Matthew 5:13

 Make Others' Lives More Pleasant

Pain That Went Away (Read Philippians 4:10-13)

"Oh, Mom, please!" begged Judy as she sat at the kitchen table looking at a catalog. "Please get me one of these neat sweatshirts! If I don't get one, I'll just die!"

Just then, they both heard a loud cry as little Jimmy came in from outside. "I got hurt at Danny's house," sobbed Jimmy. "I pinched my finger, and it hurts so bad!"

As the tears flowed, Mother asked, "Which finger is it?"

7

APRIL

Jimmy paused, looked at his hand, and wiggled his fingers. "I can't remember," he said, looking surprised. "I guess it doesn't hurt anymore!" Grinning, he turned and went back outside to play with his friends.

As they watched him go, Mother couldn't help smiling, and Judy burst out laughing. "Some 'hurt'!" she told Mother. "He couldn't even remember which finger!"

Mother turned her smile in Judy's direction and asked, "Do you remember last September, when you said you would 'just die' unless I bought something you felt you needed?"

Judy wrinkled her brows in thought. "What was it I wanted?"

"It was a pair of tennis shoes that you said everyone was wearing," Mother reminded her. "I bought you a different pair that cost half as much, and you complained for a week or two. Then you dropped the subject. Why?"

Judy blushed. "I guess I forgot about it," she admitted. "Are you trying to say that if I don't get this sweatshirt now, I'll eventually forget how much I wanted it, too?"

"Something like that," Mother replied. "It's not bad to want things. But we also need to learn to be content with what we have. When we're not content, we always want more. In a few weeks, you will want something else. Just like Jimmy, you need to learn that your 'hurt' is not as bad as you think it is!" *SLK*

HOW ABOUT YOU?

Are there things you feel you have to have in order to be happy? Think again! The Bible tells us to be content with what we have.

MEMORIZE:

"For I have learned how to get along happily whether I have much or little." *Philippians 4:11*

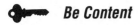 **Be Content**

Tools for Living (Read Luke 17:3-10)

"This is going to be a super tree house," declared Mark.

Roy held up a board. "I don't know," he said. "This board is too long. I tried to cut the end off, but the saw is too dull."

"Use this one," suggested Mark. He handed Roy another board.

8

APRIL

Throwing it down, Roy scratched his head. "It's too short," he said. "I give up! You're never going to build a tree house unless you get better tools!" He started down the driveway.

"Quitter!" grumbled Mark. "I won't let you play in my tree house if you don't help."

Roy kept on going. "See you," he called back.

Angrily Mark picked up the hammer and some nails, grabbed a board, and tried to fasten it onto the tree. He brought the hammer down hard. "Ouch!" he cried as the head of the hammer flew off. "My thumb!" Hanging onto his thumb, Mark hopped around. "I quit, too," he said with a sob.

That evening, Mark told his father about the problem. "That old hammer hurt me," he said, showing Dad his thumb. "Don't we have any good tools?"

"Yes, we do," answered Dad. "They're in my car. I needed them at work today, but I'll be around tomorrow. I can help you then. I'll show you how to use them. But right now let's use the tool we need for building our life."

"What is that?" asked Mark.

"I'm surprised you don't know," said Dad as he reached for the Bible they kept on a shelf in the living room. "This is the tool right here. And it's time for family devotions."

"I never thought about the Bible as a tool," said Mark. He grinned at his dad. "I suppose you could call prayer a tool, too."

Dad nodded. "That's right," he said. "When we use those tools faithfully, it makes a big difference in our life." *HAD*

HOW ABOUT YOU?

Are you using the right tools to build your life? Some television programs, movies, and books are not good for your spiritual growth. Reading and studying the Bible shows you God's way to live. Praying keeps you in touch with God so that he's able to guide you as you build your life.

MEMORIZE:

"For every house has a builder, but God is the one who made everything." *Hebrews 3:4*

 Read the Bible and Pray

Satan's Workshop (Read Proverbs 6:6-11)

Jill and David were lazily sprawled on the living room floor, watching TV. When Mother came in and sank wearily into an easy chair, David glanced at her and grinned. "What's the matter, Mom? You look tired!" he teased.

"While you two have been lying there, I have been washing woodwork, baking pies, ironing your clothes, and sorting out the laundry. It's no wonder I'm tired. I guess I should have asked you to help me."

9
APRIL

Jill yawned. "Well, we're tired, too."

"Yeah," agreed David glumly, "tired of sittin' around. We're bored."

Mother answered, "You know, my grandmother used to say, 'Idle hands are the devil's tools, and an idle mind is the devil's workshop.' I think she was right."

"What does that mean?" asked Jill.

"It means that if you don't keep busy doing worthwhile things, you will be tempted to do things that are worthless," explained Mother. "It's like . . . well . . . David, do you remember when I made you clean out your dresser drawers?"

David nodded. "You made me throw out so much stuff that I had a whole drawer left, and nothing to put in it."

"I suggested that you take some of your models out of the closet and keep them in that drawer," reminded Mother, "but when I opened that drawer this morning, I found it stuffed with junk. What a mess!"

David frowned. "Sorry, Mom," he said. "I never got around to putting my models in there, so the other stuff just kind of snuck in. That empty drawer seemed like a handy place to put things."

Mother nodded. "I know," she said. "And that's exactly what happens when you don't fill your hours with good, wholesome things—including hard work. You will end up filling your 'empty' time with all kinds of junk."

"Like these dumb cartoons," said Jill as she turned the TV set off. "Come on, David! Let's give Mom a break. I'm sure we can find plenty of work to do." *SLK*

HOW ABOUT YOU?

Do you often find yourself wasting time? Do you watch television more than you should, or gossip on the phone, or do wrong things just because you're bored? Find good things to do that will help you and others. Then you won't have time to be bored! You may even find you're having fun!

MEMORIZE:

"Never be lazy in your work, but serve the Lord enthusiastically." *Romans 12:11*

 **Don't Be Idle**

A Hurting Friend (Read Matthew 9:2-8)

10
APRIL

"Ow, it hurts! My arm hurts so bad!"

Hearing his friend's voice, Jeremy looked toward the swings. He saw Matt biting his lip as he tried to squeeze the tears back. Jeremy jumped off the monkey bars and ran to his friend. "Did you fall?" he asked. Matt nodded and clutched his injured arm. "Don't worry—it'll be OK," Jeremy comforted him. "Come on—I'll take you to the nurse." Clumsily, Jeremy grabbed Matt's good arm and started toward the school building with his friend.

Soon Matt was on his way to the doctor's office, where a cast was put on his arm.

That evening, Jeremy told his dad about Matt. "I was kind of scared—I wasn't sure I knew where the nurse's office was," he said. "But I'm glad I could help Matt."

"Why did you help him?" Dad asked.

Jeremy looked startled. "Because he was hurt," he said. "I wouldn't be a good friend if I'd just left him there!"

"Isn't Matt the friend you told me about last week?" asked Dad. "The one who doesn't go to church?" Jeremy nodded. "Have you invited him to come with you?" asked Dad.

"No," admitted Jeremy. "He says his dad doesn't believe in God, and the church is for sissies. I was afraid Matt would laugh at me if I told him I went."

"You took Matt to the nurse's office right away because you cared about him," said Dad. "Do you care about him enough to tell him about Jesus or to invite him to Sunday school so he can learn about Jesus?"

"I . . . I guess I could try," said Jeremy.

"Let's pray and ask God to give you the courage you need to invite Matt to church. He'll help you to know when the time is right." Jeremy nodded, and together they bowed their heads to pray. *LRS*

HOW ABOUT YOU?

You would immediately help a friend who was physically hurt, wouldn't you? It's sometimes harder to see when people hurt spiritually. But if they don't know Jesus, their need is great. When Jesus lived on earth, he was concerned about people's bodies and their spirits. Ask God to show you how to help your friends.

MEMORIZE:

"Therefore, go and make disciples of all the nations."

Matthew 28:19

 Bring Friends to Jesus

Cookies for Pastor Wagner

(Read 1 Peter 5:1-5; 1 Thessalonians 5:12-13)

11

APRIL

"Wow! I think these must be the very best cookies I've ever tasted." Pastor Wagner said, as he smiled at Amanda. "You're some cook! I'll have to sign you up for the next church dinner."

Amanda giggled. "Thank you, Pastor," she said. "May I ask you something?"

"Hmmm . . . I think so," agreed the pastor. "Fire away."

"In school, our teacher was talking about evolution, and I raised my hand and told the class what I believed," Amanda explained. "My teacher asked me to bring Scripture verses that proved my point. Would you be able to help me?"

"Sure," said Pastor Wagner. "How about getting a pencil and paper right now?" For several minutes, Pastor Wagner and Amanda looked in the Bible for verses Amanda could use, and by the time the pastor left, she had quite a list.

"Pastor Wagner's really nice," said Amanda after he had left. "He's always helpful. When Christy was sick last year, he visited her in the hospital almost every day. And he came to the honors program at school when I got the choir award."

"He came to our wedding, too," said Mother, laughing. "If he hadn't, we couldn't have gotten married."

"I think he should get some special reward," declared Amanda. "He spends so much time caring about others."

"Don't worry. The Lord will take care of his special award," Dad assured her. "The Bible mentions a 'crown of glory' to be given to those who feed 'the flock.' 'The flock' refers to Christians—the Good Shepherd's sheep. Pastor Wagner feeds the flock by teaching us the Word of God, by caring about us, and by loving us."

"That's neat," said Amanda thoughtfully. She grinned. "Pastor Wagner will receive that reward in heaven, but I think I'll reward him right now by making him a card." *LMW*

HOW ABOUT YOU?

Do you appreciate your pastor? Your Sunday school or Bible club teacher? Other Christian leaders? They teach you, care about you, and encourage you in your Christian life. They protect you by teaching you how to avoid sin. Let them know that you appreciate them by your attitude, actions, and words.

MEMORIZE:

"Think highly of them and give them your wholehearted love because of their work. And remember to live peaceably with each other."

1 Thessalonians 5:13

 Appreciate Christian Leaders

Not Tips—Rules! (Read Psalm 119:97-104)

12

APRIL

Jerry lay in his hospital bed, frustrated with the portable electronic game in his hands. He just could not get past this one stage. He put it down on the nightstand. "This thing's impossible, Tom," he told the boy in the other bed.

"You're not giving up so fast, are you?" his roommate asked, laughing.

As far as Jerry was concerned, he had worked on it long enough. "Here," he said, handing the game to Tom. "I'll bet you can't do it either."

Without another word, Tom began to play the game. Soon he looked up. "See?" he said. He showed Jerry that he had already completed the first stage.

Jerry laughed. "That much is easy," he said. "The rest is what's hard."

Tom said nothing, but he began to play again. In just a little while he handed the game back to Jerry. "Give up?" asked Jerry with a laugh.

"No," Tom replied good-naturedly. "Look at the score."

Jerry looked. He couldn't believe his eyes. Bewildered, he scratched his head. "How'd you do it?" he asked.

"Followed the tips in the instruction book," Tom answered. With that, he pointed to a small booklet on Jerry's nightstand. "I have this game at home, and I learned that when you follow each step just the way they tell you, you can't miss!"

Jerry looked at the game and then back at the booklet. Tom's words reminded him of something his dad had said. "God has an instruction book for us—the Bible. In it he gives rules for living," Dad had told Jerry. "Learn to follow them. When you don't follow God's rule book, you're likely to mess things up in a big way."

Jerry looked over at Tom. "Hey, thanks," he said simply. Then he picked up his New Testament. "I've got an even more important instruction book. In fact, it doesn't just have tips—it has guaranteed rules for how to win at life," he told Tom. "I'll have to tell you about it." *RIJ*

HOW ABOUT YOU?

The Bible is life's instruction book; it's God's Holy Word. Read it, study it, memorize it, and most important of all, follow it.

MEMORIZE:

"The Lord says, 'I will guide you along the best pathway for your life. I will advise you and watch over you.'" *Psalm 32:8*

 Follow God's Directions

The Unpatched Crack (Read Luke 12:1-3)

Clark's shoulders slumped and his feet dragged as he made his way home from school. The night before, he had borrowed his father's stopwatch without permission. And he had accidentally broken it. Clark had slipped it back into the dresser drawer, hoping it would be weeks before his dad needed it.

13
APRIL

As Clark entered the house, he shrugged, trying to get rid of the weight of guilt. Walking down the hall, he found his big brother, Phil, painting his room. "Neat!" exclaimed Clark. "I'll help you."

"Oh no you won't," Phil replied. "You don't know how to paint."

Clark shoved his hands into his pockets and leaned against the door frame. He watched as Phil painted over a crack that ran from the top of the window to the ceiling. "Hey, Phil. Aren't you going to patch that crack?" asked Clark.

Phil shook his head. "Naah. The paint will fill it up," he said.

"Dad always patches . . . ," Clark began.

"Get out of here and leave me alone!" said Phil. "Can't I do anything without you bugging me?"

Later Dad looked at the room. "It looks great, Phil, except for that crack over the window," he said. "Why didn't you patch it before you painted?"

"Too much trouble," Phil replied. "I thought the paint would fill it up, but it still shows, doesn't it?"

"I told him to patch it," gloated Clark.

"You'll have to patch it, Phil," said Dad, starting down the hall. "There are some things you just can't cover up."

Clark gulped as his dad's words rang in his mind. They reminded him of a recent Sunday school lesson about how you can't cover up sin forever. He knew he shouldn't really cover up his sin. He would have to tell Dad about the watch.

"Dad," he called after a moment, "there's something I need to tell you. Have you got a minute to listen?" *BJW*

HOW ABOUT YOU?

Is there something you've been trying to cover up? God says it can't be done—at least not permanently. Are you sorry for it? Then why not confess it right now?

MEMORIZE:

"**The time is coming when everything will be revealed; all that is secret will be made public.**" *Luke 12:2*

 You Can't Cover Sin

Turn on the Light (Read John 3:19-21)

14

APRIL

Jeanne was watching television one evening while Mother sat in a chair, knitting. When the commercials came on, Mother asked, "Did you finish cleaning the kitchen as I asked you to?"

"Yes . . . well, all except for washing the table," said Jeanne.

"You'd better do that now then," Mother told her. Jeanne jumped up and dashed into the kitchen. She grabbed a cloth from the sink, wiped the table, and then tossed the cloth onto the counter. She got back to her chair just as the program was coming back on.

A little later, Mother went to get a drink of water. When she turned on the kitchen light, she saw that the table was not clean. "Jeanne, come here," she called. "I thought you washed the table!"

"I did," replied Jeanne. She looked at the table in surprise. "I didn't see all those crumbs before."

"This may seem like a silly question," said Mother, "but did you turn the light on before you washed the table?"

Jeanne blushed. "Uh—well, no," she admitted. "I was in a hurry."

Mother laughed. "No wonder it didn't take you long to wash the table," she said. "Who ever heard of trying to clean something in the dark?"

Jeanne grinned. "Me," she said as she washed the table again, "but the next time I try to clean anything, I'm going to turn the light on first!"

"Good idea!" said Dad as he came up from the basement. "We all need to turn a light on in our lives from time to time, too."

"What are you talking about?" asked Jeanne.

"Well, the Bible is like a light because it shows us our sin. When we read the Bible and learn more about Christ, it shows us what areas of our lives need to be changed." *SLK*

HOW ABOUT YOU?

Do you assume that the things you do and say are all OK? Or maybe you feel that something in your life needs changing—but you're not sure what. Turn on the light of God's Word. Reading it will help you to see what needs to be changed.

MEMORIZE:

"For the word of God is full of living power. It is sharper than the sharpest knife, cutting deep into our innermost thoughts and desires. It exposes us for what we really are." *Hebrews 4:12*

 The Bible Reveals Sin

More Honey; Less Vinegar (Read Romans 12:13-21)

Anne's three-year-old brother, Bobby, caused problems for her. He sometimes went into Anne's room when she wasn't there and opened her dresser drawers, colored on her papers, and played with her jewelry. He was punished when he did these things, but it still happened. One day Anne decided she could stand it no longer. "Mom!" she yelled. "Bobby's always messing up my stuff! Could we put a lock on my door?"

15
APRIL

Mother answered, "Yes, I suppose we could, but I don't think that would be the best solution. Why don't you talk to Ken and see what he does to keep Bobby out of his things?" Ken was Anne's big brother.

"OK," agreed Anne.

When Anne asked her older brother about it, Ken smiled. "Well," he said, "an old saying goes, 'You can catch more flies with honey than with vinegar.'"

"Whatever do you mean?" asked Anne.

"It's usually easier to get people to cooperate by being nice to them than by fussing and yelling at them. Sometimes I just let Bobby come into my room to see things I'm working on. I even let him have the bottom drawer of my dresser as 'his' drawer to keep a few things in. And I make sure breakable stuff is up out of his reach. I've found that when I do these things, I hardly ever have to scold him."

"It seems like a lot of work just to keep him out of my stuff," Anne grumbled. "It's easier just to yell at him."

"It's not much work," Ken replied, "and it's worth it. It keeps him out of my things, and it makes us good friends. And like Mom is always telling us, God wants brothers and sisters to 'dwell in unity.'"

"OK, I'll try it," decided Anne. "Bobby's a pest sometimes—but I'm glad he's my brother. And I'm glad you are, too!" *SLK*

HOW ABOUT YOU?
Do you get upset when people use or misuse things that belong to you? Try being kind and sharing. You'll be surprised and pleased at the good results.

MEMORIZE:
"How wonderful it is, how pleasant, when brothers live together in harmony!" *Psalm 133:1*

 Get Along Together

Not Fair! (Read 1 Peter 2:21-24)

16

APRIL

Alex tossed his baseball cap onto the kitchen table and stormed into the family room where his parents were reading. "That's it!" he blurted angrily. "I'm through being Mr. Nice Guy!"

Alex's father looked up from his magazine. "You sound very upset about something," he said.

"Upset!" Alex exclaimed. "I'm just plain mad!" With that he dropped into a chair. "I'm the one who started this whole ball club," he continued. "I'm the one who furnished the bats and balls for that first game, and . . ."

Dad held up his hand to stop him from continuing. "So what happened to make you so upset?"

"What happened?" he asked. "What happened is that I was practically dumped from the team! Now that they've got a lot more guys to choose from, they forget that I'm the one who got things going. I even got Gem Cleaners to furnish those T-shirts for us." Alex looked over to see how his father was taking his news.

Dad shook his head. "Are the new guys better than you?" he asked.

"Well, yeah—they're OK, I guess, but I'm the guy who got things going!" Alex whined.

"Maybe it's not really fair," his father said quietly. "Things in this world aren't always fair. But try to look at this as an opportunity. Maybe if you take it calmly, the other guys will see that being a Christian makes a difference in your life and actions." Dad paused. "Do you think you could do that?" he asked. "You know, Jesus was sometimes treated badly by people, too. And he's the one who got everything in the whole universe started!"

It was hard for Alex to accept what his father was saying, and yet he knew that it was true. He knew that being bitter and angry about what was happening wouldn't change anything. But handling it calmly might make a difference. *RIJ*

HOW ABOUT YOU?

When someone mistreats you or does something that really hurts you, how do you react? At a time like that, what do your friends see in you? Ask God to help you handle the hurt.

MEMORIZE:

"Christ, who suffered for you, is your example. Follow in his steps. He did not retaliate when he was insulted."

1 Peter 2:21, 23

 Take Your Hurts to God

The Fallen Tree (Read Psalm 1)

"I don't know why we have to go to church every Sunday," Sara grumbled. She pressed her face against the car window as the family rode to church. Suddenly her attention was caught by the scene ahead. "Look at that tree!" she exclaimed, pointing to the roadside where a large tree lay uprooted on the grass.

Sara's mother looked out. "That was some wind we had last night," she said.

"Yes," said Dad, "but did you notice how shallow the roots of that tree were?"

"Yeah, they did look short and stubby for the size of the tree," agreed Sara. "Is that why it blew over when these other trees didn't?"

"Probably," replied Mother. "For some reason, it didn't grow the deep roots that would make it strong. Then, when that wind hit it last night, it toppled over."

"Sara, did you know there's a psalm in the Bible that compares a person to a tree?" asked Dad. Sara shook her head. "It says that a wise and righteous man—one who meditates on God's teachings day and night—is like a well-watered, healthy tree," continued Dad as he pulled into the church parking lot. "Such a person is like a deeply rooted tree that could withstand powerful winds."

"So I guess that's one reason we go to church—so we can learn more about God," said Sara.

"That's right," said her mom. "Then when trouble comes, we won't fall like that tree." *JKB*

17

APRIL

HOW ABOUT YOU?

Do you sometimes want to skip church? That's not unusual. But it really is important to learn about God. When you don't feel like going to church, ask God to give you a better attitude. Then go . . . and ask him to teach you at least one thing to help you grow stronger in him.

MEMORIZE:

"Let your roots grow down into him [Jesus] and draw up nourishment from him, so you will grow in faith, strong and vigorous in the truth you were taught." *Colossians 2:7*

 *Be Rooted in Christ*

Too Big a Bite (Read Mark 4:3-20)

18
APRIL

"Tomorrow evening is the mission rally at church," Dad reminded his family as they were eating at their favorite restaurant.

"I have play practice at school," said Marla.

"The last time we had a special service you had a band concert," Mother reminded her. "Perhaps we've allowed you to do too much at school."

"Why, hello." The voice of Marla's Sunday school teacher interrupted them. "I missed you Saturday morning, Marla," said Miss Willis. "We had such a good time at the nursing home." After chatting a few minutes, she left.

"Why didn't you go to the nursing home?" asked Dad.

Marla wrinkled her brow. "I was making posters for the student council. Hey, what's wrong with that man over there?" she asked suddenly.

Dad jumped to his feet and dashed across the room. "Are you choking, sir?" he asked. The man nodded frantically. "I'm going to help you," said Dad. He stood behind the frightened man and put his arms around him. With his clenched fist, he gave a couple of sharp, upward thrusts. The man gasped for air, and a moment later he was breathing normally again. Everyone applauded.

"Oh, thank you," said the man when he was able to talk. "I guess I tried to eat too fast. I was in too big a hurry."

On the way home, Marla's family talked about what had happened. "We're so busy, we even eat in a rush," observed Dad. "That makes it easy to choke. We can get involved in so many things that we choke in our spiritual lives, too."

Mother nodded. "There are a lot of things we can get involved in that are not wrong," she said. "They may even be good, unless they consume our time and energies so much that we don't have time for the things of God."

Marla was sure her parents were thinking of her. "I guess I've bitten off more than I can chew," she admitted to herself. "Maybe I'll have to drop an activity." *BJW*

HOW ABOUT YOU?

By the time you're in fifth or sixth grade, you will find many things crowding into your life. Do you still have time for prayer, Bible reading, and church? Be sure you don't get so busy with the cares of life that your spiritual life is choked out.

MEMORIZE:

"Watch out! Don't let me find you . . . filled with the worries of this life." *Luke 21:34*

 **Don't Get Too Busy**

Remembering (Read Deuteronomy 8:1-7)

When Jenna and Joseph came home from school, they found Mother sitting in the middle of the living room floor. She was surrounded by small piles of pictures. "I've finally decided to organize these snapshots," she said with a smile. "You kids can help if you'd like."

Soon Joseph and Jenna were giggling about the pictures. Some of them were taken years before they were even born. It looked funny to see their mother wearing her hair in a ponytail. And there was one of their cat, Tippy, when she was a kitten!

19
APRIL

When Dad came in, he looked discouraged. "Still no job opening anywhere!" he mumbled.

"Honey, why don't you help the kids organize these pictures while I get supper on the table," Mother suggested. So Dad joined the twins on the floor.

After supper they had family devotions, and Dad did a strange thing. Before reaching for the Bible, he took two snapshots out of his pocket. "What does this remind you of?" he asked, showing a picture of Jenna in her bathrobe.

"That was taken after my operation!" Jenna exclaimed. The family talked about how her appendix had ruptured and the doctors had said she might die.

"Wasn't God good to us?" Dad asked. "He healed Jenna." Then he showed a second picture—a snapshot of an old car.

Mother laughed. "Oh, dear! Remember all the trouble we had with that car?"

Dad smiled but looked thoughtful. "Yes, and when I saw this picture, I remembered the time the transmission had to be replaced, and we didn't have the money. Remember how God provided the money through that painting job?"

Joseph was puzzled. "Dad, what do those two pictures have to do with having family devotions?"

"Just this, Son," Dad replied. "I think God wants us to always remember what he has done for us in the past. As he was faithful then, he will continue to lead and help us in the future." *REP*

HOW ABOUT YOU?

Do you worry about the future? Sometimes a good way to avoid worrying is to remember what God has done for you in the past.

MEMORIZE:

"I recall all you have done, O Lord; I remember your wonderful deeds of long ago."

Psalm 77:11

 Remember God's Blessings

Getting Bumped (Read Matthew 5:21-24)

20
APRIL

"You dummy!" yelled Brian. "You spilled orange juice on my art project. Now I'll have to do it all over again. I wish you weren't such a stupid-head!"

"I'm sorry," apologized Jason, tears filling his eyes.

"Hey!" Brian's voice got louder. "That's not orange juice. It's punch! How come you got punch? That's what I wanted."

Hurrying into the family room, Mother confronted her angry son. "Brian, you know you're not allowed to call your brother names," she said sternly.

"Well, Jason messed up my art project," sputtered Brian. "Besides, how come he got punch and I got orange juice? The glasses looked the same."

"There was one glass of punch left over from his birthday party yesterday," explained Mother, "so I said he could have it. But you're right. You couldn't tell what was inside the glass until it got bumped. Just like we couldn't tell what was inside you until you got bumped."

Brian shook his head. "Jason didn't bump *me*," he said. "He bumped his glass, and it spilled all over my art project."

"I know," said Mother, "but when something happens to mess up our plans or efforts, it's like a bump that pushes us off course. Whatever is inside our hearts spills out. If our hearts are filled with patience and kindness, gentle words come out. But if we harbor bad attitudes or anger, harsh words spill out instead." She raised her brows. "Jason spilled punch, but you spilled harsh words. Which one is worse?"

Brian looked at the floor. Then he turned to his brother. "I-I'm sorry," he said. "Forgive me?"

Happily, Jason nodded. *LRS*

HOW ABOUT YOU?

What comes out when you "get bumped"— when things don't go right for you? If you have a selfish, impatient attitude, confess that to God and ask him to fill your heart with patience, kindness, and understanding. Then when you get "bumped," others will see the love of God coming out from within you.

MEMORIZE:

"For whatever is in your heart determines what you say."
Matthew 12:34

 Develop Good Attitudes

The Immovable Rock (Read Psalm 18:1-3)

Laurie sighed as she closed her math book. "I've studied until I can't even see the numbers on the pages anymore, Mom," she said, "but I just know I'm going to fail that math test tomorrow."

"Laurie, you've studied hard, and you've prayed about that test," said Mom. "Now just do the best you can, trusting the Lord to help you."

21
APRIL

"I guess so," said Laurie. "But I get to thinking about how terrible I am at math, and I just know I'll do the problems wrong."

Mom shook her head. "Get your eyes off of yourself and your own abilities," she said. "Trust in God, the one who never fails." She paused, then asked, "Do you still remember the time we got caught on that big rock at the beach when the tide came in and there was a storm?"

"Do I ever!" exclaimed Laurie. "That was one of the scariest times of my life. The waves were so big."

Mom smiled. "They were big all right," she said. "I think they seemed extra big to you because you were so little. Do you remember what your father said?"

"He told me not to be afraid," replied Laurie. "He said, 'We may tremble on the rock, but the rock will never tremble under us.' And he was right."

Mom nodded. "The Lord is your Rock, Laurie. When you realize how strong he is, you don't need to tremble at all as you rest on him. You can trust him to help you—even when you face a test in math."

Laurie got up and kissed her mother good night. "Well, then, I'm going to get a good night's sleep," she said. "Maybe I don't always have a big faith, but I'm trusting a big God. And tomorrow he'll help me tackle that test." *MRP*

HOW ABOUT YOU?

When you're with other Christians, do you feel sure that your needs will be met, but then begin to doubt when you face problems alone? Perhaps you begin to look at yourself or your circumstances instead of at God. He's the immovable Rock. Rest on him!

MEMORIZE:

"The Lord is my rock, my fortress, and my savior; my God is my rock, in whom I find protection. He is my shield, the strength of my salvation, and my stronghold." *Psalm 18:2*

 ***Trust Christ, the Rock***

No Directions! (Read Psalm 25:4-10)

22

APRIL

"Would you like to come to Sunday school with me next week?" Tom asked his friend Jim as they put their skateboards in Jim's garage.

"Naw," Jim answered. He pulled a big cardboard box to the middle of the garage. "I already go to school all week. I don't want to go on Sunday, too."

"What's that?" Tom asked, pointing to the box.

"It's a tricycle for my brother, Todd," Jim answered. "It's his birthday present. My folks asked me to put it together. Want to help?"

"Sure," agreed Tom.

"Hmmm. I wonder where the directions are," said Jim as he rummaged through the box. "I can't seem to find them here." He sounded a little frustrated.

"We could probably put this together without directions," said Tom with confidence.

"No way!" Jim exclaimed. "Dad made me promise to follow the directions very carefully. If I don't, Dad says I'll have the handlebars where the seat goes! He's right, too. I've made too many mistakes by not following directions. Now I never do anything without reading the directions first."

"Oh," Tom said. "Well, I wish you felt that way about the most important thing—life."

Jim looked up from the box. "What do you mean?"

"Well, in Sunday school we study the directions God gives on how we should live in this world," Tom pointed out. "Those directions are found in his Word, the Bible. If you can't put a bike together without directions, you sure can't live your life without them."

"Maybe you're right," said Jim thoughtfully. "Maybe I will go to Sunday school with you." *SLN*

HOW ABOUT YOU?

Do you think the Bible is just a list of do's and don'ts? Do you think it's just a book of nice stories? God gave us his Word so we might know how to live. Study it daily and learn to do what it says.

MEMORIZE:

"Show me the path where I should walk, O Lord; point out the right road for me to follow."

Psalm 25:4

 Read God's Directions

Moody Sue (Read 2 Peter 1:3-8)

23
APRIL

"Good morning," said Sue's mother as she tried to give her daughter a hug.

Sue avoided her mother's embrace. "Hi," she mumbled as she sat down.

After school that afternoon, Sue burst through the door. "Hi, Mom! I had a great day!" she exclaimed. And to her mother's surprise, Sue gave her a big hug.

As her parents were talking the next day, they were interrupted by a shout. "Sue is like a grizzly today," said Sue's brother, Jason. The phone rang, and he answered it. "It's for you, Grizzly," he called to Sue.

Sue came in and snatched the phone from her brother. She cleared her throat. "Hello," she said sweetly. She listened for a moment. "Oh, I'm fantastic!" she said.

Dad, Mom, and Jason looked at one another in surprise.

Sue continued to be moody. One day she was helping her dad with the grill. "Dad, the fire went out," she said. "I'll squirt some more fuel starter on the coals."

"No, don't do that. It . . ." Dad started to speak, but he was too late. Sue had already poured the starter on the hot coals. Suddenly, flames shot up at her.

"Oh!" She exclaimed, jumping back.

Dad grabbed her. "Are you OK?" he asked.

"Yeah." She nodded nervously. "But I sure didn't expect that!"

After they both had calmed down, Dad said, "You know, Sue, lately you remind me of those hot coals."

"What do you mean?" Sue asked, looking surprised.

"Well, you've been calm one minute and 'blowing up' at someone the next," replied Dad. "Just as you jumped away from that fire, your moodiness makes people want to avoid you."

"Perhaps I need to ask the Lord to help me be more even tempered," Sue said.

"That would be a good idea," agreed her dad. *SLN*

HOW ABOUT YOU?

Are you moody? Are you happy one minute and angry or unfriendly the next? You may feel sad, upset, or discouraged occasionally, but continual moodiness is not a good thing. Ask God to help you control your moods daily.

MEMORIZE:

"But when the Holy Spirit controls our lives, he will produce this kind of fruit in us: love, joy, peace, patience, kindness, goodness, faithfulness, gentleness, and self-control." *Galatians 5:22-23*

Control Your Moods

Fast-Forward Button

(Read Luke 2:51-52, Hebrews 12:1-3)

24

APRIL

Taneesha and Brittany plopped down on the sofa. "Thanks for inviting me over," said Brittany. "I was getting bored at home. I sure wanted to go to the party. It's not fair our parents won't let us go just because we're not teenagers."

"Yeah," agreed Taneesha. "They think we're still little kids. Some of the girls our age are lucky—they get to wear makeup and hang around with teenagers. Some of them even go on dates."

Brittany sighed. "I wish we could hurry and get grown up."

Taneesha nodded as she inserted a cassette into the player and turned it on. "Oh, I don't like that song," she said as the music began. "The next one's prettier." So she pushed the fast-forward button. But when she started playing the tape again, she found she'd gone too far. "Oh, now I've missed a couple of songs I want you to hear," she said. Taneesha paused, looking serious. "You know, when my mom hears me wishing I were older, she tells me I shouldn't try to 'fast-forward my life.' She says if I grow up too fast, I could miss a lot of good stuff."

Just then Taneesha's grandfather came into the room. "Hi, Grandpa," said Taneesha. She told him about the conversation they had been having. "When you were young, did you wish you could hurry up and be grown?" she asked.

"Yes, and I guess all children do," replied Grandpa. "But your mother's right. Trying to act like a grown-up too soon causes you to miss some good times and some needed learning experiences. God gives us childhood so we can grow, learning gradually how to become responsible adults. He also lets us have time for the fun of childhood. Be patient about growing up. You'll get there soon enough."

"I guess so," said Brittany with a sigh.

Grandpa smiled. "Enjoy your childhood while you can," he advised. "It's the only one you'll get." *MRP*

HOW ABOUT YOU?

Do you wish you were allowed to do what older young people do? Give yourself time to grow and learn. Even Jesus submitted to Mary and Joseph as he patiently waited for the time when his own ministry should begin. The Bible says to "run with patience the race that is set before us."

MEMORIZE:

"So let it grow, for when your endurance is fully developed, you will be strong in character and ready for anything."

James 1:4

 Enjoy Childhood

Water in the Boat (Read 2 Corinthians 6:14-18)

25

APRIL

"Come on, Tara. Let's go for a boat ride," Kevin said, coaxing his sister. Dad was taking the children out in the rowboat while Mother fixed lunch. But Tara wanted to swim. She held tightly to her pail and shovel while Dad buckled her life jacket.

Kevin rowed, and as they moved along the lakeshore, Dad pointed out some familiar landmarks. Tara wasn't interested. Instead, she took her pail, dipped up a pailful of water, and emptied it into the boat. "Stop that, Tara!" exclaimed Dad. "What are you trying to do?"

"I'm filling the boat," said Tara. "I want to swim in the water. I don't want to ride on the water."

"You can't fill the boat, Tara. And even if you could, it would sink," said Kevin.

As they ate lunch a little later, Kevin told Mother about their boat ride. When he mentioned Tara's foolish idea of filling the boat with water so she could swim, Mother smiled at the little girl. "I think Tara's given you an illustration of why you shouldn't join that neighborhood gang back home," she said. "Pretend for a minute that the water is the world and the boat is you—a Christian. As the boat is in the water, so you are in the world—you're in touch with the world, but not a part of it."

Dad nodded. "Water doesn't belong in the boat, and the world doesn't belong in your life," he added. "Too much water in the boat would cause it to sink. In a similar way, the more you join in the bad activities of the world such as drinking, using foul language, and so on, the easier it is for you to sink into its lifestyle. It's important to be friendly and kind to non-Christians. But when it comes to lifestyle and activities, we need to choose carefully when—or if—we should join in." *NEK*

HOW ABOUT YOU?

Do you know when to avoid non-Christians? Ask your parents and Sunday school teacher to guide you. Ask God to give you direction from his Word. Ask him to use you to influence those people from a distance when joining their activities might have too strong an influence on you.

MEMORIZE:

"Therefore, come out from them and separate yourselves from them, says the Lord. Don't touch their filthy things, and I will welcome you."

2 Corinthians 6:17

 Be Separate from the World

Lukewarm Christianity (Read Revelation 3:14-16)

26
APRIL

"Can I have something cold to drink, Mom?" asked Tina as she came in from the backyard.

"Oh, I don't think we have a thing," said Mom. "We're even out of milk. I need to get groceries." She opened the cupboard and took out a box of powdered milk. "Here . . . why don't you mix up some chocolate milk?" she suggested.

Tina took the box, mixed some of the powder with water, and added some chocolate syrup. Then she joined her mother at the dining room table. "I need some advice," she said. "There's a new girl at school. She's nice, but she dresses kind of weird. It's easy to be nice to her when it's just the two of us. But when I'm with the other girls and they make fun of her, I don't know what to do. She looks so hurt. But if I say something to her, I might lose my other friends." Tina took a sip of her milk and made a face. "Yuck! This tastes awful!" she exclaimed. "What's wrong?"

"Did you use any ice when you made it?" asked Mother. Tina shook her head. "You didn't heat it, either, did you?" Tina again shook her head. "When I make chocolate milk for you, I either heat it or serve it cold," said Mother. "It doesn't taste good lukewarm. And I think that may be your problem with the new girl."

"What do you mean?" asked Tina.

"I think you're being a lukewarm friend," said Mother. "You extend your friendship when you have nothing at stake but hold it back when your friends are watching. You're neither hot nor cold, but somewhere in between—afraid to take a stand for what you know is right."

Tina thoughtfully studied her glass of milk. She tasted it again, then pushed it away. "No more lukewarm milk for me. And no more lukewarm Christianity, either," she said firmly. "I'm going to be friendly . . . never mind what anybody thinks." *KEC*

HOW ABOUT YOU?
Are you willing to be bold about what you believe is right, or are you sometimes lukewarm? The Bible warns you to be strong for Jesus. Don't be afraid to stand up for what you believe.

MEMORIZE:
"And a righteous person will live by faith. But I will have no pleasure in anyone who turns away." *Hebrews 10:38*

 Be Bold for Jesus

Chuck's Lie (Read 1 John 1:8-10)

27

APRIL

Chuck paced his room. For several days he had meant to confess something to Mom. It grew harder to do each day he put it off. *I sure hate to tell her now,* he thought. *But I might as well do it and get it over with.* So he went to look for her.

When Chuck reached the kitchen, he saw that the refrigerator was out in the center of the floor. Mom was kneeling behind it with a bucket of water and a scrub brush. "What are you doing?" Chuck asked.

Mom sighed. "I'm trying to scrub away the dirt that's collected on the floor back here," she said. "It's been hidden behind the refrigerator so long that it's really hard to scrub off. I should have gotten at it sooner. Do you need something?"

Chuck took a deep breath. "I have to tell you something. Remember when my Sunday school teacher called last week? Well, he reminded me about a Sunday school party on Friday night. But I wanted to go to a baseball game instead. So I told him you were sick and I had to stay home." Mom frowned as Chuck hurried on. "Todd came by this morning and brought a get-well card for you. He said they collected money to get a gift, too. I didn't know what to do, so I took the card. I already asked God to forgive me, but I didn't know how to tell them not to buy you a gift. I'm afraid they might already have one."

"I am glad you told me the truth. But you'd better call Todd right away and tell him what you did!" said Mom. She pointed to the floor. "Remember I told you how this dirt gets worse as long as I let it hide behind the refrigerator?" Chuck nodded. "It's the same with you and this lie," continued Mom. "Your lie grew bigger when you took that card. Now it's going to be harder to 'scrub it away.' *You* will have to repay the money for the card and for the gift, too, if they've already bought one."

With a sigh, Chuck nodded. Even though it was going to be tough, Chuck was glad he had told the truth. *KEC*

HOW ABOUT YOU?

Have you ever told a lie and then had to keep lying to hide the truth? The longer you hide a lie, or any other sin, the harder it becomes to make it right. You need to confess your sin to God. Take care of it right away.

MEMORIZE:

"Confess your sins to each other and pray for each other so that you may be healed. The earnest prayer of a righteous person has great power and wonderful results." *James 5:16*

 Confess Sin Right Away

The Dirty Socks (Read 2 Timothy 3:14-17)

28

APRIL

"Dad! I don't have any clean socks!" called Steven. A few moments later, Dad walked into the bedroom, lifted up the edge of Steven's comforter, and pointed under the bed. There, in crumpled heaps, were several pairs of socks. All dirty!

"Son," Dad said, "you'll have to wash these yourself."

"I know, but I don't like to wash clothes," said Steven. "I never used to have to do stuff like that."

"You're older now, Steven," said Dad, "and it's time you assumed a little more responsibility around here, especially now that Mother is with Grandma."

After supper that evening, Steven went to the laundry room. He piled the socks and some of his dark shirts into the washer, added detergent, and pushed the button. Then he lowered the lid. He felt proud of himself.

When Steven took the clothes to the family room where he began folding them, Dad was at the desk, studying his Bible. He looked up and smiled. "Good job, Son," he said. "By the way, are you entering the Bible memory contest at church?"

Steven shook his head. "Those verses are too hard," he replied, "and Mom's not here to help me."

"Well, I'll help you when I can," said Dad. He watched as Steven finished folding his clothes. "But you can learn by yourself, too," Dad added. "You know, I wanted you to take more responsibility, and you have. I'm proud of you. Perhaps you need to take more responsibility for your spiritual growth now, too."

"What do you mean?" asked Steven.

"Well," said Dad, "you became a Christian nearly three years ago. Maybe it's time for you to work at memorizing more difficult verses on your own."

Steven gathered up his clothes. "I guess I could try," he said slowly. "I'll start as soon as I put this stuff away." *CJB*

HOW ABOUT YOU?

Do you take the responsibility of reading God's Word, praying, and learning Bible verses? Or do you wait for an adult to prod you to do those things? Why not talk to God today—tell him you're ready to become a responsible Christian.

MEMORIZE:

"Now, a person who is put in charge as a manager must be faithful." *1 Corinthians 4:2*

 Be a Responsible Christian

Riddles (Read 2 John 7-11)

"Let's see if you can figure out this riddle," suggested Laurie to her brother, Ron. "A bus with ten people stopped and picked up five more. It went two blocks, let off three and picked up four. Then it went another block and let off four. Finally, it made one more stop and picked up two." Laurie asked, "How many times did the bus stop?"

"Fourteen!" Ron promptly shouted. Then his grin faded as he realized he had been fooled. "Hey! I thought you were going to ask how many people were left on the bus. I don't remember how many times the bus stopped."

29

APRIL

Mother, who had overheard the conversation, joined in. "I have a riddle for both of you," she said. "Remember the people who came to the door the other day selling religious books?" When the children nodded, she said, "Those people were like Ron. Ron and those folks were guilty of hearing only what they wanted to hear."

The children still looked puzzled. "I know what you mean about Ron," said Laurie. "He heard only the numbers he was listening for, and he paid no attention to the rest of the story."

"Right," Mother said with a nod. "And that's not so serious—it was just a riddle. But the people who were at our door the other day claim to base their beliefs on what the Bible says, only they don't hear the whole story. They pick out some verses and leave out others."

Ron nodded slowly. "So we shouldn't believe someone just because he or she tells us the Bible says it," he observed. "We should look it up and make sure it agrees with what the rest of the Bible says."

"That's right," agreed Mother. *CV*

HOW ABOUT YOU?

Do you "hear" what you want to hear of God's Word instead of hearing what is really being taught? Pay careful attention to what the Bible really says. Don't be fooled by those who claim to believe the Bible but refuse to believe all of it. And remember, anyone who denies that Jesus is God is a false teacher.

MEMORIZE:

"That is why I tell these stories, because people see what I do, but they don't really see. They hear what I say, but they don't really hear, and they don't understand." *Matthew 13:13*

 *Hear All of God's Word*

The Faith Account (Read Romans 10:8-17)

30

APRIL

"Here are some old checks you may play with, Mindy," said Mother. "But I want you to keep them indoors and destroy them as soon as you're done with them." Mindy squealed with delight and pulled up a chair beside Mother, who was cleaning the desk drawers.

They looked up as Steve came into the room. "I was just next door, talking to Mr. Wilson," he said. "He sure has a lot of problems, doesn't he?"

Mother nodded. "Yes, he does. I told him the Lord would help him, but he says he doesn't believe God is concerned about his problems. He says God gave him sense enough to take care of himself. Unbelief robs a lot of people of blessings."

Mindy tore a check from the checkbook. "Here's a check for you, Steve. You can buy a new bicycle," she announced. "It's for a thousand dollars. Is that enough?"

Steve grinned as he looked at the check covered with scribbling. He quickly dropped it and shook his fingers. "Ouch! That burns!" he teased.

Mindy looked puzzled. "It's not hot, Steve."

Steve laughed, and Mother explained. "When someone writes a check that isn't good, Mindy, it's called a 'hot check.' You see, before you can get money from a bank, you must put money into it." She looked at Steve and added, "Faith is a little like that. When we read God's Word, our faith in him increases. We go to church where we hear his Word preached. And we listen to others tell what God has done for them. These things add to our 'faith account.' Then when we have a need, we have faith that God will take care of it."

"Mr. Wilson has never put any faith in God," Steve said slowly, "and that's why he doesn't have any faith to draw on now that he needs it." Mother nodded. "I'm going to give him a Bible and pray for him," Steve said decidedly, "and I'm going to witness to him. Maybe he'll start a 'faith account' of his own." *BJW*

HOW ABOUT YOU?

Do you have faith in God to take care of your problems? You need to start your "faith account" by first of all believing in Jesus Christ and trusting him as your Savior. Then you can build on your faith and be ready to face problems as they come.

MEMORIZE:

"So we are made right with God through faith and not by obeying the law." *Romans 3:28*

 **Build Your Faith**

Shadows (Read Mark 4:35-41)

1
MAY

The streetlight in front of Grandma's house shone through the bare branches of a tree outside the window. It cast eerie shadows across Jenny's bed. The pointed, twisted black shapes reminded her of teeth. As the wind tugged at the branches, the shadows inched their way over the covers. *Like great, big, black teeth,* thought Jenny fearfully. She swallowed. *This isn't at all like my bedroom at home. Mom turns on the night-light, and everything seems safe there.*

Then she heard a moaning sound. And underneath her bed, something clicked. To Jenny, lying there in the shadows, it sounded . . . well . . . it sounded as if a giant mouth had just snapped shut. She drew the covers up to her chin and squeezed her eyes shut. *No, I gotta keep them open,* she decided. *I gotta be ready to jump out of bed!* "Grandma!" Jenny called. But Grandma had the TV on, and Jenny knew she couldn't hear her calling. The shadows trembled. The click of teeth echoed in her ears. "Oh, Lord," whispered Jenny in prayer, "I'm really scared! Please help me."

As if in answer to her prayers, Jenny remembered stories from Sunday school—stories about times the disciples were afraid. Once, as the men sailed in a small boat, the wind roared and the waves crashed into their boat. The disciples rowed for their lives! They bailed out the water as more poured in. Like her, the disciples had been terrified. Jenny remembered what happened next. Jesus had been sleeping, but the disciples woke him up. Then Jesus said, "Peace, be still," and the wind and the sea grew calm. Jenny remembered that Jesus was Lord of everything, even shadows and scary sounds. *And he's right here with me,* she thought.

After that, things didn't seem quite so scary. In a whisper she began to sing one of her favorite Bible songs. And soon she was fast asleep. *LAB*

HOW ABOUT YOU?

Are you sometimes scared? Everyone is. What can you do to help yourself get through scary situations? Remember, our powerful Jesus is with you everywhere you go. The next time you're afraid, ask Jesus to help you know what to do.

MEMORIZE:

"Do not be afraid of the terrors of the night . . . if you make the Lord your refuge." *Psalm 91:5, 9*

 God Controls Everything

The Book of Action (Read Acts 5:12-16)

2
MAY

Glenn slammed his book shut. "This is the most boring book I have ever read," he declared. "It's about people who just sit around and talk. Half of what they say doesn't make sense."

"You should read this book." Mother held up the Bible. Glenn wrinkled his nose. "Read the Bible?" he asked. He hesitated, then added, "I think it's boring, too."

"Did you ever read the book of Acts?" asked Mother. Glenn shrugged. "Well, why don't you try reading it," she suggested. "The story of the early church is exciting. It starts with a man breaking the law of gravity and launching into space without a spaceship or suit."

Glenn sat up. "Aw, Mom, you're pulling my leg."

"No, I'm not," Mother replied. She held out the Bible. "Read the first chapter of Acts for yourself."

Glenn took the book and began reading. All was silent for a few minutes, then he grinned. "Oh," he said, "you're talking about Jesus going up into heaven."

Mother chuckled. "Right. And then there was the man in Acts whose shadow was so powerful people came from miles around to see it and have it fall on them."

Glenn shook his head. "Where do you find that story?"

"Oh," said Mother, "maybe the fourth or fifth chapter."

Again all was silent, except for the rustling of pages. Then Glenn looked up. "Tell me another one."

Mother thought a minute. "Once there was an exciting jail-break."

"Where's that one found?" asked Glenn.

"I believe you'll find that in the twelfth chapter," Mother answered with a smile. "Do you still think the Bible is boring?"

"No way!" Glenn said with a smile. *BJW*

HOW ABOUT YOU?

Do you know that the Bible is an exciting book? What is your favorite story? What is one thing you have learned about God from reading Bible stories? The Bible is full of good stories. And the best part is that they are all true.

MEMORIZE:

"Oh, how I love your law! I think about it all day long."

Psalm 119:97

 *The Bible Is Exciting*

Make Sure (Read John 3:1-16)

At the close of the children's program at Grace Church, Tim hesitantly approached Pastor Holdredge and told him he wanted to become a Christian. "I'm surprised to hear you say that," began Pastor Holdredge. He put an arm around Tim's shoulder. "I remember a night a year ago when you came forward to become a Christian," he said. "Did the Lord answer your prayer that night?"

3
MAY

"I don't know." Tim sighed. "For a while, I thought I was a Christian—I was even baptized. But I keep having doubts. Pastor, how do I know I really meant it when I asked Jesus into my heart? Maybe I should do it again, just to make sure."

"If you're having doubts, I'm glad you came to talk about it," said Pastor Holdredge. "Becoming a Christian is an important thing—the most important thing in any person's life. It's certainly not something you want to guess about."

"So you think I ought to pray again and ask Jesus to save me?" Tim asked.

"A person isn't saved by praying—or by doing any other good work," said Pastor Holdredge. "It doesn't matter if you pray one time or a hundred times, you still can't do anything to save yourself. You're saved only through faith in Christ."

Tim nodded. "You're saying that being a Christian isn't something *we* do—it's something God does for us, right?"

"Exactly," agreed Pastor Holdredge. "All you do is trust in the Lord. Do you believe that Jesus loves you and died for your sins? Do you trust in him, Tim? Or are you counting on your prayers, or maybe on your baptism, to get you to heaven?"

"I do know those things won't get me to heaven," Tim answered. "If Jesus didn't save me, I'd never be saved." Then with a smile he added, "I'm going to stop doubting and start trusting!" *SLK*

HOW ABOUT YOU?

Do you ever wonder if you're really a Christian? Have you asked Jesus to forgive you and invited him into your life? If so, then you are a Christian. Pick a verse (such as John 3:16, John 3:36, John 1:12, or Romans 10:9 or 13), and when you have doubts, quote that verse. Trust what God says.

MEMORIZE:

"For God so loved the world that he gave his only Son, so that everyone who believes in him will not perish but have eternal life." *John 3:16*

 Believe What God Says

The Good-Luck Charm (Read Exodus 32:1-8, 35)

4

MAY

"Jan!" shouted Cindy. "Did you take my cross?"

"You mean that gold one you always wear?" asked Jan. "Of course I didn't take it."

Cindy scowled. "Well, I can't find it, and I was sure I left it in my jewelry box. I just have to wear it today! I've got an English exam, and I'm afraid I won't pass it if I don't wear my cross. It always brings me luck."

Cindy's mother stuck her head in the bedroom. "Our Savior's cross was never meant to be a good-luck charm," said Mother.

"Oh, Mom," said Cindy, "I know the cross is to remind me of Jesus. But something good seems to happen every time I wear it."

Mother sighed. "I know it seems that way. But your cross doesn't have any power to help you in your test. Studying hard and praying is the best way to approach one of those."

Cindy frowned. "Well, I have studied," she replied, "and I've prayed, too. But . . . sometimes I wish we could really see or hear God. My cross gives me something I can see."

Mother answered, "Many people feel that way about God. They think that having a picture of Jesus or a statue of him in their homes will bring God's blessings on them. The Israelites did something like that—they begged Aaron to make them a god of gold like those they had seen in Egypt. They wanted to have an idol—a god they could touch and see—instead of putting their faith in the real God. God wants us to place our faith and trust only in him."

Cindy nodded. "Well, I . . . I never thought of my little cross as an idol." She closed her jewelry box. "I guess I was using it that way, though," she admitted. "When I find it, I won't wear it for a while. From now on I'll put my trust in God instead of in good-luck charms!" *SLK*

HOW ABOUT YOU?

Are you ever tempted to rely on good-luck charms—a cross, a picture, a special Bible—instead of simply trusting God? It's wrong to give that kind of trust to things—even to religious objects. God is the only one who is worthy of all our trust and worship.

MEMORIZE:

"We live by faith, not by sight."
2 Corinthians 5:7, NIV

 Trust God, Not "Idols"

God's Creation (Read Psalm 139:13-18, Matthew 10:29-31)

"Oh, Dad," said Geoffrey, "Sheba has new baby puppies!"

"That's great, Son! How many does she have?" asked Dad.

"Seven," replied Geoffrey. "Come see them." He led the way to the doghouse. Sheba and her new family were cuddled up on a warm, soft blanket. "Good girl," Geoffrey whispered.

5
MAY

"How about that!" said Dad. "Let's see—two black, two chocolate brown, two black and white, and one white pup."

"All their eyes are closed," said Geoffrey.

"Puppies are always born with their eyes closed," said Dad. "Their ears are closed too. In about ten days the pups will begin to see and hear." He smiled. "Come along," he said, "I bet Mom has supper ready."

There was much excitement during supper. Geoffrey chatted endlessly. "Mom, were my eyes closed when I was born?" he asked.

Mom and Dad chuckled. "No, Geoff. Your eyes were open," Mom told him. "But you closed them when you were asleep. And you slept a lot, just like the pups will."

"Does God know what the pups look like?" asked Geoffrey.

"Yes, he sure does," said Dad. "God created Sheba and the pups, too. He created all things, just like he created you."

"Did he know what I'd be like?" Geoffrey wanted to know.

"Yup." Dad nodded. "Psalm 139 tells us that God saw you before you were born. It also says that God knew what each day of your life would hold."

"Wow!" Geoffrey was surprised. "You mean God saw me before you and Mom saw me?"

Again Dad nodded. "And did you know that God even knows how many hairs you have on your head?" he asked.

Geoffrey giggled. "Boy, he must have a hard time keeping track of yours, Dad," he said, rubbing Dad's balding head. Mom and Dad laughed, too. *DLW*

HOW ABOUT YOU?

Did you know that you are important to God? He created you and loves you very much. He cares for you.

MEMORIZE:

"How precious are your thoughts about me, O God!"

Psalm 139:17

 God Made You Special

Behind the Scenes (Read 1 Corinthians 12:14-27)

6
MAY

"Put this blue block here," Justin suggested to Allison, his four-year-old sister. Justin was helping her build a tower with blocks. The structure was almost finished when Allison pulled out a green block from near the bottom. The tower toppled over. "You ruined it," scolded Justin. "Why did you do that?"

"I wanted that green block at the top," answered Allison.

Just then the telephone rang. "Justin, it's for you," called Mother.

When he got off the phone, Justin said dejectedly, "That was my Sunday school teacher. He wants me to come to a rehearsal for that skit they're going to do on youth night. He said he doesn't have any parts left in the skit, but they need somebody to help move props between scenes."

"What's the matter with that?" asked Mother, noting his lack of enthusiasm.

"I don't want to help," grumbled Justin with a scowl. "I'm not good enough to be in the skit, but I'm good enough to move furniture around! Anyone can do that!"

"Well, moving the props may not seem as glamorous as acting in a play, but it's a very important job," Mother told him. "The whole production could be ruined if the props aren't in the right place." She paused, then added, "It's like the block Allison took out of the tower you were building."

"What do you mean?" asked Justin.

"When Allison took just one block out, the whole building came tumbling down," replied Mother. "It was an important part of the structure even though it didn't show as much as the top blocks. And the Bible teaches us that in the church, each one of us is needed, too."

"You make it sound like moving furniture for a skit isn't so bad after all," murmured Justin. He sighed. "Well, I . . . I guess I better call Mr. Clark back and tell him I'll be at the rehearsal." *TKM*

HOW ABOUT YOU?

Do you like to do only jobs that are noticed by lots of people? Do you feel like you're not important or needed in your church? Remember that you are important in God's eyes. Do your part, even if it's not glamorous!

MEMORIZE:

"In fact, some of the parts that seem weakest and least important are really the most necessary. Now all of you together are Christ's body."

1 Corinthians 12:22, 27

 Use Your Talents for God

A Very Bad Day (Read Psalm 86:1-7)

Todd ran into his house, threw his jacket on the kitchen table, and ran up to his room. He didn't even say hi to his mom who was busy at the kitchen sink.

It had been an awful day for Todd. In fact, it was downright miserable! Billy Anderson had thrown gum in his hair on the bus, and Mrs. Harris had to use an ice cube to unstick it! Then he was late for class and got a stern look from his teacher when he clomped noisily to his seat.

7
MAY

Before going to lunch, he had to finish the work he'd missed by coming late. Since he was late for lunch, he didn't get to eat with his best friend, Christopher. Instead, he had to sit next to Madeline.

What an awful day! Todd thought.

Todd was very quiet that evening. "Is something bothering you, Son?" asked Dad as he sat beside him on the couch.

"It wasn't a very good day at school today," Todd said.

"Well, sometimes I have a bad day at work, too," Dad told him. "Do you know what I do when that happens?"

Todd turned to his dad. "Do you tell Mom?" he asked.

Dad laughed. "Yes, that's one of the things I do, and it helps," he said. "So why don't you tell Mom and me what happened to you today?"

"OK," agreed Todd. He told them about his troubles. He felt a little better. "What else do you do when you have a bad day?" he asked Dad.

"Well, Son," said Dad, "I talk to God about my problems."

"Does God really care when I have problems?" asked Todd.

"Yes, he does," answered Dad. "And it pleases him when we talk to him about them."

"Well," answered Todd, smiling, "his ears are going to be tired tonight. I have a lot to talk about." *VRG*

HOW ABOUT YOU?

When something does not go well for you, do you just keep it to yourself? You can share your concerns with a parent or friend, but God wants to hear from you, too. Tell him what's bothering you. He has promised to listen and to help you with your problems.

MEMORIZE:

"I will call to you whenever trouble strikes, and you will answer me." *Psalm 86:7*

 Talk to God about Problems

True Religion (Read 1 Corinthians 13:1-3)

8

MAY

It was a beautiful Saturday afternoon, and Grandma Holmes was hopeful. *Maybe today someone will come for a visit,* she thought. But then she frowned. *Now Vivian, don't get your hopes up again,* she scolded herself. She tried to forget about anyone coming. But she couldn't help herself because of how lonely she felt.

It had been a few years now since she had come to The Manor—a home for senior citizens. It had been a difficult change.

"I think I'll look for another good book to read," Grandma Holmes said out loud. She had enjoyed the book she had just finished. As she replaced it on the shelf, she chuckled to herself. *I remember how the grandchildren would ask me to read this one over and over.* As she reached toward the shelf, she thought she heard a knock on her door. Her heart began to pound. There it was again. *Maybe I will have a visitor today,* she thought. Excitedly, she hurried to the door. A smile spread across her face as she opened it. But no one was there. She looked down the hall and saw someone pushing a cart, bumping the wall every three or four steps.

Grandma Holmes gently closed the door and slowly walked over to her favorite chair by the window. *Vivian, I told you not to go and get your hopes up,* she chided herself again.

When she thought she heard a knock at the door a few minutes later, she didn't go to the door. The knocking continued. "Grandma Holmes! Are you there?" called a voice.

Grandma Holmes sat up straight. She hurried to the door. Opening it, she saw Melanie, her great-granddaughter, smiling at her. "Hi, Grandma," said Melanie, giving her a hug. "Got time for a visit?"

With a thankful heart, Grandma Holmes nodded, and together they went in and sat down to talk. *SKV*

HOW ABOUT YOU?

Do you know someone who lives alone or is lonely? Have you thought about visiting him or her, but you never seem to have the time? The Bible says that the highest expression of your faith is love. Giving of your time can be a great way to show love.

MEMORIZE:

"Pure and lasting religion in the sight of God our Father means that we must care for orphans and widows in their troubles." James 1:27

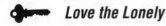 *Love the Lonely*

Before It's Too Late (Read 1 Corinthians 13:4-7, 13)

9
MAY

Sharon came home from school to find her mother changing a light bulb. "It's funny how you don't appreciate some things until you don't have them," said Mom as she twisted the new bulb into place. To her surprise, Sharon burst into tears. "What's wrong, honey?" asked Mom. She climbed down from the stool and put an arm around Sharon.

"Anna's grandma died yesterday. Anna hadn't seen her in a long time. And now it's too late," sobbed Sharon. "It made me think that someday my grandma will die, too. Then I'll feel like Anna."

"I'm so thankful each of us knows the Lord," said Mom. "We'll see each other again in heaven. But we will miss those who go to heaven before us. Anna must feel very sad."

"She does—especially since she didn't go to see her grandma for so long," said Sharon. "I don't want to feel sorry that I didn't spend more time with my grandma. I've been promising to help her clean the attic, but I've been so busy listening to my music, reading, and playing with my friends that I've been putting it off."

"It's easy to get busy and forget those we care about," said Mom. Sharon nodded. "And all of a sudden it's too late," she said. "Sometimes it works that way," agreed Mom.

Sharon wiped away her tears. "Well, I've made a decision. I'm going to spend less time in my room and more time with my family."

Mom smiled. "That's a good decision," she said.

Sharon's little sister, Julie, walked into the room. "I want to practice riding my bike. Will you help me, Sharon?" she asked.

"Not now. I want to—" Sharon clapped her hand over her mouth as she remembered the conversation she'd just had with Mom. She nodded. "I'll help you," she said, "but first I want to call Grandma to tell her I'm coming over Saturday to help her clean the attic."

KEC

HOW ABOUT YOU?

Do you love and appreciate the people God has put in your life? Think of a way to show it today.

MEMORIZE:

"So now I am giving you a new commandment: Love each other. Just as I have loved you, you should love each other."

John 13:34

 Show Your Love Today

The Cost of Education (Read Proverbs 3:11-18)

10
MAY

"Hi, Steve," Phillip said as he sat down at the kitchen table next to his big brother.

"Looks like I'm still short about a thousand dollars for college next year," Steve said.

"If you ask me, it's bad enough to have to go to school without having to pay for it!" said Phillip.

Mother looked up from the sink. "Steve realizes a good education is worth the price he'll have to pay," she said. The phone rang. "Phillip!" Mom called. "Mr. VanderStahl says Scamp got into his trash cans again. Did you tie him up after you fed him this morning?"

"I guess I forgot," groaned Phillip. "I'll go straight over and pick up the mess."

Half an hour later, Phillip returned with a sour expression on his face. "Boy, that was awful," he said. "There were old chicken bones and banana peels and everything else all over the yard. Yuck!"

Mom smiled sympathetically. "Well, Son, maybe you needed another lesson in responsibility. You do have a habit of forgetting things."

Phillip sighed. "I know, and I'm trying to do better," he said. "But can't I learn what I need to know without all that hassle?"

"Well," answered Mother, "I'm sure that having to pick up all that trash really impressed upon you the need to carry out your duties properly. But cheer up! Only a few minutes ago we were talking about the high cost of education, remember? And how it's worth the price?"

"But I'm not in college . . . ," began Phillip. Then he stopped. "Oh, you're not just talking about college now, are you?" he said. "I guess I shouldn't expect all life's lessons to be easy ones. Even if I do have hassles sometimes, I guess it will be worth it if I learn something!" *SLK*

HOW ABOUT YOU?

Do you get impatient when things don't go right? Do you wonder why God doesn't make it easier for you to learn spiritual lessons? Don't underestimate the value of the patience and other qualities God may be developing in you through your troubles.

MEMORIZE:

"Wisdom is more precious than rubies; nothing you desire can compare with her."

Proverbs 3:15

 Thank God for Lessons Learned

Let's Trade (Read Hebrews 11:24-27)

"Hey, what do you have there?" Joe said as he pointed at the bucket his friend Trent was holding.

"It's an apple tree," said Trent.

"No kidding?" Joe was skeptical. "Looks like an old dead stick to me." He changed the subject. "Hey . . . I'm going to the park to play with my new skateboard." Holding up a well-worn skateboard, he added, "Anyway, it's new to me. Want to come along?"

11
MAY

"Can't," mumbled Trent. "I'd sure rather play than plant trees, but I have to go plant this thing."

Joe looked with interest at the stick in the bucket. "You're not kidding me, are you? That really is an apple tree? How long before there will be apples on it?"

"Years and years. I got it from my Uncle Bob, and he told me how long it would take, but I've forgotten." Trent looked at Joe's skateboard. "Where'd you get your skateboard?"

"Mom got it at a garage sale," answered Joe. "Hey, how about trading?"

Trent answered, "You mean you'd trade that skateboard for this apple tree?"

Joe held out the skateboard. "Try me and see."

Trent took it quickly. "Now I'll go play while you work," he said with a grin. Then he was off to the park, whistling and thinking he had gotten the best end of the deal.

When Joe got home, he showed his mother the stick in the bucket. "You don't mind, do you?" he asked anxiously.

Mother smiled. "No—you made a wise trade. You gave up a little fun today for a lot of fruit in the future," she said. "You just better hope Trent's folks don't mind, either. If they do, you'll have to give that tree back." *BJW*

HOW ABOUT YOU?

Are you interested only in having fun right now? Do you ever give up some playtime to pray or put down your comic book to read the Bible? Do you ever give up a ball game to help with a church project? Think about doing one of these things this week.

MEMORIZE:

"For wisdom is far more valuable than rubies."

Proverbs 8:11

 Invest in the Future

Fringe Benefits (Read Galatians 6:2, 9-10)

12
MAY

"I'll never go to that church!" old Mr. Winters said as he shook his finger. "All they ever do is ask for money!"

"What a grouch!" said Brad. "All we did was invite him to church!"

The next Sunday the boys repeated Mr. Winters's words in Sunday school, and Brad mimicked Mr. Winters. "'All they ever do is ask for money!'" Then he added, "But that's not true. Our church does a lot for people."

Mr. Martin nodded. "Yes," he said. "Have any of you ever received something from the church?" Many hands went up. "Care to tell us about it?" asked Mr. Martin.

"My dad lost his job, and the church took an offering for us. They brought us groceries, too," Bobby told the class.

Brenda stood up. "I get a ride to Sunday school," she said. "If the church bus didn't come by, I wouldn't get to come."

"When our house burned down, the church rented an apartment for us and gave us clothes and furniture," offered Jerry.

"When my grandfather died, the church ladies served dinner for our family, and Pastor Davis preached the funeral," said Carl. "My uncle said he thinks the people of this church are true Christians."

"Tell your uncle that is the nicest thing he could say about us," said Mr. Martin with a smile.

"When my little sister was in the hospital, a lot of the church people prayed for her. I love our church!" Mark blushed as he sat down.

"We all love it," Brad said firmly. "All but Mr. Winters."

"Let's pray for him this week," suggested Mr. Martin. "He doesn't know what he's missing." *BJW*

HOW ABOUT YOU?

Have you ever thought about the many benefits you receive through your church? Even in the early churches, those who were able to do so shared with those who had a need. How good God was to plan the church for his children! Why not write a thank-you note to your pastor or Sunday school teacher today?

MEMORIZE:

"Whenever we have the opportunity, we should do good to everyone, especially to our Christian brothers and sisters."

Galatians 6:10

 Give Thanks for Your Church

The Safe (Read Proverbs 2:1-8)

13

MAY

Mark watched as Mother unlocked the home safe in Uncle Frank's house and took a stack of yellowed papers from it. Quickly, she sorted through them. "This is the paper the hospital needs for Uncle Frank's records," she said. She put the others back in the safe and locked it.

While Mother took care of business in the hospital office, Mark went down the hall to Uncle Frank's room. "Hi, Uncle Frank," he said.

The older gentleman raised his head from the pillow and wrinkled his brow. "Uh-h-h . . . Who are you?" He peered closely at Mark. "Why, it's little Jimmy."

"No, I'm Mark," he said. "Jimmy's my dad. He's grown up now."

"Heh? Don't mumble, Jimmy," Uncle Frank ordered.

Mark was astonished. "I'm Mark," he repeated loudly. "I've brought you the church bulletin."

Uncle Frank held the bulletin close to his face. "He that dwelleth in the secret place of the most High . . ." He put the paper down and closed his eyes. ". . . shall abide under the shadow of the Almighty. . . ."

When Mother came into the room several minutes later, Uncle Frank had just finished quoting Psalm 91.

"Uncle Frank didn't even know me. He thought I was Dad," said Mark on the way home. "Then he quoted that whole chapter from the Bible! How could he remember that when he didn't even remember me?"

"Old age has robbed Uncle Frank of a lot of information he stored in his mind," explained Mother, "but I believe that when you memorize God's Word, you don't merely file it in your mind—you store it in the 'safe' of your heart. The treasures hidden there can never be stolen away." *BJW*

HOW ABOUT YOU?

Picture each Bible verse you learn as a valuable treasure hidden in your heart. You can store up great riches by memorizing God's Word. Even after their intelligence and memory have passed away, older people can often remember and receive comfort and help from the Bible verses they have hidden in their hearts.

MEMORIZE:

"I have hidden your word in my heart, that I might not sin against you." *Psalm 119:11*

 *Memorize God's Word*

Turn Around (Read Deuteronomy 28:65-67)

14
MAY

"Meow! Meow!" Mother could hear the cat crying from the living room. "Andy, what are you doing to Muffy?" she asked, walking into the room.

"Nothing, Mom," answered Andy. "I was just petting her, but she turned around to face the other way. When I kept on stroking her, it made her fur stand up all funny, and she didn't like it!"

"I'll bet she didn't!" answered Mother with a smile. "I'm sure it makes a cat feel funny to have its fur rubbed the wrong way. From now on, try to be a little more careful."

The next day Andy looked unhappy when he got home from school. "Is something wrong?" asked Mother.

"Some of the kids in my class cheated on a test today," replied Andy. "John asked why I didn't cheat, too. I told him it makes me feel funny to do that kind of stuff—like the time I stole that candy bar. Why do I feel bad about doing things like that when nobody else does?"

"Well, Andy, it's a little like rubbing Muffy's fur the wrong way," Mother replied. "When you do something wrong, the Holy Spirit convicts you about it because you're a Christian."

"It's as if doing wrong 'rubs my fur the wrong way,' so I feel uncomfortable—guilty," said Andy.

"That's right," said Mother. "When you do what you should, you feel safe and happy instead of guilty and afraid." *DSM*

HOW ABOUT YOU?

Do you feel unhappy and guilty about something you've done? That may be the Holy Spirit working to convict you about your sin. It's as though your "fur is being rubbed the wrong way." When you feel guilty about something, confess that sin to God and tell him you're sorry. You'll feel better when you've done that.

MEMORIZE:

"People who cover over their sins will not prosper. But if they confess and forsake them, they will receive mercy." *Proverbs 28:13*

 God Convicts of Sin

The Way to Fight (Read Galatians 5:13-15, 22-26)

"Ken!" Lori shouted as she hung up the telephone. "Quit listening in on my phone calls!"

Ken hung up the extension and came upstairs. "I was just checking to see if you were finally done," he said. "You're always on the phone."

"That's not true, and you know it," snapped Lori. "You're just a big snoop."

"Blabbermouth!" Ken replied.

"Oh, you're exaggerating," said Lori. "You always do that."

Ken laughed. "I don't care what your friends think."

At that moment Mother came in from the backyard. She looked at them sternly. "I could hear you two fighting all the way outside," she scolded. She went to her room and came back with a wrinkled, faded piece of paper. "This is something your father and I wrote before we were married. It's called 'Rules for Fighting.'"

"You and Dad don't fight," objected Ken. "Not like the Allens next door. They yell and throw things."

"But we do have disagreements sometimes—everyone does," explained Mother. "That's why we made up this list. I'd like you both to read it and then each add a rule of your own!"

The list said:

1. Don't shout. "A soft answer turns away anger."
2. Be honest, but kind.
3. Don't bring up the past; forgive and forget.
4. Keep the disagreement to yourself. Leave other people out of it.
5. Don't try to hurt the person.
6. Listen more than you speak. Try to see things from the other's point of view.

"I think we could add 'No name-calling,'" said Lori.

"And 'Don't exaggerate by using the words *always* and *never*,'" added Ken.

"Agreed!" they both said in unison. *SLK*

15
MAY

HOW ABOUT YOU?

Do disagreements with your brothers or sisters tend to become "free-for-alls"? How about the last disagreement you had with a friend? How many of these rules did you break? Ask God to help you learn the "right way to fight"!

MEMORIZE:

"Let us not become conceited, or irritate one another, or be jealous of one another."

Galatians 5:26

 Fight by the Rules!

Lessons on "Tuning" (Read Colossians 3:1-4)

16
MAY

Josh watched as his father tuned a piano, but he didn't say anything. He knew not to talk or disturb him while he was working.

"You like piano tuning, don't you, Dad?" asked Josh when the two of them were in the car on their way home. Dad nodded. "But why do you like it to be so quiet while you're working?" asked Josh.

"Well, when people talk or when there are other outside distractions, my ears are not totally listening to the sound of the piano," explained Dad. "Then I might not do a good job." After a moment, he added, "You know something else?" Dad paused and waited for Josh's complete attention.

"What?" asked Josh.

"To live the kind of life God wants us to live, we have to be in tune with him," said Dad. "Sometimes Christians allow things to distract them from God's voice."

"Like sinful things?" Josh asked.

His father nodded. "Sometimes it's sinful things, and sometimes it's just things."

Josh looked up at his dad. "I don't get it," he replied.

"Anything that keeps us from giving the Lord first place in our lives is a distraction," explained Dad. "Sometimes young people—and older people, too—put things like sports, clothing, and popularity before the Lord." He paused briefly, then said, "The Bible reminds us that anything that becomes more important to us than God is sin."

"So I guess we need to stay tuned to God by reading the Bible," Josh said seriously.

"That's right," his father answered. "And by talking to him regularly and learning all we can about him." *RIJ*

HOW ABOUT YOU?

Are you in tune with God? If not, perhaps you need to turn away from things that are distracting you from him. Spend time on things that will count forever.

MEMORIZE:

"Let heaven fill your thoughts. Do not think only about things down here on earth."

Colossians 3:2

 Keep Tuned to God

First Things First (Read Luke 12:31-34)

Carrie and Ryan were on the same team for the Sunday school contest. "We're ahead," Carrie boasted as she told their parents about the current results. "The losing team has to throw a party for the winners."

"And I'm going to win the individual prize for bringing the most kids," Ryan said quickly. "Got any ideas of some more kids I could invite?"

Carrie looked at her brother in disgust. "I wouldn't tell you if I did!" she said. "I'll win that prize myself."

"Well, I know somebody you could invite, but I'm not going to tell you, either," Ryan shot back. "So there!"

Mom and Dad listened thoughtfully. Finally Dad spoke. "Why are you inviting kids to Sunday school?" he asked.

Carrie shrugged her shoulders. "We told you—there's a contest," she replied, "and there's a prize."

"The best reason for inviting someone would be because people need to hear about Jesus," said Dad.

There was an awkward hush in the room. "Well, sure, Dad," Ryan said finally. "We hope some of the kids will become Christians once they start coming."

"How important is that to you?" asked Mother. "Is it more important than your team winning or than personally getting a prize?"

Neither Carrie nor Ryan answered Mother's question. Both knew that they had wanted to bring visitors to Sunday school for the wrong reason. Their priorities had been all mixed up. They looked at each other. "Why don't you invite . . . ," they both began. Laughing, they exchanged names of children who might be interested in coming. *RIJ*

17

MAY

 Have Proper Motives

Concentration (Read Hebrews 12:1-3)

18

MAY

Thwack! The baseball sailed over the outfield fence! "Home run . . . home run . . . home run," the crowd chanted as Jacob trotted around the bases feeling like a real winner. The scoreboard flashed the winning run, and Jacob's teammates ran onto the field.

On the way home Jacob and his dad stopped to celebrate with ice cream cones. "You know, Dad," said Jacob, losing some of the excitement of the day, "I was hoping my friend Lance would come today. But ever since I invited him to church, he's been avoiding me. He's been talking to some of my other friends behind my back, too, and making fun of me. I'm kinda discouraged." Jacob said with a sigh, "I think I might as well give up trying to talk to him about God."

Dad rubbed his chin as he thought about Jacob's problem. "Do you remember how you felt when you first started to play baseball?" he asked.

"Yeah." Jacob grinned. "I thought I'd never hit the ball."

"And what did you do to get better at batting?" Dad asked.

"Well . . ." Jacob thought for a minute. "I got new glasses," he said, "so now I can see the ball."

Dad laughed. "Yeah, that probably helped a lot," he agreed. "Anything else?"

"I practiced," said Jacob, "and I practiced and I practiced! And oh, yeah . . . I had to learn to concentrate on watching the ball 'cuz I used to get distracted."

Dad nodded. "A lot of things take practice," he said, "and concentration, too. Witnessing is one of them. So keep practicing, and as it says in Hebrews, fix your eyes on Jesus—concentrate on him—when you feel discouraged."

"Do you mean I should try talking to Lance again?" asked Jacob.

"Sure." Dad nodded. "Why not?" he said. "You didn't give up when you missed a baseball. Why give up when Lance turns you down?" *BLW*

HOW ABOUT YOU?

Are you willing to try again and again to win your friends to Jesus? When they don't respond in the way you hoped, do you look to Jesus for encouragement? He understands how you feel. Keep your eyes on him so you don't lose heart.

MEMORIZE:

"We do this by keeping our eyes on Jesus, on whom our faith depends from start to finish." *Hebrews 12:2*

 Keep Your Eyes on Jesus

A Beautiful Bouquet (Read Revelation 7:9-10)

19
MAY

Kacie and her mother carried woven baskets to the flower garden. Kacie enjoyed helping Mom with her florist business. They worked together, selecting and cutting flowers in the warm sunshine. Then Kacie watched as Mom arranged them into a beautiful centerpiece. "You're so creative, Mom," Kacie said.

Mom smiled. "Thanks," she said, "but I'm not nearly as creative as God is."

"You mean because he created everything?" asked Kacie.

Mom nodded. "Yes, and he made the flowers all different," she said. "Look at these beautiful colors—white-and-yellow daisies, red-and-pink dahlias."

"Yeah," said Kacie, "and the petals are different, too—lilies shaped like trumpets, ruffly gladiolas, and baby's breath like little stars."

Mom smiled. "God made people like that, too," she said.

"Ruffly and like little stars?" teased Kacie, wrinkling her nose.

"No, silly!" Mom tickled Kacie's neck with a daisy. "He made everyone with different characteristics. He made different colors of skin, hair, and eyes. Even body shapes are different—people can be tall or short, round or thin. Their hair might be straight, wavy, or curly."

Kacie tugged on a golden ringlet. "Like mine," she said.

"Exactly," responded Mom. "Just as we gather a variety of flowers for our bouquet, the Bible says that God will gather believers from every tribe, tongue, and nation to worship him in heaven. Won't that be wonderful, Kacie, to praise the Lord among our fellow believers from the whole earth?"

Kacie's eyes widened. "Like a human bouquet!" she exclaimed.

ECK

HOW ABOUT YOU?

Do you think about how wonderful it will be in heaven, worshiping God with people from every tribe, tongue, and nation? But don't wait till then to enjoy people who look or talk in a different way than you do. Learn to appreciate God's unique creation in people. Get to know and love them now. God does.

MEMORIZE:

"After this I saw a vast crowd, too great to count, from every nation and tribe and people and language, standing in front of the throne and before the Lamb." *Revelation 7:9*

 God Loves All People

The Riddle (Read Hebrews 10:23-25)

20
MAY

Brian relaxed on the back-porch swing. "Hey, Mom! Do you know this one?" he asked. "Here is the church. Here is the steeple. Open the door and see all the people." He moved his hands and fingers to portray the words he quoted.

Mom laughed. "That's an old one, Brian," she said. "Now come look here. I have a riddle for you."

Brian slid off the swing and walked down the porch steps to where his mother was working in the flower bed. She wrote in the dirt with her finger. *CH _ _ CH.* "Do you know what that is?" she asked.

"Yeah, it's *C H blank blank C H,*" Brian said.

"Think harder. You can figure it out," encouraged Mom.

Brian scratched his head and studied the letters in the dirt. "It looks like part of the word *church,*" he said. "Is that what it means?"

"Actually, it doesn't mean anything," said Mom.

"Aw, Mom," protested Brian.

"That is," Mom added, "it means nothing until U R in it."

"Until U R . . . ," began Brian. Then he laughed. "That is a good one," he said.

"It's more than a good one, Brian," said Mom. "U R very important in our church."

"I guess I always knew church was important," said Brian, "but I never thought before about how important I was to church."

Mom smiled and nodded. "Church is a place where we can put aside our busy lives and meet with God. We can find joy in the prayers, music, sermons, and lessons. And we can encourage each other. Every person is important." *JJL*

HOW ABOUT YOU?

Do you attend church regularly? Do you experience the joy of gathering with Christian friends and with God in his meeting place? Remember CH _ _ CH means nothing until U R in it.

MEMORIZE:

"For where two or three gather together because they are mine, I am there among them."
Matthew 18:20

 U R Important in Church

Generous Jerry (Read Proverbs 11:24-28)

"You mean you really gave Matt Peters your last dollar? Boy, are you dumb!" Alan said, snapping at his young brother. "Last week you gave Amy your last fifty cents! You're always giving money away or putting it in an offering!"

21 MAY

"But Matt didn't have any lunch money," Jerry defended himself. "And Amy needed just that little bit more to buy the gift she wanted for her mom's birthday."

"So let somebody else help them!" scoffed Alan. "At the rate you're going, you'll never have anything to show for your money. I'll soon have enough to buy myself a new ball mitt!"

One Saturday a couple of weeks later, Alan came bounding into the house. "See my new mitt!" He held it up proudly. "Come play ball with me, Jerry. You can use my old mitt."

"Sorry, but I can't," Jerry answered as he put on his jacket. "Why don't you call Scott or Rick?"

"I did," replied Alan, "but they don't want to play. Why can't you?"

Jerry grinned. "Matt Peters called. His dad's company is having their picnic at Bell's Amusement Park today. Matt can bring one guest, and he invited me. The rides are free all day, and so is the food!"

Alan sighed as he threw his mitt on the couch.

"I remember you said I'd never have anything to show for my money," said Jerry, "but I guess you were wrong. I may not have much money, but I don't feel poor at all." He hesitated, then his face brightened as he looked at Alan and said, "How about you and I playing catch tomorrow?"

"OK," agreed Alan. He watched as Jerry went out the door and ran down the steps. "You can even use my new mitt," Alan called out. Maybe his brother's way was OK after all. *BJW*

HOW ABOUT YOU?

Sometimes the one with the least has the most. Do you keep everything you get for yourself, or do you share? God wants his children to be generous.

MEMORIZE:

"If you give, you will receive. Your gift will return to you in full measure, pressed down, shaken together to make room for more, and running over."

Luke 6:38

 *Gain by Giving*

Sequoias or Redwoods (Read Colossians 2:6-10)

22
MAY

Sandra and Carl walked with their father and mother along the paths of Sequoia National Forest in California. They peered up at the tall reddish brown sequoias surrounding them. "I can't even see the tops of these trees," said Sandra. "They're huge!"

The family progressed a little farther along the path. "Wow! Look!" Carl's attention was drawn to a fallen sequoia. He ran to it. "I wonder why it fell? It had plenty of roots to hold it up."

"According to this brochure I picked up, the roots were shallow," replied Dad. "They don't go far enough into the ground."

"Is that true about those redwoods we saw the other day?" asked Sandra.

Dad shook his head. "No. They're just as tall as the sequoias, but their roots reach far into the soil. It takes a lot to knock over a redwood."

Later that evening Dad called the family together for devotions. "Come on, kids," he said. "If we want to put our roots deep like those redwoods we saw, we need to spend time in God's Word."

"Roots?" asked Carl, puzzled.

Dad nodded. "The Bible says we're to be 'rooted and built up' in the Lord. One way to do this is by reading the Bible each day and then doing what it says."

"It doesn't hurt us to miss a few days though, does it?" Sandra asked as she pulled out a chair.

"Well," said Mother, entering the conversation, "if we miss very often, we won't be as solidly rooted than if we don't skip reading. We might be more like the sequoias—we might more quickly fall at the slightest temptation."

"I want to be like the redwoods," decided Carl. "I'm going to keep a picture of them in my room to remind me to read my Bible every day."

Sandra nodded her agreement. "Me too," she said. *DAL*

HOW ABOUT YOU?

Are you more like the sequoias or the redwoods? Do you miss devotions often because you feel you don't need them? Or are your heart and mind becoming deeply rooted in God's Word so that you can stand against temptations?

MEMORIZE:

"Let your roots grow down into him [Jesus] and draw up nourishment from him, so you will grow in faith, strong and vigorous in the truth you were taught." *Colossians 2:7*

 Be Rooted in Jesus

A Lesson from Blackie (Read Matthew 11:25-30)

23
MAY

Michael stood on the lawn, wishing he had someone to play with. "Timmy!" he called out to his friend next door. "Tim-m-my!"

Michael's mother appeared on the back porch. "Michael," she said, "why don't you go over and knock on Timmy's door?"

"But what if his mom answers?" protested Michael. "What if she gets mad at me for bothering her?"

"Oh, Michael!" scolded Mother. "Timmy's mother is a very nice lady."

"Well, I think I'll just play here," decided Michael.

Michael wandered behind the house to the tall maple tree in which a black squirrel lived. He often tried to get close to watch Blackie get the kernels from the ear of corn Dad had nailed to the fence post. At first Blackie always ran away. Now the squirrel didn't run until Michael was only three feet away. "Blackie's starting to trust me," Michael told his mother at lunchtime.

Mother smiled. "He's learning that you're not there to hurt him but to help," she said. "He reminds me of you. You're still learning to trust Timmy's mom. When you know her, you'll see that she's kind, too. The better you know someone, the easier it is to trust that person." She started clearing the lunch table. "You know, Michael," Mother continued, "God's like that, too. The better I get to know him, the easier it is to trust him. I learn about him by learning about Jesus. I know I can trust him to do what's best for me."

Michael thought about how Blackie was learning to trust him and how his mother was learning to trust God. He decided he had to know more about Timmy's mom, too. He went over and knocked on Timmy's door. *JKB*

HOW ABOUT YOU?

Are you afraid that if you become a Christian, God will ask you to do something you don't want to do (like volunteer to do the dishes)? When you know God's love and learn about his kindness, you'll be able to trust him. Spend time reading and learning about Jesus!

MEMORIZE:

"Take my yoke upon you. Let me teach you, because I am humble and gentle, and you will find rest for your souls."

Matthew 11:29

 Know God through Jesus

Finding the Way (Read Proverbs 3:1-8)

24

MAY

"A deer," gasped Tommy when he saw a quick flash of white in the trees. Carefully picking his way across sticks and fallen tree limbs, Tommy walked toward the deer. Glancing over his shoulder, he could still see their campsite, so he went on. As he tried to get closer to the deer, it bounded off into the trees. Tommy ran after it. Finally he stopped when he reached a small stream. Then he turned his freckled face in the direction of camp—but where was camp? Tommy was lost.

Excitement turned to terror as Tommy recalled the ranger's warning about bears in the area. And his parents had told him to stay in sight of the tent. "Dear God," he prayed, "please help me find my way back." As he looked at the stream, he remembered that there was a stream running past the campsite. Perhaps this was it. Perhaps he could follow it back to camp. He started out.

After a while he heard a voice. "Tommy!" it called.

"Dad!" he called back. He ran excitedly toward the voice.

"Where were you?" Dad asked. "We told you . . ." But the scolding stopped as Tommy's fears turned to tears. "You're OK, Tommy," Dad said, holding him tightly.

Family devotions around the campfire that night were about the need to follow God's instructions. Tommy spoke quietly. "When we don't follow God's instructions but do what we want instead, it's like when I ran off looking for the deer. I didn't mean to disobey, but I just went my own way, without thinking about how far away I was getting. When we don't think about what God says, it gets us into trouble, too, doesn't it?" Mom and Dad nodded in agreement.

DAB

HOW ABOUT YOU?

Do you hear God's Word taught in Sunday school and church? Do you read it for yourself? That's good, but here's the most important question: Do you follow the instructions found in the Bible? Knowing such instructions is not enough. You need to follow them. By following God's instructions, you follow him.

MEMORIZE:

"And remember, it is a message to obey, not just to listen to. If you don't obey, you are only fooling yourself."

James 1:22

 Do What God Says

Family Look-alikes (Read 1 Peter 1:13-16)

25
MAY

Great-aunt Louisa gave Beth a hug at the family reunion. "You're the spittin' image of your mother," she said. Beth tried to smile, but she was getting very tired of hearing this. Everyone had made the same remark. The only things the older relatives talked about were how much Beth and all her cousins had grown and who they looked like!

Things looked brighter when Uncle John organized a softball game for all the kids. Maybe this reunion wouldn't be totally boring after all!

"I'll be the pitcher!" shouted Beth as she raced toward the ball field. The game was really fun. Beth got two base hits and one home run. And because of her excellent pitching, her team won the game seven to one.

As everyone headed back to the picnic tables, Great-aunt Louisa cornered Beth again. "Well, young lady," she sputtered, "you may look like your mother, but you certainly don't act like her. She has always been a perfect lady, but you just proved what a little tomboy you are!"

For a moment Beth felt annoyed, but she managed to smile. She was glad when Mother came to her rescue this time. "Yes, Aunt Louisa, Beth may look like me," she said, "but we're very pleased that she inherited her father's athletic abilities."

On the way home that evening, Mother turned to Beth. "Dad and I were very proud of the way you acted today," she said with a smile. "I know you got tired of hearing over and over again how much you look like me, but you were very polite and friendly. In fact, I'd say you looked like someone else—your *heavenly* Father!"

REP

HOW ABOUT YOU?

Most children acquire some physical traits and some personality traits from their parents. That's fine, but if you are a child of God, you should also be learning to act as he would. Ask him to help you behave in such a way that people will say you remind them of your heavenly Father!

MEMORIZE:

"Follow God's example in everything you do, because you are his dear children."

Ephesians 5:1

 Act like God's Child

Jack's Bug Collection (Part 1)

(Read Galatians 5:13-15, 22-26)

26

MAY

It was Jack's turn to lead in prayer at supper one night. "Thank you for this food, and for Mom and Dad who work so hard," he prayed. "And please, God, help Nick to do better at school. Amen."

Mom passed the spaghetti to Jack. "How is he doing?" she asked.

"About the same," Jack replied. "Nobody likes him. He's so weird," Jack continued. Then he went on to criticize Nick and list his faults. "We're supposed to have our bug collections completed by next Monday. Nick has barely started. I think he's just lazy!"

"How many bugs do you have?" asked Allie, Jack's little sister.

"A whole bunch," said Jack. "I even have a praying mantis. We learned that they'll eat almost any kind of insect, including their own kind."

"Does your praying mantis really pray?" Allie wanted to know.

"No, it's called that because of the way it puts its front feet together," said Jack. "Do you think it said a prayer for one of its friends before eating it?"

Dad looked at Jack thoughtfully. "Some people do that," he said. "They say a prayer for someone and then they eat that person."

Jack looked puzzled. "People don't eat each other," he protested.

"Well, they don't actually eat each other," acknowledged Dad. "But criticizing and gossiping about others is called backbiting. And the word backbiting suggests eating, doesn't it?"

"I never thought about it that way before," said Jack. He felt bad for the way he had talked about Nick.

"If we really want God to help somebody, we need to find ways to help," added Dad.

"Maybe I can think of something," added Jack. *VCM*

HOW ABOUT YOU?

Is there someone who needs your help? Do you pray for that person? Do you try to find ways to help him or her?

MEMORIZE:

"No one hates his own body but lovingly cares for it, just as Christ cares for his body, which is the church." *Ephesians 5:29*

 Build Up One Another

Jack's Bug Collection (Part 2)

(Read Matthew 5:13-16)

27

MAY

Jack was excitedly telling his parents about what had happened at school that day. "I asked Nick if he'd like to work with me during study period," he reported. "Boy, was he surprised! Nobody ever wants to work with him. But he said, 'Sure.' We got all of our homework finished. I think he really liked it that somebody helped him. He's not so bad when you get to know him."

"That was very nice of you, Jack. I'm proud of you," Mother said, smiling.

"I asked Nick how his bug collection was coming along," continued Jack. "He said he hasn't caught many yet and that he doesn't know where to find more. So I offered to help him. I told him you were going to help me catch some fireflies tonight, Dad, and that I'd try to get one for him, too."

"Good," approved Dad.

"And you know what else?" Jack said, still bubbling with excitement. "I invited him to go to church with us on Sunday. He said he'd like that. He's really quite a nice guy."

After supper Jack and Dad went out to the backyard to catch fireflies. After they had several in a jar, they sat on the porch. "I'm glad to see that instead of acting like a praying mantis, you acted like a firefly today," said Dad.

"What does that mean?" asked Jack.

"Well," said Dad, "what do fireflies do? They let their lights shine, right? And you let your light shine for Jesus by the way you treated Nick."

Jack grinned. "You know something, Dad?" he said. "It feels a whole lot better being a firefly than a praying mantis." *VCM*

HOW ABOUT YOU?

Do you let your light shine for Jesus? What can you do to show a friend what Jesus means to you? Perhaps you could help with schoolwork. Perhaps you could include that person in a game (even if he or she is not so good at it). Or maybe you could just be a friend.

MEMORIZE:

"In the same way, let your good deeds shine out for all to see, so that everyone will praise your heavenly Father."

Matthew 5:16

 Let Your Light Shine

Only When It Hurts (Read Psalm 105:1-5)

28

MAY

John chattered as he and his mom drove home from church, but she was quiet. When they reached home, she stopped the car and turned to face him. "Your Sunday school teacher told me you haven't been memorizing your Bible verses lately," she said solemnly. "I'm disappointed. I thought you reviewed your verses when you had your personal devotions each day."

John squirmed under Mom's gaze. "Sometimes I do," he said, "but I haven't had anything to pray about lately. And sometimes I forget to read my Bible."

"I see. And how about when things aren't going so well?" asked Mom as they got out of the car.

"Then I remember. Like last month when Pixie ran away . . . I put an ad in the paper and prayed every night," said John. He followed Mom into the house. As he let the screen door shut, it slammed against his fingers. John let out a howl of pain.

Mom looked at John's hand and went to get an ice bag. "Hold this on your hand to keep it from swelling too badly," she said.

"This really hurts bad," he said. "I'll be glad when it starts to feel better."

"I will, too. But then you won't need me anymore," Mom said sadly.

John looked startled. "Why won't I need you?" he asked.

"Because your hand will be all better," replied Mom.

"But I'll still need you!" exclaimed John. "You make meals for me and take me places. And besides that, I love you."

"I'm so glad you do," Mom said. "But don't you love God, too?" she asked.

John looked puzzled. "Of course I do."

"But you said when everything is OK you forget to pray and memorize your verses," said Mom. "Don't you believe God is still taking care of you when everything is going well?"

John nodded. "I see what you mean," he said slowly. *KEC*

HOW ABOUT YOU?

Do you talk to God and allow him to talk to you through his Word when things are pleasant for you as well as when you're hurting or in trouble? Remember that God has many things to teach you, and he's always ready to hear your prayers and praise. Spend time with him in good days as well as in bad.

MEMORIZE:

"Search for the Lord and for his strength, and keep on searching." *Psalm 105:4*

 Spend Time with God

Shedding Bad Habits (Read Colossians 3:8-14)

"Grandma! Grandpa!" Casey and Tyler yelled as they ran outside to greet their grandparents.

"Did you have a good time on your trip?" Grandma asked.

"We sure did—and come see what we brought home," said Tyler. He led his grandparents to the family room. "Look," he said, as he pointed to a covered glass bowl filled with living green plants.

29
MAY

"Nice plants," Grandpa said. "Very nice."

"Look again, Grandpa," suggested Casey. "Look right there." He pointed to a small branch resting on the bottom of the bowl.

Grandpa looked where Casey pointed. He grinned. "I see it," he said. "It's a chameleon. God colored chameleons so they could blend in with their surroundings. He gave them camouflage uniforms!"

"It looks almost like a little leaf," Grandma said in amazement.

"Chameleons are interesting creatures. Their skin doesn't grow," Grandpa said. "When they get too big for their skin, they begin shedding it."

"Yeah—we learned about that in school," said Tyler. "They get rid of their old skin, and soon they have all new skin."

"Kind of like what we should do, isn't it?" observed Grandma.

Casey and Tyler looked at her. "We should get rid of our skin?" asked Tyler.

"No," Grandma said, laughing. "I guess I was thinking out loud," she said. "As the chameleon sheds his skin, we are to shed sinful things. And as the chameleon puts on new skin, we are to put on new, godly characteristics."

Casey nodded. "We learned a verse about that in Sunday school," he said. "The Bible says we're to put off 'the old man' and 'put on the new.'"

"Good for you!" approved Grandpa. "But . . . this old man's hungry. What's for lunch?" Laughing, they headed for the kitchen.

LJR

HOW ABOUT YOU?

Are you shedding sinful habits that you know do not please God? Are you putting on the characteristics that do please him? Knowing Jesus should make a difference in the way you behave.

MEMORIZE:

"What this means is that those who become Christians become new persons. They are not the same anymore, for the old life is gone. A new life has begun!" *2 Corinthians 5:17*

 Shed Old, Bad Habits

Roots (Read Ephesians 3:14-21)

30
MAY

Louise and her brother were helping their dad pull stumps in an area behind their house. It was such hard work! Louise leaned on her shovel and looked at the hole she was digging around the stump. "Is it ready yet?" she asked, sighing.

Dad came over and checked her stump. "Not quite ready," he said.

"I've got a root for you, Dad!" said Tim.

Dad grabbed the ax and went to Tim's stump. Chips flew as he chopped the root. "This one looks ready to pull," said Dad when he finished chopping. He hooked a heavy chain to the stump. Then he hooked the chain to the truck. Tim and Louise cheered as the stump pulled out easily.

Louise kept digging around her stump while Dad chopped the roots she uncovered. Finally he decided it was ready to pull, too. He hooked it up to the truck. This time the tires spun, and Louise groaned. But eventually the stump came out.

After supper that night, Dad reached for his Bible. He turned to Ephesians and read several verses emphasizing one phrase, "being rooted and grounded in love." Dad looked up. "Does this verse remind you of anything?" he asked.

Louise and Tim groaned and rubbed their backs. "It reminds me of all those roots we dug up and had to chop out," said Louise.

Dad smiled. "That was such hard work because the roots were strong and went deep into the ground," he said. "Now . . . this verse is talking about having strong roots in Christ. How do we get strong roots in Christ?"

"By reading the Bible." Tim and Louise spoke together.

"That's one way," agreed Dad. "What's another?"

"Ah . . . by praying?" suggested Tim.

"And by witnessing to our friends?" asked Louise.

"Those are all good," Mom said. "How about by going to church?"

"Good," said Dad. "We all know how to have strong roots!" *HFL*

HOW ABOUT YOU?

Are you growing strong roots in Christ? Do you have devotions regularly? Do you pray often and attend church faithfully? Work on developing your "root systems," so you can stand strong when Satan tempts you.

MEMORIZE:

"But grow in the special favor and knowledge of our Lord and Savior Jesus Christ. To him be all glory and honor, both now and forevermore. Amen."

2 Peter 3:18

 Grow Strong Roots in Christ

Casting Nets (Read Psalm 55:1-2, 16-17, 22)

Wide-eyed, Jason and his sister, Heather, watched the fisherman on the long pier casting his net out and over the Gulf of Mexico.

"That's quite a skill you have there," Dad told the fisherman.

The man chuckled as he pulled the dripping net back in. "Would your kids care to try it?" he asked. Eagerly, Jason and Heather nodded. The man showed them how to place the net on the pier and then how to cast it out. However, instead of landing smoothly out over the water, it bunched up close to the pier. The man smiled. "You hung on a little too long, but not bad for a first try," he said.

After watching a little longer, Jason, Heather, and Dad continued their walk along the sparkling gulf. They were enjoying their weekend vacation, but a cloud of sadness hung over Jason and Heather. Their mother was sick.

"I wish Mom could walk out here with us," said Jason. "Dad, when will Mom get better?"

Dad answered, "I don't know. The doctors don't, either," he said, "but I know what we have to do during this time."

"What?" asked Heather eagerly. "We want to help."

"Remember how that fisherman cast his net way out over the water?" asked Dad. "It reminded me of a different kind of 'casting.' Psalm 55:22 says, 'Cast your cares on the Lord and he will sustain you.' That's what we have to do."

"But, Dad, we already pray every day for Mom," said Jason.

Dad nodded. "We'll keep doing that, of course," he said, "but when we've finished praying, we also need to leave our worries with God. Too often we cast out our worries the way the two of you cast that net; we keep hanging onto them even after praying about them. But remember how the net sailed from the fisherman's hands, way out over the water? That's the way we need to cast our worries—far away from ourselves and onto God." *CEY*

31

MAY

HOW ABOUT YOU?

Do you stop worrying after you pray about something? If the worry comes back, take it to the Lord again.

MEMORIZE:

"Cast your cares on the Lord and he will sustain you; he will never let the righteous fall."

Psalm 55:22, NIV

 Cast Cares onto God

A Special Award (Read 3 John 1-8, 11)

1

JUNE

All the students of the Thomas Jefferson Elementary School were sitting in the auditorium for the end-of-the-year awards assembly. Library awards were given first, then music awards, and then spelling awards. Joe King thought the list would go on forever! He was anxiously awaiting the attendance awards. Finally the principal began reading the names of those who hadn't missed a day all year. "And now we have a very special attendance award to give out." Principal Howard smiled. "Joe King has not missed a day of school since he had the chicken pox in kindergarten. He is now in the sixth grade." Everyone clapped as Joe went up front to receive his perfect-attendance certificate.

As soon as Joe got home from school that afternoon, he showed the award to his mom. "That's neat, Joe." Mother smiled. "You probably stay so healthy because of all that spinach I make you eat." Joe laughed. Everyone in the family liked spinach, except him! "You know, Son," Mother continued, "it's good to be physically healthy, but it's even more important to be spiritually healthy. It's been a long time since you were physically sick. But I wonder, how is your spirit doing?"

"Not as good as my body," admitted Joe.

"I'm afraid we all have to say that about ourselves," said Mother. "Staying spiritually healthy involves reading our Bibles and listening to our Sunday school teachers and the pastor. Then, if someone tries to teach something that goes against God's Word, we will recognize that it is wrong. Being spiritually healthy helps us live the way the Lord wants us to live."

"You know what, Mom?" Joe said. "From now on, I'm going to try to keep myself healthy, both spiritually and physically!" *LMW*

HOW ABOUT YOU?

How is your spiritual health? Don't neglect the most important part of your life. Be a healthy Christian by allowing the teaching of God's Word to control your life.

MEMORIZE:

"Dear friend, I am praying that all is well with you and that your body is as healthy as I know your soul is." *3 John 1:2*

 Be Spiritually Healthy

Mexico or South Street (Read 2 Timothy 4:1-5)

2
JUNE

The Hansen family was at the airport, saying good-bye to seventeen-year-old Becky. Along with some other young people from her church, she was going to spend the summer in Mexico, helping missionaries teach vacation Bible school. Becky's brother, Steve, wished he could go, too. He was only in fifth grade, but already he felt quite sure the Lord wanted him to serve as a missionary someday. He stood thoughtfully, watching an airplane taxi down the runway.

"What's wrong, Son?" Dad asked. "Are you going to miss Becky?"

"Sure, but that's not why I'm feeling sad," answered Steve. "I'm feeling sad because I wish I could be a missionary, too."

"Why, Steve! I think you're already a missionary!" exclaimed Dad. "You bring your friend Dan to church, and he's even going to Bible camp with you."

"That's true, but . . ."

"And you often go down to Mrs. Field's house and help her," added Dad.

"Well, yes, but . . ."

"And how about those two children that moved next door last month?" continued Dad. "I heard you telling them about the Lord just yesterday."

"But I want to be a real missionary," sighed Steve.

"Son," Dad said gently, "someday you'll probably have the opportunity to go to another country, just as Becky is doing this summer. But being a missionary has nothing to do with going far away. Being a missionary is sharing the gospel of Christ with those around you. You are a real missionary already, Steve."

Steve smiled. "Thanks, Dad. I guess I am. Becky is going to be a missionary in Mexico, and I'm being a missionary on South Street!" *LMW*

HOW ABOUT YOU?

Do you want to be a missionary? Being a missionary is simply sharing the gospel with those around you. You can be a missionary on your own street. And if you do become a missionary in another country someday, think of all the good training you will have had!

MEMORIZE:

"Preach the word of God. Be persistent, whether the time is favorable or not. Patiently correct, rebuke, and encourage your people with good teaching." *2 Timothy 4:2*

 Be a Missionary Today

Available Comfort (Read Psalm 46)

3
JUNE

As David watched his father at his workbench in the garage, he knew Dad still felt bad about losing the promotion he had expected. Dad always whistled when he worked happily on a project. Today Dad looked discouraged. David wished he knew how to cheer his dad up. In fact, he had even asked God for an idea of how to help, but nothing happened.

Just as Dad turned off his power saw, a bird flew into the garage. "Go away," Dad said. "This is no place for you." Dad tried to chase it out with a broom. The bird darted under the workbench.

"I think he's trying to find a place to hide," David said.

"Open the door farther," said Dad. "Maybe the wide open space will attract him."

As soon as David opened the door, the bird flew up into the attic of the garage. "Oh no," said Dad. "I should have closed the door to the attic. I'm afraid I'll never get him out now." Dad went up into the attic, but he couldn't even find the bird. "He's probably hiding in the rafters," said Dad as he began working again. "If only he could know how much I want to help him get free!"

An idea began to form in David's mind, but he wasn't sure how to express it. Finally, he decided to do the best he could. Clearing his throat, David began. "Dad, I don't know how to say this, but I was thinking about what you said. You wished the bird could know how much you wanted to help it. Maybe God wishes you to know how much he wants to help you feel better about your job."

Dad finished drawing a line on a piece of lumber and then turned his full attention to David. "You said it very well, Son," he said. "Thank you."

A few minutes later, David grinned as he heard his Dad whistling. But he grinned even more when he saw the bird fly out of the garage. *EMB*

HOW ABOUT YOU?

Do you know someone who is hurting? Why don't you remind him or her of how much God cares? Don't pretend that trusting God will miraculously make all the pain go away. Just let the person know that God wants to share the pain. He cares.

MEMORIZE:

"Give all your worries and cares to God, for he cares about what happens to you."

1 Peter 5:7

 God Cares and Wants to Help You

Tried and True (Read Hebrews 11:1-6)

"Mmmm . . . smells good in here," said Monica as she and Kayla stepped into the kitchen. Monica had come home from church with Kayla.

Kayla nodded. "Yeah, what's cooking, Mom?" she asked.

"Beef stew," Mom answered. Monica made a face and cast a worried glance toward Kayla.

4
JUNE

"Uh oh!" said Kayla. "Monica told me just the other day that she doesn't like beef stew." Then Kayla added, "Not to worry, Monica. You'll like this. Mom's a great cook."

As the family began to eat, Monica saw that Kayla ate heartily, so she took a bite. To her surprise, it was good!

"Our Sunday school lesson today was about faith," said Kayla when the girls were helping Mom with the dishes after dinner. "But how do we know our faith is in the right place—or person?"

"Good question," said Mom. "Our faith as Christians is based on what the Bible teaches."

"But not everyone believes in it," continued Monica.

"No," said Mom, "but that doesn't change what's true." She grinned. "You didn't want to believe there was stew in my crockpot, but it was stew just the same." Her eyes twinkled. "When I first told you girls what we were having for dinner, Kayla was delighted. She has faith in my cooking because she's tasted it before," said Mom. "Monica, you were willing to try the stew because of Kayla's testimony about it, but it wasn't until you tasted it yourself that you really believed it was good, right?" Monica nodded. "In a way, it's like that with our faith," continued Mom. "We become interested in God because of what others tell us. But each of us needs to step out in faith and taste the goodness of God for ourselves to really believe."

Monica grinned. "I think I would like to learn more about God. Could I come to Sunday school next week?"

"Of course," Kayla said with a smile. *GDB*

HOW ABOUT YOU?

Have you wondered if you have the right "set of beliefs"? There are many things that point to the fact that the Bible is truly God's Word. Others have put faith in it, but you need to decide for yourself whether you will believe it or not. By faith, accept all God allows you to experience.

MEMORIZE:

"So, you see, it is impossible to please God without faith."

Hebrews 11:6

 *Walk by Faith*

Caught in the Whirlpool (Read Proverbs 1:10-15)

5

JUNE

"Push harder!" Seth called. "The faster we move in this direction the stronger the whirlpool will be." Seth and his friends ran through the water, circling the inside of the family swimming pool. "OK! Turn around," called Seth. Quickly the kids faced the opposite direction, but some couldn't move against the current.

"I can't fight it," Tobin said, laughing, while he and Seth let the water carry them along.

When the water had relaxed, Seth asked his father, who was watching, if they could make another whirlpool. Dad shook his head. "Not today," he said. "I heard of a pool that split after several whirlpools in one day. I'd rather not take any chances. I'm not sure about our pool's strength." After the other boys had left, Seth grinned at his dad. "This was a fun day even though you wouldn't let me hang around the mall with those other guys from school," he said. "They probably spent pockets full of quarters in the Game Alley anyway."

"It would have cost you more than money to be with those boys," said Dad.

Seth hated it when his father talked like that. "I wouldn't have done anything bad," he said defensively.

"I'm sure you wouldn't intend to," Dad said, "but if you hang around guys who use filthy language, make rude comments about girls, and sneak cigarettes, you might find yourself picking up some of their bad habits."

"Oh, Dad," grumbled Seth.

"After circling in the pool in one direction today, what happened when you tried to go the other way?" asked Dad.

"We almost couldn't," Seth said.

"That's right," Dad agreed. "It was easier to go with the current than to struggle against it, wasn't it? It works that way with friendships, too. If you hang around the boys who do wrong things, it's much easier to let yourself go their way than to turn back and do the right things." *NEK*

HOW ABOUT YOU?

Do you wish you could hang out with some of the kids who get to do whatever they want? Remember that God wants you to walk only one way—and that's his way.

MEMORIZE:

"**Mark out a straight path for your feet; then stick to the path and stay safe.**" *Proverbs 4:26*

 Go God's Way

What You Can't See (Read 1 Peter 1:3-5)

6

JUNE

Luke sneezed. He put down the book he was reading and reached for a tissue. A bad cold had kept him home from Sunday school, and his nose felt sore. "How are you feeling?" asked Mother as she came in with a glass of juice.

Luke sneezed again and reached for another tissue. "I keep sneezing," he said. "But I got this cold from Rick, and he feels OK now. So I guess I'll feel better in a day or two." He frowned. "Something else bothers me, though."

Mother sat beside Luke. "Something I can help with?" she asked.

"Well, the other day I asked Rick if he wanted to come with me to Sunday school sometime," said Luke. "Rick said he doesn't believe in things he can't see. He asked how I know there's a God or such a place as heaven since I can't see them. I told him I just know . . . and I do, but . . . how do I know, Mom?"

Mother thought a moment. "You said Rick had a cold last week, right?" she asked.

Luke nodded.

"I bet Rick has read about germs that cause colds and diseases," said Mother. "You might ask if he's ever seen those germs."

Luke grinned. "Oh, yeah! Good idea," he said. "I bet he believes those germs are what made him sick."

Mother nodded. "There are germs living around us all the time in a tiny world of their own. Just because we can't see them, it doesn't mean they aren't there. It's the same with God and heaven. God describes heaven in the Bible. It's a world we can't see, but that doesn't mean it's not there."

"I'll tell that to Rick, and I'll ask him to Sunday school again next week," said Luke. "Maybe he'll want to learn more about other things he can't see. And someday, maybe he'll even see heaven." Luke grinned. "I know I will," he added. *KEC*

HOW ABOUT YOU?

Do you believe only in things you can see? Actually, you believe in lots of things you can't see—TV and radio sound waves, the wind, electricity, and germs. Evidence that God exists and that his Word is true is all around you in the world that he created.

MEMORIZE:

"No eye has seen, no ear has heard, and no mind has imagined what God has prepared for those who love him." *1 Corinthians 2:9*

 God and Heaven Are Real

Two Impostors (Read Ephesians 2:4-10)

7

JUNE

Tyrone scanned the hymnal pages. *Isn't Pastor Karlson ever going to end the message?* he thought to himself. *He's been preaching for hours.* When the congregation finally bowed their heads for the closing prayer, Tyrone went on daydreaming as he swung his legs back and forth.

Pastor Karlson's voice traveled over the audience. "If you know without a doubt you are saved, please raise your hand," he said. Out of the corner of his eye, Tyrone saw many hands go up. Quickly his hand shot up, too. Then Pastor Karlson gave an invitation to those who were not saved, but Tyrone scarcely heard him. His mind was too busy with other things.

The next day Tyrone went out to the garden and picked spinach for a salad. When he helped Mother wash the leaves a little later, Mother frowned. "Tyrone, some of these aren't spinach leaves," she said.

"I picked them out of the spinach row," insisted Tyrone.

"They look a lot like spinach," Mother agreed, "but they're weeds."

"Weeds!" exclaimed Tyrone. "I picked some weeds?"

Mother nodded. "Impostors in the spinach row," she said as they began to sort out spinach leaves from those of the weeds. "You know what?" added Mother as they worked. "These impostors in the spinach row remind me of the impostors in the church row."

"What do you mean?" asked Tyrone.

"Being in the spinach row didn't make these spinach," replied Mother, "and being in a church row doesn't make anyone a Christian."

Tyrone remembered that he had raised his hand to say he was saved. Suddenly he realized that always being in church with his mom didn't mean he was a Christian—in fact, he knew he wasn't. There were two impostors here—the weeds and him. He knew he needed to do something about that. "Mom," he began, "I need to talk about something. . . ." *DAL*

HOW ABOUT YOU?

Are you an impostor? Are you acting like a Christian, yet you've never accepted Jesus as your Savior? It's an individual decision. If you're interested, talk to a trusted adult to find out more about what it means to become a Christian.

MEMORIZE:

"If you confess with your mouth that Jesus is Lord and believe in your heart that God raised him from the dead, you will be saved." Romans 10:9

 Don't Be an Impostor

God's History Books (Read Joshua 6:1-5, 20)

"You'd better study now, Rick." Mother looked over her shoulder into the back seat of the car. "Once we get to the reunion, there won't be time."

Rick picked up his book. "History is stuffy and boring," he said.

"But very important," said Dad. "It's been said that we're the sum total of those who lived before us."

"Sounds more like math than history," grumbled Rick, "and I don't like math, either."

8
JUNE

All was quiet for several miles. "Enough of that!" said Rick at last. He slammed his book shut. "I can't wait to get to Grandpa's house. He sure has some neat stories to tell. I love to hear about when he came to the United States with only a few dollars. And he could only speak half a dozen English words. That took courage." Rick looked out the window. "Will Grandpa's brother from Sweden be at the reunion?" he asked. "I'll bet he's got some good stories to tell, too."

Dad laughed. "Rick, do you realize that the stories Grandpa tells are history?"

"Oh no, Dad!" exclaimed Rick. "Grandpa tells exciting stories."

"Yes, and they are history," insisted Dad. "What Grandpa tells you is the history of our family. What you're reading in that textbook is the history of our country."

Rick looked surprised. "I guess some history can be interesting then," he said.

"Yes, it can," agreed Mother. "*God* gave us an interesting history book, too."

"The Bible," said Rick.

"That's right," agreed Mother. "The Old Testament books from Joshua through Esther tell the history of God's special people—the Jews. Some of the most exciting stories in the Bible are found there. Like the story of Joshua and the battle of Jericho."

Again Rick was surprised. "I love that story," he said. "Maybe I'll have to take back what I said about history being stuffy." *BJW*

HOW ABOUT YOU?

Did you know about those twelve books of history in the Old Testament? Memorize their names. Read them. You might be surprised what you find there.

MEMORIZE:

"Study this Book of the Law continually. Meditate on it day and night so you may be sure to obey all that is written in it."

Joshua 1:8

 Read the Old Testament

A New Addition (Read Matthew 19:13-15)

9

Margaret and her younger sister, Wanda, looked curiously at Dad as he cleared his throat. "We have a surprise for you," Dad told them mysteriously. Margaret hoped this meant a new, big screen TV, while Wanda envisioned a trip to Disneyland.

Mom clasped Dad's hand. "I am going to have a baby," she said, smiling.

"Really?" Wanda jumped up and down excitedly. "Yipee!"

"You've got to be kidding!" said Margaret.

"We thought you'd be happy," said Mom. "You enjoy other people's babies."

"That's different!" insisted Margaret. "They're not around all the time getting into my stuff. And I'll probably have to change its diapers and baby-sit all the time. Everything will be different with a baby around."

"That's true," said Mom. "But I'm sure we all have plenty of love to share."

Princess, one of the family's two cats, crawled up into Margaret's lap. Rodney, the older cat, lay napping nearby, curled into a ball.

Looking at his daughter and the kitten, Dad had a thought. "Do you remember when Princess became our pet?" he asked. "And do you remember how Rodney responded when we brought Princess into the house?"

"Well . . . sure," said Margaret slowly. "Rodney didn't like it much at first because she invaded his territory. But before long they became good friends." Margaret began to understand her father's meaning. "So you think I'll like having a new brother or sister once he or she comes?" she asked.

Mom and Dad nodded, then Dad added, "We'll ask God to help us all to look forward with joy to that event."

"OK," agreed Margaret. "What will we name it? I hope it's a boy." She noticed her parents' smiles. "I guess I'm more excited about the baby than I realized." *EJH*

HOW ABOUT YOU?

Are there others you can love—like a baby brother or sister? Or maybe a new person at school? Jesus loved everyone. He even took time to hold and speak with little children. He knew that babies are a gift from God.

MEMORIZE:

"But Jesus said, 'Let the children come to me. Don't stop them! For the Kingdom of Heaven belongs to such as these.'" *Matthew 19:14*

 Welcome New Family Members

Shawneesha's Fear (Read Matthew 6:26-29, 34)

10
JUNE

It was Shawneesha's birthday. As she stared at her very first bike, her mom and brother, Hank, were grinning at her. "You can learn to ride it right after breakfast," said Mom. "OK?"

Shawneesha nodded, but secretly she wished they hadn't given her a bike.

When Mom went inside, Hank plopped down on the steps beside Shawneesha. She looked unhappy.

Hank smiled. "I'll help you learn to ride," he offered. "You'll learn fast." Shawneesha looked away. She was afraid to ride a bike. When she had visited her cousins the year before, she had tried, but she had fallen and broken her arm. She was sure Hank knew she was afraid. He put an arm around her.

"I'm afraid I'll fall again, Hank," said Shawneesha, tears in her eyes.

"You probably will," agreed Hank. "I fell a lot when I was learning to ride." Shawneesha tried not to cry. "It's OK to be afraid, Shawneesha," said Hank.

"You weren't afraid to learn," replied Shawneesha.

"No, I wasn't," admitted Hank. "But do you remember when Mom took us horseback riding last year?"

"Yes!" Shawneesha smiled. "That was fun!"

"Well, I was really scared then," said Hank. "But I asked God to help me."

Shawneesha thought for a minute. "I never thought about asking him for something like that," she said. "It seems so small."

"Remember the verses Mom read the other night about how God takes care of the birds and lilies in the field?" asked Hank. "And how about your hair? God even knows how many hairs are on your head. Those things are small, too—really small! But not too small for him to care for."

Shawneesha smiled. "OK, Hank. I'll ask Jesus to help me not be afraid," she said. Even though her fear was not gone, she knew Jesus would help her. *MKH*

HOW ABOUT YOU?
Do you remember that nothing is too small to talk to God about? He's interested in every detail of your life. Tell him your hopes and fears. Trust him to help with even your smallest concerns.

MEMORIZE:
"And the very hairs on your head are all numbered."
Luke 12:7

 Jesus Cares about Little Things

Unexpected Fruit (Read Mark 4:14-20)

11

JUNE

"Mom! Dad!" Justin called, racing into the house. "Come quick! I think a watermelon is growing in our backyard!"

"Really?" asked Dad. "That ground out back is so poor and rocky—I wouldn't think a watermelon could grow there."

"There is one though," insisted Justin. "Come look."

"We'll look later," Dad said. "Right now we have to get to the Rescue Mission or we'll be late for chapel."

Justin's family had agreed to lead the Rescue Mission's afternoon chapel service once a month. Grumbling, Justin went to his room and got his trumpet and sheet music.

On the way home a couple of hours later, they discussed the service. "No one at the mission seemed to be paying attention today, and no one accepted Jesus," said Justin. "I think it was a waste of time for us to go."

"We still need to share the gospel," Mother said. "You never know when someone's heart will be ready to accept the Lord."

As soon as they reached home, Justin persuaded his parents to go with him to look at the watermelon plant. Sure enough, there was a vine with one very small watermelon. "This must have grown from some seeds we threw out here last year," said Justin.

Dad nodded. "I thought all the soil back here was good for nothing, but it looks like one of those seeds fell on ground that was just right for watermelon growing."

"Today at the mission we scattered seed, too," added Mother. "That seed was the Word of God. Some of the men didn't seem to be paying attention, but we don't know the condition of their hearts. Perhaps that seed will bring forth fruit, too." *NEK*

HOW ABOUT YOU?

Do you feel as though it's useless to share the Lord with people who don't seem interested? It's your responsibility to keep sharing. You may be speaking to someone whose heart is getting ready to accept Jesus.

MEMORIZE:

"The good soil represents the hearts of those who truly accept God's message and produce a huge harvest."

Matthew 13:23

 Spread God's Word

The Big Picture (Read Genesis 50:15-20)

Anna watched the TV screen eagerly. Her mom's office was going to be shown. "I don't think that looks like your office," Anna told Mom. "Your office is bigger than that. All you can see on the TV screen is your boss's desk and that picture behind it."

"Well, they can show only a small part of what's really there, you know," said Mom. "Kind of what God does with us in life sometimes."

12
JUNE

"What do you mean?" asked Anna.

Mom turned the TV off. She continued, "Well, sometimes things happen that make us sad, and we don't understand why they happen. But, just like the TV picture doesn't show the whole office, we don't see the whole picture of our lives," explained Mom. "And when sad things happen, we can trust that God still loves us and has a good plan for our lives."

Anna was thoughtful. "I've been sad lately because Grandpa isn't here anymore," she told Mom. She felt tears coming to her eyes as she thought about Grandpa. "Why did he have to die in a plane crash?"

Mother answered, "I don't know why, Anna. Only God knows that. But I know you're sad because you miss him. And that's OK for now. But life won't always be sad. Now, let's read the verse for today," Mom said as she picked up her devotional.

Anna read, "'For I know the plans I have for you,' says the Lord. 'They are plans for good and not for disaster, to give you a future and a hope.' Hmmm, I wonder if God has any good plans for me?"

"I think he does," answered Mom with a smile. "And just like the TV only showed a little bit of my office, God is only showing you a little part of your life. Who knows what may be just around the corner!"

"I'm glad God can see the whole picture," Anna said with a smile. *KRA*

HOW ABOUT YOU?

Are you unhappy about a situation in your life? Could you have a false impression about it? God sees the whole picture and will do what's best for you. Trust him.

MEMORIZE:

"'**For I know the plans I have for you,' says the Lord. 'They are plans for good and not for disaster, to give you a future and a hope.'**" *Jeremiah 29:11*

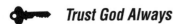 *Trust God Always*

Apple of Your Eye (Read Proverbs 7:1-4)

13

JUNE

Sarah shut her eyes tight and ducked quickly when she saw the pencil flying through the air toward her. When she heard it bounce off her desk onto the floor, she sat up and glared at Kent, who was grinning. "That almost hit me in the eye," Sarah said crossly.

"Kent . . . Sarah . . . what's going on here?" Mrs. Newton asked as she walked up to their desks.

"Kent just threw a pencil and almost hit me in the eye!" said Sarah.

"I didn't mean to," said Kent quickly.

"Did too," accused Sarah.

"Did not," insisted Kent. "I was just playing." He scowled.

"Kent," said Mrs. Newton sternly, "you could have hurt Sarah, even though you thought you were just having fun. And, Sarah, can you see that Kent didn't intend to hurt you?" asked Mrs. Newton. Sarah glanced at Kent and nodded.

"I think this may be a good time for a lesson on eyes," said Mrs. Newton as she walked back to her desk. "Class, let's get out our health books."

At home that evening, Sarah told her parents about the lesson. "We learned that we all have a built-in instinct that tells us to shut our eyelids and move when something comes toward our faces," she reported. "That's because our eyes are sensitive and easily damaged. If we didn't do that, some people might even be blind today."

Mother nodded. "We all try to take very good care of our eyes because they're important to us," she said.

Dad asked, "Did you know that God refers to his people as the 'apple of his eye'? That gives an indication of how important we are to him. And the Bible also says we should guard his teachings as the 'apple of our eye.'"

Sarah smiled. "I guess we should take good care of our eyes so we can see well. And we should treat God's Word as we would our eyes, as a precious possession," she said. *JJB*

HOW ABOUT YOU?

How do you treat God's Word? Is it important to you? Try to read it each day this week.

MEMORIZE:

"**Keep my commands and you will live; guard my teachings as the apple of your eye.**"

Proverbs 7:2, NIV

 Care for God's Word

Clean Inside and Out (Read Psalm 119:9-16)

It was bath time at the Berens home. And as usual John and Christie were complaining about having to take a bath.

"I hate taking baths!" said John.

"Me too," Christie added. "They always interrupt what I'm doing." But both kids got their baths and were glad they had a little time left to play.

Then Mom called them to the family room. "It's time for family devotions," she said.

14

JUNE

"Oh, Mom," whined Christie. "Do we have to? I want to work on my crossword puzzle."

"Why do we have to have devotions every single day anyway?" complained John. "It takes so much time!"

"It's interesting that you should ask," Mother replied, "because the verses I was planning to read talk about that." She opened the Bible to Psalm 119 and read verse 9. "'How can a young person stay pure? By obeying your word and following its rules.'"

"That's good advice. We need to keep our lives clean as well as our bodies," said Dad. "The Bible tells us how God wants us to live, and it helps us see the dirty spots of sin in our life. We could say God's Word is like a mirror to help us see where we need washing."

"And confessing sin through prayer is like soap making dirt come loose," suggested Christie.

"And God's forgiveness is like water rinsing away all the dirt or sin," finished John.

"Right," agreed Dad. "Does that answer your question? Do you see why it's important to read the Bible and pray every day?" John and Christie nodded. Mother turned to her Bible to read some more verses. *CEY*

HOW ABOUT YOU?

Do you wash yourself carefully on the outside but not bother about the inside? Your body needs daily cleansing with soap and water. And your life needs daily cleansing through reading God's Word and then obeying it.

MEMORIZE:

"How can a young person stay pure? By obeying your word and following its rules."

Psalm 119:9

 **Read the Bible**

Quiet Surprise (Read Matthew 10:29-31)

15

JUNE

Finally the Helm family arrived at Grandpa's. Ryan jumped out and ran to the door. He was excited! Just the night before, Grandpa had called and told Ryan he had a special surprise.

As soon as Grandpa came to the door, Ryan asked, "Where's the surprise, Grandpa? Can I see it now?"

Grandpa laughed. "Come on," he said. "I'll show it to you." He headed toward a part of the yard where Ryan was not allowed to play because it was where Grandpa kept his bird feeders. He didn't want Ryan scaring the birds. Grandpa held Ryan's hand out flat and put a sunflower seed in his palm. "Now stand still, and don't move an inch," he instructed.

Ryan did as he was told. He waited a few minutes, and his arm began to get tired. But then a little gray-and-white bird hopped on his finger, grabbed the sunflower seed, and flew away. "Wow!" exclaimed Ryan. "That was neat!"

"You just fed a chickadee," his grandfather explained.

"It was so tiny, it was almost as if it wasn't really there," Ryan said. "Chickadees sure are cute!"

Grandpa nodded. "Yes, they are," he agreed. "In fact, chickadees are my favorite bird. They're one of the easiest birds to tame, and they *are* small! You know, when I'm out here feeding the birds, I'm reminded of those verses in the Bible that tell us about God's care for the birds and us. Imagine, if he cares for a little chickadee, how much more he must care for us."

"God sure does care a lot about us, doesn't he, Grandpa?" said Ryan as he put another sunflower seed on his palm. *LMW*

HOW ABOUT YOU?

Do you sometimes feel lost and alone in the world—confused about things that are happening? Do you feel as if no one really cares about you? Don't think that. The Lord knows and cares about the tiny birds, and you are much more important to him than birds. God cares about you—all the time!

MEMORIZE:

"So don't be afraid; you are more valuable to him than a whole flock of sparrows."

Matthew 10:31

 *God Cares for You*

Out of Reach (Read 2 Timothy 2:20-25)

16

JUNE

"No more candy before supper, Allen," said Mom as she took a hot dish out of the oven.

Allen absentmindedly nodded and chewed on a caramel as he set the table. He was thinking about the invitation he had received to go to a party the coming weekend. All the popular kids would be there.

"Let's go—we'll have a great time," his friend Jeff had urged. "And why don't you stay at my house overnight? Then we can play my new video game, too."

It sounded tempting, but Allen had seen some of the kids who were invited to the party smoking and drinking after school. He was quite sure they would do that at the party, too. He knew his parents would say no if they knew about it.

"So don't tell 'em," said Jeff. "Just say you're coming over to my house."

Go ahead, an inner voice whispered to Allen. *You don't have to do anything you don't want to at the party.*

"I guess I can go as long as I really do spend a lot of time at your house," Allen had finally agreed. But now that he was home, his conscience was bothering him. Reaching for another piece of chocolate, he brushed the doubts from his mind.

"Allen, I said no more candy," Mom scolded. She took the unwrapped candy from his hand. "I guess I'll have to put it out of your reach so you won't be tempted," she added.

Temptation, thought Allen. *That's right! I know things like smoking and drinking are wrong, but what if the guys convince me to try it "just once"? I'd feel awful later and wish I'd stayed home. I'm going to call Jeff right now and tell him I'm not going to the party. That way I'll be out of temptation's reach. SLB*

HOW ABOUT YOU?

Do you sometimes put yourself in tempting situations that could easily be avoided? Saying no when asked to do something wrong is important, but God also wants you to avoid tempting situations when you can. Follow his advice and, whenever possible, flee—run away from—situations where you'd be tempted to sin.

MEMORIZE:

"Run from anything that stimulates youthful lust."

2 Timothy 2:22

 Turn from Temptation

Just like Dad (Read Ephesians 4:30-32; 5:1-8)

17

JUNE

One day when Nathan and his father were shopping, an elderly man walked up to them. "Excuse me," the man said. "I'm Bill Cook. I've been watching the two of you, and I can't help noticing how much both of you look like a school chum I had years ago. His name was Nathan Noble. Are you related to him?"

"That's my name, and my dad's, too!" blurted out Nathan. "He's Nathan Nobel, Jr., and I'm the third," he added proudly. "But you look too old to have gone to school with Dad."

The two men laughed. "I'm sure this gentleman is talking about your grandfather, Nathan," explained Dad.

"I just knew you must be related," said Mr. Cook after they had talked a few minutes. "Your boy here, with his red hair and freckles, looks very much like old Nate did in grammar school. Both of you walk and talk like him, too."

After Mr. Cook left, Dad smiled at Nathan. "It was a real compliment, Nathan, to be recognized as my father's son," he said. "I've always admired him very much, and I guess I've imitated his ways more than I realize. I'm really proud to be just like Dad."

"Yeah—wasn't that something?" asked Nathan. "Mr. Cook hasn't seen Grandpa in years, and yet he recognized how much we were like him."

Dad looked very thoughtful. "There's someone else we should be like, Nathan," he said. "The Bible says that others should be able to tell that God is our Father just by watching our actions and hearing our words."

"But he's perfect, and he can do all kinds of miracles," said Nathan. "We can't be exactly like him."

"That's true," agreed Dad, "but with God's help, we can show his kind of love, kindness, and forgiveness to others. We should also do our best to live the way God would want us to live. Then surely some people will say, 'There goes a child of God.'" *MRP*

HOW ABOUT YOU?

Have you been told that you look, sound, or act like one of your parents? Can people also tell by watching you that you're a child of God? In every way possible, Christians are to be like their heavenly Father. After all, that's the only way others can see what God is really like.

MEMORIZE:

"Follow God's example in everything you do, because you are his dear children."

Ephesians 5:1

 Be like Your Heavenly Father

Light in Darkness (Read John 1:1-5, 9-12)

The Moore family had just settled down in the den for nightly devotions when suddenly the lights blinked, and then everything went black. "Oh, wow!" Jeff wailed. "The storm knocked out our power. What do we do now?"

"Sit tight," Dad instructed. "I'll get us some light."

"I'll come, too," offered Jeff. He jumped up, took one step, and tripped over a footstool. "Ow!" he exclaimed, sinking back into his seat.

Soon Dad came back, carrying a candle in each hand. A warm circle of light filled the room. "There . . . how's that?" asked Dad as he carefully set the candles down on the coffee table. "Now we can see again."

"That's much better!" exclaimed Sarah. She leaned back in her chair. "It's creepy when it's so dark that you can't see anything."

"Well, it's a little dim yet, but I think we can get back to our devotions now," said Dad. "I'll read some of the verses that talk about Jesus being the Light of the World." He opened the Bible. "Not knowing Jesus as Lord and Savior is like living in a dark room all the time," he observed after reading the verses. "Choosing to live our lives without Jesus keeps us from seeing clearly. We might even think everything is OK, but it isn't."

"Yeah," agreed Jeff, "like tonight—I thought I could see well enough to walk around, but I fell over the footstool!"

Mom nodded. "A lot of people think they can get along just fine without Jesus," she said, "but sooner or later their sins 'trip' them up."

"But when we confess our sins to God and give our lives to Jesus, it's just like having all the lights come back on," Dad added, closing the Bible. "And the best part is that his light never goes out!" *LML*

18 JUNE

HOW ABOUT YOU?

Do you have the light of Jesus in your life? You can make the decision to let Jesus take away the darkness inside by asking him to forgive your sins and by trusting him to be your Savior.

MEMORIZE:

"Jesus said to the people, 'I am the light of the world. If you follow me, you won't be stumbling through the darkness, because you will have the light that leads to life.'" *John 8:12*

 Jesus Is the Light of the World

Generous Pansies (Read 2 Corinthians 9:6-8)

19

JUNE

"What are you going to do with that?" Tiffany asked when she saw her sister slip some money into her Bible.

"It's for our special missionary project," Tara told her. "How much are you giving?"

Tiffany got up to leave the room. "That's none of your business," she mumbled. She certainly didn't want to admit that she was giving only a few pennies. If she gave any more, she wouldn't have enough to buy that new outfit she wanted.

As they returned home from church that morning, Mother pointed to the flowers along the front walk. "Look at my pansies," she said. "Aren't they pretty?"

"How can they have so many flowers already?" asked Tiffany. "You just picked all the pansies two days ago."

"Pansies need to be picked often," said Mother. "The more they give, the more they have to give. It makes me think of our gifts to the Lord. When we give generously and cheerfully to him, he gives back to us. It seems as though the more we give, the more we have from which to give."

Tiffany stooped to pick a pansy as she thought about that. "You mean if we give lots of money, God will send more money to us?" she asked.

Mother smiled. "Well, I can't promise you that," she said. "But sometimes he may give extra blessings to us in some other form. Maybe he'll give a special sense of joy and peace and well-being."

Tiffany thought about her sister, who was always generous and happy. Then she thought about how grumpy she often felt herself. *Perhaps I need to start giving like the pansies, too,* she thought.

MRP

HOW ABOUT YOU?

Do you give cheerfully to the Lord, or do you grumble and complain about giving money? The Lord loves a cheerful giver. He's promised to give you more than you give him. It may not be money, but it will be whatever blessings you need most.

MEMORIZE:

"Give, and it shall be given unto you; good measure, pressed down, and shaken together, and running over."

Luke 6:38, KJV

 Be a Cheerful Giver

The Second Mile (Read Matthew 5:38-42)

Heather and Jessica were special friends. Both were Christians, but neither of their families attended church.

"Jessica," said Heather one day, "let's start a Second Mile Club like Mrs. Jenner suggested in Sunday school yesterday."

"Second Mile Club?" asked Jessica. "How?"

20
JUNE

"Going the second mile is putting Matthew 5:40-41 into action," explained Heather. "If someone asks us to do something, let's do more than they ask."

Jessica frowned. "If my brother asks me to carry his books home, I should?"

Heather nodded. "Yes, and even offer to carry his jacket and hang it up when you get home. If Mom asks me to wash dishes, I will, and then I'll sweep the floor. See what I mean? We go the 'first mile' because we're asked, and we go the 'second mile' because we want to."

Jessica hesitated. "I'm not sure I *do* want to."

"But it'll be fun. Think how shocked everyone will be!" Heather grinned. "Besides, Jess, we talk about showing God's love to our families, but what do we ever do about it? Let's try it for a week."

The girls didn't see results from their efforts the first few days, but before the end of the week, Jessica's dad commented on her improved attitude. She overheard her mother saying that she "might go to church with Jessica one of these days." Her brother Tim was about to burst with curiosity. He was sure Jess was "up to something," but he couldn't figure out what. And Heather heard her dad say that "maybe Heather's religion is real after all—we'll have to wait and see."

"One week is up," Heather reminded Jessica the following Monday. "Do you want to stop?"

Jessica looked shocked. "Stop? Jesus didn't say to do this for a week. He wants us to live this way all the time."

Heather nodded. "Even if we goof up sometimes, let's keep trying—for life!" *BJW*

HOW ABOUT YOU?
Would you like to belong to the Second Mile Club? All you have to do is "a little bit extra." Even if you don't see results right away, don't quit. Why not try it for a week? You might want to be a lifetime member, too.

MEMORIZE:
"If someone forces you to go one mile, go with him two miles." *Matthew 5:41,* NIV

 Do More Than Required

Proper Dress (Read Ephesians 6:10-17)

21
JUNE

"Billy!" called Dad. "Want to go with me on a bike ride?"

"Sure, in a minute," Billy called back. "I'm just getting out of the shower."

Dad walked toward Billy's room. "Let's go," he called again.

Billy opened the bathroom door. "Like this?" he asked with a grin as he hugged his bathrobe tightly around him. "Don't worry, Dad. I'll get dressed fast."

Soon Billy hurried out to the garage where Dad was waiting. "Oh no," said Billy, "I forgot my helmet." He ran into the house and grabbed his bike helmet. Back outside, he said, "OK, Dad. Let's go."

Dad leaned on his bike. "You're sure you're finally ready?" he asked.

"I think so," replied Billy. "I've got my biking shorts on, and my shoes. And I've got my helmet so my head will be protected in case of an accident. I'm all set."

"All right!" said Dad. He grinned at Billy. "This reminds me of the Scripture we read last night."

"Scripture?" asked Billy, thinking. "Oh . . . yeah. It talked about putting on the armor of God, didn't it? It even mentioned a helmet. You said we need to always put on God's armor every day."

"That's right," agreed Dad. "We do that to be properly prepared for all the experiences we'll have during the day. It's as important as being properly dressed for a bike ride. Sometimes we forget that." He wheeled his bike out of the garage. "Let's go," he said. "We both have our biking clothes on. As we ride, maybe we should review the pieces of the armor God provides and make sure we've also put them on today." *NJF*

HOW ABOUT YOU?

Do you put on the armor of God every day? It provides protection for you as you face the experiences of life. Don't be in such a hurry that you don't take time to pray and read the Bible.

MEMORIZE:

"Put on all of God's armor so that you will be able to stand firm against all strategies and tricks of the Devil." *Ephesians 6:11*

 Put on the Armor of God

Burning Candles (Read Matthew 5:13-16)

22
JUNE

Jenny was so excited that she could hardly sit still as she waited, eyes closed, for Mom to bring in her birthday cake. "OK, sweetie! Open your eyes!" said Dad at last.

Jenny blinked as her eyes adjusted to the light created by the glowing candles in the dark. It was the most beautiful birthday cake she had ever seen! Nine colorful frosting angels each held a flickering candle.

"Make a wish and blow the candles out!" said Dad with a smile.

Jenny closed her eyes and made a secret wish that all her days would be as happy as this one! She opened her eyes and blew out the candles. But as she reached for the cake knife, she saw that, somehow, every candle had started burning again! "Look! The candles!" exclaimed Jenny. "I thought I blew them out, but they all started up again!"

Jenny's father tried not to laugh. "Better blow them out again, Jenny!" suggested Mother.

"Yeah, I guess so!" Jenny took a deep breath and blew extra hard this time. Once again all the candles went out. Jenny watched the cake. One by one, each candle sparked and was soon burning again. Jenny was speechless! She carefully lifted one candle from the cake and examined it closely.

Her father burst into laughter. "Got ya, Jenny," he teased. "I put special candles on your cake!"

"I should have known," said Jenny. "That's what my friends Jerry and Annie did to their dad on his April 1 birthday."

Jenny and Dad tried blowing them out again. They laughed together as the lights kept coming back.

Jesus wants us to be like the candles on Jenny's cake, always shining for him. *MJL*

HOW ABOUT YOU?

Are you a Christian? If so, did you know that you were chosen by God as his "special candle" to share his message with others? Have you been doing that? Don't be embarrassed or uncomfortable talking about him—don't let your Christian light flicker! Ask Jesus to help you always shine brightly for him!

MEMORIZE:

"In the same way, let your good deeds shine out for all to see, so that everyone will praise your heavenly Father."

Matthew 5:16

 Shine for Jesus

A Long Life (Read Psalm 71:5-9, 14-18)

23

JUNE

Nervously, Jeff carried his stand to the platform and arranged his music sheets. He was going to play a special number at church for the first time. He looked out over the audience and saw his dad and mom and his great-uncle Roger. Uncle Roger was ninety-one years old and was highly respected in the community and in the church. He wasn't able to get to church often anymore, but on this day he had made the effort because of Jeff's solo.

After the service Uncle Roger complimented Jeff.

"Fine job, Jeff. Fine job," the old man said. "You know," he added with a grin, "when I was just about your age, my sister Mary and I sometimes sang in church. I've never been sorry I took those opportunities when I was young." He had a faraway look in his eyes as he remembered the times so long ago.

"How long have you been a Christian, Uncle Roger?" asked Jeff.

"Let's see," his uncle murmured, "it's been a long time—more than eighty years. There's something special about becoming a Christian as a child and having an entire life to live in service for the Lord." He thumped Jeff on the back. "Yep," he said, "you can waste your life on unimportant things, or you can live it for the Lord. Make the right choice, boy. Make the right choice! Perhaps the Lord will give you as many years to serve him as he has given to me."

Jeff thought about what Uncle Roger had said. Jeff didn't know how many years were ahead of him, but he decided right then that he, too, would use them to serve the Lord. *LMW*

HOW ABOUT YOU?

If you're a Christian, start now to serve the Lord. Take advantage of opportunities to sing or play solos, to participate in junior choir, to help with senior citizens, and to invite friends to join you in Sunday school or Bible club. Don't wait until you're older. How wonderful to have an entire life to serve Jesus!

MEMORIZE:

"O God, you have taught me from my earliest childhood, and I have constantly told others about the wonderful things you do." *Psalm 71:17*

 Live for Jesus Now

Amazing Grace (Read Romans 8:1-4)

One Sunday, as the Walker family finished devotions, Jeff turned to his dad with a puzzled look. "Sometimes we read how God used to punish sin in the old days," he said. "Like when he struck people dead because they sinned, or when other people were supposed to stone them to death. It always sounds so awful. Why did he do that?"

"That's a very good question," Dad answered. "And there is no easy answer." He tapped his fingers on the table as he thought about it. "It was important for the Israelites to know that God really meant what he said and that the laws he had given them could not be broken without severe consequences. He had to show them how bad sin really was. Sometimes he sent sickness—even death—as a warning of the terrible consequences of disobeying God. He punished people so others, including future generations, could learn from it."

24
JUNE

Jeff looked confused. "Why doesn't God punish us that way now?" he wondered.

"Another good question," admitted Dad, "and also a hard one to answer. Perhaps there are several reasons. For one thing, we have the Bible now, and we learn from it just how much God hates sin. The Bible also tells us that God is gracious and merciful to those who have accepted his Son as their Savior. We must remember, too, that God does still punish sin, though perhaps not in exactly the same way. As Christians, we are his children, and he disciplines us when we need it. No, we can't get away with sinning. However, his relationship with us today is one of grace and freedom, not of law and bondage. Isn't that good news?"

"It sure is!" Jeff exclaimed. "That makes me want to obey God all the more—not because I'm afraid of him but because I love him!"

SLK

HOW ABOUT YOU?

Do you realize just how much God hates sin? His attitude toward sin has never changed—all sin must be severely punished. But Jesus came and took the punishment for your sins. What he has done should cause you to obey and serve God out of love, not out of fear.

 *Thank God for His Grace*

MEMORIZE:

"But now we have been released from the law, for we died with Christ. . . . Now we can really serve God, not in the old way by obeying the letter of the law, but in the new way, by the Spirit." *Romans 7:6*

Katie's New Clothes (Read 1 Peter 3:8-12)

25

JUNE

As Grandma and Grandpa pulled out of the driveway, Mother turned to Katie. "I want to have a word with you about your manners," she said.

"What's wrong with my manners?" asked Katie.

"You didn't say much of anything to your grandparents. You acted as though you weren't at all glad to see them," explained Mother.

"Well, it's easier to talk to my friends," pouted Katie. "What am I supposed to say, anyway?"

"How about 'I'm glad to see you' or 'How are you feeling?'" asked Mother.

"Oh, Mom, I'd sound like a robot!" cried Katie. "I'd feel silly talking like that!" And she stormed out of the room.

A few days later Mother suggested that Katie wear some new clothes to a youth meeting. But Katie came out wearing the old skirt and sweater that she wore almost every week. "I hate wearing new clothes," she said. "This is more my style. I don't want everybody staring at me."

Mother frowned. "Those clothes are not only worn out, they're dirty," she said. "Go put on your new ones." So Katie did, but she didn't like it.

After the meeting Katie was smiling. "Everyone loved my new outfit."

"Good," said Mother with a smile. Then she added, "Along with the new clothes, there's something else you should try on."

"What's that?" asked Katie.

"A new set of manners," said Mother. "Like new clothes, they may feel strange at first, but after you get used to them, I think you'll enjoy them."

"OK," laughed Katie. "I'll start by writing a nice note to Grandpa and Grandma." *SLK*

HOW ABOUT YOU?

Do you have old habits that need to be changed? Do you ignore certain people or act bored when you're with them? Don't wait until you *feel* like doing the right thing. Make an effort to be courteous and friendly toward others. Before long, you'll find you really like the "new you." Others will, too!

MEMORIZE:

"Finally, all of you should be of one mind, full of sympathy toward each other, loving one another with tender hearts and humble minds." *1 Peter 3:8*

 Learn Good Manners

Charged Up (Read Psalm 19:7-11)

After shopping at the mall for a few hours, Karen and her mother had lunch together and then headed for the parking lot.

"What's the matter with the car?" cried Karen in alarm as her mother tried to start it. The car made a growling sound, but that was all.

Mom shook her head. "I don't know," she said, checking over everything on the panel in front of her. Suddenly she spotted it! The light button was pulled out! "Oh, dear!" she exclaimed. "We used the lights because it was foggy when we came to the shopping mall. I forgot to turn them off. Now the battery is run down."

26

JUNE

Calling a garage did not take much time, but waiting for help to arrive seemed to take forever. Finally a mechanic came. Soon the car was running, and they were ready to leave. "If you're not going very far, you might want to take your car to your service station and get a quick charge," suggested the serviceman before he left them.

"What's a quick charge?" asked Karen as they started home.

"When the battery has been run down, they sometimes hook it up to a battery charger," Mother explained. "I can't tell you how it works—only that the charger puts new power back into the battery so that it will work again."

That evening Karen excitedly told her father about their car trouble and the quick charge they had needed. "The service station man says the battery should be OK now," she reported.

"Good," said Dad. He reached for the family Bible. "And now it's time for our 'quick charge,' too," he said. Karen looked at him curiously. "Sometimes we need to get 'charged up' in our spirits through reading the Bible," added Dad with a smile. "Reading it, studying it, and meditating on it helps to put power in our life and make us strong Christians." *RIJ*

HOW ABOUT YOU?

Do you take time to read God's Word each day? Do you think about the things you've read? Do you look for more verses on the same subject? Do you look for verses about problems you are facing? Doing these things will help keep you "charged up" for God.

MEMORIZE:

"Work hard so God can approve you. Be a good worker, one who does not need to be ashamed and who correctly explains the word of truth."

2 Timothy 2:15

 *Study to Learn*

Cheer Them On (Read Romans 12:10-17)

27

JUNE

Blake watched as the other children lined up for the foot race. *If it hadn't been for Marlo, I'd be running, too,* he thought. She had left her skates on the porch, and he had tripped over them and fallen down the stairs. Now, with a broken arm, he couldn't enter the race at the school picnic. He kept his eye on his sister. *She's to blame for my broken arm, but she gets to run. It's not fair!*

Marlo glanced at him. "Cheer for me," she called.

"I hope she doesn't win," Blake grumbled to himself.

The whistle blew, and the runners began their race. Blake's sister didn't seem to get a good start. That made Blake feel good. But as the race went on, Marlo gained speed, and in a few minutes she was in front. Then something happened! Marlo tripped and fell! The others passed her, and another girl won.

Marlo got up slowly and ran to the sidelines where Blake was standing. "Tough break," Blake said offhandedly. He glared at her. "Now you know how I feel."

Marlo looked at him sadly. "I'm sorry," she said. "I wanted to win the prize for you."

Somehow Blake didn't enjoy the rest of the picnic very much. *It's because I can't do anything with this broken arm,* he told himself. But whenever he saw Marlo, he felt especially bad. "It's not my fault she lost," he muttered under his breath. "Besides, I'm glad." But he wasn't glad; he was unhappy. And deep down he knew that it was his own attitude that made him unhappy.

Just then he saw the boys and girls lining up for the crabwalk race—another activity he couldn't enter. But Marlo was entering. Blake walked over to watch. "Go, Marlo, go!" he yelled as the whistle blew. And he meant it! *RIJ*

HOW ABOUT YOU?

Are you happy when someone else does a better job than you do? The Bible teaches that you should be glad with them even though that may be hard to do. Ask God to help you.

MEMORIZE:

"When others are happy, be happy with them. If they are sad, share their sorrow."

Romans 12:15

 Cheer for Others

The Storm (Read 1 Thessalonians 5:16-24)

28 JUNE

Big, dark clouds moved in front of the sun and cast a shadow over the Carlsons' picnic. A streak of lightning flashed across the sky. "Oohhhh, it's going to storm," wailed Marcy.

"Don't be a baby!" scoffed Davy. "I'm younger than you, and I'm not scared of storms. I'm not even scared of thunder!" A big rumble filled the air. "Not . . . too much anyway," he added as he ran for the car.

They had barely started home when the rain began pouring down so hard that Dad could hardly see. The wind was strong, and he had trouble keeping the car on the road.

"Oh, I'm scared! Ask Jesus to stop the rain," Marcy begged fearfully.

"But, Marcy, we really need the rain," said Mother. "Many people have prayed for rain."

An extra loud clap of thunder made Davy jump. "I don't like . . . ," he began. He was interrupted by an especially bright streak of lightning and another mighty roar of thunder.

Dad slowed the car. "That was close," he said.

"There's a large tree across the highway behind us," Mother said, looking back.

"Thank you, Lord," breathed Dad.

Marcy was still trembling. "Daddy, why are you thanking God?" she asked.

"I'm thanking him because the tree blew down *behind* us, not on top of us or in front of us," her father replied.

A few miles down the road, they drove out of the storm. "Look!" Marcy pointed at the sky. "A pretty rainbow. Now, Daddy, you can pray again. Now you can really thank God!" *BJW*

HOW ABOUT YOU?

Do thunderstorms frighten you? How about the storms—or troubles—of life? Do they frighten you, too? Maybe you have to go to a new school, or you're changing churches. Maybe there's sickness in your family, or your dad has lost his job. Remember, God will take care of you, and soon the sun will shine again.

MEMORIZE:

"No matter what happens, always be thankful, for this is God's will for you who belong to Christ Jesus."

1 Thessalonians 5:18

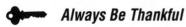 *Always Be Thankful*

God's Armor (Read Proverbs 4:5-9)

29

JUNE

Jason squatted behind the batter and watched the ball sail toward his glove. He raised his mitt to catch it. Suddenly the batter swung wildly and lost his grip on the bat. He missed the ball, and his bat hit the bottom of Jason's mask. Jason fell backward. He felt dizzy.

Everyone rushed forward to see if Jason was OK. Someone lifted the mask, and he heard his mother saying, "Jason, are you all right?"

Jason rubbed his chin. "I think so," he said. He got up and put his mask back on. The game went on, and Jason's team won.

After supper the next Wednesday night, Jason hesitantly approached his mother. "Can I . . . ah . . . skip youth group Bible study tonight?" he asked. "There are a lot of other things I could be doing. I'm a Christian now, and that's what counts anyway, isn't it?"

Mother looked at Jason. "It is most important that you've accepted Jesus," she agreed, "but Bible study is important, too. It will help you grow in your faith." She paused, then asked, "Remember when that batter accidentally hit you with the bat?"

Jason rubbed his chin. "I sure do."

"You don't want to quit wearing your catcher's mask now, do you?"

"Of course not," said Jason. "But what does that have to do with Bible study?"

"The catcher's mask offers protection when you play ball, and studying the Bible offers protection in your everyday life," said Mother.

Jason frowned. "I don't get it," he said.

"As you grow up, people may question your faith, and if you don't have a solid belief in the Bible, you may begin to doubt," explained Mother. "Understanding God's Word is protection for your faith."

Slowly Jason nodded. "So I keep wearing my catcher's mask to protect my head, and I keep going to Bible study to protect my faith, right?" He grinned. "OK," he agreed. "I'm on my way." *KEC*

HOW ABOUT YOU?

Do you learn all you can about God and his Word? What you learn from the Bible can protect you when troubles or temptations come along.

MEMORIZE:

"A final word: Be strong with the Lord's mighty power."

Ephesians 6:10

 Use God's Word as Armor

The Polishing Process

(Read Proverbs 27:17; Ephesians 4:1-6)

30
JUNE

Jeremy sighed as he perched on the edge of his dad's chair. "Is something wrong, Jeremy?" asked Dad as he glanced up from his newspaper.

"I'm tired of trying to be nice to Ryan," replied Jeremy. "He's always bugging me. Today in Sunday school he kept poking my arm."

"Is Ryan the boy who accepted the Lord at Bible camp?" Dad asked.

Jeremy nodded. "Why can't he grow up?" he grumbled.

Just then his younger brother, Bryce, dashed into the room. "Hey, Dad! Can we go and look at my rocks now?" Bryce asked.

"Bryce, it takes five or six weeks to polish stones," Jeremy reminded him. "If you take them out now, they won't be polished."

"That's right," agreed Dad. "The rocks have to tumble day and night for several weeks before they'll be smooth and shiny."

Bryce's smile faded away. "That's a long time," he complained.

"Be patient," Jeremy encouraged his brother. "You'll think it was worth the wait when you see how pretty they are after they're finished."

Bryce sighed. "OK," he murmured as he left the room.

Dad thought a moment. "I guess Ryan isn't polished yet, either," he said.

Jeremy's head shot up. "What do you mean?" he asked.

"He's a new Christian, and it takes a lot of polishing to make human beings like Jesus," explained Dad. "We won't be perfected until we reach heaven. In the meantime, we're all in different stages of our spiritual growth. Those of us who have been Christians longer need to have more patience with new Christians."

"So you're saying that I need to be more patient with Ryan?" asked Jeremy.

Dad nodded. "Perhaps God is using him to help you grow in love and understanding," he said. "Just like the grinding agent works to make the rocks smooth, God sometimes uses people to polish each other." *LRS*

HOW ABOUT YOU?

Do you tend to lose patience with Christians who don't act the way you'd like them to? Remember, none of us is perfect yet. Ask God to help you to be forgiving and kind to others.

MEMORIZE:

"Instead, be kind to each other, tenderhearted, forgiving one another, just as God through Christ has forgiven you."

Ephesians 4:32

 Be Patient and Forgiving

Buried Treasure (Read Proverbs 2:1-5)

1
JULY

"Hey, check this out, Steve! An old baseball card!" Brian said. "Go ask Grandpa if we can have it," he urged. His little brother disappeared down through the trap door in their grandfather's attic. Brian kept looking though the pile of old boxes, letters, and other stuff. Maybe there were more cards to find!

"Grandpa says we can have it," reported Steve when he returned, "and he said we can have any other cards we find, too!" He started helping Brian dig through the dusty piles. "Here's another one!" he yelled after a moment. "This is like looking for buried treasure, isn't it, Brian?"

"It *is* buried treasure," Brian told him. "These cards could be worth a lot of money." The boys kept on digging.

Soon their grandfather asked, "Find any more cards?"

"Lots and lots!" said Brian. "You sure you want us to keep these?"

"Keep every one you find, boys," Grandpa said. "Just be careful."

"We will," promised Brian.

"Yeah," agreed Steve. "Then they wouldn't be treasures any more!"

At noon, Grandpa called the boys for lunch. As they ate, Grandpa reached for the old family Bible. "You know, boys," he said, "it's good to read your Bible the way you guys were looking for baseball cards today."

"What do you mean, Grandpa?" Brian asked.

"Well, just as you search carefully for the 'card treasures,' you need to search God's Word carefully," said Grandpa. "It's 'treasure,' too, but of a different kind."

Brian and Steve looked at each other. "Treasure worth money?" asked Steve.

Grandpa chuckled. "Steve, the treasures of God's Word are worth more than money," he said. "God offers treasures such as his promises, his wisdom, his comfort, and encouragement." Grandpa opened the Bible. "Let's see if we can find some treasure right now." *MTK*

HOW ABOUT YOU?

Do you find the Bible to be a boring book? Maybe it's because it's hard for you to understand. If you don't have a children's or student's Bible, ask your parents about getting one for you. Then try reading it again. God's Word is full of hidden treasures. Go find some today!

MEMORIZE:

"I have rejoiced in your decrees as much as in riches."

Psalm 119:14

 God's Word Is Treasure

Good-bye Castles (Read Psalm 49:16-20)

While the rest of his family swam and soaked up the sun at the beach, Ben worked on his sand castle. He packed and molded sand for hours. He was making it like the medieval castle with soaring towers and a deep moat that he had seen in the history book.

The castle was quite tall when Ben noticed that the ocean's waves were slipping in. Each wave rolled in slightly closer than the one before. "Help, Dad!" shouted Ben. "Help me protect my castle. The water's going to get it."

2 JULY

Dad shook his head. "It's no use," he said. "The tide is coming in, and the waves will come a lot higher before they go back down."

But Ben didn't want to believe that. He dug a large trench all around his castle. Then he erected a sand barrier to protect it. But soon water filled the trench as waves crashed over the barrier. They splashed against the edge of the castle, pulling it apart with watery fingers.

"I worked all morning to make my castle," Ben moaned sadly. "Now it's gone in no time."

Dad nodded. "That's the way it goes with all earthly possessions," he said. "Many people work all their lives to get more and more things. They build their 'castles' bigger and bigger. But nobody can keep them forever. Soon they'll be gone."

"I guess nothing lasts forever," said Ben.

"One thing does—your relationship with Jesus," Dad told him. "When our lives here on earth are done, then we will go to live in heaven with him forever. It's too bad that so many people worry more about their lives now than what will happen to them after this life is over." *PIK*

HOW ABOUT YOU?

Do you worry about having the right kind of clothes, the right hairdo, or a nice house? These things must not take too much of your time and attention. Do you hope to make lots of money some day? What is truly important is having a good relationship with Jesus.

MEMORIZE:

"And how do you benefit if you gain the whole world but lose your own soul in the process?"

Matthew 16:26

 Don't Hold Tightly to Earthly Things

Storm Tossed (Read Romans 5:1-5)

3
JULY

Boom! A clap of thunder shook the house, and rain began to pour down outside. "That sounded awfully close!" exclaimed Hope fearfully. "I hate storms."

Grandma nodded. "I know," she said. "When I was your age, I'd go hide my head under the covers. I felt safer if I didn't have to see the lightning or hear the thunder."

"Why do we have to have storms anyway?" asked Hope. "Why can't it just rain without all the thunder and lightning?"

"Well, did you know that when lightning hits the ground it puts nutrients into the soil?" asked Grandma.

"Really?" asked Hope. "I didn't know that."

"That's what I've read," said Grandma, "so that means the lightning has a part in helping plants grow." She smiled. "Actually, storms remind me of life," she said.

Hope looked at her grandmother. "Of life?" she asked.

Grandma's eyes twinkled. "Think about it," she said. "As I see it, one of two things can happen when we get hit by the 'storms' of life. We can either get buried under the problems, or we can ask God to help us grow from the nutrients life's storms bring us. If we ask for his help, we learn to lean on him. Then when the storm is past, we're left with a better understanding of God and a closer walk with him. The stormy time turns out to be the time we grow most spiritually."

"Maybe so, but it doesn't make it any easier when you're in the storm, does it?" asked Hope.

"Oh, but it does," said Grandma quickly. "It makes it easier when we know that God is right there with us and that he'll not only see us through but also teach us something through the experience." *CPH*

HOW ABOUT YOU?

Are you going through a hard time right now? Are you in the "middle of a storm"? If you know Jesus, you're not alone. He's right there with you. Talk to him about your problems. Ask him to help you grow through the trial.

MEMORIZE:

"For when your faith is tested, your endurance has a chance to grow." *James 1:3*

Grow through Trials

Lights in the Sky (Read Genesis 1:14-19)

Boom! Boom! Andy grinned as the loud sound of the fireworks was followed by a shower of colorful sparks cascading downward.

Carol covered her ears. "I don't like the noise," she said. "But the fireworks sure are pretty!"

The fireworks display at the county fairgrounds was an event that Andy and Carol looked forward to each summer. Everyone would gasp as the rockets whistled through the air, then burst into umbrellas of brilliant, jewel-like sparks. It seemed like hundreds of bombs were going off at the same time in a grand finale. The sky filled with millions of brightly colored lights.

4
JULY

All too soon the sparks flickered and died before they reached the ground. Smoke vapors trailed off into nothing. The fireworks display was over. Everything was dark except for the beams of flashlights as people made their way back to their cars. Above, the stars shone brightly—higher than any fireworks could reach.

Andy pointed upward. "See that airplane?" he asked.

Carol nodded. "I wonder what the pilot saw from way up there."

Mom smiled. "I wonder what God thought about the fireworks from his viewpoint," she said. "Maybe he said, 'Quite impressive, folks, but have you considered the lights I put in the sky? They can be seen all over the earth. And they don't die out—the sun, moon, and stars are as bright as when I placed them there.'"

"They don't appear only on special occasions like the Fourth of July, either," added Carol.

Dad nodded. "People make fireworks with explosive chemicals, but God created his lights by simply speaking a word," he said. "People can't seem to agree on how the world as we know it came to be. But all they have to do is read the first chapter of Genesis."

BLK

HOW ABOUT YOU?

Are you confused by what you read or hear concerning where the sun, moon, stars, and our world came from? Remember that people can make many things, but they can only make them from materials that God has already created. He is the Creator of everything.

MEMORIZE:

"The heavens tell of the glory of God. The skies display his marvelous craftsmanship."

Psalm 19:1

 God Created Everything

Persistent Squirrel (Read 2 Timothy 2:3-10)

5
JULY

"Billy, look at all the birds at the feeder!" said Jan excitedly. "Aren't those red ones pretty?"

"Yeah—they're cardinals," said Billy. "Oh, look! There's a big, frisky, gray squirrel—what's he up to?"

The children watched as the squirrel ran to the pole and climbed up to the bird feeder. Then he began chattering and chattering, chasing the birds away. Soon he was eating from the bird feeder and dropping shells all over the ground.

When Dad came home from work, Jan and Billy told him about the squirrel. "Can you stop him from stealing the birds' seed?" they asked.

"I'll try," promised Dad.

When the squirrel returned the next day, he was surprised. The pole was slippery. He could not get up to the feeder. He tried again and again but fell down the pole. Dad had not only put a metal squirrel baffle around the pole, he had put oil on it.

But the squirrel did not give up. The children watched as he climbed up a tree, then jumped from the tree and landed on the bird feeder.

That evening Dad moved the feeder away from the tree—too far for the squirrel to jump to it from the branches. But the squirrel climbed the tree and tried jumping several times. Each time, he crashed to the ground. Finally, he gave up and sat in the tree chattering and scolding whoever would listen to him.

"Interesting!" said Dad when Jan and Billy told him about it. "Did you learn anything from him?"

"Like what?" asked Billy. He grinned. "How to be a thief?"

"No," said Dad, playfully mussing Billy's hair. "Did you notice that he didn't give up just because things became difficult? He was not a quitter."

"He sure wasn't," agreed Jan.

"Persistence—not quitting—is a quality God approves of," said Dad. "He says we should 'endure'—he wants us to stick to things we start, even when it's hard." *HCE*

HOW ABOUT YOU?

Do you stick with a job until you've completed your assignment, or do you quit when the going gets tough? The next time you feel like quitting, ask God to help you endure. You'll be glad you did.

MEMORIZE:

"Endure suffering along with me, as a good soldier of Christ Jesus." *2 Timothy 2:3*

 Don't Be a Quitter

Visiting Pappy (Read 1 Corinthians 12:22-27)

Chad signed his name as he entered the Mount Hope Nursing Home. Every Sunday he and his parents went to visit his grandfather, who had lived there since he had had a stroke. "Is Pappy ever going to get better?" asked Chad, using the pet name for his grandpa.

Mom and Dad looked at each other. "It may be that Pappy will get completely well only in heaven," said Chad's mom.

6
JULY

Chad noticed that Dad was carrying a big leather book. He recognized their family photograph album. "Why'd you bring that?" he asked.

"We thought we'd show Pappy some pictures," said Dad.

When they walked into Pappy's room, he was sitting in his wheelchair. He looked up but didn't say anything.

Chad's father placed the album on the table in front of Pappy and opened it. His parents talked cheerfully and pointed to pictures. Pappy stared down at the photographs.

"That's me!" exclaimed Chad, pointing to one of the photographs. "I was really little then." He looked more closely. "What's Pappy doing?" he asked.

Chad's dad chuckled. "He was trying to teach you how to play checkers."

"All you wanted to do was eat the game pieces," added Mom.

Chad laughed. "Looks like we were having fun," he said.

The next Sunday when Chad visited his grandfather, he took Pappy's old checkerboard. He set it on the table in front of the wheelchair. "Don't worry, Pappy," he said. "I'll move the pieces for both of us."

Chad glanced at his grandfather's face. He wasn't sure, but he thought he saw a little smile. *LLZ*

HOW ABOUT YOU?

Do you know people who are sick or elderly? They are important to Jesus even if they can't do all the things you can do. God is pleased when you show special kindness to them.

MEMORIZE:

"**We must help the weak, remembering the words the Lord Jesus himself said: 'It is more blessed to give than to receive.'**" *Acts 20:35*, NIV

 Love Those Who Are Suffering

Ready for Rain (Read Psalm 86:1-7)

7
JULY

"I've got to call the repairman," Jennie's father announced at breakfast. "I want him to check out a leak in the roof over the kitchen."

Jennie was surprised. It was a very sunny day, and it had not rained for several days. She looked up at the ceiling. It was as dry as could be, though there was a mark where the water had come in. "Why must the repairman come?" she asked. "It's not leaking now. Maybe it's OK."

Dad shook his head. "It can hardly be OK when we haven't done anything to correct it," he told her. "Maybe it doesn't show right now, but as soon as it rains or snows, the moisture will come in again."

Later that day Jenny became angry with her sister, lost her temper, and said things that she was sorry for later. "Oh," she moaned, "things were going so well—I hadn't gotten mad for so long I forgot that I have to watch out for my temper."

Dad nodded. "It's like the roof," he said. "We forget all about the leak when it's not raining, but that doesn't change the problem. The leak is still there. And your temper is still there, too—even when there are no problems."

Jennie sighed. "I guess so," she agreed.

"I need to get that leak fixed now, even though it's not giving us a problem today. Otherwise we'll have trouble when bad weather comes," said Dad. "And you need to commit your temper to the Lord each day—even when you're not feeling angry about anything. Ask him to take charge of it and change it. Then when you get mad, he can help you express your anger appropriately. And you and I can talk about ways to do that, too."

Slowly Jennie nodded. "Be ready when the 'rain' comes, right?" she asked.

Smiling, Dad nodded. "You've got the idea," he said. *RIJ*

HOW ABOUT YOU?

Is there something in your life that needs fixing? Maybe you have a temper too. Or maybe you have some other problems—a lazy nature or a sassy attitude. Whatever your problem is, Jesus is willing to help you learn how to change, but he is waiting for you to call on him to do the "repair" work.

MEMORIZE:

"Be merciful, O Lord, for I am calling on you constantly."

Psalm 86:3

 *Ask God for Help Daily*

A Different Look (Read Luke 19:1-6)

Hearing the doorbell, Matt looked out the front window. Trenton stood on the front porch, bouncing his basketball. *All right!* thought Matt excitedly. *Trent's back! The summer's been so boring without him.* Trent had been visiting his dad in another state. *I can't wait to see him!* Matt raced toward the door. But suddenly he stopped and stood still.

Mother came in from the kitchen just in time to see Matt remove his glasses, put them on the hall table, and head for the door. "Whoa!" said Mother. "Put your glasses on, Son. You know the doctor said you should wear them all the time." Matt had gotten glasses only a few weeks earlier, and he still didn't like wearing them.

8
JULY

"But it's Trent, Mom," protested Matt. "What if he thinks I look weird?"

"You do not look weird," said Mom. "Do you remember the Bible story about Zacchaeus?" she asked. "I bet his friends teased him—maybe they called him Shorty. But when Jesus found him sitting in the tree, he wanted to be his friend. What was in Zacchaeus's heart is what mattered to Jesus, not his appearance. I'm sure it's that way with Trent, too." As Matt continued to fidget, Mother asked, "Would you still want to play with Trent if *he* wore glasses?"

"Well, of course," replied Matt, "but he doesn't." He sighed as the doorbell rang again, then picked up his glasses and put them on. Matt opened the front door. There stood Trent, a shiny, silver grin on his face. "Braces!" said Matt in surprise.

"Glasses!" exclaimed Trent.

"When did you . . . ?"

"A month ago," they chorused at the same time. Then they both started laughing. *DJS*

HOW ABOUT YOU?

Do you wish your hair was a different color? Would you like to be taller, more popular, a star athlete, or a better student? Do you need glasses? braces? Such things don't keep God from loving you. Never let such things come between you and a friend either.

MEMORIZE:

"I praise you because I am fearfully and wonderfully made." *Psalm 139:14,* NIV

 True Beauty Is Within

The Boomerang (Read Luke 6:27-31)

"Mmmm! Cookies!" exclaimed Megan as she opened the kitchen door after school. "Chocolate chip! May I have one?"

Mother nodded. "How was school today?" she asked as she poured a glass of milk for Megan.

"Oh, all right," said Megan. "But Greg makes me mad! Right after the last recess he put a worm on my notebook. I almost smashed it when I reached inside my desk. Then he laughed at me. I'll think of something to do to get even with him. But first I have to write a report on how something works," she said. "What can I write about?"

"I have an idea," said Mother. "I saw something interesting about boomerangs in the book Grandma gave you last week. Maybe you could write about that."

"I'll look at it," said Megan as she headed for her room.

Before long, Megan returned to the kitchen. "That didn't take too long," she said. "Want to hear my report?"

"Sure," said Mother.

Megan read, "A boomerang is a weapon still used by some tribes in Australia. Boomerangs are flat, curved objects that are made of hard wood. They can be thrown in such a way that they curve around and come back to the one who throws them. Sometimes, though, people are hit by the boomerangs they themselves have thrown."

"Our actions can 'boomerang,' too. It's something we need to remember when we feel like getting even with people we're mad at," said Mother.

Megan stared at the floor. She felt her face turn red. "OK," she said. "I know you're talking about me and Greg. But how can I keep him from playing more tricks?" She looked at the cookies Mother was putting into the cookie jar. "I know!" she exclaimed. "Mom, may I have two or three cookies to take to Greg tomorrow?" *MMP*

HOW ABOUT YOU?

Have your actions boomeranged when you've tried to get even with someone? God is pleased when we get rid of an enemy by making a friend of him or her. Remember—good actions "boomerang," too.

MEMORIZE:

"Don't let evil get the best of you, but conquer evil by doing good." *Romans 12:21*

 *Don't Get Even*

Alike but Different (Read 1 Corinthians 12:4-7, 14-19)

10
JULY

"Mom, I'm so stupid," wailed Kelly when she arrived home from school. "Why do I have to be so dumb?"

"What's wrong, honey?" asked Mother.

With tears in her eyes, Kelly handed Mother her paper. It was a math test, and she had failed it. "I got the worst score in the whole class," she moaned.

"Oh, Kelly, I'm sorry!" said Mother. "I know you really studied hard for that test too." Mother gave her a hug. "But that doesn't mean that you are stupid."

"Yes it does," insisted Kelly. "No one else has so much trouble with math. Why can't I be like everyone else?"

Mother looked out the window. "It's snowing," she said. "Do you remember the report you did on snowflakes a while back?" Kelly nodded. "Snowflakes have a lot of things in common," continued Mother. "They're all formed by a certain process, they all melt, and they fall from the clouds. So they're all alike, right?"

This time Kelly shook her head. "No two are alike—I had that in my report. Don't you remember?" she asked.

Mother smiled. "I do remember," she said. "And Kelly, God made us like those snowflakes—no two alike. Each snowflake is beautiful, and as God's creation each person is beautiful and special, too. Take you, for instance. You love to play the piano, and you can play music that kids twice your age can't play. If we were all the same and were all good at math, then who would play the music?" *CPH*

HOW ABOUT YOU?

Do you realize that God has made you as you are for a purpose? Do your best in all your subjects, and take advantage of all the opportunities offered you. But don't expect to excel in everything. Use your talents for God's glory, and thank him today for making you who you are.

MEMORIZE:

"There are different ways God works in our lives, but it is the same God who does the work through all of us."

1 Corinthians 12:6

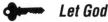 *Let God Use You*

When the Radio "Died" (Read Psalm 119:9-16)

11

"Everything's loaded," said Mark as he tossed his backpack into Grandpa's van.

"Let's double-check," Grandpa said. "Sleeping bags, the tent, food, fishing poles. Yep, it's all there. There's just one thing left to do before we go—pray."

Mark groaned. "Oh, Grandpa, can't we forget about that for once?" he begged.

"We don't want to neglect our best friend, do we?" asked Grandpa. Mark shook his head and tried to listen as Grandpa prayed.

Soon they were on their way, and at first it was fun. Then Mark began to ask the same question again and again. "How much farther is it?"

Finally Grandpa reached over and turned on the radio. "There's usually a good Bible story at this time of day," he said. "Let's listen."

"Well, OK." Mark sighed. "I hope it's not one I've heard sixteen times, though."

Even though Mark didn't really want to listen, he began to enjoy the story. Then the station started to fade in and out. It would go blank for a minute and then come back on the air, but only for a short time. "Can you fix the radio?" asked Mark. "I want to hear the rest of this story."

"I think we're getting too far from the station," said Grandpa. The sound got worse, and Grandpa turned the radio off. "We'd have to turn around and get closer to the station to hear any more of that program," he said. "And you know, Mark, that's a little like what happens when we begin to move away from the Lord. We still hear his voice for a while. Then it seems to fade, and we hear it only sometimes. Soon we no longer hear when God tries to talk to us. The only way to regain what we've lost is to get close to him again. How do we do that?"

"By reading the Bible, listening to Bible stories, and praying. Right?"

"Right!" Grandpa answered back with a smile. *MMP*

HOW ABOUT YOU?

Do you talk to Jesus and let his Word help you every day? Praying and reading the Bible are two things you need to do to stay close to Jesus. If you've wandered away from him, turn back. Tell him you're sorry and begin to spend more time with him.

MEMORIZE:

"I listen carefully to what God the Lord is saying." *Psalm 85:8*

 Stay Close to Jesus

Dust It Away (Read John 8:31-36)

Hannah enjoyed cooking, but she didn't care much about cleaning and dusting. Still, there was a certain feeling of pride in making the house look nice. "I really appreciate the way you help with the work," said Mother one day after Hannah had helped her.

Hannah smiled and glanced around the newly cleaned living room. The sun shone brightly through the window. "Oh no!" she exclaimed as she looked at the lamp table. "I missed a spot when I dusted this morning. It took the sun to show it up." She ran to get the dust cloth.

12
JULY

"You know something?" asked mother. "That's a good illustration of something that happens in our spiritual lives. As Christians, we may think our lives are good and that everything is all right. Then all at once, the Son—God's Son—points out a sin that needs to be cleaned away, almost like the dusting you're doing."

"I can dust away the spot on the table, but only Jesus can 'dust away' the sin in our life, right?" asked Hannah.

"Right!" Mom agreed. *RIJ*

HOW ABOUT YOU?

Has Jesus pointed out things that need to be changed in your life—a lack of kindness, a need for obedience, or a tendency to tell half-truths? Whatever it is, do you ask him to "dust it" right away? When the Son shows you a sin, confess it. Ask Jesus to free you from it, and then put it aside.

MEMORIZE:

"If the Son sets you free, you will indeed be free." *John 8:36*

 The Son Shows Our Sin

Brandon's Puppy (Read John 4:4-14)

Brandon's puppy was sick. The veterinarian prescribed some medicine and told Brandon he must also get his puppy to drink lots of water.

Brandon eagerly tried to follow the vet's orders, but to his dismay, the puppy refused to drink. "How can I make Rusty drink water?" Brandon asked his mother. "I've been trying, but he won't drink."

13
JULY

"I'm not sure," Mother replied, "but I remember that once when you were little, you wouldn't drink water either, so the doctor said to give you a saltine cracker. It worked. The dry, salty cracker made you realize you were thirsty."

Brandon ran to try it. It took a lot of coaxing, but the puppy finally ate the salty cracker. He looked at Brandon mournfully as he opened and closed his dry mouth. When Brandon offered water, the puppy turned his head. Brandon sighed. Then it happened! The puppy stuck his nose in the water. He licked his chops, then turned to the water again and had a good drink.

"Hey, look, Mom!" exclaimed Brandon happily. "Rusty's drinking."

"Good!" replied Mother. After a moment she said, "Didn't you have a Sunday school verse about drinking water?"

Brandon nodded and quoted it out loud. "Whoever drinks of the water that I shall give him will never thirst. But the water that I shall give him will become in him a fountain of water springing up into everlasting life" (John 4:14).

Mother nodded. "That was Jesus talking," she said. "He's the Living Water that everybody needs. A lot of people are 'thirsty' for lasting peace and joy in their hearts, but they don't always realize it. Even boys and girls may be so busy with school, clubs, baseball, and other activities, that they hardly know they're 'thirsty.' But none of their busy activities can really satisfy them for long. Only Jesus can satisfy their spiritual thirst." *RIJ*

HOW ABOUT YOU?

Have you ever realized that you are spiritually "thirsty"? The Bible says you are to come to Jesus, the "Living Water," and drink. Have you come to Jesus for this everlasting water? Talk to a trusted adult to find out how you can do this.

 Jesus Gives "Living Water"

MEMORIZE:

"The Spirit and the bride say, 'Come.' Let each one who hears them say, 'Come.' Let the thirsty ones come—anyone who wants to. Let them come and drink the water of life without charge." *Revelation 22:17*

A Good Ending (Read John 14:1-6)

Shawn and his sister, Kelly, begged to be allowed to stay up late to watch a TV show about a shipwreck. "I'll watch it with you," decided Dad. "I'm not sure what it will be like. We'll turn it off if it gets too scary for you two," he said.

"It won't scare me," Shawn boasted. "But Kelly will probably scream through most of it. She's such a chicken!"

"I am not!" Kelly scowled.

14
JULY

Sure enough—when the storm got really rough and it was apparent that the ship would go down, Kelly just yawned. And when the passengers made it safely to an island, only to discover that it was inhabited by wild animals, Kelly smiled. Shawn couldn't believe it! "What's with you?" he asked. "Usually you scream and cover your eyes over nothing! Why aren't you scared?"

"I probably would be," admitted Kelly, "except that my friend LaDonna saw this program before, and she told me about it. I know it has a good ending."

After the program Dad decided to watch the news, and he let Kelly and Shawn stay up, too. As they heard the reports of wars, accidents, kidnappings, and murders, Kelly shivered. "Now, those are real horror stories," she said.

"Yeah," Shawn agreed. "That's what makes them so scary."

"Oh, I'm not scared," Dad said.

Shawn looked at him curiously. "Why not, Dad?" he asked. "Just because we're Christians doesn't mean things like that couldn't happen to us, does it?"

"No," replied Dad, "but I'm not afraid, because I know what will happen in the end. The Bible says that we who are Christians will eventually be in heaven with Christ."

"Wow, Dad—-that's neat!" exclaimed Kelly. "I'm glad our family knows Jesus. Scary things aren't so scary when you know there's a good ending!" *SLK*

HOW ABOUT YOU?

Do you worry that something bad might happen to you? Relax! If you know the Lord as your Savior, you know what the "ending" of your life will be—eternal happiness in heaven. True, now you may sometimes have problems, but thinking about your joyful future will help you through them.

MEMORIZE:

"Don't be troubled. You trust God, now trust in me." *John 14:1*

 Trust God's "Good Ending"

Let Them See (Read John 1:37-47)

Every night Sally's family gathered for prayer, Bible reading, and a story. One night the story Sally's father read caught her attention more than any she had heard in a long time.

15
JULY

The story was about a blind man living in a far-off country. When he heard about a missionary doctor who could operate on eyes, he walked many miles until he reached the mission station. After many tests, the doctor finally operated on the man's eyes. It was a long time before he was allowed to take off the bandages, but when he did, he could see!

"And what did the blind man do?" read Dad. "Just enjoy his sight? No, he went around to all the villages and found other people who were blind. He led them on the long walk to the village where the missionary doctor was living. 'I have brought many people to you,' he said, introducing them to the surgeon. 'They need to see, too.'"

Dad closed the book. "Just as the blind man brought others to the doctor for help, Christians need to bring others to Jesus," he said. "People who don't know Jesus are spiritually blind, and they're even worse off than those who are physically blind."

Sally was still thinking about the story when she went to bed that night. She thought about some of the kids in the neighborhood. There was her friend Julie, who didn't ever go to Sunday school. And Phyllis—she went only when her folks made her go. Neither of these girls knew Jesus as Savior. "Help me to do what the blind man did," Sally prayed before going to sleep. "Help me bring my friends to Jesus." *RIJ*

HOW ABOUT YOU?

As you read today's Scripture, did you notice that when Jesus called men to follow him, they brought others? That is the job of every Christian. Andrew brought Peter. Philip brought Nathanael. Whom have you brought?

MEMORIZE:

"Then Andrew brought Simon to meet Jesus. Looking intently at Simon, Jesus said, 'You are Simon, the son of John—but you will be called Cephas' (which means Peter)." *John 1:42*

 Bring Others to Jesus

Finding the Way (Read John 1:1-9)

16
JULY

"Good-bye," said Jeremy as he walked toward Rick's back door. "See you tomorrow."

"OK. Bye," replied Rick as Jeremy opened the door. "Hey . . . don't you have a flashlight?"

"No." Jeremy stepped outside and looked around. The night was black—no moon, no stars. "It's not that far home. I don't need one," he said confidently

"Are you sure?" Rick asked. "You could borrow mine."

"Naw, I'll be fine," Jeremy answered. "See you at school tomorrow." He started down the steps and headed home.

Jeremy lived just across the woods from Rick's house. The path was overgrown and a bit hard to find in the darkness, but he soon found it and began to walk quickly. Then . . . *thunk!* "Owww!" Jeremy had walked into a branch. As he rubbed his forehead . . . *Zzzzkt! Zzzzkttt! What was that?* he wondered. Usually he wasn't afraid of the dark, but these sounds seemed different . . . threatening. He forced himself to continue walking. His head ached, and his eyes strained to see ahead. *Where are the lights from my house? I should be close enough to see them by now!* he thought. *I should have borrowed Rick's flashlight.* He sighed with relief when he finally saw the lights of his home, warm and welcoming.

Later, just before climbing into bed, Jeremy opened his devotional book and Bible. As he read the devotional for the day, a smile spread slowly over his face. The verses he read proclaimed Jesus as the light of the world. *And we sure need his light,* Jeremy thought, *even when we think we don't! KRL*

HOW ABOUT YOU?

Are you following Jesus, the Light of the World? God says the world is in darkness because of sin. The only way to overcome darkness is to turn on a light. Jesus is the light that God has provided. Accept him as Savior, and then follow him each day. By receiving him you will be able to reach your home in heaven.

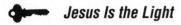
Jesus Is the Light

MEMORIZE:

"Jesus said to the people, 'I am the light of the world. If you follow me, you won't be stumbling through the darkness, because you will have the light that leads to life.'" *John 8:12*

The Sandstorm (Read Hebrews 6:9-12)

17

JULY

Wind and sand swirled around the car as the Reynolds family traveled home. It was very hard to see anything.

"That car was on the wrong side of the road!" gasped Mom when a car they were meeting narrowly missed them. "Maybe we should wait till this sandstorm is over." Then she pointed. "Oh, look! There's a car up ahead. Let's follow them."

The drivers of two other cars had the same idea. But Dad didn't want to go that fast, so he continued to move along at a slower pace. "Look at that!" he exclaimed suddenly. "That first car drove right off the road! And the other two followed!"

Sure enough, three cars had slipped down a steep incline.

"Let's stop, Dad," Marti said, her voice trembling slightly.

"That might be a good idea," agreed Dad, "but I need a place to pull off or we could be hit from behind." He edged closer to the middle of the highway until he could see the median. "Until then, I'll go slowly and keep my eyes on the median. That way I'll be sure to stay on the road. Sandstorms generally last only a few minutes. We'll soon be able to get on home."

Dad was right. A few minutes later the sandstorm had passed. When they came to the next gas station, they reported the cars that had gone off the road.

Mother breathed a sigh of relief. "I'm glad you didn't follow those cars as I suggested," she said.

"I'm reminded of what Jesus told his disciples once," replied Dad. "If the blind lead the blind, they both fall into the ditch. It's a good reminder that we need to be careful about whom we follow—not just on the road, but also in life." *KRL*

HOW ABOUT YOU?

Whom are you following? Where are those you follow leading you? Do their words and actions cause you to feel close to Jesus? If not, you may be heading toward a "ditch"! Instead, surround yourself with those who love Jesus.

MEMORIZE:

"Then you will not become spiritually dull and indifferent. Instead, you will follow the example of those who are going to inherit God's promises because of their faith and patience." *Hebrews 6:12*

 Follow Those Who Follow Christ

The Driver (Read Psalm 25:1-10)

18
JULY

"Watch it! Oh!" Uncle Jack gasped. "Slow down, Dawn!"

In the backseat, Jill turned to Matt and grinned. This was fun. Uncle Jack had offered to let their sister drive his new car. Dawn was a pretty good driver, even though she'd had her license for only a week. But as she drove, Uncle Jack instructed her nonstop the whole time.

"There's a stop sign up ahead. It's a little hard to see, so I'm telling you ahead of time," Uncle Jack said. He paused only a moment. "I usually slow down when I pass this fire hydrant. . . . Oh, and two lights down we'll turn to the right. Be sure to hug this side of the curb when you turn this way . . . and you have learned that the best way to pull into the parking places is . . ." Uncle Jack hardly stopped talking long enough to breathe!

When they reached the store, Dawn handed the keys to Uncle Jack. She smiled and winked at Jill. "I think you should drive home, Uncle Jack," she said. "You're more familiar with the car."

"Well, dear, are you sure?" Uncle Jack asked as he took the keys.

"Yes, I'm sure," Dawn answered. Later she turned to Jill and Matt. "It's usually a lot of fun to drive, but, somehow, with Uncle Jack . . ." She rolled her eyes, and they all laughed.

That night Mother smiled when they told her about the incident. "You know, we're all a little like Uncle Jack sometimes," she said. "We invite God to take over our life, and then we sit beside him and tell him exactly how to run it."

Jill was thoughtful. "You mean . . . like wanting to do things our own way? And getting upset when things don't happen the way we want them to?"

Mother nodded. "If only we would remember that God knows how to manage our life—better than we do!" *KRL*

HOW ABOUT YOU?

Do you want things your own way? We all do at times. If you will give up your own way, and let God "drive," your life will honor him. He knows just how to get you where he wants you to go. You don't know where the curves are, or what may be around the next corner, but God does. Trust him.

MEMORIZE:

"Show me the path where I should walk, O Lord; point out the right road for me to follow."

Psalm 25:4

 Trust God with Your Life

Drive It Deep (Read Colossians 2:6-10)

When Robb and his dad arrived at their campsite, Robb quickly got the tackle box and his rod and reel. "C'mon, Dad," he said as he ran to the lake.

"Hey!" Dad called after him. "We've got to get the tent up first."

"Aw, can't we fish a little now?" Robb asked.

Dad shook his head. "Fun follows work," he said with a smile.

Robb reluctantly put down his fishing gear, and together he and Dad stretched out the tent and began to pound the stakes into the ground. Robb finished before Dad, but soon they were both ready to go.

During the next couple of hours they pulled in several good-sized fish. Suddenly the wind came up, and when a light rain began to fall, Robb and his dad hurried back to the tent. Much to their surprise, one side had collapsed—the side that Robb had worked on. "What happened?" he asked.

Dad stooped over and picked up a stake that was lying on the ground. "See this?" he said, pointing to the ground. "You didn't pound it deep enough." Robb was embarrassed. He knew he had been in too big a hurry.

Putting up the tent was more uncomfortable this time, because they had to work in the rain. Robb knew it was his fault. "Sorry, Dad," he apologized.

As they cooked the fish later, Robb grinned at Dad. "We studied some verses in Sunday school," said Robb. "Something about being rooted in Christ and established in our faith. Our teacher said if our spiritual stakes go deep and we are well rooted in Christ and in God's Word, we won't be tossed about by 'winds' of false teachings or by difficult circumstances."

Robb's father smiled broadly. "Well," he said, "you may not be too great at pounding in a tent stake, but if you continue listening and learning as well as you did last Sunday, I don't think I'll have to worry about your spiritual stakes." *RIJ*

HOW ABOUT YOU?

Are you easily swayed if someone tries to tell you that something in the Bible is not true? Are you soon discouraged when troubles come? You can pound your spiritual stakes more deeply by reading God's Word, listening well in church and Sunday school, and by praying.

MEMORIZE:

"Let your roots grow down into him and draw up nourishment from him, so you will grow in faith, strong and vigorous in the truth you were taught."

Colossians 2:7

 Be Rooted in Your Faith

Friend in the Street (Read Proverbs 1:1-7, 20-23)

"Whew! It's so hot!" Paul said, wiping a hand across his forehead. "I absolutely detest picking green beans, don't you?" he asked his brother, Mike, who was kneeling in the row next to him.

"Yeah," groaned Mike. "You almost have to stand on your head to find them." He waved his arms wildly around his head. "And when you have a pesky deerfly buzzing around you, it's worse yet."

20
JULY

"Those deerflies love sweaty people," said Paul.

Grandpa, who was picking tomatoes, had been listening to the boys. "Hey, fellas!" he called to them. "Listen!"

The boys paused from their work and then suddenly cheered up. "It's the ice-cream truck!" they squealed. They went running and jumping over rows of carrots and onions to reach Grandpa. "Can we get something?"

Grandpa handed them some money. "Get each of us a fudge bar."

When the boys came back to the garden, they all sat down under a nearby tree to enjoy their treats. "You know," said Grandpa as he unwrapped his fudge bar, "every time I hear that ice-cream truck coming down the street, I'm reminded of a verse in Proverbs. It says that wisdom calls out in the street."

"Wisdom?" asked Mike. "Is the ice-cream truck wise?"

"Well, I sure thought it was wise of us to get this ice cream," put in Paul. He took a big bite.

Grandpa laughed. "I agree. That ice-cream truck 'calls out in the street' because it has something refreshing for you when you're hot and tired. The book of Proverbs says wisdom 'calls out in the street' with something even better for you," he explained. "I hope you're just as eager to get wisdom as you were to get ice cream."

Mike frowned. "How do we do that? Go to school?"

Grandpa nodded. "To God's school—to God's Word, the Bible," he said. *SLN*

HOW ABOUT YOU?

Do you know what wisdom is? It is knowing God's truth and doing what it says. To know God's truth, you must study his Word and follow it. The Bible says, "Happy is the person who finds wisdom." Proverbs 3:13.

MEMORIZE:

"Getting wisdom is the most important thing you can do! And whatever else you do, get good judgment." *Proverbs 4:7*

 God's Word Gives Wisdom

Keep It Mowed (Read James 1:12-15)

21

JULY

One summer Todd's family stayed at a lake cottage for a whole month. Todd became friends with Mike, a boy from another cottage. One day Mike said, "I'm sure hungry for a candy bar, and I know where we can get the money. Come on!" Mike led Todd into his big brother's room. He pulled a shoe box filled with coins from under the bed. "Skip will never notice if we each take a little," said Mike.

Todd knew it was wrong to steal, but he wanted candy so badly that he took two quarters. The next day, the boys again took money for candy bars. Todd still felt guilty, but it was easier this time. Several times they helped themselves to Skip's money, and soon it didn't bother Todd nearly so much.

One day the boys quietly crept into the bedroom. They opened the box as usual, but then a loud voice roared, "So you're the thieves!" It was Skip, who had hidden in order to catch the person who had been robbing him.

Todd's parents were shocked and disappointed in him, and Mike's parents were angry, too. Both boys were punished. How Todd wished he had never taken that first quarter. He felt so ashamed!

When Todd's family returned to their home in town, he stared in disbelief at the empty lot next door. He had always kept it mowed so he and his friends could play baseball there. But while he had been at the cottage, the weeds had grown thick and high. Playing ball would be impossible. "What happened?" he asked his dad.

"Let weeds go, and they'll take over," Dad chuckled. "They never got this high before, because you kept mowing them." Todd sat down under a tree and stared at the tall, straggly weeds that were choking the baseball field. "In a way, this is what happened to you at the lake," continued Dad. "If you had said no to Mike's first suggestion to steal money, you probably wouldn't have taken any at all. But because you didn't mow down that temptation, it got a good start."

"From now on, I'm going to mow down temptation right away," said Todd. *CEY*

HOW ABOUT YOU?

Do you give sin a chance to grow? Learn to say no to temptation as soon as it is suggested. That's how God wants you to fight sin. Mow "weeds of sin" down before they get so big that they take over your life.

MEMORIZE:

"So humble yourselves before God. Resist the Devil, and he will flee from you." *James 4:7*

 Mow Down Sin

Lighthouse in a Storm (Read Matthew 5:13-16)

22
JULY

Kyle and Andy felt the cool water spray into their faces as the bow of the boat bobbed along. Andy's parents often invited Kyle on boat outings, and he was always eager to go. Time went by quickly as the sleek boat sliced through the water, leaving rolling waves behind.

Andy's dad looked up at the sky. "I'm afraid there's a storm brewing in those dark clouds, and it might come up fast," he said. "We'd better head for shore."

Soon the wind began to churn the water, and the boat's bow slapped hard on the waves. Water whipped into the boys' faces, and they ducked down to escape it. It grew darker and darker, and soon it was raining hard. "Help me watch for the lighthouse, boys," called Andy's dad. Andy and Kyle strained their eyes, looking for the warm light from the lighthouse to guide them. But it was hard to see.

Kyle was scared. Right out loud he prayed, "Dear Lord, please help us find the lighthouse and get safely to shore."

A few minutes later, Andy shouted, "There it is!" Soon the boat was safely in harbor, where Kyle's father was waiting to take him home.

"Bye, Kyle," said Andy. "And thanks for praying in the boat."

"Did you hear that, Dad?" asked Kyle excitedly as they drove away. "I was so scared that I prayed out loud that God would help us. Before this, I've never mentioned God to Andy. I thought he wouldn't like me anymore if I did. But maybe now he might want to hear about God."

"Maybe," said Dad, "you can be a lighthouse to Andy."

"A lighthouse?" asked Kyle. "Oh, I get it. I can point out the way to Jesus."

"That's right," said his dad with a smile. *CEY*

HOW ABOUT YOU?

Do you stand up for the Lord in front of friends? You can be a lighthouse to others, pointing them to Jesus. Don't be afraid to speak up for him, even though you fear you'll lose a friend. It may be the only chance that person has to hear about God's love.

MEMORIZE:

"You are the light of the world—like a city on a mountain, glowing in the night for all to see." *Matthew 5:14*

 Be God's Lighthouse

A Cry for Help (Read Proverbs 22:2-9)

23
JULY

"Here comes the ice-cream truck. C'mon, Sheila!" yelled Jason as he ran out of the room. When he returned, licking an ice-cream bar, he asked, "Why didn't you come?"

"I didn't have any money," Sheila replied. "I paid for Dana's lunch today."

Jason snorted. "Those Brown kids never have a cent. Vic didn't have any money, either, but I sure didn't pay for his lunch. Let him get a paper route like me."

"You know he can't do a paper route with his crippled leg," said Sheila.

"Well, his dad doesn't have a crippled leg," retorted Jason. "Those Browns are just plain lazy."

"Jason!" exclaimed Mother. "You are not to talk like that. God has blessed your father with good health and a good job. We should be thankful for what we have but not proud. And we need to be willing to help those who are struggling. The Browns are going through a hard time right now. I am very proud of what Sheila did today at school. The Bible says, 'Blessed are those who help the poor.' And I don't know how or when, but God is going to bless her."

BJW

HOW ABOUT YOU?

Do you look down on those who have less than you do or who are not as smart as you are? Do you refuse to help them? God's way is to help those in need, and he blesses those who do. You, too, may have special needs someday. If you help others, others will help you.

MEMORIZE:

"Blessed are those who help the poor." *Proverbs 14:21*

 *Help Those in Need*

Down the Drain (Read 1 Peter 1:17-23)

24
JULY

Matt's cousin, Eric, was spending the week with him. After supper the first evening, the boys were anxious to go swimming, but Matt's mother said, "I'd like you boys to do the dishes first."

"Aw, do we have to?" they groaned.

"Washing dishes is the only job you'll have to do this week," Mother replied with a smile. "You'll survive."

"I'll survive if I can get past all that food in the sink!" Matt told Eric. "Look at those pieces of soggy lettuce, potato peelings, and celery," he observed.

"Yeah," added Eric, "and noodles and bits of hamburger!"

"That mess makes me sick to my stomach," groaned Matt. "Mom, if you'll rinse this stuff down the garbage disposal, I'll gladly wash the dishes."

Mother laughed. "OK, I'll do that, but remember—no more complaints about doing dishes this week!"

"Right," chorused the boys, and Eric added, "Nothing's worse than all that garbage in the sink!"

"Actually, there is," said Mother. "Sin is much worse. It's so bad, God can't stand to look at it. And he has said that no one who sins will be able to live with him in heaven."

"But isn't God happy with us if we do good, and try not to be bad?" Eric asked.

"A lot of people think that," said Mother. "But we need to ask Jesus to be our Savior. He was the one who took the punishment for our sin. All the good things we do won't get us into heaven. But each person has to choose whether to accept Jesus or not." *SLN*

HOW ABOUT YOU?

Do you think you're pretty good? The Bible says no one is good. We all do wrong things. God hates sin, but he loves you. Confess your need to him. Ask him to cleanse you from sin, and he will do it.

MEMORIZE:

"For God sent Jesus to take the punishment for our sins and to satisfy God's anger against us."

Romans 3:25

 *God Hates Sin*

The Price of Faith (Read Hebrews 11:32-40)

25
JULY

"Hi, Mom!" called Jan as she slammed the screen door behind her. "Aunt Sue and I stopped at a garage sale. See what I got?" Jan held up a little figurine. "This cost only fifty cents. I thought it would be a good toy for Betsy."

Later that afternoon Aunt Sue called and talked to Jan. "Guess what?" said Jan after she hung up the phone. "Aunt Sue said her friend has a figurine exactly like mine. She paid twenty dollars for it at an antique store! I'm going to put mine up on a shelf where it won't get broken."

"Sounds like that little figurine is more valuable than what you thought," observed Mother. "That reminds me of this book I'm reading."

Jan looked at the paperback book in Mother's hand. The title of it was *Foxe's Book of Martyrs*. "Is that book really valuable, Mom?"

"No—the book isn't, but it tells about people who paid a very high price for something we often take for granted," replied Mother.

"What's that?" asked Jan.

"Our Christian faith," said Mother quietly. "This book describes how believers were persecuted during the early years of the church. They had their lands and houses taken away, they were put in prison, tortured, and even killed—all because they refused to deny their faith in Christ. Their faith cost them a lot."

Jan nodded her head thoughtfully. "Wow! I guess I never realized just how special it is to know Jesus. And to think I grumble sometimes when it's time to have my devotions!" Then she smiled. "I'm going to take better care my Bible. It's a lot more valuable than that figurine!" *SLK*

HOW ABOUT YOU?

Even today many Christians face prison or death for meeting together for worship or sharing their faith with others. Take advantage of the freedom you have—and thank God for your precious Christian faith!

MEMORIZE:

"But he said, 'Why all this weeping? You are breaking my heart! For I am ready not only to be jailed at Jerusalem but also to die for the sake of the Lord Jesus.'" *Acts 21:13*

 Your Faith Is Valuable

A Little Dirt (Read 1 Corinthians 5:6-8)

26
JULY

Trevor poured himself a glass of apple juice. He enjoyed having a snack each day after he finished his paper route. As he drank his juice, he watched his mother repotting an African violet at the other end of the kitchen table.

"Hi, Son," said his father as he came through the back door. "I'm glad you're here." He took three magazines from the kitchen counter as he added, "I've been looking at these cartoon books you got in your trade with Tim. Some of them are all right, but these three contain some bad language."

"Aw, Dad," Trevor protested, "you know I don't use that kind of language. A lot of guys do, so that's why the characters in the cartoons talk that way."

"Do you really think it's OK to read these magazines?" asked Mother. "Foul language doesn't honor God."

Trevor's face turned a little red. "Well, there aren't very many bad words, and the jokes are funny," he argued. "I just ignore the bad words."

"That may not be as easy as you think," Dad said. He took a pinch of potting soil and held it over Tim's glass of juice. "If I dropped this in your juice, even though it's a tiny amount, would you still want your juice?"

"Of course not!" exclaimed Trevor.

Dad nodded. "The Bible says a little leaven, or yeast, 'leavens the whole lump.' In this case, a little dirt would ruin the whole glass of juice." He put the three magazines on the table. "Just a little dirt can do a lot of damage, can't it?" he asked.

Trevor was thoughtful. "I see your point, and I'll put these in the trash. And I'll try to be more careful in the future."

"Good idea!" said his mom and dad together. *RM*

HOW ABOUT YOU?

Do you read magazines or books that contain bad language? You may not intend to use profanity or other bad words, but if you read or listen to them, such words may slip out. Ask God to help you "clean up your act." Praise him with your lips.

MEMORIZE:

"May the words of my mouth and the thoughts of my heart be pleasing to you, O Lord, my rock and my redeemer."

Psalm 19:14

 **Use Clean Speech**

The Flame (Read James 4:13-17)

27

JULY

Oh, not another essay! Shelley groaned to herself as the teacher wrote the subject on the chalkboard: What I Want to Be When I Grow Up. *I hate writing essays. Anyway, I don't know what I want to be.*

At dinner that night, the family discussed the news of the day. A couple of blocks away, a house had burned to the ground. The fire had been started by two little boys playing with matches.

Then Shelley complained about having to write the essay for school. "I don't know what I want to be when I grow up, and I don't really care," she said.

"You should care," said her dad. "Life is a very precious gift from God. It must be lived very carefully, for it can be used for great good or evil." He found a match and struck it. "Look at this flame, Shelley. Can you think of something good it could do?"

"It could light a fire to cook food or to warm people," answered Shelley.

Dad nodded. "Some people's lives have been saved because they had a match to start a fire. But the house that burned today shows the great harm one little flame can do." He paused and looked at his daughter. "Your life is like this flame. Do you know what I mean?"

Shelley nodded. "I think so," she said slowly. "I can use my life for either good or bad. I guess I could be asking God what I could do with it." *MRP*

HOW ABOUT YOU?
Have you thought about what you want to do when you grow up? You don't need to decide right now, but it's not too early to begin asking God what he wants you to be. Be willing to serve him in whatever way he chooses for you, both right now and in the future.

MEMORIZE:

"If you search for good, you will find favor; but if you search for evil, it will find you!"

Proverbs 11:27

 *Choose God's Will*

The Smoking Wick (Read Colossians 3:8-11)

Grandmother glanced up as Jacob stomped into the house. "You look as angry as those thunderheads in the west," she said.

"Thunderheads?" asked Jacob.

Grandmother stood up. "Guess you were too busy storming yourself to notice them. Help me close the windows." As they shut the last window, the storm struck.

28
JULY

As Grandmother began supper, she asked, "Why are you mad, Jacob?"

Jacob's face flushed. "Chuck won't let me borrow his calculator."

Crash! A loud roll of thunder shook the house, and lightning flashed. Jacob and Grandmother jumped. "The lights are out!" Jacob wailed.

"Sit still," Grandmother said as she rummaged in the cabinet. "I have an old lamp somewhere. Ahhhh, here it is. Now for a match . . . here they are." As she lit the lamp and set it on the table, she continued, "Isn't Chuck the boy who's coming to Sunday school with you next Sunday?"

Jacob nodded. "Yes. I mean, no. I doubt if he'll come now. I yelled at him." Jacob coughed. "What's wrong with the lamp, Grandma? It's smoking and not putting out much light."

Grandmother fanned the smoke away from the lamp with her hand and lifted the globe off with a pot holder. She turned a little knob and adjusted the wick in the lamp. Then she cleaned the globe. As she worked, she explained what she was doing. "I had the wick turned up too high," she said. "When the wick is too long, it smokes up the globe so the light can't shine through." When the lamp was burning brightly again, she looked at Jacob. "The light of God's love can't shine through you when you're angry, Jacob," Grandmother told him. "Your temper has smoked up your witness."

Jacob hung his head. "I know," he admitted. "I'd better tell Chuck I'm sorry." *BJW*

HOW ABOUT YOU?

If your friends don't seem to listen when you witness to them, take a look at your life. Are you doing something that "smokes up" your witness? If so, now is the time to clean up your act and let the light of God's love shine through.

MEMORIZE:

"In the same way, let your good deeds shine out for all to see, so that everyone will praise your heavenly Father."

Matthew 5:16

 Let Your Witness Shine

Slogans and Actions (Read Galatians 5:16-25)

29

JULY

On their vacation trip, Ken and Sandy passed time by watching for signs and slogans beginning with the letters of the alphabet. "I got one for *H*," Sandy shouted. "See—that bumper sticker says 'Honk if you love Jesus.'"

As Ken glanced at the car, the driver angrily blasted his horn at another driver. "That man better change his slogan," observed Ken.

A little later Dad stopped for gas. "Service with a smile," Ken read on the sign. "That's an *S* for me." But they had to wait a long time for service. Then the attendant grumbled about the heat and the business. "He forgot the smile," declared Ken as they drove away.

The family checked into a motel for the night, and the next morning they attended church. The sign out front said "Friendly Gospel Church." No one greeted them, but they enjoyed the service, including the special music, which included the words "They'll know we are Christians by our love." The pastor shook hands with them as they left, but very few others did.

As they ate lunch, they talked about the fun they were having on their trip and the things they had seen. "Now let's think of something we've learned while we traveled," said Dad.

"One thing is that we better live up to what we say. We sure saw lots of slogans and signs that nobody seemed to pay any attention to. Even that church we went to—the sign said they were friendly, but they really weren't," said Ken.

"True," agreed Mom. "What things do we say that we need to live up to?"

"Well, that we're Christians," suggested Ken.

Dad added, "I wonder if people look at us and say, 'What's the difference between you and me?' They need to see the fruit of the Spirit in our life." *JLH*

HOW ABOUT YOU?

If you're a Christian, can people tell it by your life as well as by your lips? Are you friendly? faithful to the Lord? firm in your beliefs? quick to serve Jesus and others? Is the fruit of the Spirit evident in your life? Can people tell that you "have been with Jesus"?

MEMORIZE:

"The members of the council were amazed when they saw the boldness of Peter and John, for they could see that they were ordinary men . . . who had been with Jesus." *Acts 4:13*

 Show the Fruit of the Spirit

The Nail and the Toothpick (Read Psalm 27:1-5, 14)

The boys of Bay Street were cursing and telling dirty jokes and stories. Andy stood there, hating it all, but saying nothing. "Didn't you get the point?" asked one of the boys when Andy didn't laugh at his joke.

Andy swallowed hard. "I got it," he said. "It's late; I have to go." He mumbled a good-bye and hurried away. *Why didn't I tell them to stop their dirty talk?* he thought. *It's sure hard to be the only Christian boy in the neighborhood.*

30
JULY

Running fast with his head down and his mind on his troubles, Andy didn't see Pastor Flint until he smacked right into him. "Oh, I'm sorry, Pastor!" he said.

"Where are you going in such a hurry?" asked the pastor.

"No place—just getting away from the fellows. They're talking dirty," said Andy. "It's really hard to stand for the Lord all by yourself."

"Yes, it is," agreed Pastor Flint. He took a toothpick from his pocket. "You're like this toothpick. Here—see if you can break it." Andy broke the toothpick easily.

"Yeah, I'm like that," he agreed. "I'm the only Christian, and I'm not strong enough to say anything."

"But you're not alone," said the pastor, holding out a nail and another toothpick. "Now, can you break this toothpick with the nail alongside it?"

"Oh no," answered Andy. "But who's the nail like?"

"Jesus," said Pastor Flint. "He's always there to help you."

Andy was thoughtful. "That's my trouble—I haven't been depending on Jesus," he admitted, looking at the nail. "Say, Pastor, how'd you happen to have a nail in your pocket?"

"I brought it along to show this object lesson to Ralph Folmer," said Pastor Flint. "He's having trouble with the Bay Street boys, too. You see, he thinks *he's* the only Christian boy in the neighborhood." *MRP*

HOW ABOUT YOU?
Do you have trouble standing up for what's right? You can have the strength you need if you trust Jesus. With his help, you can find the courage to speak out against sin.

MEMORIZE:
"We also pray that you will be strengthened with his glorious power so that you will have all the patience and endurance you need. May you be filled with joy." *Colossians 1:11*

 Be Strong in the Lord

God's Gift (Read Luke 10:25-37)

31
JULY

Cassie sat on the beach with her seagull and stroked his snowy feathers. Tears streaking her cheeks, she looked up at her mother. "I'm not sure I can let Edgar go, Mama," she said. "He's about the only friend I've got!"

Mother sat down next to Cassie. "Now, what makes you say that?" she asked.

Cassie looked down. "The kids at school called me a dummy because I go to special classes. Mama, why can't I be smart like the other kids?"

Mother put her arm around Cassie. "Honey, it may be true that you have a harder time learning than some kids. But God made you with your own gifts and talents," she said.

Cassie wiped her eyes. "I don't have any gifts or talents."

Mother smiled. "You like to care for others. I think that's your special gift!"

"It is?" asked Cassie.

Mother nodded. "Your father and I have noticed that you are very helpful to others. When Grandma broke her hip, you went to her house almost every day to help out. At the dinner table, you always remember to pray for kids at school who are sick. And look at Edgar here. . . ." Cassie looked down at the seagull in her arms. "Edgar was almost dead from a fishing line twisted around his neck, and he had a broken wing," continued Mother. "Yet you nursed him back to health."

Cassie shrugged. "Those are things anyone would do."

Mother shook her head. "I wish that were true," she said, "but few people are that sensitive to the needs of others. Those kids who teased you certainly don't have the gift you have, or they never would have said those things."

Cassie was starting to feel better. She looked at Edgar again. "Well, Edgar, how would you like your freedom?" she asked. She stood up and tossed Edgar into the air. He floundered a bit at first, then straightened out. He squawked what must have been a thank-you and sailed out over the lake. *AJS*

HOW ABOUT YOU?

Do you treat other people as special gifts from God? Or do you tease them about something they can't help? Remember, you are special to God, and he wants you to remember that every other person is special, too.

MEMORIZE:

"There are different kinds of spiritual gifts . . . but it is the same Lord we are serving."

1 Corinthians 12:4-5

 Each Person Is Special

Run Away! (Read 2 Timothy 2:19-22)

"Mom, may I have a cookie?" asked Jodi.

"No, honey," replied Mom. "It's nearly time for lunch."

"But I'm hungry now!" whined Jodi.

"Yes, but I want you to wait so you'll eat a good lunch," said Mom.

Jodi climbed onto a stool and rested her elbows on the counter with her chin on her hands. She stared at the plate full of cookies right in front of her. *I'll just sit here and look at them,* she thought to herself. *I don't know why I can't have just one.* As Jodi sat there, all she could think of were the cookies and how yummy one would be. As she stared at them, her hand reached out and touched one. She took it in her hand and looked at it. She smelled it. The next thing she knew, she was eating it. "Mmmm," she murmured. It was good.

1

AUGUST

"Jodi! What are you doing?" Mom asked as she came back into the kitchen.

Jodi stopped chewing. She could not look into her mother's face. "Oh, Mom, I meant to just look at the cookies. Then suddenly I was eating one!" she cried. "I just couldn't help myself!"

"Why do you think that happened?" asked Mom.

"Because I forgot to run away from my temptation."

"That's right, Jodi. If you had been playing somewhere else, you could have forgotten about the cookies. Remember the Bible says, 'Run from anything that stimulates youthful lust.' That means to get away from something that might cause you to do what's wrong. And God will help you to do that if you ask him for help."

"I'm sorry, Mom," Jodi said.

"I'm sorry, too," said Mom. "I hope you'll remember how important it is to run away from temptation. You'll be facing even harder ones as you grow older, Jodi, but every time you run away from one, you'll become a little stronger. Then it may be easier to say no the next time." *EMM*

HOW ABOUT YOU?

Are you learning to say no to things you know are wrong? Are you running away from them? When you do, God will help you overcome any temptation. If you remember that, it will help you to trust him when the next temptation comes.

MEMORIZE:

"Run from anything that stimulates youthful lust."

2 Timothy 2:22

 Run from Temptation

Waiting to Hear (Read Matthew 28:16-20)

2
AUGUST

Angela started toward the mailbox at the road in front of her house. This was her third trip out here. She had checked for mail at eleven and again around noon. "I don't think the mail carrier has come yet," said Mother. "I see the Nelsons still have mail for her to pick up."

"She should have been here long ago," Angela insisted, and continued on her way. Finding the box still empty, she returned to the house. "I think it's awful that the mail is late. Mail carriers should be more prompt. I should get a letter from Gloria today, and I can't wait to hear from her!"

Mother smiled as Angela sat down on the front steps. "This reminds me of the story Pastor Blaine told one Sunday during missionary conference," she said. "Remember how he explained that Christians are somewhat like mail carriers? We have the most important message ever given, and we're to deliver it to all the people of the world."

As she spoke, a car rounded the corner. "There she is," squealed Angela, running to the road.

The mail carrier waved. "Sorry I'm late," she apologized. "I had car trouble. I can see you've been waiting for me, and you didn't wait for nothing." She grinned as she handed Angela the letter she was expecting.

As the mail carrier drove on, Angela became quiet and thoughtful. At last she spoke. "I wonder if people in other lands are waiting for us to come and give them God's message."

Mother nodded. "There are so many waiting and so few to go," she said with a sigh. "I'm glad you have dedicated your life to the Lord. Perhaps he'll send you into missionary work." *RIJ*

HOW ABOUT YOU?

Are you a good carrier of God's message? You may be too young now to go to a foreign country with the message, but what about sharing with your friends? Do that faithfully. Perhaps someday you will travel to faraway places as well. Be alert and ready to go wherever God wants to send you.

MEMORIZE:

"Go into all the world and preach the Good News to everyone, everywhere."

Mark 16:15

 Share God's Message

Not like a Robot (Read Numbers 24:3-5)

3

"Look, Dad," said Andy as he set his new toy car on the patio. "I can make it go anywhere I want." He pressed the lever on the remote control, and the shiny red Mustang shot backward and forward. As he rotated the lever on the control pad, the car sped in a circle around Andy's feet.

"Hey! What a smart car!" exclaimed Marissa, who was watching. "It just runs by itself."

"Not really," said Dad as he carried a platter of hamburgers to the grill. "It does what it's told. Basically the car receives messages Andy is sending from the remote control unit. Certain signals mean left and right, for instance. When the car receives the signals, it obeys the command."

"It's sort of like a robot, isn't it?" Andy asked as the car buzzed around the patio. "I tell it what to do, and it does it."

"That's right," agreed Dad. "The car has no life of its own. It can't think for itself, so it just goes through the motions." He paused. "Just like people sometimes," he added.

"What do you mean, Dad?" asked Marissa.

"As Christians, sometimes we don't put any life into our actions," Dad replied. "It's almost as though we're robots programmed to act as Christians. Going to church and repeating memorized prayers without thinking about them are a couple of examples."

Andy thought for a moment. "You mean like . . . saying a memorized prayer at bedtime or before we eat?"

Dad nodded. "That's right," he agreed, "unless you really mean the words you're saying. Let's think of other ways we can be less like robots." *SLB*

HOW ABOUT YOU?

Saying memorized prayers is often a good way to learn to pray, but think about what you're saying and begin to add some thoughts of your own, too. Attending church is also important. Benefit from it by thinking of the meaning of the songs you sing and the sermon you hear.

MEMORIZE:

"And I will give them singleness of heart and put a new spirit within them. I will take away their hearts of stone and give them tender hearts instead." *Ezekiel 11:19*

 Listen to the Word

Always-Present Family (Read 2 Timothy 4:16-18)

4

AUGUST

The Holmes family was having a reunion. People were everywhere. Alexa loved it. All these people were family— aunts and uncles and lots of cousins. Having all these people around meant there was always someone to be with her.

Aunt Marty agreed to play a game with Alexa, but when they started, Stevie, Alexa's little brother, kept climbing onto the game board. "Stevie, *stop!*" screamed Alexa. Suddenly, Uncle Paul scooped Stevie out of the way. Alexa and Aunt Marty began the game again. But then cousin Wendy ran around the corner and fell. *Oh, great! Now Aunt Marty will have to take care of her,* thought Alexa. But Grandpa picked up Wendy. Aunt Marty and Alexa played the game until lunchtime.

After lunch Alexa's "bully cousin," Jake, wouldn't leave her alone. He said something that hurt her feelings. Alexa went to her mother. She found her frosting a cake while talking to Aunt Phyl and Uncle Joe. "Jake hurt my feelings," Alexa whispered to her mother.

"I'm sorry," said Mother, "but I can't help you right now."

Aunt Phyl took Alexa's hand. They went out the back door and down a quiet road. They talked about how it feels when your feelings get hurt and how nice it is to have someone to comfort you.

"At home, Mommy is busy most of the time," said Alexa. "Here there's always someone to talk to. I like that."

"Well," said Aunt Phyl, "what about God?"

"God?" asked Alexa.

Aunt Phyl nodded. "God is like a big family all in himself—he's always there to comfort you," she explained.

Alexa thought about that. She smiled. She had forgotten what a good friend and comforter God is! *MLD*

HOW ABOUT YOU?

Are you lonely sometimes? Perhaps your parents are busy, or your best friend won't play? Does it sometimes seem as if nobody cares when you get hurt or get a bad grade? Jesus cares. You can say, "Please God, I need you to put your arms around me for a minute." He wants to comfort you.

MEMORIZE:

"I, even I, am the one who comforts you." *Isaiah 51:12*

 *God Is Always There*

A Tiny Flame (Read Matthew 5:13-16)

5

As soon as Jason left Keith's house, he ran all the way home. He hadn't been so excited since moving to Kentucky. "Mom! Mom!" he called as he entered the house.

"Yes, Jason, I'm here," Mom called from the laundry room.

Jason helped Mom fold the sheet she had in her hand. "Mom, Keith's family invited me to go with them to Mammoth Cave a week from Saturday. May I?"

"Sounds like fun," said Mom. "I'm sure it will be fine."

"I'll call Keith and tell him." Jason started for the phone.

"While you're talking to Keith, why don't you invite him to come to Sunday school and church with us?" suggested Mom.

Jason thought about that. He didn't want to be teased about going to church as he had been in his previous school. He didn't want to say that to Mom because she would talk about letting his light shine for Christ. *I do love the Lord,* thought Jason. *But I don't think the little light I could give would make much difference.*

The trip was as much fun as Jason expected. Exploring the cave was a real adventure. When the group reached a room deep in the cave, the tour guide turned out the single bulb in the area. "I want you to experience total darkness," she said.

"Are you there, Jason?" whispered Keith.

"Yeah," Jason whispered back.

The tour guide lit a match, and every eye focused on the tiny flame. As they stood there, Jason was surprised at how much light that one little flame gave off.

On the drive home, Jason thought about the tiny flame. *I guess small things can make a difference,* he admitted to himself. "Keith," he said finally, "would you like to go to Sunday school and church with me sometime?"

Keith was quiet for a moment, then he said, "I guess so."

"Great!" said Jason. *Maybe my light will make a difference after all,* he thought. *EMB*

HOW ABOUT YOU?

Do you realize that your light—your witness—can make a big difference in someone's life? If you're a Christian, ask God to show you how to let your light shine for him. Maybe it will be by talking to someone about the Lord, inviting someone to church, or just being kind and helpful.

MEMORIZE:

"You are the light of the world."

Matthew 5:14

 *Shine for Jesus*

A Little at a Time (Read 2 Timothy 3:14-17)

6

AUGUST

Devon sat on the front step with a pocketknife in one hand and a block of wood in the other. Turning the wood in his hand, he studied it intently. After looking at it from all angles, he began to carve. He worked for quite a long time. Slowly the shape of a duck began to emerge.

"What ya working on, boy?" Startled, Devon looked up. He had been concentrating so hard on his work that he had failed to hear his grandfather's approach. Devon held out his carving.

Grandpa turned it over and over in his hands. "You're doing a good job, Son," he said, handing back the half-finished duck. "Before you know it, the duck that's in your mind is what you'll be holding in your hands."

"I guess so," said Devon, "if I don't make a mistake and goof it up—or quit. I really like carving, but I wish it didn't take so long. A chip off here, another off there. . . . It seems to take forever."

"Oh, I hope you won't quit," said Grandpa quickly. "I know it's a slow process, but the only way to get it right is to chip off just a little at a time." After a moment he added, "Aren't you glad God doesn't quit when he's working in our life?"

"What do you mean, Gramps?" asked Devon. Grandpa always was weaving God into their conversations.

"God sees in us what we can be—what we can develop into—just as you see a special object in a block of wood. Little by little God shows us things that need to be chipped away to make us more like him," explained Grandpa. "I guess you could say that he is carving our life, a little at a time, just the way you're carving that block of wood."

Devon looked at the half-finished duck he held. "And we're only half-finished, too, aren't we?" he asked with a grin.

Grandpa nodded. "That's right," he said. "But you can be sure God'll finished the job!" *CPH*

HOW ABOUT YOU?

Are there bad habits that need to be chipped away out of your life? Let God work in you so that you may be more like him. Obey him when he shows you what is right to do, and avoid the things that he shows you are wrong.

MEMORIZE:

"But you must remain faithful to the things you have been taught." *2 Timothy 3:14*

 God's Still Working on You

A Picture to Remember (Read 1 Corinthians 11:23-26)

7

AUGUST

Kelli was thoughtful as her family arrived home after church. There had been a Communion service that morning, and she had some questions. "I know the Lord wants us to take Communion to remind us of his death and resurrection, and he says we're to do it until he takes us to heaven," she said. "But won't we take Communion when we get to heaven, too?"

Dad shook his head. "No, Kelli, we won't."

"Why not?" asked Kelli. "I don't understand."

Dad thought for a minute, then pointed to a picture on top of the piano. "Before Uncle Doug and Aunt Laura left for Africa as missionaries, we promised we would pray for them each time we looked at their picture, remember?"

Kelli nodded. "Yes, and I look at it a lot!" she said.

"That's good," said Dad. "Remember last summer when they spent a couple of weeks with us? It was at the time our rosebushes were blooming. Mom picked so many roses for the house, we had roses everywhere!"

Kelli laughed. "I remember! We even put Uncle Doug and Aunt Laura's picture away for a while because we needed the space on top of the piano. But it didn't matter then, because we didn't need their picture—they were here in person. That's better than a picture any day!"

"That's exactly it, Kelli—and Communion is like a picture to help us remember the Lord's death and resurrection," Dad explained. "When we're in heaven, we'll be with the Lord Jesus Christ. We'll no longer need the 'picture'!"

"Oh, I get it!" exclaimed Kelli. "That makes sense." *LMW*

HOW ABOUT YOU?

If you have questions about the Communion service, ask your parents, Sunday school teacher, or pastor. When you participate, do so with thanksgiving, joyfully looking forward to the time when the picture will no longer be needed because you'll see Jesus in person.

MEMORIZE:

"For every time you eat this bread and drink this cup, you are announcing the Lord's death until he comes again."

1 Corinthians 11:26

 Communion Gives a Picture of Jesus

Use the Entrance (Read John 10:7-10)

8

AUGUST

Tyler was visiting his grandparents. He was outside playing when he noticed that the rose trellis reached nearly to his bedroom window on the second floor of the large brick farmhouse.

Suddenly Tyler had an idea. He could climb up that trellis, stretch up to the windowsill, pull himself up on it, and then crawl through the open window into his room! Tyler scrambled to his feet and darted toward the trellis. He positioned his foot on a low trellis slat, pushed away a few roses, and began to climb. Higher and higher he went. He stretched his arms, caught the windowsill, and swung himself up. Then suddenly he lost his grip and fell. He landed in the flower bed with a loud thud. Grandma and Grandpa came running.

"Tyler, can you open your eyes?" asked a voice from far away.

Tyler blinked his eyes and groaned at the sharp pain in his head. "What happened?" whispered Tyler.

"You had a nasty fall," said Grandpa. "I think we should see the doctor."

"Tyler, why did you climb the rose trellis?" asked Grandma.

"I wanted to climb through the window to get into my bedroom," he replied.

"But why?" asked Grandma. "Why didn't you just go in the door?" Tyler had been dreading these questions and didn't have a good answer. He felt ashamed. He had hurt himself, and he had upset his grandparents, too.

For devotions that evening, Grandpa turned to John 10. "These verses tell us that Jesus is the door to heaven. But there are a lot of people that try to get there by doing good works. That's sort of like you, Tyler, trying to get to your bedroom up the rose trellis instead of using the door. And like you, those people are going to get a hurtful surprise. Good works won't get you into heaven. Only believing in Jesus will. I'm glad he's our Savior." *LAT*

HOW ABOUT YOU?

Do you know Jesus is the only way to heaven, or are you trying to get there some other way? Jesus loves you and died for you. If you are interested in asking him to be your Savior, talk to a trusted adult to find out more.

MEMORIZE:

"I am the door: by me if any man enter in, he shall be saved." *John 10:9,* KJV

Trust Jesus as Savior

Parents and Teachers (Read Proverbs 4:1-11)

Danny and his friend Shane were riding their bikes past the neighborhood school yard when Danny began to talk about the coming school year. "I'm going to be in Mr. Simon's class," he said. "How about you, Shane?"

Shane shrugged. "I'm not going back to school in the fall," he replied.

9

AUGUST

"Aw, come on," said Danny. "Everybody goes to school."

Shane explained that his parents were going to teach him at home. "It'll be different, but I think I'll like it. You can learn a lot from your parents."

Back home, Danny thought about what Shane had said. *What have I learned from my parents?* he thought. *They taught me to walk, talk, and ride a bike. Hmmm. Those were pretty good things. I wonder if there are other things they could teach me now?* With that thought in mind, he went to the kitchen where his mother was cooking. "Hey, Mom," he said after watching her for a few minutes, "why do you mix the flour and water in that cup before you dump it in the pan?"

"I do it so there won't be lumps in the gravy," she explained. "Then when I add the flour mixture to the hot liquid, I have to stir it quickly, like this." She demonstrated. "It needs a little more flour—want to try it?" she asked. Danny laughed and took the spoon she offered. By the end of the impromptu cooking lesson, both were laughing and feeling closer than they had for a long time.

"I'm going down to watch Dad at his workbench," Danny decided. "You never know—I might learn something."

"Yes, you might," agreed Mother, "but right now it's dinnertime. You can call your dad to the table. I'm glad you're so eager to learn, though. I'll tell you what—right after dinner you can learn how to wash the dishes!" She laughed at Danny's groan as he went to call his dad. *SLK*

HOW ABOUT YOU?

You have many teachers—schoolteachers, Sunday school teachers, perhaps a piano teacher or baseball coach. Your parents are probably the most important teachers of all those God has given you. They'll teach you many everyday lessons that will help you for the rest of your life. Be a good student.

MEMORIZE:

"My children, listen to me. Listen to your father's instruction. Pay attention and grow wise." *Proverbs 4:1*

 Learn from Parents

Dark Glasses (Read 1 Corinthians 13:9-13)

10

AUGUST

Sandy had spent the afternoon at the beach with her girlfriend. "We had such fun!" she declared when she got home. She plopped down in a chair and described the good time she'd had. She looked around the room. "Why is it so dark in here?" she wanted to know.

Her brother let out a whoop. "Because you're still wearing your sunglasses, dummy," he told her, laughing. Sandy laughed, too, and removed the glasses.

Her father smiled. "I just thought of something, Sandy," he said. He reached for a Bible and opened it. "Put those glasses back on and come here a minute. I'd like you to read some verses for me." He pointed to the text with his finger.

Sandy looked at the Bible. "You mean with my glasses on?" she asked. Her father nodded.

Sandy held the Bible a little closer. The page wasn't very clear, but she managed to read it. "For now we see through a glass, darkly; but then face to face: now I know in part; but then shall I know even as also I am known." She stopped reading and grinned at her father. "Seeing through a glass darkly describes me all right," she said.

"It describes all of us," said Dad. "When your cousin Jason died last month, we all were very upset and even angry, weren't we?" Sandy nodded her head. "And we all had questions—we wanted to know *why,* didn't we?" Again Sandy nodded, and her father continued softly, "In this life we see the events occurring around us as though we had dark glasses on. Things are unclear, and we wonder *why.* But when we meet the Lord in heaven, we won't have questions like that anymore. We'll truly understand that God does all things well." *RM*

HOW ABOUT YOU?

It's easier to trust God when you see things clearly, isn't it? But God appreciates faith that trusts him when things *don't* seem clear. Ask God to help you trust him, regardless of how things may appear. God loves you so much he *can* be trusted.

MEMORIZE:

"For now we see through a glass, darkly; but then face to face: now I know in part; but then shall I know even as also I am known." *1 Corinthians 13:12,* KJV

Trust God Even in Hard Times

Facing Your Goliath (Read Psalm 3:3-8)

11

AUGUST

Stacey was spending the night at her grandma's house. It was dark and quiet in the bedroom. She lay alone in the dark, seeing strange shadows on the wall. In the corner of the room she saw a big, dark shape that looked like a bear.

Keeping her eyes on the bear, Stacey slid out of bed and dashed out of the bedroom door and down the hall. She heard her grandmother singing in the kitchen. Stacey raced into the kitchen. "There's a big, dark shape in my room. It looks like a bear," she said breathlessly.

Grandma smiled at Stacey. "Do you remember the story in the Bible about David and Goliath?" she asked. Stacey nodded. "How do you think David had the courage to fight the giant?" asked Grandma.

"He knew God was with him," replied Stacey.

"Right," agreed Grandma, "and God is with you, too. Do you see that Bible on the shelf?" Stacey nodded. "Take it with you, and we'll go back to the bedroom," said Grandma. "I want you to carry it like the armor of God."

As they walked to the bedroom, Stacey held the Bible tightly in her hand. Grandma switched on the light, and Stacey looked for the bear. But there was only a large stuffed chair in that corner of the room.

Grandma tucked Stacey into bed again. Then she turned off the light and left. The "bear" came back. Stacey quickly turned on the light, and the "bear" disappeared. She knew now that, in the dark, the chair looked like a bear. She looked at the Bible. It reminded her of all the times God had helped people. "I want to be brave and trust you. Help me, please," she prayed. Then she switched the light off again, turned over, and went to sleep. *KEC*

HOW ABOUT YOU?

Do you remember that God is the same today as when he took care of David? Ask him to walk beside you and help you conquer your fear. He will.

MEMORIZE:

"I prayed to the Lord, and he answered me, freeing me from all my fears." *Psalm 34:4*

 Trust God When You're Afraid

The Key Piece (Read Acts 17:24-28; Ephesians 4:14-18)

12
AUGUST

As Jack and Judy played in their grandmother's attic one day, Jack found a small case filled with an assortment of carved wooden shapes. "Look at this!" he said to his sister. "It looks like some kind of puzzle."

"Grandpa did carving when he was a boy. He probably made it," Judy said. "Let's see if we can put it together." As they worked, Jack tossed aside a piece that was painted red and looked different from the other pieces. "This must belong to another puzzle," he said.

Some time later Judy looked up and sighed. "This just won't go together," she said. "Let's put them back." It wasn't until the last piece was in the box that Judy remembered something.

"Hey!" she said. "What about that red piece you threw away?" She looked around. "Here it is! Maybe it does belong, after all." Once again the children set to work. To their surprise, the other pieces fit easily around the red piece, and soon they put the entire puzzle together.

When they went downstairs, they showed the puzzle to their grandmother and told her about the curious red piece. "That sounds just like your grandpa—painting the key piece red so it would be easier to find," she said with a smile. "But you two threw it out because it was 'different.' It reminds me of the way some people treat the Lord."

"I don't get it," said Judy.

"Many people go through life searching for answers," explained Grandma. "They want to know how they got here, where they're going, and whether there's any purpose to their lives. The trouble is, they reject God and Christ and try to find the answers for themselves. They don't understand that the pieces of their lives will never 'fit together' until they put Christ in the center, where he belongs." *SLK*

HOW ABOUT YOU?

Have you wondered what life was all about? Have you tried to be happy without accepting Christ as your Savior? Your life won't make sense or be all that God wants it to be until you accept Christ and put him in the center of it. It will not "fit together" unless the key piece—Jesus—is in place.

MEMORIZE:

"For in him we live and move and exist. As one of your own poets says, 'We are his offspring.'" *Acts 17:28*

 Make Jesus the Center of Your Life

Making a Mark (Read Psalm 17:1-6)

As Shawn and his friends walked to the ballpark, they cut across the lawn of a large brick house on a corner lot. One day the owner of the house was working outdoors when they came by. "I know it's a big temptation to cut corners," said Mr. Black, "but I'd appreciate it if you would use the sidewalk so there won't be a path worn in the grass. OK?"

13

AUGUST

"Sure thing," agreed the boys.

But the next day they crossed over Mr. Black's lawn again. "Hey," said Shawn, suddenly remembering their promise, "we said we'd use the sidewalk."

"So what? The old man didn't catch us," snapped one of the boys. "Anyway, how much harm can we cause just walking across his lawn once in a while?" Day after day the boys used the short cut. By the end of the summer, a definite path appeared in the area where they had walked.

As Shawn passed the house on his way home one day, Mr. Black was working on his lawn. "You boys didn't keep your promise," said Mr. Black.

Shawn shrugged. "I guess we didn't think that walking on the grass once a day would do much damage."

Mr. Black answered, "Doing it over and over has a way of making a mark. Guess it's like a bad habit." He looked at Shawn from beneath bushy eyebrows. "Some habits leave much worse marks than the path worn in the grass," he said.

Shawn thought of the temptations he sometimes faced—temptations to smoke, try drugs or alcohol, or participate in questionable "fun." He was surprised to hear Mr. Black's next words. "You know bad habits aren't always big things," said Mr. Black. "But God wants to help us overcome any habit that keeps us from following him." *RIJ*

HOW ABOUT YOU?

Do you find it easy to stay away from smoking or swearing? How about throwing clothes on a chair rather than hanging them up in the closet? talking back to your parents? putting things off until "tomorrow"? Bad habits are hard to break, but with God's help you can do it.

MEMORIZE:

"My steps have stayed on your path; I have not wavered from following you." Psalm 17:5

 Stop Harmful Habits

A Lie Is a Lie Is a Lie . . . (Read Luke 12:1-3)

14

AUGUST

"Did you pick up your toys, David?" asked Grandma.

"Yes, ma'am," said David as he popped up on a kitchen stool. "What are you making?"

"Cinnamon rolls," replied Grandma.

"Oh, yummy!" exclaimed David. He watched as Grandma tore open a small package and poured its contents into a cup of water. "What'd you just put in there?"

Grandma laughed. "Yeast. It makes the dough grow, so the bread will be light," she explained as she poured the liquid into a large bowl. Then she sifted several cups of flour into it. When she set it aside and began cleaning up the kitchen, David asked, "Why are you quitting?"

"We have to let the dough rise for about an hour," Grandma answered. "Then we'll make the rolls."

Later, Grandma went into the bedroom to see if David had picked up his toys as he said. She smiled, for there was not one toy in sight. But when she opened the toy chest, she frowned. There was not one toy in the chest! Picking up the edge of the bedspread, she sighed. There, under the bed, were the toys.

When Grandma called David to help finish the rolls, he bounded into the kitchen. His eyes grew big as he looked at the bowl in his grandmother's hands. "The dough has grown so big that it's about to spill over!" he exclaimed.

"That's what the yeast did to the dough." Grandma punched down the dough with her fist as she continued. "David, why did you tell me you had picked up your toys?"

David answered, "What I meant is I put 'em out of sight."

"What you did is lie about it," Grandma said sternly, "and a lie is like the yeast in this dough, David. It grows and grows. One lie leads to another. Now—you need to do a real cleanup job before you can help me with the cinnamon rolls." *BJW*

HOW ABOUT YOU?

Are you kidding yourself by saying, "It was just a 'little' lie—it won't hurt anything"? No sin is little in God's sight. If you have told a lie, make it right by telling the truth now. Don't wait until it grows into more lies.

MEMORIZE:

"But it takes only one wrong person among you to infect all the others—a little yeast spreads quickly through the whole batch of dough!"

Galatians 5:9

 **Don't Tell Lies**

Truthful Pictures (Read Ecclesiastes 11:9-10; 12:1, 13-14)

"Oh, goody!" squealed Heather when Dad arrived home with pictures of their camping trip. She took them and began to look at them. "Oh no! How awful!" she cried.

Heather's brother, Mike, peered over Heather's shoulder. He started to laugh. "Why, Heather! You look nice!" he teased.

"I do not!" Heather sniffed. "I look terrible!" She shuffled through more of the photographs. Then she grinned as she pointed to a picture of Mike. "Remember when you tripped and fell while we were hiking?" She giggled.

15

AUGUST

"Yeah," Mike said with a nod, "but I didn't know Dad was taking a picture of me then! I was covered with mud!"

"I wanted to get some candid shots," said Dad with a smile, "not just posed ones. There's Mike in his favorite outfit—plaid pants, striped shirt, and silly orange hat. And here are Heather and Mom standing on the picnic table, trying to escape that ferocious six-inch-long grass snake."

Heather groaned. "Next time I'm going to be careful not to let you get pictures of me looking so bad," she said.

"A photograph can record things the way they really are," commented Dad. Then he added, "Pastor Davis talked about a sort of 'picture-showing session' we'll attend someday—do you remember that?"

"What pictures are you talking about?" asked Heather.

"I remember," said Mike. "He was talking about the time God will judge the things we've done. He said it would be like viewing pictures of our lives."

"Right," agreed Dad. "We won't be able to hide or change anything, no matter how much we might want to. Perhaps we should ask God to help us live wisely!" *SLK*

HOW ABOUT YOU?

Do you realize that God is keeping a record of the things you do, say, and think? You may hide your sins from others, but you're not fooling God. Live in such a way that you will be glad to give an account of your life.

MEMORIZE:

"God will judge us for everything we do, including every secret thing, whether good or bad." *Ecclesiastes 12:14*

 God Will Judge Everything

Dirty and Scuffed (Read Matthew 23:25-26)

16
AUGUST

Chad came through the back door and grunted a hi at his mom. He headed for his room and slammed the door as he tossed his books down on the bed. He caught a glimpse of himself in the mirror on his wall. His hair stuck out in all directions, and his shirt was torn. His hands were filthy from digging in the dirt on his way home. His scuffed tennis shoes were untied, and there was a tear in his pants. It probably came from sliding into second base in the ball game at recess.

Just then there was a knock on his bedroom door. "Chad," his mother called, "may I come in?"

"Sure, Mom," Chad replied, trying to repair some of the "ugliness" he saw in the mirror.

"What's wrong, Son?" asked Mom.

"I'm angry with Linda. I passed her on the way home from school, and she said I was an ugly sight," said Chad. "She oughta remember that it doesn't matter what you look like on the outside. It's the inside that counts."

"Hmmm. I guess I'll have to have a talk with Linda," said Mother. "That was no way for her to talk to you. But you know what? If you had taken a moment to stop in the boys' rest room before coming home, you could have cleaned up a bit."

"But that's not so important," insisted Chad. "Like my Bible verse last Sunday said, 'People judge by outward appearance, but the Lord looks at a person's thoughts and intentions.'"

"I agree that the inside is more important," said Mother. "However, as your verse said, people look at the outward appearance. It's all they can see. And if you want to influence people for Christ, it's important to take care of your 'outside,' too." *CV*

HOW ABOUT YOU?

Are you careful to be clean and neat? Or are you sometimes careless about your appearance? It's a good habit to take care of yourself "inside" and "outside."

MEMORIZE:

"But the Lord said to Samuel, 'Don't judge by his appearance or height. . . . People judge by outward appearance, but the Lord looks at a person's thoughts and intentions.'"

1 Samuel 16:7

 Be Clean Inside and Out

Who's That Talking? (Read Proverbs 26:21-28)

17

AUGUST

Megan was excited! She had gotten a tape recorder and several blank tapes for her birthday. "Hey, Andy," she called to her brother. "Let's pretend we're doing a radio program. You tell your favorite jokes, and I'll sing a solo." Andy agreed, so they started to record their show. Andy had only finished telling one joke when Mother called them to supper. "I didn't even get my turn," Megan complained.

"I'm sure you'll have time after supper," Mother told her.

But Megan didn't want to wait. All through supper she pouted. Afterwards she had a big argument with Andy over whose turn it was to wash the dishes. "I washed them last night!" she yelled.

"I did!" Andy shouted back.

"That's not true," insisted Megan angrily. "I remember that I washed them because we had spaghetti, and I had to clean up all that messy tomato sauce."

Mother came into the kitchen. "I don't want to hear another word out of the two of you," she scolded. "I'm tired of your fighting. Megan, you wash the dishes. Andy, you dry."

Finally the task was done, and the children went back to the tape recorder. Megan rewound the tape to listen to Andy tell his joke before recording something new. But she got a big surprise. She discovered that she had left the tape recorder running all through supper. She heard not only Andy's joke but also all the complaining and angry words she had said during supper and while doing the dishes. She couldn't believe how grouchy she had been. It certainly didn't sound anything like the girl she wanted to be!

"I'm glad you bought me this recorder, Mom," Megan said as she erased her whiny voice from the tape. "It has already taught me a good lesson!" *LMW*

HOW ABOUT YOU?

How do you think you sound to other people? How do you sound to God? Are your words gentle and kind, or are they angry and whiny? Listen to yourself. Notice how you treat the other members of your family—especially your brothers and sisters. The Bible says a Christian is to be gentle. Practice gentleness.

MEMORIZE:

"The Lord's servants must not quarrel but must be kind to everyone. They must be able to teach effectively and be patient with difficult people."

2 Timothy 2:24

 **Be Gentle**

Candy Apple (Read Psalm 145:13-19)

18
AUGUST

Laura had gotten a new bicycle for her birthday. It was her first two-wheeler! On the way home from the store, Dad asked, "Are you sure you don't want training wheels—or shall I help you at first? Learning to ride a two-wheeler takes practice."

"Oh no, Dad," Laura declared. "I'll catch on fast. I can do it by myself." Laura pictured herself zooming down the block, pretending she was on a beautiful horse!

"Since I can't have a horse, Dad, I'll pretend my bike is one. Its name is Candy, short for Candy Apple, because it's red."

As soon as they arrived home, Laura wheeled the new bike to the front sidewalk. She put one foot on a pedal and shoved off. She lifted her other foot and was surprised to find that she just couldn't keep her balance. She started to tip over every time and had to quickly put her feet back on the ground. Again and again Laura tried to ride the bike, but it kept tipping over. She choked back tears.

Laura was feeling very discouraged when she heard approaching footsteps. "Looks like you could use a helping hand with this bucking bronco," said her father. "Whoa, Candy Apple!" Laura giggled as Dad held the bike steady so she could seat herself. Then he held onto the seat and ran along as she began to pedal slowly down the sidewalk.

Later, Laura and Dad were resting on the front steps. "Thanks a lot, Dad," said Laura. "I thought I could learn to ride my bike all by myself, but I needed your help."

Dad smiled. "A lot of people think they can handle their problems all by themselves," he told her, "but God wants to help them just as I wanted to help you."

"Candy Apple will be a good reminder that my heavenly Father wants to help me," Laura agreed. She tugged at Dad's hand. "Come on—let's go practice some more." *DAF*

HOW ABOUT YOU?

Is something bothering you? Poor grades? Being "picked on"? Inability to get along with family members? Ask your heavenly Father for help and then trust him. He may remove your problems—or he may give the strength to handle them. He wants to help you.

MEMORIZE:

"The Lord helps the fallen and lifts up those bent beneath their loads." *Psalm 145:14*

 *Depend on God*

Merry-Go-Round (Read Ecclesiastes 2:4-11)

19

Paul and his parents munched freshly made caramel corn as they wandered about on the first day of the Harvest Fair. "Well, Paul," said Dad, "today you can ride on three different things. What would you like to try first?"

"The merry-go-round," Paul decided. Soon he was in line, waiting to get on. When the attendant opened the gate, Paul quickly found the horse he wanted to ride. As the merry-go-round began to turn and pick up speed, he bounced in the saddle. The ride ended all too soon. "That's my favorite ride!" he exclaimed as he rejoined his parents. "I want to use the rest of my tickets for it, too." And he did.

A little later Paul walked over to a bench where Mother and Dad were waiting with cups of apple cider. "I think I should have tried something else," he said with a sigh. "After the second ride, it got a little boring. I guess it was because it wasn't a real horse, and I really didn't go anywhere—just round and round."

"That reminds me of what our life is like when we try to live it without Jesus," said Mother. "We try to make ourselves happy with new toys, clothes, or exciting experiences. These things satisfy for a short time, but sooner or later we tire of them. We go round and round looking for something better."

"That's right," agreed Dad. "We're just going in circles, the way you were doing on the merry-go-round. Even all of King Solomon's riches didn't bring him happiness. Only Jesus can do that." *DAF*

HOW ABOUT YOU?

Have you felt you would be satisfied if only you had a certain toy—yet later you grew tired of it? If you're looking for contentment in possessions, you won't find it. Only when Jesus is in control, can you stop searching and be satisfied. Turn your life over to him.

MEMORIZE:

"[Jesus said,] My purpose is to give life in all its fullness."

John 10:10

 Only Jesus Satisfies

Puzzle Pieces (Read Romans 8:28-32)

20
AUGUST

"Hi, Mom," said Brooke. Then she frowned. It seemed strange to see Mom in a hospital bed. "You feel OK?"

"Sure." Mom nodded. "They only did tests today. The surgery isn't until tomorrow." She noticed a box under Brooke's arm. "What did you bring?"

"You said to bring something we could do together," Brooke reminded her. She dumped the pieces of a small puzzle onto Mom's bedside table, and they began searching out the pieces that went around the edge of the picture.

Brooke frowned as she worked. So many questions filled her mind. Would Mom's surgery hurt her? Would it make her well? And the question that bothered Brooke the most—could Mom die during the surgery? But she didn't want to worry Mom with her questions at a time like this.

"I can't figure out where this piece goes," Brooke said, still frowning.

Mom smiled at her. "I'm glad you brought a puzzle," she said. "It's kind of like my life right now. Being ill and needing surgery is like that piece of the puzzle—I don't know where it fits into the picture of my life." Mom's words also described what Brooke was feeling. "But I've seen how God has put many other pieces of my life together already," Mom continued. "That helps me trust him to work this piece in, too."

"What do you mean?" asked Brooke.

"Remember how worried we were when Dad lost his job?" Brooke nodded. "God provided Dad with a job in this city where Dr. Campbell practices," Mom continued. "He's the best doctor in the country to perform my surgery. Do you think that happened by accident?"

"No. God was taking care of you," Brooke answered slowly. "And he'll take care of you tomorrow, too." *KRA*

HOW ABOUT YOU?

Are there events in your life that you don't understand? Take comfort—God sees the total picture of your life, and he's fitting the pieces into just the right places. He'll work everything out for your good, even though you may not see it now.

MEMORIZE:

"And we know that God causes everything to work together for the good of those who love God and are called according to his purpose for them." *Romans 8:28*

 Trust God to Work

Scars to Remember (Read Hebrews 12:5-11)

Adam hesitated as his friend Stephen held up a video he and some other boys were going to watch. "Come on, Adam," urged Stephen.

Adam was curious about the popular horror movie. However, he wasn't anxious to break his parents' rule about not watching horror movies.

21

AUGUST

"Wimpy! Wimpy!" the boys chanted. Adam gave in.

When he got home, he felt guilty. "How did it happen, Lord?" he prayed. "I didn't mean to disobey. I should have said no. Please forgive me."

Adam went to bed with a clear conscience and fell right to sleep. But then the dream came—a terrible dream in which the monster from the movie was after him with such reality that Adam was terrified.

"Adam, wake up." Adam heard Dad's voice over his own cries. Dad's words were comforting, but the terror was still with Adam, and he couldn't stop crying. Through his tears, he told Dad about the movie and how it had brought on the dream. "I asked God to forgive me. Why didn't he? Why did he let me have that bad dream?" Adam asked.

"Remember the lamp you broke playing ball in the house?" asked Dad. Adam nodded. "We forgave you for breaking it, but the lamp will always have a scar—the crack in its base," said Dad. "Tonight you asked God to forgive you for watching that movie when you knew you shouldn't. He has forgiven you, too, but that doesn't mean there will be no scars."

"The dream was a scar, wasn't it?" asked Adam.

"I think so," said Dad. "Often God allows us to experience the consequences of our sin. I think it's part of his discipline to keep us from sin that has even worse consequences. He does that because he loves us." *KRA*

HOW ABOUT YOU?

Have you done wrong things because you were curious or because others pressured you? Accept God's forgiveness when you repent, but also recognize his discipline when he allows you to experience the consequences of that sin. His discipline helps you remember that sin is dangerous.

MEMORIZE:

"I am the one who corrects and disciplines everyone I love. Be diligent and turn from your indifference." *Revelation 3:19*

 Accept God's Discipline

Not Everybody (Read 1 Kings 19:9-18)

22

AUGUST

In amazement, Mother stared out the kitchen window. Renee and her friend Janis were twisting and writhing on the back lawn. Mother raised the window. "Girls, whatever are you doing?"

Both girls sat up. "We're just break dancing, Mother," Renee answered.

"I want you to stop," said Mother.

"Oh, Mother . . . ," Renee began, but Mother had shut the window. Later, Renee came into the house. "Janis was teaching me to break dance, Mother. You embarrassed me when you made us stop," she accused.

"Well, I surely didn't like the looks of what you were doing," Mother said firmly. "I don't want you doing it anymore."

"But, Mother," Renee protested, "everybody's doing it."

Mother raised her eyebrows. "Oh? And if everyone does it, that makes it right?"

"Well, if everyone does it, it surely can't be too bad," Renee argued weakly.

Mother handed Renee a pencil and paper. "Let's take a poll, Renee. Write down the names and telephone numbers of your friends." Renee looked puzzled, but obeyed. When finished, she handed the list to Mother. "Now call each one," Mother instructed. "Ask one question, 'Do you break dance?' Write down the answers."

An hour later Renee came into the kitchen with a strange look on her face. "Seven said no. Three said yes. And one wasn't home," she reported.

Mother nodded. "One of Satan's biggest lies is 'Everybody's doing it.' Maybe the loudest crowd is doing it, but if we check, we usually find that 'everyone' is not doing it. Even if they were, it would not make wrong right. But there is comfort in knowing that many people are standing for right." *BJW*

HOW ABOUT YOU?

Elijah believed he was the only one doing right, but God had a surprise for him. There were seven thousand others who had not worshiped Baal. Don't be afraid to stand for right. You can be sure that many others are standing with you.

MEMORIZE:

"So now the Lord says, 'Stop right where you are! Look for the old, godly way, and walk in it. Travel its path, and you will find rest for your souls.'"

Jeremiah 6:16

 *Not "Everybody" Does It*

Way to Go (Read Psalm 119:9-16)

23
AUGUST

"I read a helpful verse in my Bible this morning," said Mom as the family car moved along on the second day of their vacation. After she shared her verse, Dad told about what he'd read in his daily Bible reading.

"What did you read about today?" Mom asked Rick.

"I . . . I forgot to pack my Bible," Rick said uneasily.

"You may borrow mine," suggested Mom.

"I hate to read in the car," said Rick, refusing the Bible she offered. "Besides, I read my Bible all the time. I won't forget what it says during the short time we're on vacation." His parents exchanged glances but said nothing.

After a while Mom saw an exit sign. "Isn't this where we turn off?" she asked.

"No, I don't think so," said Dad. "Double-check with the map." He reached for the map, but it wasn't there. Mom and Rick looked all over the car, but the map wasn't to be found. Mom suggested stopping to buy another. "Let's not take time," said Dad. "I studied the map carefully before we left. I'm sure this isn't the right exit."

After traveling a while longer, Dad finally agreed to get another map. They discovered that Dad was wrong. They should have turned off long before. Rick felt angry when he heard how far out of their way they'd gone.

"Studying a map regularly is better than relying on memory," said Mom.

"That's for sure," agreed Rick.

"Traveling down the highway on our vacation reminds me that we are also traveling down the 'highway' of life," said Mom. "The Bible shows us the way we should go—if we refer to it regularly."

Dad returned, and they soon were on their way. As they drove off, Rick spoke. "I'm ready to borrow your Bible, Mom," he said. "I'd better review the 'map' to see what I need to know." *KRA*

HOW ABOUT YOU?

Do you feel you've studied the Bible so much that you remember all you need to know? Do you find excuses for neglecting daily Bible reading? God provided a wonderful guide when he gave us the Bible. He expects us to refresh our memories by reading it regularly.

MEMORIZE:

"I will delight in your principles and not forget your word." *Psalm 119:16*

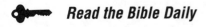 *Read the Bible Daily*

The Best Job (Read Ephesians 6:5-10)

24
AUGUST

Clarissa sat at the piano to practice. "May I stay home from school for the next two weeks?" she asked her mother while opening her music book.

Mother smiled. "Does this question have anything to do with the two-week-long responsibility Mrs. Murphy assigned you?" she asked.

Clarissa sighed. "It would be neat having the same job every day for that long if it were a good job," she said. "But who wants to pick up all the scraps of paper and other stuff that falls under our desks?" Clarissa placed her hands on her hips. "Martha gets to wash the chalkboard. Robin gets to clap the erasers. Smitty gets to be the last one out of the room so he can close the door. But me—I have a dumb job."

"When I was young, your granddad had a truck that he used for picking up old furniture," Mother said thoughtfully. "He fixed up and sold some pieces, and he chopped up others for firewood. Our backyard was piled full of old desks and chests of drawers and upright pianos from other people's houses. I was embarrassed. One day I told your grandmother I was going to run away till all those things were gone."

"You did?" gasped Clarissa.

Mother nodded. "Your grandma reminded me that the old furniture provided a living for us," she continued. "And many times your granddad served God by giving wood to people who didn't have any. Sometimes he also gave the mended furniture to people who needed it."

"I think Granddad had a neat job," Clarissa said.

"He made it neat by choosing to be happy and to serve God with a task that others saw as lowly," Mother said. "He knew that serving God was the best job."

Clarissa began to practice her scales. "I suppose my job could help make the janitor's work easier," she said.

"Then does this mean you'll be going back to school tomorrow?" Mother asked, and they both laughed. *NEK*

HOW ABOUT YOU?

Do you ever think that some of your chores are "dumb"? Are you embarrassed doing jobs you feel too grown up to do or that don't look important? Decide now to be willing to serve God in any way. Ask him to help you.

MEMORIZE:

"Work hard, but not just to please your masters when they are watching. As slaves of Christ, do the will of God with all your heart." *Ephesians 6:6*

 Serve God in All You Do

Open Your Mouth! (Read Luke 12:22-31)

25

AUGUST

"Just a minute, Cindy. Your bottle's almost ready," called Julie from the kitchen. She was watching her baby sister so Mother could work in the garden. Julie tested the bottle to make sure it was the right temperature. Then she got Cindy out of her crib and took her to the sofa. She laughed as she saw Cindy sucking on her hands. "Take your hands out of your mouth, silly!" she said. "How can I give you your bottle when your mouth is full of your own fingers?" Finally, she held the baby's hands down while she placed the nipple in Cindy's mouth. At last Cindy settled down and began to drink her bottle.

"What was wrong?" asked Mother when she came in. "I heard Cindy crying." Julie told her how Cindy sucked her own fingers instead of taking the bottle. Mother smiled. "Even older people sometimes act that way," she said.

"Older people refuse their food and suck their hands?" asked Julie with a laugh.

"In a way they do," replied Mother. "Christians often try to meet their own needs instead of letting God provide for them."

"Like how?" asked Julie. "Oh," she added, "I know! Like when you and Dad told me I couldn't hang around with Becky anymore because she was a bad influence. For a while, I was mad. I told you I had to run around with Becky, or I wouldn't have any good friends."

Mother nodded. "That was trying to meet your own needs," she said. "It wasn't long before God helped you find a new best friend." She looked at Cindy, who was now sleeping on Julie's lap, as she added, "Sometimes we forget that God always wants what's best for us." *SLK*

HOW ABOUT YOU?

Do you think you need clothes, money, a new friend, or maybe a feeling of being important? God can provide you with everything you need. Instead of trying to make yourself happy, turn to him in obedience. Remove those things from your life that may be interfering with his plan. Trust him. He will provide.

MEMORIZE:

"And this same God who takes care of me will supply all your needs from his glorious riches, which have been given to us in Christ Jesus." *Philippians 4:19*

 God Meets All Needs

Why Mosquitoes? (Read Genesis 1:21-31)

26

"I hate mosquitoes!" Nancy said, slapping her arm. All evening she and her brother, Jason, had been bothered by the pesky insects, but the kids didn't want to go inside the cabin. They only got to spend one week each summer at the lake, and they didn't want to spend it inside! They decided to spray themselves with more repellent, so they ran up the hill to the cabin.

Their parents were sitting on the porch. "You two tired of playing already?" asked Dad.

"No, but we're getting eaten alive! We have to put more repellent on our arms and legs," Nancy explained.

"Why did God have to make mosquitoes anyhow?" Jason wondered.

"Well," Dad said, "mosquitoes might be a nuisance to you, but they are very important to dragonflies."

"And to purple martins," Mom said, smiling.

"And there are certain kinds of fish who eat mosquito larvae," Dad added.

"Wow!" Nancy said. "I didn't realize that!"

"Remember what God said after he created the earth?" Dad asked.

"Sure," said Jason. "We learned that in Sunday school. 'Then God looked over all he had made, and he saw that it was excellent in every way.'"

"Right," agreed Dad. "Everything God made has a purpose, but the fulfillment of that purpose has been affected by sin. That's why some things in the creation are now harmful and irritating. Someday in the future, God will restore harmony within creation. Then mosquitoes will no longer be a nuisance."

"Hmmm, I never thought about it that way, Dad!" Nancy said, grinning. "I can't wait for that day!" *LMW*

HOW ABOUT YOU?

Do you ever wonder why God made flies, mosquitoes, snakes and spiders? He made all things to be part of his plan, but sin has affected that plan. There is still a balance, however, and creation is dependent on itself for nourishment. And someday God will again restore harmony to the creation.

MEMORIZE:

"Then God looked over all he had made, and he saw that it was excellent in every way. This all happened on the sixth day." *Genesis 1:31*

 Everything Has a Purpose

Special Blood (Read Romans 5:6-11)

Zak was excited! He was spending a weekend with his grandparents. He loved them dearly, but one thing was wrong. Grandpa didn't know Jesus as his Savior. Grandpa said he'd made his own way all his life, and he sure didn't see any need to change now. Zak prayed that God would help him be a good witness.

27

AUGUST

On Saturday morning Grandpa and Zak went for a hike in the woods. They were having a fine time, when suddenly Grandpa tripped over a tree root. He fell on a piece of glass and cut his leg. Blood gushed out!

"Grandpa!" Zak exclaimed. "You need a doctor."

"Don't need a doctor," Grandpa grunted. "Never needed one before, and I don't need one now!" He attempted to stop the bleeding, but it appeared to be a very deep cut.

"Grandpa, you need help," Zak insisted.

"No one to help us anyway," Grandpa said faintly. He got up and tried to walk, but he soon had to sit down again.

"I'm going for help," Zak declared, and he rushed off. He murmured a prayer of thanks when he met some campers just entering the woods. They quickly offered their help, and soon Grandpa was on his way to the hospital. Later Zak told him what had happened. "You lost a lot of blood and needed a transfusion," Zak said. "Since you have a rare type of blood, they had to send to another hospital to get it. Without that blood, you would have died!" Zak saw Grandpa looking at the tubes carrying blood into his veins. "You know, Grandpa," Zak said, "that reminds me of Jesus' blood. You needed this blood to keep your earthly life, and you need Jesus' blood to save you and give you eternal life."

Grandpa blinked. "I always thought I could live on my own," he murmured, "but now I realize I can't. Tell me more about your Jesus." *JLH*

HOW ABOUT YOU?

Do you think you can manage your life by yourself? You can't get to heaven without Jesus. His blood was shed to purchase your salvation. Have you accepted his offer of eternal life?

MEMORIZE:

"In fact, we can say that according to the law of Moses, nearly everything was purified by sprinkling with blood. Without the shedding of blood, there is no forgiveness of sins."

Hebrews 9:22

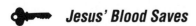 *Jesus' Blood Saves*

An Unjoyful Sound (Read Psalm 100)

28

As Eric and Darrin worked together painting a raft they had built, Darrin started singing. "Where in the world did you learn that?" Eric asked.

"Oh, it's on the latest album by the Mid Knight Witches," answered Darrin. "I bought it yesterday at the mall."

Eric looked up. "But you're a Christian!"

"So? The Bible doesn't say you can't listen to Mid Knight Witches' songs," replied Darrin. "Besides, I don't pay attention to the words."

Eric looked surprised. "You must pay some attention to them. You just got the CD yesterday, but you already know the words. Listen to what you're singing—'I'm going to steal you, kill you, chill you. . . .' Those words sound awful brutal."

"They don't mean anything, Eric," protested Darrin.

"They must mean something," retorted Eric.

The conversation with Darrin still bothered Eric that night. As he sat down to supper, he told his parents what Darrin had said.

"That's interesting," said Dad. "I just read an article in last night's paper about the Mid Knight Witches. The lead singer was quoted as saying he enjoyed the power the group had over young people's minds. He also said that violence was one of their major themes."

Eric was thoughtful for a few minutes, and then he said, "Darrin told me that the Bible doesn't say anything about listening to Mid Knight Witches' music, but it does! The Lord tells us to make a joyful noise, and the Mid Knight Witches' album certainly isn't joyful!"

"It also says we are to make melody in our heart to the Lord," his mother reminded him. Eric smiled and nodded. He had some important verses to show Darrin! *LMW*

HOW ABOUT YOU?

What kind of music do you listen to on your radio? What kind of albums do you buy? Do you think rock music is OK because you don't pay any attention to the words? Be careful! Often the lyrics in rock songs are not pleasing to the Lord. There are many good songs that are fun to sing.

MEMORIZE:

"Then you will sing psalms and hymns and spiritual songs among yourselves, making music to the Lord in your hearts." *Ephesians 5:19*

 *Choose Music Wisely*

Bouncing Quarters (Read Isaiah 53:3-7)

After Terri's big brother, Chad, led her to Jesus, they became best friends. Together they prayed for their parents who were unsaved.

When Chad left home to go to college, Terri was very upset. "Oh, Chad! How am I going to get along without you?" she cried. "I'm not a strong enough Christian yet to talk to Mom and Dad about my faith! I need you to help me!"

29
AUGUST

"Aw, c'mon, kiddo. You're stronger than you think," encouraged Chad. "Besides, the Lord is within you, and he'll help you. Remember the verse we learned that says, 'The Spirit who lives in you is greater than the spirit who lives in the world'? And keep busy with your friends from church—they'll help you, too."

The first days after Chad left were lonely ones for Terri. When her folks made cutting remarks about her faith in Jesus, she tried to do what she knew Jesus and Chad would expect her to do.

One day a letter came for Terri. "Hi, Sis," it said. "Miss me? Well, I hope so, 'cause I miss you! I have a nice roommate, and he says he's going to teach me to make a bed properly before the year is over. What do you think of that? His mom taught him that the sheets should be pulled so tight and tucked in so that if he drops a quarter on the bed, it will bounce. He said she used to inspect his bed, and if a quarter wouldn't bounce, he'd have to make the bed over again. Know what, Terri? The bouncing quarters made me think of you. It's almost like Mom and Dad are constantly inspecting your Christianity. If they 'drop' mean remarks on you and they bounce right off (in other words, if you don't get mean in return), then you passed that inspection. Just remember, Terri, Jesus told us to rejoice in persecution and pray for those who persecute us. I'm praying for you. Love you, Chad." *REP*

HOW ABOUT YOU?

Do you pass inspection when cruel remarks come your way? Jesus gave the best example when he patiently suffered for us. Surely we should be willing to do as much for him. Next time someone teases you because you won't fight or join in worldly activities, let the remarks bounce off.

MEMORIZE:

"God blesses you when you are mocked and persecuted and lied about because you are my followers." Matthew 5:11

 Don't Answer Back

The Box of Paints (Read 1 Corinthians 12:27-31)

Why didn't God give me musical talent too? thought Melissa as she listened to her family give a musical program. *I couldn't carry a tune if it were in a bucket.*

30

AUGUST

After church, she complained out loud. "It's not fair. All of you can play and sing, and I can't," she grumbled. "I feel stupid sitting there—the only Miller not in the program. I wish I could have a part, too."

"We'd like you to join us, Melissa, but . . . we don't know how to use a bullfrog," teased her brother.

"That was uncalled for, Bill," said Mother, noticing the hurt look on Melissa's face. "Melissa may not have musical talent, but she has other talents." She turned to her daughter. "You like to draw pictures," she reminded Melissa. "Maybe that's a special talent God has given you."

"That's nothing," protested Melissa. "I want to be musical, like all of you."

The next afternoon when Dad came home, he handed Melissa a box. "Here are some paints for you," he said.

"Thanks, Dad!" squealed Melissa. Quickly she opened the box. "There must be a mistake," she wailed. "There's only blue here. I can't paint pictures with only one color."

"It takes different colors to paint pretty pictures, doesn't it?" agreed Dad. He handed her another box.

Melissa nodded as she eagerly looked over a variety of colors in the second box. "But why did you give me only blue at first?" she asked.

"I wanted you to see how uninteresting it would be if all people were alike," answered Dad. "God gives each person different abilities for doing his work."

Slowly Melissa nodded. "Like having only one color to paint with," she said. "I guess God would rather have me paint than sing. So I'll try to do the best I can." *MRP*

HOW ABOUT YOU?

Have you discovered your own special talents? Maybe you can't sing or paint, but perhaps you're good at math or helping with housework. Whatever your abilities are, develop them the best you can. God may have a special use for them someday.

MEMORIZE:

"Whatever you do, do well. For when you go to the grave, there will be no work or planning or knowledge or wisdom."

Ecclesiastes 9:10

 Use Your Talents

Warm-Water Drink (Read Revelation 3:14-19)

It was still dark when Dennis woke up. *I'd sure like a cold drink of water,* he thought to himself. Getting out of bed, he stumbled to the bathroom. *The light will hurt my eyes,* he thought sleepily. *I can find a cup in the dark.* He did. Then he turned on the water and let it run a bit so it would be nice and cold. He took a sip, but immediately spat it out. "Yuk!" he said. Instead of nice, cold water, it was warm! Dennis realized he had turned on the hot water faucet by mistake and had let it run just long enough to get warm. He quickly turned on the cold water. This time he tested it with his finger before filling his cup. *Ahh, that's much better,* he thought.

31
AUGUST

The next morning Dennis told his family about his warm drink. Everyone chuckled, and Dad reached for his Bible. He turned to Revelation 3 (see today's Scripture) and read that passage for family devotions. "Dennis, I think you've helped us understand these verses," he said. "You see, God was telling a group of Christians that they were not very excited about him. To him, they were like lukewarm water."

"Apparently their worldly possessions made them feel self-sufficient," added Mother, "and their love for God became lukewarm. I wonder if a lot of us aren't like that."

"I'm afraid so," said Dad. "We know we should serve God, so we do."

"But when we don't do it very enthusiastically we're like lukewarm water, right?" asked Dennis.

"Right," said Dad. "Let's be sure the real reason we serve him is because we love him and not because we feel it's our duty."

CLG

HOW ABOUT YOU?

Are you a lukewarm Christian? Do you go to church only because your parents make you go? Do you hurry through devotions? Do you give your money to God just because you know you're supposed to? Ask God to increase your genuine love for him.

MEMORIZE:

"I know all the things you do, that you are neither hot nor cold. I wish you were one or the other!" *Revelation 3:15*

 **Love God Sincerely**

Treasure for Trinkets (Read Hebrews 11:23-29)

1

"You may take this for show-and-tell, Jill, but take good care of it," said Mother as she handed her daughter a book. "Grandma Andrews used this reader when she was in third grade."

Jill eagerly took the book as she and her brother, Jason, started for the door.

When the children came home from school that afternoon, Jill was all smiles. "Just look what Nikki brought for show-and-tell," she squealed, pulling a music box from her schoolbag. She wound it, and a little bird on the top spun around as the music played. "Isn't it cute?"

"Yes," said Mother, "but what are you doing with Nikki's music box?"

"We traded," said Jill happily. "I gave her Grandma Andrews's reader."

"Oh, Jill, you didn't!" interrupted Mother. "You can easily replace a music box like that, but you can't buy a reader anywhere that would be as valuable to me as the one Grandma Andrews used!"

"I'm sorry!" said Jill as tears filled her eyes.

Mother sighed. "Well, you should have known better than to trade," she said as she left the room to answer the telephone. When she returned, she was smiling. "That was Nikki's mother. She recognized the value of Grandma Andrews's reader. Take Nikki's music box to school tomorrow, Jill, and she'll return our book."

"OK," agreed Jill, but she looked sadly at the music box.

"What you did reminds me of what we studied in history," said Jason. "When the French traders first came to America, they tricked the Indians into trading things like gold and silver for worthless little trinkets."

Mother sighed. "I'm afraid we all do things like that," she said. "We often have more time for things like TV, video games, and soccer than we have for Sunday school lessons and devotions. Which do you think are the most valuable?" *BJW*

HOW ABOUT YOU?

How do you spend your time? Do you make time to spend with Jesus each day? Your relationship with him is your most valuable treasure.

MEMORIZE:

"And how do you benefit if you gain the whole world but lose your own soul in the process? Is anything worth more than your soul?" Matthew 16:26

 Hold on to What's Truly Valuable

Eyes on the Highway (Read Psalm 5:1-8; Hebrew 12:1-3)

2

SEPTEMBER

Drew, who had recently gotten his driver's license, was taking his young brother, Tyler, to a ball game. All the way, Tyler kept up a constant chatter about the upcoming game. He was excited because he was the starting pitcher on his team. "I know I can strike all of them out," he boasted.

Keeping his eyes on the road, Drew replied, "Don't be so sure. This team beat you badly last year."

"Yeah, but we've really practiced hard this year," said Tyler. "We'll win this time."

As Tyler continued to talk, Drew nodded his head in agreement from time to time. "I'd like to get so good that I could be in the big leagues!" exclaimed Tyler. "Wouldn't that make you proud of me?" Then Tyler frowned as he looked at his big brother. "Hey, Drew, I don't think you're really paying attention," he complained. "You're not looking at me."

Drew laughed. "Oh, I'm listening all right," he said. "But Dad gave me some pretty heavy instructions before letting me take the car. One of the things he said was that I should be sure to keep my eyes on the highway at all times. In fact, I practically got a whole sermon on that subject!"

"Yeah?" asked Tyler.

"Yeah," said Drew. "Dad said driving was sort of like living for Jesus. He said many people have wrecked their cars by letting their eyes stray from the highway—just as people have wrecked their lives by letting their eyes stray from Jesus."

"Oh," murmured Tyler. Suddenly he sat up straight. "Now in baseball, you have to keep your eyes on the ball. . . ." *BJT*

HOW ABOUT YOU?

Do you study God's Word, listen to your Sunday school teacher and pastor, read Christian books, listen to Christian broadcasts, and learn how to live for God? You can't live as the world lives and let Jesus have the place he should have in your life.

MEMORIZE:

"Let us fix our eyes on Jesus, the author and perfecter of our faith." *Hebrews 12:2,* NIV

 Keep Your Eyes on Jesus

Brownies and Anger (Read 1 Corinthians 13:1-7)

3

SEPTEMBER

Janet sat with her family at dinner and picked at her food. Even the brownies, her favorite dessert, didn't interest her.

It was Janet's night to do dishes. She silently loaded plates into the dishwasher and washed and dried pans. "What's the matter, honey?" Mother asked as she set aside a brownie for Janet and handed her the empty pan.

"It's Sharon!" exclaimed Janet angrily. "She knew how much I wanted the lead part in the play, so she wasn't even going to try out. Then today she changed her mind, and Mrs. Parker gave her the lead. I got the part of her sister, and I have only a few lines."

"Well, honey, maybe Sharon really wanted that part as much as you did," said Mother. "Maybe she waited to try out because she couldn't make up her mind about doing it, since she knew you wanted it."

"Well, I think it was really mean of her to take it," insisted Janet. "I'm going to call her tonight and tell her what I think of her."

Mother watched Janet scrubbing at the pan the brownies had baked in. There were places where they had stuck and baked on tight. "Why don't you let that soak till morning?" suggested Mother. "It will come off quite easily then." After a moment, she added, "I think you should let your anger 'soak,' too. Before you call Sharon, why don't you pray about it tonight and see how you feel in the morning? Ask the Lord how he wants you to handle things." Janet looked doubtful, but she agreed.

When Janet washed the brownie pan the next morning, she turned to Mother. "You're right—this washes easily now," Janet said with a grin.

"Good," said Mother. "And how about Sharon?"

"You were right about that, too," admitted Janet. "I realize she didn't try out for the part just to hurt me. I'm glad I didn't call her. Next time I'm mad, I'm going to remember the brownie pan and let my anger 'soak' before I say anything!" *KEC*

HOW ABOUT YOU?

Do you remember that love is patient and kind? When you're angry with someone, do you let your anger "soak" while you pray for a solution?

MEMORIZE:

"A fool gives full vent to anger, but a wise person quietly holds it back." *Proverbs 29:11*

 *Let Anger "Soak"*

Who Gives God Counsel? (Read Romans 11:33-36)

4

SEPTEMBER

Justin parked his bike in the garage. He could hear his mom on the phone talking with a friend about praying for rain for the dry yards and gardens. When he went in, she motioned for him to begin shucking the ears of corn that were lying on the table.

"Mom, I don't care if you pray for rain," said Justin a little later. "But please don't pray for it to come on Saturday. That's the day of our big soccer game, and I don't want it rained out. Besides . . ." Justin chuckled, "if you pray for rain and I pray for sunshine, God might be pretty confused!"

Mom stopped stirring the pudding and turned to look at Justin. "I'm not going to pray for rain on Saturday. But even if I did, I don't think God would be confused." She pointed to the ears of corn. "How much corn do you have there, anyway?"

Justin counted the ears. "Nine ears," he said.

"Well," said Mom, "what if you and Dad wanted three ears of corn, and Sarah and I each wanted two? Would there be enough?"

"No. We'd be one short. And besides, Dad always gets three ears because he needs more food than we do. You'd probably tell me no," Justin answered.

"That's right," replied Mom. "But if you asked for another ear, I might buy you an extra one next time. But tonight I'd have to say no because Dad needs more food than you do. God is kind of like that, too. If you ask for sunshine and I ask for rain, God would have to say no to one of our requests, but it would not confuse him. He is the wisest person in the whole universe. Now let's get this corn on the stove so we can eat it," she said. *PEJ*

HOW ABOUT YOU?

Have you ever wondered if God gets confused about how to answer prayers when people ask for opposite things? Because he is all-wise and all-knowing, it's not a problem to him. Read Romans 11:33 and 34 again. Remember, God knows everything, and nothing confuses him!

MEMORIZE:

"Oh, what a wonderful God we have! How great are his riches and wisdom and knowledge! How impossible it is for us to understand his decisions and his methods!" *Romans 11:33*

 God Is All-Knowing

Watch Out! (Read Titus 2:1-8)

5

SEPTEMBER

Mr. Brock's van was packed full of kids—his own children plus several of their friends. They were on their way to Kids' Club, and the noise level in the car was at its usual high pitch. Mr. Brock listened to the chatter good-naturedly until he pulled onto Route 40. "OK, kids," he said, "I'm going to ask you to be quiet for the next few miles. The road is under construction here, and I need to pay close attention—especially where it narrows to one lane."

"Your dad says that every week," Mandy whispered to Jason.

For a while, the kids were quiet. Then one of the boys playfully punched another boy. That boy punched back. Before long, a book went flying through the car, hitting Mr. Brock on the back of the head. He jerked the steering wheel, and the van gave a crazy turn toward the oncoming lane of traffic. "Watch out!" someone screamed.

Mr. Brock gripped the wheel and pulled off on the side of the road. Then he talked to the children about how important it was for them to sit quietly.

When they arrived at Kids' Club, the children were still excited over what had happened. Their teacher, Mrs. Grady, heard all about it. She shook her head. "You know," she said, "it's not easy driving a car full of boys and girls. In fact, it's a huge responsibility. And Mr. Brock needs all of you to act like mature young people. When the apostle Paul wrote to Titus, he said that one of the qualifications of a maturing young person is wise thinking. In your situation, what would have been the wise thing to do?"

"To talk softly and not to goof around when Mr. Brock was driving," answered Mandy.

"That's right," replied Mrs. Grady. "And fortunately, you'll get a retest on the way home tonight. And I hope you all will pass the maturity test!" *LMW*

HOW ABOUT YOU?

Do you ride on a school bus? Or do your parents or a friend's parents drive you different places? Do you goof off or fight or yell? Next time you're in a bus or car with other kids, be courteous and quiet. Thank the driver for picking you up. Thank the Lord for that driver, too.

MEMORIZE:

"In the same way, encourage the young men to live wisely in all they do." *Titus 2:6*

 Be a Courteous Passenger

Things That Hurt (Read Matthew 7:9-11)

6

SEPTEMBER

Brian stomped into the kitchen. "I didn't make the soccer team, Mom," he said.

"Oh, Brian, I'm so sorry," his mother said, trying to console him.

Brian punched his soccer ball. "I practiced every day for a month," he said. "Jason and Matt made the team. Now they'll be gone all the time, and I won't have anybody to hang around with."

"You can still be on the city team," Mother reminded him.

Brian threw himself onto a chair. "You know what hurts the most?" he asked. "I prayed every day about it. God knows how much I wanted to make the team, and he didn't let me. Why, Mom?"

Just then the screen door slammed, and Brian's new puppy, Chessie, bounded into the room, followed by Brian's dad. Dad set his briefcase down. "Brian, did you remember that we have an appointment with the vet today?" he asked. "Chessie needs to get a rabies shot."

Brian stared at the puppy's dark trusting eyes. "That shot will hurt Chessie, Dad," he protested. "I don't want to take him. Maybe he won't like me anymore."

Dad sat down next to Brian. "Would you rather take a chance on letting Chessie get rabies and die?" Brian solemnly shook his head. "Son," continued Dad, "even though the shot will hurt for a moment, Chessie trusts you."

Brian picked up Chessie and headed for the door. "OK, Dad. Let's go," he said.

Mother broke in. "I know you hate to do anything that allows your dog to suffer, even though you know it's the best for him," she said. "But have you ever thought how hard it must be for God to let something happen that may hurt you—even though he knows it's best for you?"

Brian paused. "So . . . I guess I need to trust him about this soccer thing. It'll be tough, but I'll try."

"That's all he asks," Mother answered with a smile. *LRS*

HOW ABOUT YOU?

When disappointments come, do you wonder if God still cares about you? Remember that God always knows what's best. Ask him to help you trust him even when you're disappointed.

MEMORIZE:

"Trust in the Lord with all your heart; do not depend on your own understanding." *Proverbs 3:5*

 God Cares and Knows Best

Do You See What I See? (Read Hebrews 10:25-37)

7

SEPTEMBER

Kelly skipped home with her new library book. Her ponytail bounced along behind her as she came to her driveway. "Mom! Mom! I got it! It's finally my turn to have the Magic Eye book," she called.

"What's a Magic Eye book?" Mom asked.

"Oh, they're these books that are only pictures. If you look long and hard, there's another picture that comes out," explained Kelly.

"Oh, I know what you mean," said Mom, "but I never can see the picture."

"Here . . . hold it up to your eyes like this," said Kelly, holding the book right up to her mom's face. "Then pull it away real slow. Keep your eyes in one spot—you'll probably feel like you're getting cross-eyed." She paused. "It's a cat. Can you see anything yet? Sometimes it takes a while."

"I don't see anything but squiggly lines of color," Mom said.

Kelly's dad came into the kitchen, and Kelly handed him the book. Then she explained how to look for the cat. He found it on the fourth try. Mom tried again, but she soon gave up.

When they sat down to eat, Dad thanked God for the food. "You know, Kelly," he said, "your Magic Eye pictures remind me of how hard it is to tell people about Jesus. We know he's there, but sometimes it's hard to explain that to people and get them to see him."

Kelly nodded thoughtfully. "I tried and tried to help Sarah understand about Jesus," she said, "but she just didn't get it."

"Well, I had to try four times before I could see the cat, but I finally found it," said Dad. "So keep trying to explain to Sarah about Jesus. We'll pray about it, too, because it's really God who helps people to understand about him." *NMS*

HOW ABOUT YOU?

Do you get tired of trying to tell your friends about Jesus? Do you feel as though you're not getting through to them? You must keep trying. Sometimes it takes a while before they understand.

MEMORIZE:

"Patient endurance is what you need now, so you will continue to do God's will. Then you will receive all that he has promised." *Hebrews 10:36*

 Keep Telling about Jesus

Whipping Boy (Read Isaiah 53:3-12)

The Whipping Boy. Keeshan read the title of the book Mother had brought from the library. "Mother, what's a whipping boy?" he asked.

Mother smiled. "I didn't know that myself," she told him, "but look . . . here on the back cover it says that royal families used whipping boys. It says it's a boy who was educated with a prince and punished in his place."

8

SEPTEMBER

Keeshan frowned. "You mean he was punished for the wrong things the prince did? I bet that made him mad! I wonder if the boy in this story ran away," said Keeshan.

"I don't think so," said Mother. "According to the description on the cover of the book, this story is about a boy who *offered* to take the place of one who deserved to be punished."

"Who would do that?" exclaimed Keeshan. "It's so unfair."

"Yes," agreed Mother. "But I know someone who had so much love for others that, in a way, he volunteered to become a whipping boy."

Keeshan stared at Mother to see if she was serious. "I thought that was something people did long ago," he said. "Who do you know that did that?"

"I was thinking of Jesus," answered Mother quietly. "The Bible doesn't use the words 'whipping boy,' but I think of what Jesus did for us. He willingly went to the cross and died for us."

"That's right!" exclaimed Keeshan. "Jesus wasn't just whipped for our sins, he *died* on a cross for us because he loved us, didn't he?"

Mother nodded. "And that means we can be forgiven and go to live with him in heaven," she said. "How we should thank him that he cared that much about us! And how we should show our appreciation by living to please him!" *MMP*

HOW ABOUT YOU?

Have you thanked Jesus for taking your "whipping" and dying for you? Have you asked him to forgive your sins? If not and you're interested in finding out more, talk to a trusted adult.

MEMORIZE:

"Christ also suffered when he died for our sins once for all time. He never sinned, but he died for sinners that he might bring us safely home to God."

1 Peter 3:18

 Jesus Took Your Punishment

Spilled Milk (Read Matthew 7:1-5)

9
SEPTEMBER

"You'll never believe what Carl did in school today," announced Eric.

"What did he do this time?" asked Dad. Eric's family was getting used to hearing about Carl every night at dinner.

"First, he got sent to the principal for cheating on the spelling test," said Eric. "Then when he came back, he wrote a nasty poem about Mrs. Sanderson and passed it to the kid in front of him. He got caught and had to go to the principal again!" Eric said. "I would never do the things he does."

Just then Eric's little brother, Tim, bumped his glass. Milk spilled into Eric's lap. "Hey, clumsy!" yelled Eric. "These are my new jeans!"

"You don't need to yell, Eric," said Dad, as Eric jumped up and Tim began to cry. "It was an accident. And please don't call your brother names," Dad added.

"He should be more careful," snapped Eric.

After the mess was mopped up and Eric had changed his jeans, Mom said, "You know, Eric, you've been telling us about all the bad things Carl does and how you would never do those things. But it seems to me you have the same problem Carl has."

Eric was stunned. "What do you mean?" he demanded. "I'm not like Carl at all."

Dad nodded. "Yes, you are," he said. "The Bible tells us we're all sinners. And it warns us not to judge others when there's sin in our own lives. After all, who's to say what's worse—cheating on a test or hurting someone with our anger?"

Eric's face turned red. "I . . . I'm sorry, Tim," he mumbled.

Dad smiled. "The difference between you and Carl may be that you know Jesus as your Savior; perhaps Carl doesn't. Instead of judging him, we need to pray that he'll come to know Jesus, too."

LJO

HOW ABOUT YOU?

Do you easily notice the sins of others but have a hard time admitting your own sins? Acknowledge your sin to God and ask him for forgiveness and help in overcoming it. Then be careful not to judge others.

MEMORIZE:

"Stop judging others, and you will not be judged." *Matthew 7:1*

 *Admit Your Own Sin*

Letting Go (Read Psalm 20:1-7)

Jen dug her paddle into the water with powerful, even strokes. "Dad! Look over there!" she exclaimed as their canoe reached a rough stretch of water. Up ahead, an overturned canoe was drifting downstream. A woman was desperately clinging to a tree that had fallen partially across the river.

"Help me!" cried the woman as Jen and Dad approached.

"Jen, if we get too close to her, she might panic and grab our canoe," Dad warned. "It won't help her if we tip over too. We need to maneuver around and get just downstream from her." With Jen's rapid strokes providing forward momentum, Dad expertly turned their canoe around the tree and just beyond the stranded woman. "Let go of the tree limb, and let the river take you downstream!" Dad shouted. "We'll pick you up."

"I can't," replied the woman fearfully. "The current will pull me under."

"Your life jacket will keep your head above water," Dad assured her. He finally persuaded the young woman to release her hold from the tree, and she floated downstream to safety.

Later that afternoon Jen couldn't stop talking about what had happened. "That lady was so scared, Mom," she said. "She was hanging onto that tree like her life depended on it. But that tree couldn't get her to safety. She had to let it go and trust her life jacket. When she did, it took her to safety."

"She was relying on the wrong thing for help, wasn't she?" asked Mom. "Sometimes we're just like her. When things go wrong, we rely on things we shouldn't—we become desperate. Only when everything else we try has failed do we ask God for assistance. God should be our first resort, not our last."

"He is sort of like our life jacket," added Jen.

"That's right," said her dad. "When we depend on him, he will carry us safely through life's currents." *LMM*

10

SEPTEMBER

HOW ABOUT YOU?

When you have a problem, do you turn to God right away? Or do you first try everything else you can think of? Do you figure your parents, teachers, or friends will take care of your problem? They can be a help, but you also need to depend on God. He is always with you and ready to help.

MEMORIZE:

"Keep me safe, O God, for I have come to you for refuge."

Psalm 16:1

 Turn to God First

No Comfort (Read Romans 3:19, 23-28)

11

SEPTEMBER

One day Greg noticed that two of his friends, Randy and Bob, were passing notes back and forth in their class at school. *They better watch it,* he thought. *Mrs. Barnes doesn't like that. She said anybody passing notes has to stay in at recess.* Greg decided to warn the other boys, so he wrote a note reminding them to be careful.

As Greg slipped his note to Randy, Mrs. Barnes looked up. "Greg, Randy, and Bob—you will all stay in at recess time today," she said sternly. And stay in they did.

That evening Greg complained about his punishment. "All I wrote was one little note!" he said. "The other boys wrote a whole lot more."

"But you did write one, and so you did deserve the punishment, didn't you?" asked Mother. Greg had to admit that was true.

"As you stayed in, did you find any comfort in the fact that you were not, as you say, as bad as the other boys?" Dad wanted to know. Greg shook his head. "I didn't think so," said Dad. "You see, what happened to you at school reminds me of Pastor Rogers's sermon last Sunday. He pointed out that some people think they're not so bad—and maybe they really aren't as bad as someone else. But God says that no one is good enough to get to heaven. All deserve to be punished and cannot enter heaven apart from accepting Jesus. When a person stands before God, the thought that someone else was worse than he will be of no comfort either."

HWM

HOW ABOUT YOU?

Do you think that others are worse than you? That won't make you feel any better when you are punished. But believing that Jesus died to take your punishment and accepting him as Savior will make all the difference in the world! Talk to a trusted adult about it.

MEMORIZE:

"For all have sinned; all fall short of God's glorious standard." *Romans 3:23*

 Everyone Is a Sinner

What's Inside? (Read James 2:1, 5, 8-9)

Tammy carefully placed a small cardboard box in her desk at school. She had brought it to show the class. It contained an art project she had done at home. With just a little help from Grandma, it had turned out nicely.

When Mrs. Sims finally called on Tammy to show the class her project, she took the box out of her desk, carried it to the front of the room, and set it on the table. She opened the lid and carefully lifted the art project out of the box. "This is a cocoon," she said. "I made it out of papier-mâché."

12
SEPTEMBER

"It sure is ugly!" one of the boys called out.

"Well, cocoons are ugly," replied Tammy, "but you haven't seen all of it yet." She tore open the back side of the cocoon and brought out a tiny white-and-yellow ceramic butterfly.

"Hey! Neat! That's really pretty!" one of the girls exclaimed.

"Nice job, Tammy," said her teacher. "The beautiful butterfly that develops inside the cocoon is a good reminder that outer appearances aren't as important as what's inside."

That afternoon Tammy walked home from school with her friend Sarah. "What do you think of the new girl in our class?" Sarah asked.

Tammy shrugged. "I talked to her for only a few minutes at recess, but she seemed nice to me."

"She sure dresses funny," observed Sarah. "And those glasses she wears make her look real goofy."

Tammy frowned. "Well, as Mrs. Sims said when I showed my art project . . . appearance isn't so important. We talked about that in Sunday school too, remember? We learned that God looks at our heart and not at our outward appearance. We need to try to do that with the new girl, too." *WEB*

HOW ABOUT YOU?

Do you judge people by what they're like inside, not by the way they look? Remember that God looks at the heart, and so should you. You can't look inside people the way God can, but you can talk with them and get to know them. Don't make hasty judgments.

MEMORIZE:

"**Stop judging by mere appearances, and make a right judgment.**" *John 7:24,* NIV

 Don't Judge by Outer Appearance

Spiritual Muscle (Read Isaiah 40:28-31)

13

<small>**SEPTEMBER**</small>

Michael tried to slip into the house quietly after school, but Mom heard the door close and called out, "Is that you, Michael?"

"Yes," answered Michael reluctantly.

"Come tell me about your day," said Mom.

"I finished the book I was reading for my report. I did well in track practice. And my coach says I might win the fifty-yard dash next week."

"That's great. Did you tell your teacher about the mistake on your grade?" Mom asked.

Michael stared at his shoe. "No. I sorta forgot," he mumbled.

"You forgot?" she asked.

Feeling ashamed, he said, "I didn't really forget. . . . It's just that math is my lowest grade. If I tell Mr. Thomas about the mistake, I'll have an even lower grade on my report card." He sighed. "I know it's the right thing to do, but I couldn't make myself do it."

Mom set some cookies in the oven and turned to Michael. "Do you remember how sore your legs were when you first started running track?" she asked.

"I sure do!" exclaimed Michael. "It's not so hard now, though."

"Developing the muscles of your spirit is like developing the muscles of your body," Mom told him. "At first it's hard. But if you keep at it, you get stronger. Doing what's right is hard, too, but you get stronger in your spirit when you practice."

"Even if it hurts at first?" asked Michael.

"Even if it hurts," said Mother.

Michael nodded. "I'll tell Mr. Thomas tomorrow," he promised, "even if it hurts." *KEC*

HOW ABOUT YOU?

Do you develop your spiritual muscles by choosing to do what is honest and right? The more you practice, the easier it becomes. Don't forget to exercise your spirit as well as your body.

MEMORIZE:

"The Lord is more pleased when we do what is just and right than when we give him sacrifices." *Proverbs 21:3*

 Do What Is Right

Gone Fishin' (Read John 6:32-35)

Donnie sighed. He wished a fish would take his bait. When the line finally jiggled, he jerked it up quickly, but there was no fish and part of the worm was gone. "That's the one that got away," said Grandpa with a chuckle. "Try again." Grandpa helped Donnie bait the hook.

After a while Donnie pulled up a fish. "I got one this time," he yelled.

After Donnie and Grandpa caught several more fish, Grandpa stuck the oars in the water and rowed for shore.

14

SEPTEMBER

"Did you know that Jesus once talked to his disciples about fishing?" asked Grandpa as he rowed. "Some of them had fished for a living, so they understood fish talk. Jesus told them they could be fishers of people."

Donnie wrinkled up his nose. "I know," he said. "We sing that song in Sunday school, but I don't get it. How do you fish for people?"

"You offer them food—spiritual food—just like you offered worms to the fish," replied Grandpa. "Jesus called himself the 'Bread of Life,' so telling others about him is like offering them food."

"Sometimes they don't bite, though, do they?" Donnie asked.

Grandpa shook his head. "Nope," he said. "Some don't want to hear about Jesus at all. And others are like the fish that only nibble. They're sort of interested, but not too much, and they leave after hearing only a little about Jesus. But other people are like the fish we caught." Grandpa's eyes sparkled like the water around the boat. "They want to know all they can, and they eventually receive Jesus as Savior."

Donnie grinned as he admired the fish in the bucket. "So we have to keep fishin', don't we?" he said. "Even when it seems like they're not bitin'. We have to keep telling people about Jesus."

CEY

HOW ABOUT YOU?

Would you like to be a fisher of people? Then watch for opportunities to talk about the Lord. When you get a chance, mention little things about God. You might say you're thankful for the beautiful day God has made. Or you can tell someone about something special God has done for you.

MEMORIZE:

"Come, be my disciples, and I will show you how to fish for people!" *Mark 1:17*

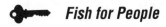 **Fish for People**

No More Jonahs (Read Jonah 3:1-4, 10; 4:1-4, 11)

15
SEPTEMBER

Jean was almost home when she suddenly felt water splashing on her as the new boy next door whizzed by and slammed on the brakes in his driveway. He had raced his bike right through the big puddle next to the sidewalk. He laughed as he looked back to see her reaction. *No, I won't say anything,* Jean thought. *I won't even look at him.* Shaking off as much water as possible, she ran up the walk and around to the kitchen door.

Mother looked up in surprise as Jean entered. "Look what Joe the Jerk did," Jean wailed. "And they want *me* to invite *him* to the youth rally next Saturday. Well, I'm not going to do it!"

Mother came over to help her daughter dry off. "It wasn't very nice of him to do this," she said, "but I think he does need to be invited to the rally."

"Then let someone else ask him," Jean said. "He's too mean."

"Maybe that makes him a good candidate for the rally," suggested Mother. "He needs to see that he has to have his sins forgiven."

"Well, I don't want him to be forgiven!" Jean cried. "I want him to be punished."

Mother sat down. "You sound like Jonah," she said.

"Jonah?" asked Jean. "How am I like that?"

"Jonah was supposed to give the people in the city of Nineveh God's warning of destruction, and at first he refused. After his episode with the fish, he did tell them, and they repented and were saved. But Jonah didn't like that. He thought they should be punished. He seemed to think he knew better than God how they should be treated."

Jean looked at her mother. "Oh . . . right," she said slowly. "I guess I don't want to be a Jonah." She sighed. "I'll change my clothes and go see Joe the Jerk—I mean Joey—and invite him to the rally." *HAD*

HOW ABOUT YOU?

Are you willing to tell everyone the good news of Jesus? Or are there some kids you want to see punished someday? What if someone had decided not to tell *you?*

MEMORIZE:

"And then he [Jesus] told them, 'Go into all the world and preach the Good News to everyone, everywhere.'"

Mark 16:15

 Tell Everyone the Good News

The Rough Edges (Read 2 Peter 1:5-11)

"Mornin'. What have you got there?" called Mr. Walker.

"Good morning, Mr. Walker. This is a porch swing," said Brent as Mr. Walker came up onto the porch.

"Looks a bit worn out," observed Mr. Walker. "You fixin' to paint it?"

"Yes, sir," Brent replied. "Mom got it at a garage sale."

"Paintin' it white, eh? If it was me, I'd paint it green."

Brent took a deep breath. "My mother wants it white."

"You gonna paint wearin' that good shirt?" Brent ignored the comment as he dipped his brush into the paint. Then Mr. Walker grabbed his arm. "Wait a minute there. . . . You can't paint yet. Where's your sandpaper?"

"I don't need sandpaper," said Brent through clenched teeth.

"Sure you do. You've gotta sand it down before you put on the new paint."

Brent was about to tell the old man to mind his own business when Mother called him to the telephone. After he finished his phone call, Brent exploded. "Mr. Walker makes me so mad! He criticizes everything I do." He mimicked the old man. "You shouldn't wear that good shirt when you paint! You shouldn't paint without sanding first."

"Hmmm, sounds like good advice," she said. "That is a good shirt, so please change it. And you do need to sand off the rough spots and the peeling paint. If you paint right over the peeling paint, the new paint won't last long."

"Mom, you're criticizing, too," Brent complained.

"Criticism isn't always bad, Brent," said Mother. "It's a little like the sandpaper you're going to use. God can use criticism to knock rough spots off our characters. Accepting constructive criticism helps us to grow."

Brent sighed. "Well, between you and Mr. Walker, I ought to become a pretty smooth character," he teased as he went to change his shirt and look for sandpaper. *BJW*

16
SEPTEMBER

HOW ABOUT YOU?

Do you resent criticism? It's a sign of spiritual maturity when you can take it with a good attitude. The Lord will often use others to show you where you need to change. Accept constructive criticism to knock off the rough spots in your character.

MEMORIZE:

"Fools think they need no advice, but the wise listen to others." *Proverbs 12:15*

 *Accept Criticism*

Do It Right (Read Galatians 6:7-10)

17

SEPTEMBER

Tammy was proud of the cake she had baked. She lifted it from the oven and set it on the cake rack. "Can I turn it out on a plate now?" she asked Mother.

Mother shook her head. "This recipe says to let it cool a little first," she said.

After Mother left the kitchen, Tammy looked at her lovely cake. It was smooth and round on the top. She couldn't wait to frost it! So using pot holders, she picked up the cake pan and shook it over a plate. To her surprise, only a part of her beautiful cake fell onto the plate. Tammy stared at it in horror. Then she burst into tears.

Mother hurried into the kitchen. When she saw what had happened, she shook her head. "You didn't wait, did you?" she asked. "You know, honey, waiting is the only way to do some things right."

"But it's hard to wait," wailed Tammy.

"It *is* hard, but it pays," said Mother. "Do you remember last year when we grew those giant sunflowers and you were going to roast the seeds? The first time you tried it, they weren't quite ripe enough. Remember what happened?"

"I remember," said Tammy. "They were hard to get out of the shells."

"What happened when you waited two weeks and tried again?" asked Mother.

"They fell right out into my hands," said Tammy.

Mother nodded. "That's right," she said. "Through nature, God shows us the importance of patience. He knows how much happier we'll be—how much more content—when we've learned that lesson." She picked up the cake pan and used a spatula to get the rest of the cake out. "You know what?" she said. "We'll glue this cake together with extra frosting, and no one will notice that it broke."

Tammy grinned. "All right!" she said. "And after this I'm going to remember to let cakes cool and to let sunflower seeds ripen and . . . and . . . and to be patient about everything!" *KEC*

HOW ABOUT YOU?

Are you a patient person? God wants you to be. He wants you to do your best in all that you do, and that often takes time.

MEMORIZE:

"Be patient with everyone."

1 Thessalonians 5:14

 **Develop Patience**

The Night Desert (Read Joshua 1:7-9)

18

SEPTEMBER

Sondra pushed open the screen door of the ranch house and started down the desert path to their nearest neighbors, the Stricklins. She was going over to play with Kellie Stricklin, her best friend. "Get home before dark," Mom called.

"OK," replied Sondra. She had no intention of being out after dark anyway. She loved the desert. She loved the prickly plants, the shining rocks, and the hot sand. But at night, desert breezes whistled eerily through the brush. It was easy to imagine stumbling over a rattlesnake or feeling the fuzzy legs of a tarantula. Also, coyotes prowled the edge of the ranch during the night looking for a lone calf. Their eyes glowed in the moonlight, and their way of slinking along told Sondra that they were up to no good.

As Sondra approached the Stricklins' ranch, Kellie saw her coming and ran to meet her. "Want to swing?" asked Kellie. "And did you bring your swimsuit? Mom said we could run through the sprinklers if we want to." Soon the girls were squealing and shouting as they played.

Later, while Kellie's mom cooked, the girls sat at the kitchen table, coloring. "I need to leave soon," said Sondra as she glanced out the window. But she became so interested in what they were doing that she forgot the time.

When Kellie's dad came in from work, Sondra realized it was already getting dark outside. She jumped up. "I've gotta get home!" she exclaimed. She thought of the cactus, the rattlesnakes, and the tarantulas. When she thought of the coyotes, tears filled her eyes.

Mrs. Stricklin noticed. "Don't be afraid, Sondra," she said, giving her a hug. "Kellie and her dad will walk home with you while I finish supper."

"Right," agreed Mr. Stricklin, and soon they were on their way.

Having Mr. Stricklin along did not change the desert at night, but Sondra was no longer afraid. She had become strong and courageous. Why? Because she no longer faced the desert night alone. *DSK*

HOW ABOUT YOU?

Do you ever feel fearful when you're faced with a new or scary situation? If you're a Christian, you don't have to face it alone. God is with you always.

MEMORIZE:

"Take courage and work, for I am with you, says the Lord Almighty." *Haggai 2:4*

 God Is with You

The Right Season (Read Ecclesiastes 3:1-8)

19

SEPTEMBER

Angie moped around the house. She was bored and lonely. Becky, her older sister, was on a weekend camping trip with a group of girls her age. "They could have asked me to go," muttered Angie as she kicked a shoe across her bedroom floor. She went to find her mother. "I'm too young to do anything fun!" she complained to Mother. "I'm too young to go camping. I'm too young to ride my bike in the street. And I'm *never* old enough to do the things Becky does. It's not fair!"

"You'll get to do those things soon enough," Mother told her. "Don't try to rush through life. That will only make you unhappy." Mother picked up some pattern pieces. "When you were a baby and your sister was a toddler, I tried to sew," she said. "I spread my patterns on the floor and pinned them down. But I got interrupted so often that I never got anything done. You needed feeding, or your sister needed a drink. It was the wrong season of my life to try to sew, so I put my patterns away."

"You sew now, though," observed Angie.

"Yes, I do," said Mother, "because it's the right time now. You and your sister are older and don't need as much care anymore, so now I can sew." She smiled at Angie. "You see, God gives us 'seasons of life' as he gives us seasons of the year. Food won't grow if it's planted in the wrong season—and we can't be happy if we try to live in the wrong season. If you'll patiently wait for the right season to do the things Becky is doing, you'll be much happier."

Angie sighed. "OK," she agreed, "but it must be the right time for me to do *something.*"

"It is," said Mother. "I think you're just the right age to help me make cookies." *KEC*

HOW ABOUT YOU?

From the time you were a baby until you get very old, you will pass through many seasons. God has things for you to enjoy in each one of them. Take pleasure in doing what you can do now. Look forward to doing other things when you get older. Be happy where you are.

MEMORIZE:

"Yes, there is a time and a way for everything." *Ecclesiastes 8:6*

 Accept Each "Season" of Your Life

In God's Hand (Read Isaiah 41:10, 13)

20

As Adam finished his Sunday school lesson and closed his workbook, Dad looked up from his newspaper. "Got it done already?" he asked. "Have you memorized your verse?"

"Sure," said Adam. "It's an easy one this time." He quoted it. "I am holding you by your right hand—I, the Lord your God. And I say to you, 'Do not be afraid. I am here to help you.'"

Dad nodded. "And do you understand what it means?" he asked.

Adam frowned. "Well . . . not really," he said.

"Here, give me your hand," said Dad. As Adam held out his hand, his father clasped it firmly in his own. "See, when you let me hold your hand, you are secure. If you fall, I'm here to help you."

"Yeah," said Adam. "I can understand that. But God can't really hold my hand, can he? Not like you do."

Dad smiled. "He doesn't hold it physically, like I do," he agreed. "But by trusting God, you allow him to hold your hand. That doesn't mean things will always be easy, but he will take care of you even through hard times." *RIJ*

HOW ABOUT YOU?

Do you allow God to "hold your hand"? Are you willing to trust him to take care of you? to go where he wants you to go? to be what he wants you to be? Yield your life and will to him now. You couldn't be in better hands!

MEMORIZE:

"I am holding you by your right hand—I, the Lord your God. And I say to you, 'Do not be afraid. I am here to help you.'"

Isaiah 41:13

 ***Trust God***

Monkeys, Mongooses, and Boboes!

(Read Philippians 4:8-13)

21

SEPTEMBER

Hannah, whose parents were missionaries, lived in the Central African Republic. She was enjoying many new and exciting experiences. But one day Hannah got a letter from Shandra, a friend in the States. "We took a trip to Disney World," wrote Shandra. "I wish you could have been with me, Hannah. You're missing so much."

Hannah sighed as she read about the exciting rides Shandra had enjoyed. They did sound like fun! Shandra's favorite was the African Safari river ride. "There were make-believe elephants that sprayed water at us," Shandra wrote, "and monkeys chattering in the trees. It seemed so real."

Just then Benji, Hannah's cape monkey, snuggled up to her. Benji loved being around her and would often follow her to church and school. That was a no-no of course, and when that happened, Hannah had to chase Benji back home. Now she gave him a little squeeze. "You're better than a mechanical monkey," she told him. "You're real."

Hannah thought about her other pets. Besides Odie, the dog, there were Frisky, the baby antelope, and Rollo, the mongoose. Rollo was so roly-poly and cute. Her favorite food was eggs. One day Hannah's mom threw her a Ping-Pong ball. Rollo quickly caught it, lifted it with her front paws, and smacked it down hard on the ground. After a couple of tries, she realized it was fake and gave up. Rollo sometimes annoyed them by chirping a lot, but she made up for it by eating cockroaches and little flying termites called "boboes." When she got bigger, she would eat snakes! Hannah grinned. *Not many kids have a pet like that!* she thought.

Hannah turned back to Shandra's letter. She smiled as she finished reading. She realized that the Lord was giving her so many fun things to see and do right where she was! She was content with what she had. *CV*

HOW ABOUT YOU?

Do you often wish you could be somewhere else—or even be someone else? Or have you learned the secret of being content with what you have? Learn to enjoy all the little things God has placed right around you, and thank him for each one of them.

MEMORIZE:

"Not that I was ever in need, for I have learned how to get along happily whether I have much or little." *Philippians 4:11*

 Enjoy Little Things

Always There (Read Psalm 139:3-10)

22

"Don't be scared, Donnie," Esther said to comfort her little brother. "Jesus will be with you when you're getting your teeth fixed, won't he, Mother?"

Mother smiled. "That's right," she agreed. Donnie followed the dentist into the inner office.

When he came out, Donnie was smiling. "It didn't hurt too bad," he said.

"See? I told you Jesus would be with you," said Esther as they left the office. "I get to sit in front with Mother," she added, running ahead to the car.

"No! I do!" protested Donnie.

"I said so first," insisted Esther.

"But I had to go to the dentist, so I get the front seat." Donnie tried to push past his sister and get into the car. She shoved him away, and he shoved back.

Mother pretended not to notice the children fighting as she went to her own side of the car. "God is with me today," she sang. "God is with me always. He's with me when I work, and he's with me when I play. He sees all I do, and he hears all I say. God is with me right now." She emphasized the words *right now.* Donnie and Esther looked uncertainly at each other. "Sing it with me, kids," encouraged Mother.

Esther didn't join in the singing as she climbed slowly into the back seat. "I know Jesus is with us when we're afraid," she said finally, "or when we need help with something, but I never thought about him being with us when we fight. He is, though, isn't he?"

"Oh yes," answered Mother. "He promised never to leave us. But we often forget that."

"I'm sorry I was mean to you, Donnie," said Esther. Then she began to sing the song. "God is with me today. . . ." *HWM*

HOW ABOUT YOU?

If you're a Christian, Jesus is always with you. That's a great comfort when you take a test or go to a new school or have to be home alone. But don't forget—he's there through all the ordinary, routine things you do too. Will he be pleased with what he sees you do today? Will he be pleased with what he hears?

MEMORIZE:

"**For God has said, 'I will never fail you. I will never forsake you.'**" *Hebrews 13:5*

 God Is Always with You

Leaving the Nest (Read Proverbs 4:1-13)

23

SEPTEMBER

Caitlyn held her mother's hand, and her dad carried her baby brother, Timmy, as the family walked to church. It was a sunny fall morning. The leaves were beginning to turn orange and gold. "I'm glad we live close to church. It's fun to walk," said Caitlyn as she bent to collect a handful of colorful leaves. "I know the way to church all by myself," she added confidently. Mother smiled and nodded.

When they reached the church steps, Mother turned to Caitlyn. "You're a big girl now," she said. "You know the way to church, and you know the way to your Sunday school room. Dad and I are taking Timmy to the nursery and going to our class. I'm going to let you take yourself to your room today."

Caitlyn clutched her mother's hand tightly and shook her head. "I want you to take me," she pleaded.

"I'll watch you go, but learning to do things by yourself is part of growing up," Mother told her. Mother pointed to a large, black bird that was circling in the sky. "That bird wasn't able to fly when he was born. Like Timmy, he was carefully taken care of. His parents fed him in a nest until he was big enough to try his wings."

Caitlyn watched the bird while Mother continued. "He grew little by little, and after a while, the mother bird knew he had enough feathers to fly by himself. She let him take short trips that she knew were safe. Finally, he could fly anywhere he needed to go." Mother smiled at Caitlyn. "God wants his little birds to learn to fly, and he helps them do that. And he wants little people to learn how to take care of themselves as they grow, too. God didn't give you wings, but he gave you good, strong legs and a smart mind that will help you find your way. Remember, he'll go with you."

Caitlyn thought about what Mother had said. She did know the way to her room. She knew she could find it. She let go of her mother's hand. "I can do it," she said. And she did. *KEC*

HOW ABOUT YOU?

Do you remember that it is God's plan that you do more for yourself as you grow up? Trust God as he gives you new abilities. Remember not to rely on others for what you can do for yourself.

MEMORIZE:

"For wisdom will enter your heart, and knowledge will fill you with joy." *Proverbs 2:10*

 Trust God to Help You as You Grow Up

Not a Baby (Read Luke 12:13-21)

Belinda was having a problem as she baby-sat her little brother and sister. First, three-year-old Judith grabbed a stuffed toy from her brother, causing him to cry. Belinda suggested that they play with the blocks. The two children stacked blocks for a while. Gordon, however, started knocking them down and grabbing them. "Gordon, don't grab the blocks!" scolded Belinda.

24

SEPTEMBER

When Mom got home, Belinda was exasperated. "Babies naturally want what someone else has," said Mom when Belinda told her about the little ones' behavior.

When Belinda came home from school a few days later, she went straight to her room. She slammed her door and kicked her stuffed bear. *Thud!* He bounced off the wall.

Mother knocked, then opened the door. "What's going on?" she asked.

"Connie was voted in as president of our class. I wanted to win so bad," Belinda pouted.

"I'm sorry about that," Mom said, "but being bitter about it will only make you feel worse."

"Oooooh!" A loud wail came from the living room, and a moment later, Gordon toddled into the room, clutching a teddy bear. "Gordy took Petey!" cried Judith, close behind him. "Give him to me, Gordy."

Mom sighed and soon took care of the problem. She shook her head. "Like I said before, babies tend to want what someone else has," she said. "They need to learn to be content with what they have." She solemnly looked at Belinda.

"I have been acting like them, haven't I?" Belinda said. "Well, I guess I will need to learn to be content with not being class president." *LJR*

HOW ABOUT YOU?

Are you angry because someone else got picked to sing a solo part? Are you cross because all your friends got new outfits, but your mom said you didn't need one? Maybe you didn't make the basketball team, but your best friend did. Being happy with your circumstances isn't easy. But God can help you. Ask him.

MEMORIZE:

"Stay away from the love of money; be satisfied with what you have. For God has said, 'I will never fail you. I will never forsake you.'" *Hebrews 13:5*

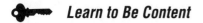 *Learn to Be Content*

Just a Nice Kid (Read Philemon 1:1-7)

25

Allison's next-door neighbor, Mrs. Henderson, was an elderly lady who didn't get out very often. So each day after school, Allison would stop to say hello and tell her what had happened that day. Usually Allison's friend Christy stopped with her, but some days Christy had music lessons right after school.

One rainy Tuesday Allison ran up Mrs. Henderson's front steps and knocked on the door. "Mrs. Henderson, I'm here!" she called as she opened the door.

"Good afternoon, Allison," the old lady greeted her. She was in her favorite chair with an old quilt wrapped around her.

"You look warm and comfortable." Allison smiled. "Would you like me to fix you a cup of tea? I have a couple of cookies, too. I helped make them last night."

"Sounds like we're equipped for a real party," said Mrs. Henderson.

Later, as they were sipping their tea, Mrs. Henderson asked Allison where Christy was. "Oh, she has flute lessons," Allison sighed. "She's so talented! She can sing and play the flute, and she draws well, too. I can't do anything!"

"Why, Allison, that's not true!" Mrs. Henderson exclaimed. "You have a special gift, the ability to make others feel good. It was such a dreary day today—until you came. You're like a bit of sunshine! You remind me of Philemon in the Bible. The apostle Paul wrote that Philemon refreshed all those who knew him. And that's the way you are, too, Allison. You make others happy, just by being you. You make others happy by showing God's love in the way you live. That, Allison, is one of the very best gifts you could possibly have."

Allison gave Mrs. Henderson a hug. "Thank you for telling me that," she said. "I like making others happy, but I never thought about it being a special gift from God before." *LMW*

HOW ABOUT YOU?

Do you make others happy? Do you smile at people often? Is it refreshing for others to have you as a friend? Look around you. Find someone that you can encourage just by being a friend. Being a friendly, contented person is a good way to share God's love with others.

MEMORIZE:

"**I myself have gained much joy and comfort from your love, my brother, because your kindness has so often refreshed the hearts of God's people.**" *Philemon 1:7*

 **Be a Cheerful Person**

Exchange Program (Read Matthew 6:1-4)

After school one day, Lauren walked into the house with a scowl on her face instead of her usual smile. Mom looked up from ironing. "What's wrong, Lauren?" she asked.

"Mrs. Berry put Claire Adams and me together on a science project," replied Lauren. "She's a new girl, and she seems so weird. No one likes her."

"Maybe you can help Claire fit in," suggested Mother. Lauren knew her mother might say something like that.

26
SEPTEMBER

Lauren shrugged. "The other girls say I should ask Mrs. Berry to give me a different partner," she said. "If I don't, they'll think I'm weird, too."

"Maybe," Mom said as she started ironing again. A moment later, she said, "Lauren, have you looked in your bank recently?"

"Not since the other night when I took out money for that book I wanted," Lauren answered. She wondered why Mom had changed the subject.

"Why don't you look now?" suggested Mom.

It seemed a strange thing for Mom to ask, but Lauren took her bank from the shelf, just as she had done when Dad said she needed to pay for the book if she wanted it. It had taken almost all of her money. When she opened the bank, though, she found a surprise.

"Mom, where did these dollar bills come from?" Lauren asked as she rushed back to her mother.

"After you gave Dad the money for the book, he slipped those into your bank when you weren't looking," Mom told her. "He wanted you to be willing to spend your own money, but he wanted you to have that money, too." After a moment she added, "It reminds me of how God works. If it costs us to do right, he'll make it up to us—not always in just the way we might choose. And we don't always see it right away, either. But he does repay us sooner or later. You can count on it." *EMB*

HOW ABOUT YOU?

Are you afraid to do what is right because you think it will cost too much? When you're unselfish, obedient, honest, or kind, it may seem like you're getting a bad deal at first. But God knows all about it, and someday your efforts will be rewarded.

MEMORIZE:

"Trouble chases sinners, while blessings chase the righteous!"

Proverbs 13:21

 You Can't Outgive God

The Field Trip (Read Romans 7:14-25)

27

SEPTEMBER

Rob and the others in his class climbed into the bus for their field trip to the zoo. *How could I have lost my temper like that?* Rob thought as he looked out the window. *Greg didn't mean to break my pencil. Why did I yell at him? I got so mad at my sister yesterday, too. I've been a Christian for three months now, and I've still got a terrible temper. Will I ever learn to control it?* Even after arriving at the zoo, he continued to be upset with himself and had a hard time concentrating on what Nels, their tour guide, was saying. But when they saw a baby elephant, even Rob was interested.

"Aw, isn't he cute?" squealed several of the girls.

"He's just learning to use his trunk," Nels told them. "Watch." The kids giggled as they watched the elephant calf try to drink water. First he blew bubbles in the water rather than sucking it into his trunk. When he finally did get some into his trunk, he missed his mouth and sprayed his face. "It will take time for the calf to be able to use his trunk properly," said Nels. "But he'll keep trying, and it will come. After all, he's only three months old."

That's kind of like me, thought Rob. *I'm just a new Christian. Maybe it's going to take more time to get rid of this bad temper than I thought. I'll keep trying . . . just like that baby elephant. With the Lord's help, I'll overcome the problem.* SLN

HOW ABOUT YOU?

Do you find yourself doing a particular sin over and over again? Don't be discouraged. Old habits are hard to break. Keep working at overcoming, but do realize that you can't do it by yourself. Ask the Lord to help you. In time, as you learn to yield to him, you will be victorious.

MEMORIZE:

"The Lord will work out his plans for my life—for your faithful love, O Lord, endures forever. Don't abandon me, for you made me." *Psalm 138:8*

 You Can Overcome Sin

Calling It Quits (Read 2 Thessalonians 3:7-13)

28

SEPTEMBER

"I'm bored, Mom. I need something interesting to do," complained Cliff.

"You could finish the model ship or the birdhouse you started. Or you could work on your Bible memorization program," suggested Mother. "I've noticed that you seldom finish what you start. That could be a problem later on in life."

Cliff answered, "You're always making mountains out of molehills, Mom. Not finishing those little things won't make me a failure in life."

Mother started to reply but stopped. Instead she said, "You have an appointment with Uncle Don tomorrow."

"Oh no!" Cliff howled. "I hate going to the dentist, even if he is my uncle."

As Cliff sat in the dentist's chair the next afternoon, Uncle Don said, "You've got to have a filling." Cliff groaned, and Uncle Don began the work. But about halfway through, he put down his tools. "I think that's all I'm going to do for now," he said to his assistant. "I want to go fishing." He started to leave the room.

Cliff sat up straight. "What do you mean?" he asked. "You're not finished with my tooth."

Uncle Don shrugged. "I'll finish another day," he promised. "I feel like fishing now."

"But you can't quit now," protested Cliff. "You have to finish filling this tooth, or it'll start to hurt!" Then he noticed that his uncle seemed to be trying not to laugh. Suddenly he understood. "OK, Uncle Don! I know you've been talking to Mom," he said. "She put you up to this, didn't she?"

Uncle Don grinned, but he said soberly, "Cliff, you need to learn now to finish what you start. I wouldn't be a dentist today if I had called it quits the first time I felt like it. You see, it's important to develop good habits now."

Cliff nodded. "I get the message. Now how about finishing my tooth?" *BJW*

HOW ABOUT YOU?

Do you finish what you start? Doing so teaches you responsibility, discipline, and consistency—big words and big lessons that will make a big difference in your life. If you have a hard time finishing what you start, ask God to help you.

MEMORIZE:

"I have fought a good fight, I have finished the race, and I have remained faithful."

2 Timothy 4:7

 Finish What You Start

Sheltered (Read Psalm 91:1-10)

29

SEPTEMBER

Dark clouds covered the sky, and thunder boomed in the distance. "Look at Henny-Pen, Mom," said Michelle, pointing to the little coop near the barn. "She's clucking for her chicks. I guess she wants to protect them from the storm." The mother hen stood in the doorway of the coop, clucking loudly. The chicks ran to her from all directions. Then she led them into the coop and settled down, covering them with her wings. A heavy gust of wind and a spattering of rain sent Michelle and her mother scurrying into their house.

"We're under a tornado warning," Dad told them. "I just heard it on the radio. Let's go to the basement."

From their basement, the family heard the storm increasing in fury. The wind raged and howled, and lightning flashed again and again. Michelle moved close to her father. "Hold me, Dad," she begged. "I'm scared."

At last the storm passed, and they all hurried upstairs, thankful that the house was still standing. "I was really afraid, Dad, but I felt safer in your arms—sort of like the chicks, safe under their mother's wings," said Michelle.

"Henny-Pen sheltered her chicks, Dad sheltered you, and God shelters his children," observed Mother.

"Yes," said Dad. "You'll go through many storms in life, Michelle, and there will be times when things get tough and scary. I may not always be there to put my arms around you. But just remember what the Bible says of your heavenly Father: 'He will shield you with his wings.' He's always there to watch over you in life's storms."

"That's right," agreed Mother. *MRP*

HOW ABOUT YOU?

Are you afraid of something—storms, darkness, a new school, getting lost or hurt? Remember that God promises to be with you always. He's there to shelter you and take care of you. Trust him to do that.

MEMORIZE:

"He will shield you with his wings. He will shelter you with his feathers. His faithful promises are your armor and protection." *Psalm 91:4*

 *God Protects You*

The Kid Who Was Different

(Read Galatians 5:13-15, 22-26)

30

SEPTEMBER

Miss Norris sighed as she surveyed her Sunday school class. Jason had left a vacant seat between himself and Joey. On the other side of Joey was another empty chair. Although surrounded by boys, the Asian boy was alone. Across the room, Annie, who was mentally retarded, was being ignored by a group of chattering girls.

Miss Norris taught the lesson with a heavy heart. As the class was dismissed, she said, "Next week I want you each to bring one leaf for the bulletin board."

As her students gathered around the bulletin board the next Sunday, Miss Norris picked up a leaf. "This is a beautiful leaf," she said.

"I brunged it." Annie beamed.

Several of the students snickered.

Miss Norris picked up another leaf. "This one is not as pretty, so we'll put it aside." Jason frowned. He wasn't pleased at having his choice discarded. "And this one is not big enough," Miss Norris said as she set another one aside. She studied another critically. "We don't want oak leaves."

"Why not?" asked Natalie, who had brought it. "What's wrong with it?"

"Oh, it's different," said Miss Norris as she picked up the first leaf and compared the two. "See how different it is?"

"Sure, it's different," Nathan said. "God made leaves that way."

Jason picked up his leaf. "Annie's leaf isn't any better than mine," he said.

"Nor mine," Stephanie declared as she picked up the small leaf.

To the children's surprise, Miss Norris nodded and smiled. "You're right. 'Different' does not mean better or worse. I'm glad you see that," she said. "Neither is one person better than another. God made everyone different, and he made everyone special."

Miss Norris began to arrange all the leaves on the bulletin board as she added, "Let these leaves remind us how nice it is that everyone is different." *BJW*

HOW ABOUT YOU?

Are you kind to others, even those who seem "different"? Look in the mirror. Have you ever seen anyone who looks exactly like you? Of course not, because you are different yourself. Just as you are unique, so is each person. God loves us all.

MEMORIZE:

"Then Peter replied, 'I see very clearly that God doesn't show partiality.'" *Acts 10:34*

🔑 *God Made Everyone Special*

What's after Death? (Read Ezekiel 18:30-32)

1

Aaron clutched Dad's hand as they quietly walked into the church for the funeral. Mr. Connors, who had lived down the street from them, had died. Aaron had often helped the elderly man with work around his house and yard. In fact, just last Saturday the two of them had cut wood for the winter. But now Mr. Connors was in heaven.

Only the soft tones of the organ broke the silence as the family walked past the casket. Mr. Connors looked strange among all the flowers, and Aaron was glad when his dad led him to a seat. A lady sang, and then Pastor Brown spoke. Aaron listened closely as the pastor talked about the things Mr. Connors had done for the church and for the Lord. Pastor Brown also talked about God's promise that all Christians would someday be reunited in heaven.

Aaron was silent as the family drove to the cemetery. "Dad," he said finally, "what does a pastor say if the person who dies isn't a Christian?"

"That's a sad occasion," Dad told him. "But we must remember it's not for us to judge who is a Christian and who isn't one. Only the Lord knows. When a person hasn't made a known commitment to Christ, all the pastor can do is leave it with God. He should make sure those still living know the way to heaven."

Aaron nodded. *Thank you, Lord,* he prayed silently, *that Mr. Connors did know you as Savior. And, Lord, I am so glad you are my Savior too.* LFW

HOW ABOUT YOU?

Do you know how to become a Christian? If not, and if you are interested, ask a trusted adult to tell you more.

MEMORIZE:

"And just as it is destined that each person dies only once and after that comes judgment, so also Christ died only once as a sacrifice to take away the sins of many people." *Hebrews 9:27-28*

 Make Sure of Heaven

No Doubt about It (Read Psalm 103:8-12)

Jared sat on the beach watching the big waves come in and go out. But his mind was elsewhere. When his friend Jim had teased him about being a "church boy" and asked him how he could be sure he was going to heaven, Jared began to think about it. "You sing a song about your sins being 'rolled away.' Aren't you afraid they'll roll right back again?" Jim had asked with a laugh. Jared wasn't quite sure how to answer. How *did* he know for sure?

2

OCTOBER

As Jared stared at the water, he suddenly realized someone had joined him. He turned to find his grandfather sitting beside him on the sand. "As I look out over those waves," said Grandpa, "I'm reminded of how God has forgiven my sins."

Jared looked up at him. "How does the ocean remind you of that?" he asked.

"Can you see where the ocean ends?" Grandpa asked.

Jared cupped his hands over his eyes and looked into the distance. "Yeah," he said. "I see where it ends."

His grandfather disagreed. "No, Jared," he said. "You see to a place where it seems that the water and sky meet, but that's not the end. That's only as far as you can see." Jared continued to squint as Grandpa spoke. "Do you remember when we were out in the boat yesterday? We were so far out that we could see only sky and water in every direction. It seemed a long, long way from one 'edge of the sky' to the other. But that distance is nothing compared to the distance God has removed our sins from us. You know, no matter how far east you go, you can still keep going east forever. And no matter how far west you go, you can still keep going west forever. Yet God says that a Christian's sins are removed as far away from him as the east is from the west. Isn't that great?"

Jared nodded. "They can't come back again, either, can they?" he asked.

"Sure can't," Grandpa answered firmly. *RIJ*

HOW ABOUT YOU?

Have you ever wondered if you are really a Christian? Remember, if you've accepted Jesus as Savior, God's Word says he has removed your sins far from you. Aren't you glad?

MEMORIZE:

"He has removed our rebellious acts as far away from us as the east is from the west." *Psalm 103:12*

 God Removes Sin Forever

Foolish Frogs (Read 1 Corinthians 10:1-13)

3

OCTOBER

As Jason dangled his fishing line into the pond, he watched two frogs that seemed to be fighting over a place to sit on a log. Jason laughed as both frogs fell into the water.

A moment later Jason noticed a large snake slither onto the log to sleep in the sun. The frogs swimming nearby also noticed the snake and moved quickly away. But little by little they came closer again, as if they were checking to see if the snake were really sleeping. The snake seemed to pay no attention to their antics, and gradually they came so close that they were within his reach. The snake suddenly came to life and grabbed the nearest frog. That foolish frog was soon swallowed, and the other swam away quickly. Jason later told his parents what he had seen.

The next day Jason came home from school with news. "Remember Brian? The kid I used to play with sometimes?" he asked. "Well, he got caught with a knife in school, and now he's suspended." Jason shook his head. "I don't know how he got so messed up," he added.

Jason's father put an arm around his shoulders. "Remember the frogs and the snake?" he asked. "How did the frog happen to get caught?"

"Well, the frogs just kept getting closer and closer to the snake, until they got too close," replied Jason.

Dad nodded. "That's sort of how the devil likes to 'catch' us," he said. "First he might suggest that we tell a lie, then to take something that doesn't belong to us. It goes on and on from there. That's probably what happened with Brian."

Jason looked thoughtful. "Is that how kids get started on drugs and drinking and smoking?" he asked.

Dad nodded. "Yes, and other things, too. Just like the frogs, they get too close to the things that are wrong—and before they know it, they're caught by those things." *MPC*

HOW ABOUT YOU?

Do you get too close to things you know are wrong? Be careful. Living close to sin is dangerous. Be smart. Stay far away from it.

MEMORIZE:

"So, if you think you are standing firm, be careful that you don't fall!"

1 Corinthians 10:12, NIV

 Stay Away from Sin

Trapped (Read Philippians 4:11-13)

Dave watched as his grandfather tightened the final screw on the birdhouse they had made. Then they mounted the completed birdhouse on the trunk of a maple tree in Grandpa's backyard.

Later that afternoon Grandpa grinned at Dave and said, "If you keep pacing back and forth to that window, you'll wear holes in your tennis shoes."

"I want to see what kind of birds come," replied Dave. "Hey!" He pointed out the window. "A squirrel is trying to get into the birdhouse!"

4

OCTOBER

"Don't worry. The bird book says the hole is too small for that furry fellow," Grandpa reassured Dave. "He can't chew the entrance larger, either, because we nailed a piece of metal around the hole."

Grandpa and Dave laughed as they watched the squirrel wiggle, squirm, and turn circles, trying to get into the birdhouse. Suddenly, to their amazement, the squirrel squeezed through the hole! He disappeared for a few minutes. Then he stuck his head back out. Once again they watched as he struggled and squirmed and stretched, trying to get back out. But he could not escape.

"Well," said Grandpa, "let's go rescue Mr. Squirrel." They went out to the yard, and Grandpa blocked the hole in the birdhouse and took it down. After releasing the squirrel, they decided they had better make the hole in the birdhouse a little smaller.

"You know, Dave, sometimes we're like that squirrel. We squirm and struggle to get what we want, too, whether it's what God wants or not," said Grandpa as he worked. "Then sometimes God will let us have what we think we want. When we get it, though, we find it doesn't make us happy after all." *DAB*

HOW ABOUT YOU?

Do you beg your parents to let you take part in questionable activities or to go places that you know you shouldn't go? Do you plead with God for more and more things, rather than thanking him for what you already have?

MEMORIZE:

"And [God] gave them their request, but sent leanness into their soul." *Psalm 106:15,* KJV

 Want What God Wants

Imperfect Pictures (Read 1 Peter 1:7-9)

5
OCTOBER

Celeste quickly opened the package she had received in the mail from her Aunt Ginny. "Oh, look . . . a new Bible story-book," she said, holding it up. She leafed through several pages. "Look, Mom," she said, stopping at one page. "This must be Jesus, but it doesn't look the same as other pictures I've seen of him."

"Well, there were no cameras when Jesus was on earth," said Mother. "All the pictures we have are ideas of how the artists think Jesus looked."

"I wish I knew what he really looked like," said Celeste. "Then it would be easier to read the Bible and pray."

"You don't need to know how Jesus looks in order to talk to him," said Mother. "You talk to Aunt Ginny on the telephone, but you don't know how she looks. You've never seen her because she lives so far away."

"I saw pictures of her in the photo album," said Celeste.

Mother nodded. "Yes, but all of those pictures were taken quite a while ago," she said with a grin. "You'd think we'd have some more recent pictures, but she seems to be camera shy. She always avoids having her picture taken." She paused, then added, "But when Aunt Ginny writes a letter, you like to read it, don't you?"

Celeste nodded.

"That's a little like the kind of relationship we have with Jesus," said Mother. "We can talk with him in prayer and read his Word, the Bible." After a moment she added, "Suppose Aunt Ginny sent a picture, and you didn't think she was very pretty . . . would you be disappointed?"

Celeste shook her head. "It doesn't really matter how she looks," she said. "And I guess it doesn't matter how Jesus looked when he lived on earth, either." *PLR*

HOW ABOUT YOU?

If someone you love were in an accident and covered with scars or burns, you'd still love that person. That's because you love the person for who he or she is. Even though you can't see Jesus, you love him for who he is. The better you get to know him, the more you'll love him.

MEMORIZE:

"You love him even though you have never seen him." *1 Peter 1:8*

 Love God for Who He Is

More Precious (Read Proverbs 1:7-10, 29-33)

Jane excitedly waited for Andrea, the most popular girl in school, to arrive.

When Andrea finally came, she had something to show Jane. "Look at this necklace!" she squealed. "It came from my Uncle Derick." Jane was impressed, and she wanted to impress Andrea, too. So she proudly told Andrea about a ring she had just inherited from her grandma. "Let me see it," demanded Andrea.

6

OCTOBER

"Well, I'm not supposed to get it out without permission," answered Jane doubtfully. "And Mom's gone to the store."

"Don't be such a baby," said Andrea. So Jane got the box and opened it. There lay her precious ring. "Oh, Jane," cried Andrea, "it's beautiful! Let me try it on." Jane hesitated, but she handed Andrea the ring. "I want to wear it for a while," declared Andrea.

The girls decided to go to a nearby park. After a while, Jane suggested they return home. "Give me the ring before we go in," she said. "I don't want Mom to see you wearing it."

"OK," agreed Andrea. She took off the ring. As she turned to give it to Jane, she let go too soon. And the ring dropped into a storm water drain.

Jane gasped. She ran home and tearfully explained what had happened. Mom hurried out but couldn't even see the ring. Then she called the city sewer department, but no one was able to help them. Andrea went home. Jane lay across her bed and cried.

"Oh, Dad," sobbed Jane that evening. "I knew it was wrong to let Andrea wear my ring. Now it's lost forever!"

Dad replied. "Before long you'll be a teenager, and more and more 'friends' will be wanting you to do things that you know are wrong," he said. "If you listen to such friends, you may lose things more valuable than that ring."

"Like what?" asked Jane.

"Well," said Dad, "if you do the wrong things they want you to, it could result in serious consequences. Never take the advice of friends if it goes against what you know to be right." *RJC*

HOW ABOUT YOU?

Do you allow friends to influence you to do things that displease God? That's very foolish, and it can have unhappy, long-lasting consequences.

MEMORIZE:

"My child, if sinners entice you, turn your back on them!"

Proverbs 1:10

 Sin Has Serious Consequences

The Bad Week (Read 1 Peter 4:14-19)

7
OCTOBER

Joel and Michael were at Ben's house getting ready to study for a math test. "This has been one terrible day," Ben told his friends. "The guys in gym class razzed me because I wouldn't look at a magazine one of them brought. Somebody's dad got it at the adult bookstore."

"My day wasn't so great either," said Joel. "My science teacher made fun of me because I wrote about creation in one of the essay questions on the test yesterday."

Michael took a cookie from the plate. "Today was pretty good for me," he said, "but yesterday I got laughed at, too. I bought baseball cards at the hobby store, and the clerk gave me too much change. My cousin was with me, and he said I was a real dummy for giving the extra money back." He sighed. "How come everyone's giving us a hard time for doing the right thing?"

Ben's dad had been working at his computer and overheard the boys talking. "I'm really not surprised to hear that you boys are being persecuted because of the right things you do," he said. "In fact, that's good."

Ben, Joel, and Michael stared at him. "It is?" asked Ben.

"Yep!" Dad nodded. "The Bible says we can expect that. You see, your obedience to God sometimes makes other people uncomfortable, so they try to make you uncomfortable, too. But God says to be glad when that happens!" Dad grinned at the boys.

Joel frowned. "I'm not sure I get this," he said. "We're supposed to be glad because people are making fun of us?"

"That's right," said Ben's dad. "I know it seems hard when it's happening. But the Bible promises a blessing to those who suffer for doing the right thing." *LJO*

HOW ABOUT YOU?

Do you get frustrated and upset when others tease you or get angry with you for doing the right thing? Keep on obeying God, and pray for those who persecute you. God will bless you, and perhaps he will use you to talk to them about Jesus.

MEMORIZE:

"Blessed are you when people . . . persecute you . . . because of me. Rejoice and be glad, because great is your reward in heaven." *Matthew 5:11-12,* NIV

 *Suffer Joyfully*

Cakes and Kids (Read Exodus 31:1-11)

"Put more frosting on Donald's nose, Megan!" demanded three-year-old Ryan. He clapped his hands with delight as his sister put the finishing touches on his birthday cake. Then he raced out of the room yelling, "Daddy! Daddy, Megan made me Donald Duck for my birthday!"

8
OCTOBER

Mother laughed, but Megan just sighed. "What's wrong?" asked Mother.

"I was just wishing I had a special talent," Megan answered. "Marsha is spending the weekend at a gymnastics competition. Cindy is going to the state music contest tomorrow. All I'm doing this weekend is baby-sitting." Just then the phone rang, and she went to answer it. "Hello," she said. "This is Megan." After a moment she added, "Oh, hi, Mrs. Conners. Saturday afternoon? Well, I'm already baby-sitting at six o'clock, but I guess I could help you out in the afternoon." A slow smile crept over her face as she continued to listen. "Oh, tell Jenny not to worry," she said. "I'll be there. Good-bye."

"What was Jenny worried about?" asked Mother.

Megan laughed. "Mrs. Conners said Jenny was afraid they wouldn't be able to get me to baby-sit tomorrow."

Mother smiled. "Mrs. Conners told me Jenny and Emily don't want any other baby-sitter because they think you tell such good stories," she said, giving her daughter a hug. "Megan, God's gifts to us aren't always noticeable talents, like music or sports," she continued, "but he gives each of us abilities that will make people around us happier. He's given you the skills of baking and decorating. You also have the important gift of caring for children."

"Oh, Mom!" Megan was a little embarrassed but very pleased. "Thank you," she said. "I guess I should thank God, too, for making me the way I am." *LRS*

HOW ABOUT YOU?
Do you sometimes wish God gave you more—or different—talents? He gives each of us skills like sewing, carpentry, telling stories, or baking so we can help other people. Ask him to show you what you do best and how to use that skill to help others.

MEMORIZE:
"Whatever you eat or drink or whatever you do, you must do all for the glory of God."
1 Corinthians 10:31

 Do Your Best for God

A Puzzling Gift (Read Proverbs 3:1-8)

The mailman delivered a package to Juanita and Pablo. It was from Grandma and contained two envelopes and two huge jigsaw puzzles—one for each of them. The envelopes were taped shut, and on them were printed the words "Don't open till you've worked the puzzles!"

Juanita and Pablo dumped their puzzles on the floor and busily put them together. It took quite a while, but finally they were almost done. "I'm missing a piece," said Pablo, as he added the last piece he had to his puzzle.

"Me too," said Juanita. "There's a hole in my puzzle."

Juanita looked all over the floor while Pablo searched the wrapping paper and boxes, but they couldn't find the missing pieces. Finally their mother suggested they look in the envelopes. They opened them quickly and read, "I'm missing something, too! I miss each of you and feel like there's a hole in my life! I'm coming to visit next week. Love, Grandma."

When Grandma came, she handed Juanita a tiny package. Inside, Juanita found the missing puzzle piece and a gold chain. Then Grandma gave Pablo a package containing his missing piece and a small key chain. "All right! Now we can work our puzzles, and they won't have any holes in them," said Juanita.

Grandma nodded. "Just don't forget," she said, "that I miss you when I don't see you or hear from you." She gave them each a hug. "Do you know who else sometimes misses hearing from you?" she asked.

"Our friends?" asked Juanita.

Grandma nodded. "I'm sure they do," she agreed, "but I was thinking of Jesus. He misses you when you forget to pray or read the Bible." *KHW*

HOW ABOUT YOU?

Are you ever sad when a friend promises to play or call and then forgets? Are you sometimes the one who forgets to call your friend? Don't be the "hole"—the missing piece. Be faithful to your friends. Above all, be faithful in spending time with the Lord and in reading the Bible and talking with him.

MEMORIZE:

"My child, never forget the things I have taught you. Store my commands in your heart."

Proverbs 3:1

 Keep in Touch with Jesus

The Body-House (Read John 11:21-27)

10

"Dad, I was reading in the book of John this morning," said Stephen. "It says that if somebody believes in God, he will never see death. But people who are Christians die. Like Grandpa Potter. I'm sure he loved God, but last year he died anyway. Does that mean there's a mistake in the Bible?"

Dad shook his head. Then he reached over and pinched Stephen lightly on the arm.

"Ouch!" exclaimed Stephen. "Why did you pinch me?"

"I didn't," said Dad. "I only pinched the house you live in."

"What do you mean?" Stephen asked.

"Well, Son, you are more than a body," explained Dad. "God made you with a mind to think and a spirit to know him. Right?"

"Yeah, I guess so," said Stephen.

"Then," Dad went on, "God gave your mind and spirit a house to live in on earth. We call it a body. The real you lives inside your body-house."

"Oh," said Stephen thoughtfully.

"Stephen, when you believed on Jesus Christ and asked him to forgive your sins, he gave everlasting life to your spirit—to the real you. Will something that is everlasting die sometime?"

"No," Stephen quickly replied. "It lasts forever and ever."

"That's right. But, Son, your body was not made to last forever. So at the very moment your body dies, God will take you out of your body-house and into his home in heaven. The real you will not see or go through death—not ever."

Stephen was quiet for a few minutes. His dad was quiet, too, so Stephen could think. "So . . . then Grandpa didn't really die, did he? He just moved on to heaven," said Stephen. "And now he's seeing Jesus! Wow!" *EMM*

HOW ABOUT YOU?

Have you asked Jesus to be your Savior? If you have, the real you can never die! And you will live with Jesus forever. If you haven't yet, talk to a trusted adult to find out more!

MEMORIZE:

"And whoever lives and believes in me will never die."

John 11:26, NIV

 Believers Never Really Die

Speed Bumps (Read Romans 13:1-7)

"Mr. Cox is making me do my whole assignment over because I didn't show how I got my answers!" Jason complained. "I'll never get to go swimming today!"

"Speed bumps," said his older brother, Chip.

"What?" asked Jason.

11

OCTOBER

"You know those built-up humps in the parking lots that force you to go slow?" asked Chip. Jason nodded. Chip continued, "Speed bumps are good because they keep a driver alert. If he's going too fast, they remind him to slow down."

"So?" asked Jason.

"So maybe Mr. Cox is forcing you to slow down so you'll be more careful, too," Chip told his brother. Jason didn't answer. *How can Chip understand?* he thought. *He's always been good in math.* "Look," Chip said, turning to go, "I'll be ready to go swimming in about an hour. Try to get your homework done by then."

"Yeah, right," said Jason. He was sure that was impossible.

Jason pulled out his math book. When he carefully checked his first problem, showing all the steps he took to get the answer, he discovered he had added when he should have subtracted. In another problem, he had forgotten the decimal point. He had expressed one answer in inches instead of feet.

"Almost finished?" asked Chip when he came back. He pulled up a chair. "Hey, Jason, did I ever tell you about *my* fifth-grade math teacher? His name was Mr. Cox."

Jason stared at his brother. "The same Mr. Cox?" he asked.

Chip nodded. "A lot of math is just being careful and checking your work. Mr. Cox taught me that." He gave his brother a playful nudge. "I guess God knew all along that Mr. Cox is the kind of teacher you need," he said.

Jason grinned. "And he knew you were the kind of brother I need. As soon as I get over these speed bumps, I'll race you to the pool." *MEU*

HOW ABOUT YOU?

Do you realize that God puts people in your life for your good? Perhaps they're providing the "speed bumps" you need. Honor God by submitting to those he puts in authority.

MEMORIZE:

"For the Lord's sake, accept all authority." *1 Peter 2:13*

 Submit to Authority

The Tough Shell (Read 1 Samuel 16:6-13)

Tap! Tap! Tap! The two hammers hit the soft, spongy walnut shells. Randy and his dad were stripping the shells from nuts they had gathered.

"Gross!" Randy exclaimed, looking at the stains on his old gloves. "These nuts sure are messy, aren't they, Dad?"

"Yep," Dad murmured, busy with his own pile. "But just think of how good these black walnuts will taste in Grandma's special cake. We'll think they're worth the work when we taste that."

12

OCTOBER

As they worked, Randy talked about school, his soccer team, and his friends. "I like Steve," Randy said. "But Jeff is weird!"

"What's wrong with Jeff?" asked Dad.

"Oh, he always talks so loud. And he thinks he's so tough. I just don't like him," declared Randy.

Dad kept working in silence for a while. Then he picked up a nut and held it out. "Maybe Jeff's a little like this nut," he told Randy.

"How?" asked Randy.

"Maybe on the outside he seems hard, but what about inside?" asked Dad. He tapped the nut with his hammer. "Walnuts grow with this mushy covering and a hard shell," he added. "We can't see the good nutmeats inside. Maybe Jeff is like that."

Randy answered. "You mean maybe he's just putting on an act? That he's really nice inside?"

"He may be nicer than you think," Dad answered. "Sometimes when people are afraid or insecure, they act rough and tough to hide that from others. We see only the outside, but God made Jeff—and under that hard exterior is a soul that God loves. Perhaps with God's help, you can find what's good in Jeff." *JKB*

HOW ABOUT YOU?

Do you have trouble liking someone? Ask God to help you see something good about that person, and then compliment him or her on that good thing. Who knows? Maybe you'll discover someone nice under that outer covering. Best of all, you may be able to share God's love with that person.

MEMORIZE:

"People judge by outward appearance, but the Lord looks at a person's thoughts and intentions." *1 Samuel 16:7*

 Look through God's Eyes

The Coach's Voice (Read Deuteronomy 5:32-33)

13

OCTOBER

The ball bounced down the court and into Stephanie's outstretched hands. This was her first season on the junior high team. Her heart pounded with excitement as she scooted around the other team's defensive players. She heard someone yell, "Play number 5!" Stephanie recognized the voice of Coach Howard and remembered the play they had practiced. But the basket was so close! How thrilling it would be to actually score some points in a game! So Stephanie went toward the basket.

Suddenly the defense closed in around her, and her opportunity to score was gone. With a quick pivot turn, she thrust the ball hard toward the basket. The crowd groaned as a tall girl on the other team grabbed the ball and started dribbling fast toward the opposite end of the court.

After the game Coach Howard sat down on the bench beside Stephanie. She didn't look up. She knew she had let the team and the coach down. "Did you hear me call the play number?" the coach asked gently.

"Yes, I did," admitted Stephanie. "But I thought I had the perfect chance to make some points! I'm sorry."

Coach Howard nodded. "I think you've learned a good lesson," he said.

Stephanie went to the locker room, changed her clothes, and ran out to ride home with her dad, who had come to see the game. "Good game, Steph," he said.

Stephanie sighed. "Thanks, but I shouldn't have tried for the basket. I heard Coach Howard call a play, and I should have listened."

Dad was quiet for a moment. "Steph, I think I know how you feel," he said. "Sometimes I respond that same way to God by letting my desires become more important to me than God's voice."

Stephanie sighed. "I guess I've done that, too," she said. Then she smiled and added, "Coach Howard let me stay in the game, though. And I'm sure glad God keeps letting me play in his game, even when I mess up!" *JJB*

HOW ABOUT YOU?

Do you hear God's voice through his Word and through wise people? Do you listen and obey, or do you go your own way instead? God wants you to listen to his commands and obey him. His plan is much better than yours.

MEMORIZE:

"We will serve the Lord our God. We will obey him alone."

Joshua 24:24

 Listen to God and Obey

A Strong Hand (Read Psalm 71:12-16)

14
OCTOBER

"Wow, Dad! Did you see those fish?" Nathan's eyes sparkled as he lifted his face out of the water and adjusted his snorkeling mask.

"I sure did!" Dad grinned.

"I almost touched one of those yellow-and-black-striped ones," Nathan said.

Dad looked at the setting sun. "Well, it's getting late," he said. We better start swimming back to shore. Are you ready?"

"So soon?" asked Nathan. "Bet I can beat you back."

But it was farther to the shore than Nathan had realized. After a while he called to his father. "Dad, can we rest a minute?"

His dad stopped swimming and shook his head. "If we do, this current may take us too far offshore. Here . . ." He stretched out his arm for Nathan to grab. "Hold onto me, and I'll pull you along." Soon they reached the shore, tired but safe.

As they loaded their snorkeling gear into the car, Dad turned to Nathan. "It's a good thing I was with you to pull you along, wasn't it?"

"Uh-huh," agreed Nathan. "I was getting tired."

Dad smiled. "You know, I think living the Christian life is sometimes a little like swimming," he said. "Once in a while you may get tired of doing things you know are right. Where do you suppose you can get encouragement and help then?"

"From you," Nathan answered promptly.

Dad chuckled softly. "Right," he said. "I'll help all I can. And other Christians can be a help, too. Where else can you get help?"

"From the Bible and the Lord," said Nathan.

"That's a good answer, Son," said Dad. "When I ask the Lord for his help, I sometimes feel as if he says to me, 'Here . . . I'll pull you along.' We can always depend on him." *RSM*

HOW ABOUT YOU?

When you get tired and discouraged as you try to live for the Lord, do you look to other Christians for encouragement? They can be a lot of help to you. And be sure to ask the Lord to help you too. He will always reach out his hand and help you when you depend on him.

MEMORIZE:

"Don't be afraid, for I am with you. . . . I will strengthen you. I will help you. I will uphold you with my victorious right hand."

Isaiah 41:10

 Get Help from God

The Odd Stamp (Read John 15:18-21)

15

OCTOBER

"That Brian Farley is really odd, and I told him so," Tiffany announced as she slammed the front door behind her. "We'll never get our science project done if he keeps being such a 'Holy Joe' about everything."

"What happened?" asked Mother.

"Brian and I were assigned to do a report on television programs for teens," said Tiffany, "and Brian told our teacher that some of the programs are bad for our mind and that teens shouldn't watch so much TV. Imagine! He said that in front of the whole class! I was so embarrassed!" Before Mother could reply, Tiffany stormed off to her bedroom. She came out a few minutes later. "Where did this come from?" she asked, holding up a small, square object.

Mother smiled. "Uncle Ray knows you like stamps, so he wanted you to see this one."

"What's special about it?" asked Tiffany. "It looks like a plain, ordinary stamp. It isn't pretty or anything."

"Take a good look," said Mother. "Some of the printing is upside down, and that's what makes it different and very unusual. It's actually valuable because it's so rare." She paused as Tiffany studied the stamp with new respect. "You know, your friend Brian is a bit like this stamp."

"Huh?" grunted Tiffany. "How?"

"He may seem odd to some people, but I think he's a much finer person than you gave him credit for," Mother explained. "He had the courage to speak up for what he believes. You should be proud to be Brian's friend. He's one in a million!" *SLK*

HOW ABOUT YOU?

Are you afraid of being considered "weird" because of your beliefs? Are you willing to take a stand that is different from most of the kids? Christ was rejected by the world, and his followers are sometimes rejected too. Judge yourself—and your friends—by God's standards, not the world's standards.

MEMORIZE:

"The world would love you if you belonged to it, but you don't." *John 15:19*

 "Different" Can Be OK

Milk Time! (Read Psalm 119:33-40)

Tonya put the orange juice into the refrigerator. She tried to close the door, but her baby brother, Danny, was in the way. When Tonya nudged him over a few inches, Danny whimpered.

When Tonya opened the door a few minutes later to put the butter away, Danny scooted over. "What is it you like so well in the refrigerator?" Tonya asked as she moved him back again. Danny started to fuss.

16

OCTOBER

Just then Mom entered the room. "Time for our bottle," she said to Danny as she reached for the refrigerator door. She took out a bottle and walked over to the cupboard. Fussing even more loudly, Danny scooted after her.

"Oh, I bet he wanted his milk," said Tonya.

"He's a smart little guy," said Mom with a smile, "especially when he wants to eat." She picked up the baby, who was crying and reaching for the bottle in her hand. His mouth opened wide as the bottle was offered to him.

Tonya grinned. "You know, Mom," she said thoughtfully, "Mrs. Johnson talked about babies and milk in Sunday school a couple of weeks ago. We had to learn a Bible verse about it."

"As newborn babes, desire the sincere milk of the word, that ye may grow thereby (1 Peter 2:2)," said Mother.

"So, you know that verse, too," said Tonya. Then she added, "Mrs. Johnson said we should be just as eager to learn about God as a baby is eager to get milk. And watching Danny, I think I know what she means!" *RLV*

HOW ABOUT YOU?

Do you read your Bible? Do you like to go to church? Do you listen while you're there? Do you talk about what God's Word says? A Christian should love God's Word just as a baby loves to drink milk.

MEMORIZE:

"As newborn babes, desire the sincere milk of the word, that ye may grow thereby."

1 Peter 2:2, KJV

 Be Eager for God's Word

Too Late (Read James 4:13-17)

17

OCTOBER

"Can I watch TV?" asked Eric one evening as he and his parents sat in the family room.

"Well, let's see . . . I think that documentary about the *Titanic* is on now," replied Mother. "I want to see it, too."

"Aw, Mom! There must be something better on than a dumb old documentary!" protested Eric.

"I think you'll find this one interesting," insisted Mother. "Do you know what the *Titanic* is?"

"Sure—it was a big ship, and they thought it was unsinkable, but it sank," replied Eric. "Whatever made them think it couldn't sink?"

"Let's watch the program and find out," said Mother.

"Oh, all right," grumbled Eric, as he sprawled out on the floor, "but I know it'll be boring." Soon, however, he was caught up in the story of the *Titanic.*

When the program was over, Eric stood up and stretched. "I can't believe they were so stupid!" he declared. "They didn't even have enough lifeboats. Wouldn't you think they'd at least have put more of those on board? I mean . . . when you're out at sea and your ship is sinking, it's too late to get them then!"

Dad nodded. "It's so easy for us to see how foolish they were. Yet many people are just as foolish today. They think they're 'unsinkable,' too—that they can put off thinking about God until the end of their lives. But the truth is, none of us knows when that day will come." *BRE*

HOW ABOUT YOU?

Are you putting off accepting Jesus as your Savior? Do you think you have "plenty of time"? You may be wrong! Accept Christ today, before it's too late!

MEMORIZE:

"How do you know what will happen tomorrow? For your life is like the morning fog—it's here a little while, then it's gone." *James 4:14*

 Don't Wait to Be Saved

Good-Luck Penny (Read Matthew 10:29-31)

As Chase and Devon walked along, they saw a penny on the sidewalk. Chase picked it up. "You can't do much with a penny," he said. "But at least I won't have bad luck today."

"What does a penny have to do with luck?" asked Devon.

"You know that poem," answered Chase. "See a penny, leave it lay—have bad luck all the day. See a penny, pick it up—all day long, have good luck."

18

OCTOBER

"Hah!" scoffed Devon. "I don't believe in luck. I believe God controls events in our life."

"Nah," grunted Chase. "I suppose he thinks about big things like wars, earthquakes, floods, and stuff like that, but I'm sure he can't bother about all the details in the lives of the millions of people down here. Can he?"

"He's watching everything," insisted Devon. "We learned in Sunday school that God even watches over little birds."

"You're kidding!" exclaimed Chase.

"Nope," Devon said, shaking his head. "Hey! Want to come to Sunday school with me this week and hear more about God?"

"OK," agreed Chase as they reached his house. "If Mom will let me. And here." He tossed the coin. "Have a penny!" *CEY*

HOW ABOUT YOU?

Do you think "luck" controls your life? Or do you put faith in God and trust him to take care of you? God made the earth and everything in it, including you. He controls all things. He sees and knows about everything, even the little birds. And he cares about you.

MEMORIZE:

"So don't be afraid; you are more valuable to him than a whole flock of sparrows."

Matthew 10:31

 God Cares about Everything

Proper Balance (Read James 1:21-25)

19

OCTOBER

Andy, Joy, and Mother took off on horseback down the dirt road—Andy and Joy on Midnight, and Mother riding Lady. Andy glanced back. "Look," he said. "Dad is feeding Buster some grain." Buster was an older pony, and when he ate with the other horses, he often got pushed away from his own grain by Lady, who was the boss of the barnyard.

"Oh, good," said Joy. "For once he gets to enjoy his afternoon treat." She patted Midnight. "You sure don't need it, do you, Midnight?" she asked.

Mother smiled. "I've noticed that, too," she said. "Your dad says it's because all she does is eat. He says what she needs is to be ridden or exercised every day."

"Can we canter?" asked Andy.

"That would be good for her," Mother agreed.

As they unsaddled the horses later, the children told Dad about their ride. "One of us is going to exercise Midnight every day," Andy said, and Joy nodded.

"Good," approved Dad. "She needs it. She's like some Christians I know."

Andy looked at his father. "You're not making sense, Dad," he said.

Dad grinned. "Some Christians are like Midnight—they eat all the time but don't get much exercise," he explained. "They 'eat' by going to church a lot and reading their Bibles. But they fail to 'exercise' their faith. They hardly ever witness or do anything to serve the Lord. They're just getting fat spiritually."

Mother joined the conversation. "Good point," she said as she patted Buster. "And there are also Christians like Buster. He gets enough exercise, but he doesn't always get enough to eat. Christians like him may do a lot of things to serve the Lord, but they don't take time to get spiritual food. They don't read the Bible on their own or attend church. They're getting 'spiritually skinny.'"

Dad nodded. "We need a proper balance between food and exercise," he said, "not only physically, but also spiritually." *TJE*

HOW ABOUT YOU?

Are you reading the Bible and praying? Are you faithful in attending church? Do you have Christian friends? That's good. Are you also exercising your faith? Are you spreading God's Word and doing his work? Jesus wants you to be a well-balanced Christian. Ask him to show you what area you need to work on.

MEMORIZE:

"Do not merely listen to the word. . . . Do what it says."

James 1:22, NIV

 Hear God's Word and "Do" It

One Little Step (Read Romans 8:1-6)

When Steve and his friend Brian got home from the store, Steve put a bag of groceries on the counter. "Here's your change, Mom," he said.

Mother counted the change. "This is a dollar short," she said.

20

OCTOBER

Steve gulped. "The clerk must have made a mistake," he muttered. "I'm going out to play with Brian."

Soon Steve's little brother, Mark, came into the kitchen. "Mommy, I want an ice-cream bar, too," he said. "Steve and Brian had one."

"Where did you get that idea?" asked Mother.

"I saw them throw away the sticks. I want an ice-cream bar, too," whined Mark.

Mother called Steve into the house and asked him about the ice cream. "Brian bought them," Steve lied. "He . . ."

At that moment Brian stuck his head in the doorway. "I've got to go home, Steve," he said. "Thanks for the ice cream."

There was silence in the kitchen after Brian shut the door. Finally Mother spoke. "I'm sorry, but you are grounded for the next two weeks," she said. "Not only did you spend the money without permission, you lied about it—twice."

"One little mistake around here, and you're treated like a criminal," grumbled Steve as he went to his room. Dad, who was coming down the hall, heard him.

"Come with me, Steve," said Dad when he learned what had happened. "I want to show you something." In silence they drove downtown to a construction site. The large steel skeleton for a tall building rose into the air. "See that man way up there? What if he got careless and thought, 'What difference does it make how I walk? What difference will one little step make?' What could happen?"

"Well . . . he might fall," Steve answered.

Dad nodded. "It's important for him to walk carefully," he said. "The Bible tells Christians to walk very carefully in this world. Telling lies could have serious consequences. And one lie often leads to another. So be careful, Son." *BJW*

HOW ABOUT YOU?

Do you try to excuse yourself for doing wrong by saying, "Well, it was just a little sin" or "a little lie" or "a few pennies"? In walking with God, every step is important. Be careful how you walk.

MEMORIZE:

"So be careful how you live, not as fools but as those who are wise." *Ephesians 5:15*

 Every Action Is Important

A Strange Blessing (Read Psalm 34:1-3, 8)

21

OCTOBER

After enjoying a picnic lunch at a park, Adam and Sara talked Mom and Dad into tossing a Frisbee around with them. Adam and Mom teamed up, trying to keep it away from Sara and Dad.

Adam and Sara ran, laughing and grabbing for the spinning disk. Adam jumped and came down with a thud. "Ohhh!" he groaned. "My ankle!" He grabbed his foot with one hand and held tightly to the Frisbee with the other.

But Mom and Dad both stopped playing. "I think you better sit down and let me have a look at that ankle," said Dad. "You came down pretty hard on it."

"I'm OK," insisted Adam. But when he took a step, it hurt.

"I think it's beginning to swell," said Mom.

Dad nodded. "We need to get that taken care of," he said. "Wait here, and I'll drive up as close as I can and then help you to the car." Adam wasn't happy about the decision to leave, but his ankle did hurt badly.

Much later, Adam lay on the couch at home, surrounded by his family. "Does it hurt very much?" Sara asked anxiously.

"Not as much as it did," Adam replied.

"Pain is a blessing," said Mother as she brought Adam a pillow.

"A blessing?" Adam said. "You're kidding!"

"No, I'm not," replied Mother. "Pain is a built-in alarm, telling us something isn't right. If your ankle hadn't hurt, you would have continued to walk on it. Then you might have hurt it even worse."

"Mom's right, Adam," agreed Dad. "Pain is a blessing—a strange one, but nevertheless a blessing. A headache, a stomachache, a toothache—all are warnings that something is wrong and needs care. Pain often saves people from death."

"Thank God for pain!" Adam grinned weakly, then added, "I guess." *BJW*

HOW ABOUT YOU?

Have you ever thanked God for pain? Probably not. It's hard to give thanks when you're hurting, but even pain has a purpose. If you give more thanks and do less complaining, you may find you feel better much faster.

MEMORIZE:

"And you will always give thanks for everything to God the Father in the name of our Lord Jesus Christ." *Ephesians 5:20*

 Thank God for Pain

Correction! (Read Colossians 1:9-14)

Jenny tore the paper from her printer and crumpled it up. "I have to do a history report this weekend," she told Mother. "I thought I might get a better grade if I typed it on the computer. But every time I get a few lines typed, I make a mistake."

"Why don't you use the spell check?" Mother asked.

"How does it work?" asked Jenny.

"Like this," said Mother. She showed Jenny how to have her computer search for misspelled words.

22
OCTOBER

"That's neat!" exclaimed Jenny. "I'll get this done yet!"

An hour later Jenny asked Mother, "Do you want to read my report?"

When Mother began to read, a strange look passed over her face. "Did you read this over?" she asked. She showed it to Jenny. "George Wash was our first president," she read aloud. "He was called the fat of our country."

"Oh no!" laughed Jenny. "The computer knew when a word wasn't spelled right. But it didn't know that *Wash* and *fat* weren't the right words to replace them with."

Mother smiled. "You'll need to open your file again. You're responsible for doing the final checking, you know." She added, "This will make a good illustration for my Sunday school lesson."

"How's that?" asked Jenny.

"The computer can remove mistakes, like the blood of Christ removes our guilt," explained Mother. "But we need to check our life every day to be sure that we don't keep on doing wrong things. Just as you need to replace the wrong words on the computer with right words, all of us need to replace wrong actions with right actions." *SLK*

HOW ABOUT YOU?

Have you accepted Christ's sacrifice on the cross for your sins? His blood is sufficient to erase all of your guilt. But he also wants to use your life to accomplish his will. Don't just get rid of your sin—allow Christ to put something good in its place.

MEMORIZE:

"Then the way you live will always honor and please the Lord, and you will continually do good, kind things for others. All the while, you will learn to know God better and better."

Colossians 1:10

 You're Saved to Serve

Grandpa's Cotton Patch (Read 1 John 1:8-10; 2:1-2)

23

OCTOBER

"Look, Dad," said Tommy, as they walked through Grandpa's cotton patch. "There's an odd-looking, gray thing on this cotton boll. It's awfully small, but it looks like it has a long nose. What is it, Dad?"

Tommy's father closely examined the cotton boll. "That small, pesty insect is called a boll weevil," he said.

"What do boll weevils do?" asked Tommy.

"They feed on the cotton plant," replied Dad. "They lay a lot of eggs, too. Then the eggs hatch and become baby boll weevils. Those things destroy a lot of plants."

"We better tell Grandpa about those old weevils so he can stop them before they ruin his cotton," said Tommy.

"Yes, we better," agreed Dad.

When Grandpa heard about the boll weevils, he frowned. "I'll have to take care of that right away," he said.

Soon it was time for Tommy and Dad to leave for home. "Good-bye, Grandpa," said Tommy. "Don't forget to get rid of those boll weevils."

"I won't," Grandpa assured him. Then he grinned. "I have a riddle for you," he said. "What comes into our life and multiplies just like those boll weevils if we don't get rid of it soon?"

Tommy thought for a moment. "I don't know," he said.

"Then I better tell you," said Grandpa. "It's sin. When we realize that some sin has crept into our life, we need to get rid of it right away. On the cross, Jesus made that possible. We can confess our sins and receive forgiveness. Through him, our sins are completely wiped away." Grandpa gave Tommy a hug. "I'll take care of those boll weevils," he said, "and let's both remember to confess our sins every day and not let them multiply in our life, OK?" Tommy nodded. *WWS*

HOW ABOUT YOU?

When you do something wrong, do you quickly confess it? If you don't, you're likely to repeat it. God wants you to repent of your sin and turn from it. Ask him to help you to repent.

MEMORIZE:

"But if we confess our sins to him, he is faithful and just to forgive us and to cleanse us from every wrong." *1 John 1:9*

 Unconfessed Sin Is Often Repeated

Too Much Money (Read Romans 12:9-21)

"That's eight seventy-five, nine dollars, ten, and twenty dollars," the clerk counted. Dennis's eyes widened as he quickly stuffed the bills into his pocket. He picked up the small sack of groceries and hurried out the door.

"Wow!" he whistled. "She thought I gave her a twenty-dollar bill when I only gave her a ten. Now I'll be able to buy that tennis racket I've been wanting." When he arrived home, he gave his mother her change and hid the extra ten dollars in his desk drawer.

24
OCTOBER

That night he skipped devotions—he didn't feel like thinking about God. But he couldn't shut out the voice in his head which said over and over, *That was stealing. Take it back. Take it back.*

The next morning Dennis took the money from his bank and added the ten dollars to it. He planned to stop at the sporting-goods store on the way home from school. But as he entered his classroom, he overheard Staci talking to their teacher. "I won't be able to go on our class trip, Miss Martin," said Staci. "My sister was going to pay my way, but at work yesterday she came up ten dollars short at her register. She had to pay it."

Dennis's heart almost stopped. It was Staci's sister who had given him too much money. "It's not my fault," he tried to tell himself. "I didn't take it—she gave it to me." But he really knew that by keeping money that didn't belong to him, he was stealing just as surely as if he had taken it out of the register himself. And he suddenly realized that any time something was stolen, someone had to pay. "If I keep the money, Staci will have to pay for it by missing the class trip," he murmured. "Then how can I enjoy going? As a Christian, how can I enjoy anything I'd buy with that money?" And so he stopped at the grocery store after school to give back the money instead of going to the sporting-goods store. And he went home with a happy smile instead of a tennis racket.

BJW

HOW ABOUT YOU?

Have you stolen things? It's possible to steal in different ways—not only by taking things that do not belong to you, but also by failing to return things that belong to someone else. God is as displeased with one method of stealing as with another. Do you need to return something?

MEMORIZE:

"We are careful to be honorable before the Lord, but we also want everyone else to know we are honorable."

2 Corinthians 8:21

 **Be Honest**

Patti's Talents (Read Matthew 25:14-23)

"I'll have to be in the hospital at least a week for the operation," said Mother from her wheelchair as she watched Patti clear the table. "Aunt Wilda says you and Brad can stay with them."

"Ohhh," groaned Patti. "Do we have to?"

"You can't stay by yourselves," Mother reasoned. "Why don't you like it there?"

Patti hesitated. Then she blurted out, "It's just that Marci is so . . . so . . . pretty and smart and popular. When I'm around her, I feel like a big fat zero!"

Before Mother could reply, a scream pierced the air. "It's Brad!" As Mother turned her wheelchair, Patti ran out the door. Almost instantly she returned with the sobbing little boy in her arms. "He cut his finger, but it's not very deep." Patti carried Brad into the bathroom, and soon his cries were replaced with giggles.

A few minutes later, Brad proudly displayed a bandaged finger. "See, Mommy! Patti fixed it. She's a good nurse."

Mother nodded. "I know. She's a good cook and a good house-keeper, too. She has taken excellent care of us since I've hurt my leg. Aunt Wilda says she's glad you and Patti will be staying with them a little while because Patti is such a good influence on Marci. She thinks Patti is one of the sweetest, most talented girls she knows."

"Me too," Brad agreed. "She even knows how to make chocolate chip cookies."

Patti laughed. "All right. I get the hint, little brother. I'll go make some cookies. And I get the message you're giving me, too, Mom. I'll be thankful for the talents God has given me and use them for him instead of complaining and wishing for what he's given to someone else." *BJW*

HOW ABOUT YOU?

Do you ever feel like a big fat zero? God has given everyone at least one talent. What talent has he given you? The ability to sing or speak? to spread joy through a cheerful smile? to help others? Whatever your talents, use them for God's glory.

MEMORIZE:

"The master said, 'Well done, my good and faithful servant. You have been faithful in handling this small amount, so now I will give you many more responsibilities. Let's celebrate together!'"

Matthew 25:23

 Use Your Talents

The Band-Aid Kid (Read Psalm 32:1-5)

26
OCTOBER

Dad sighed as he saw Monty sweeping the garage. When Monty did work without being asked, it sometimes meant he'd done something wrong. "Hi," he said, greeting his wife. "Anything happen today?"

"Travis has chicken pox," she announced, "and Monty shot Mr. White's dog with Kyle Roe's BB gun."

Dad frowned. "I've told him over and over not to play with Kyle's gun! Did he hurt the dog?"

"No—just scared him and made Mr. White angry," replied Mother. "He's coming over this evening."

Dad grimaced. "I knew something was wrong when—"

"Look at me! Look, Daddy!" interrupted three-year-old Travis. Mother's mouth fell open, and Dad roared with laughter when he saw Travis. "I got the chicken poxes. See? I put Band-Aids on them."

"How dumb can you get!" grumbled Monty as he entered the room and saw his brother. "You can't cure chicken pox by covering up the spots!"

"That's true," agreed Dad. "And you can't cover up sin with 'good deed Band-Aids' either. I've noticed that whenever you do something wrong, you try to cover it up by doing something good," continued Dad. "You've been sweeping the garage as if that would make up for what you did this afternoon."

"Kyle dared me, and he said . . ." Monty stopped.

"When you do something wrong, Monty, don't blame it on anyone else. Be big enough to admit it," Dad said. "The only cure for sin is repentance."

Tears filled Monty's eyes. "I'm sorry, Dad. Do you suppose Mr. White will forgive me?"

Dad sighed. "I surely hope so. You also owe Jesus an apology, Monty. When you wrong someone, you sin against the Lord too."

Monty gulped. "I'll go talk to the Lord now." *BJW*

HOW ABOUT YOU?

Are you a "Band-Aid kid"? Don't try to cover your sins with good deeds or excuses. You need to repent and ask God to forgive you.

MEMORIZE:

"People who cover over their sins will not prosper. But if they confess and forsake them, they will receive mercy." *Proverbs 28:13*

 Confess and Forsake Sin

Moving Pains (Part 1)

(Read 1 Thessalonians 2:17; 3:9-13)

27

OCTOBER

Kurt's father had been assigned to a new job in another town, and this would be Kurt's last day with his church friends before he and his family moved. He was eager to see his friends once more, but he hated good-byes.

"Someday all of us will be moving," said Mr. Rogers as he began the lesson. "If you know the Lord Jesus as Savior, your move will take you to live with him in heaven." He looked from one student to another. "Wouldn't it be great to have a class reunion there? I wonder—would you all be there?"

It was quiet in the room for a moment, then Kurt spoke up. "I would," he said. "I accepted Jesus as my Savior, so I'll see you again in heaven."

Suddenly the class time turned into a testimony service. One after another the members told how they had accepted Christ as Savior and were sure of going to heaven. Some mentioned that they looked forward to seeing their grandparents there. Kurt smiled. His grandparents were Christians, so he would see them in heaven too.

At the end of the Sunday school hour, the class gave Kurt an oversized card with the signatures and addresses of every member. They promised that if he would write to them, they would answer. "I'll miss you guys," Kurt said.

"We'll miss you, too," Mr. Rogers told him, "but judging from the testimonies we've heard here, we can look forward to all being together in heaven someday."

Kurt smiled. *RIJ*

HOW ABOUT YOU?

Have you or people you know ever had to move away? It's natural to feel sad then, but you can pray for one another, write to each other, and look forward to visits. Best of all, if you're both Christians, you can be sure you'll be together in heaven someday.

MEMORIZE:

"For though I am far away from you, my heart is with you. And I am very happy because you are living as you should and because of your strong faith in Christ." *Colossians 2:5*

 Christians Have Lasting Fellowship

Moving Pains (Part 2) (Read John 9:13-25)

28
OCTOBER

Kurt softly hummed the old song "When We All Get to Heaven" as he got ready for school on Monday morning. He was thinking about his friends in Sunday school. Suddenly he stopped as a new thought struck him. *What about the kids in my class at school? How many of them know the Lord?* Kurt began to think about them one by one. *I've never asked any of them, but if they don't know the Lord, I might never see them again after I move away.* It was then that Kurt made a silent commitment to God. "Help me, Lord, to use my last week at school to talk to my friends about you," he prayed. But he was scared. *What if they laugh at me?*

As Kurt thought about his friends again, another thought struck him. *What if they ask questions I can't answer?* Then he remembered a story about a blind man whom Jesus had healed. People had asked him all kinds of questions that he couldn't answer. He just told them he didn't know the answers to their questions and ended by saying, "One thing I know . . . I was blind; now I see." *That's what I'll do,* decided Kurt. *I'll tell them I don't have all the answers, but there's one thing I'm sure of: once I was separated from God because of sin, but now I'm God's child.*

Before the bell rang that morning, Kurt had his first chance to witness. His friend Jim asked what he had done with himself the day before. "I went to church and Sunday school and said good-bye to my friends there, but I'll see them again in heaven someday," replied Kurt. He took a deep breath and added, "I hope I'll see you there, too. Do you know Jesus?"

To his amazement, Jim nodded. "I wish I'd known you were a Christian sooner," he said. "I'm sure sorry you're going to move away. Now I'll probably be the only Christian in our room."

Kurt stared at Jim. Jim was a Christian too? Neither of them had said anything before! "I wish I'd said something sooner too," said Kurt. *RIJ*

HOW ABOUT YOU?

Have you ever asked any of your school friends if they are Christians? Are you afraid of being laughed at or of not knowing what to say? Ask God for courage. Then let them know where you stand. Perhaps your witness will give another shy Christian courage to speak for Jesus too.

MEMORIZE:

"'I don't know whether he is a sinner,' the man replied. 'But I know this: I was blind, and now I can see!'" *John 9:25*

 Speak Up for Jesus

Moving Pains (Part 3) (Read Ephesians 6:10-17)

29

OCTOBER

By noon on the first day at his new school, Kurt was wondering if he would ever make any friends there. He saw a number of boys leaning against the building a short distance away. *Well, if I want friends, I guess I better be friendly,* he thought. He walked up to them and spoke. "Hi, my name's Kurt Carlson."

The other boys looked him over carefully. Finally one of them spoke up. "Do you have any connections?" asked the boy. "Can you get your hands on any grass?"

Kurt was shocked. *Grass?* he thought. *He means marijuana. Do you have to use or sell drugs to "get in" with the guys in this school?* Kurt hesitated only for a moment. *I want friends, but . . . well, I guess I better look somewhere else for them.* He was about to turn and walk away when he remembered that he had asked God to help him be a good witness in this new school. Well, this sure was an opportunity!

Kurt took a deep breath. "If you guys think I use drugs," he said boldly, though he was trembling inside, "then you've got me sized up all wrong." He took another deep breath. "I'm a Christian, and I don't need anything to get me high. I'm happy with life just the way it is because I know Jesus."

Kurt turned and started to leave. As he did, there was a roar of laughter from the group, but Kurt felt good inside. In his old school he had never been faced with the temptation to mess around with drugs. Here the temptation had come on his very first day, but God had helped him be strong and not give in. As he walked away, he silently thanked the Lord for helping him—and he also asked the Lord to show him where he could find the right kind of friends.

RIJ

HOW ABOUT YOU?

Have you ever been tempted to become involved with drugs? with alcoholic drinks? with shoplifting? with stealing from someone's desk? Satan has many ways to tempt you. Don't give in. Use all the provisions God has made to resist temptation. Be strong in the Lord.

MEMORIZE:

"A final word: Be strong with the Lord's mighty power."

Ephesians 6:10

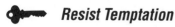 *Resist Temptation*

Moving Pains (Part 4) (Read 1 Timothy 1:12-15)

As Kurt left the boys who had talked about drugs, he noticed that one of them broke away from the group and was calling to him. Kurt stopped and waited.

30

OCTOBER

The boy offered a slight smile. "Hi! My name's Eric Keyes. You had a lot of courage speaking up like you did back there," he said. "If I'd done that my first day here, I'd be a lot better off. I used to go to church and Sunday school every week. But then I got to hanging around with this gang, and things really changed. My folks didn't care if I went to church or stayed home." He stopped and swallowed hard.

Kurt decided this was his opportunity to speak. "Hey, why don't you come to church with me next Sunday?" he urged.

But the boy shook his head. "Too late now," he said.

"It's not too late. Just because you goofed in the past doesn't mean you have to leave things that way," said Kurt. "If you'll come to Jesus and confess that you're a sinner and ask him to come into your life, he will." Kurt stopped briefly. "You do consider yourself a sinner, don't you?"

"Me? A sinner?" said Eric scornfully. "I'm the worst! That's what makes me a hopeless case."

"No one's hopeless," Kurt assured him, at the same time praying silently for guidance. "Why don't you ask the Lord to forgive you and change your life? That's what I did."

Eric sighed and shook his head. "Not now. I gotta get back to my friends," he said. "But you're OK! Stick to your guns. See ya."

Kurt watched as Eric walked away. One thing he knew for sure, he was going to pray for Eric every day and be a friend to him every chance he had. *RIJ*

HOW ABOUT YOU?

Do you feel like a "hopeless case"? Have you done even worse things than your parents know about? Well, then Jesus came to save you. He changed Saul, who was persecuting Christians, into Paul the apostle. He wants to make a new person out of you, too. Give your life to him today.

MEMORIZE:

"This is a true saying, and everyone should believe it: Christ Jesus came into the world to save sinners—and I was the worst of them all."

1 Timothy 1:15

 The Worst Sinner Can Be Saved

The Right Clothes (Read Revelation 19:5-9)

31

OCTOBER

Rachel and Jack were excited about the costume parade and contest their youth group was having on Saturday night. "I hope I win first prize," said Rachel as she worked on her princess costume.

"No chance," declared Jack. "I'm going to win. See—I just finished this bow to go with my Robin Hood costume," he said, proudly displaying his handiwork.

Rachel grinned. "We'll see," she said.

Both worked hard on their costumes. They wanted every little detail to be just right. "You both look great," declared Mother.

After the party, Rachel and Jack rushed into the house. "Guess what?" shouted Jack. "We both won. The judges couldn't decide which was best, so they gave us a tie!"

"Yeah," said Rachel. "We kinda hogged the prizes, I guess. I almost feel guilty—almost, but not quite!"

"Well," said Dad, "I'm glad you kids had fun. Did you learn something worthwhile, too?"

Jack nodded. "For our devotions, Mr. Perry talked about all the work that went into costumes for this one day of fun. Then he said we should make sure we have the right 'clothes' for something even more important."

"He was talking about being ready to go to heaven," added Rachel, "and about the 'robes of righteousness' we're given when we accept Jesus as Savior. He said that means we're covered with Christ's righteousness, which makes us presentable in God's sight."

"That's right," agreed Mother. "And how glad I am that all of us have our 'heaven clothes' already!" *HWM*

HOW ABOUT YOU?

Did you dress up in a costume and have a good time today? It's fun to go to a parade or party all dressed up so nobody will know you, isn't it? Have you taken as much care to be ready to go to heaven? You need the proper "garments" for that occasion too—you need Christ's righteousness. Think about it today.

"Dress" for Heaven

MEMORIZE:

"I am overwhelmed with joy in the Lord my God! For he has dressed me with the clothing of salvation and draped me in a robe of righteousness. I am like a bridegroom in his wedding suit or a bride with her jewels." *Isaiah 61:10*

God Knows Best (Read Psalm 25:8-13)

Matthew kicked an empty box out of the way as he walked into his father's study. He dropped down into a chair and stared out the window at the icicles hanging from the roof. "I think God made a big mistake sending us here," he said.

"What makes you say that, Son?" his dad asked. "You know your mother and I feel that God clearly showed us it was time to move on to a new ministry."

"But everything's so different here," complained Matthew. "We had a big church back home with lots of people. Hardly anybody comes to this church, and they don't have all the neat programs we did back home."

"This church is just getting started, Matthew," said Dad. "As the church grows, we'll have more programs for kids like you. Right now we just need to trust God that we're in the place he intended for us."

"Mail call!" Matthew's mother walked into the room and handed several letters to Dad and one to Matthew. "I got a letter, too," she said. "It's from Grandma Ryan. She sent a new cookie recipe."

Matthew's mouth watered as he remembered the last time he had milk and cookies in Grandma Ryan's kitchen. "Can you make some soon, Mom?" he asked eagerly.

"Wait a minute there, Son." Dad reached up to take the recipe out of Mom's hand. "Are you sure you want any of these? What if Grandma sent us a bad recipe? What if this recipe makes the worst cookies you've ever eaten?"

"It won't—Grandma tried it," said Matthew. "She wouldn't send us a recipe unless she knew it would turn out good."

A wide grin spread across Dad's face. "And do you think God would send us into a new ministry if he didn't already know that it would all work out for good?"

Matthew grinned back. "All right . . . I get it," he said. *EMO*

HOW ABOUT YOU?

Do you think of God as a loving heavenly Father or as a mean old bully who ruins your plans? Even when things aren't going as you'd like, remember that God loves you. He wants the best for you and all of his children.

MEMORIZE:

"The Lord leads with unfailing love and faithfulness all those who keep his covenant and obey his decrees." *Psalm 25:10*

 *God Can Be Trusted*

When Life Hurts (Read 1 Peter 5:6-7, 10-11)

2 NOVEMBER

Eric stood crying in a field on his grandpa's farm. They had come to bury his pet. Rascal had been a beautiful golden retriever. Eric had raised him from a puppy and trained him to fetch, shake hands, and sit. Unfortunately, Eric had not been able to keep him from chasing cars.

One afternoon Mother had found Rascal dead on the highway.

At first, Eric had been shocked and sad. "I should have found a better way to keep him safe," he moaned.

But now, as he stood between his parents on his grandpa's farm, he began to feel angry. "God knew how much I loved Rascal. Why did he let this happen?" The words burst from his mouth.

Dad knelt down beside Eric. "The way to love Rascal is a little like the way we love you," he said. "Even though we love you, we can't keep you from getting hurt sometimes. Is it our fault when you fall off your bike or you bump your head?"

Eric shook his head. "No," he said.

"Of course not," agreed Dad. "We could try to make sure you never got hurt by keeping you in bed all the time. But you wouldn't like that, and you need a certain amount of freedom to grow. You did your best to keep Rascal safe by fencing in the backyard. Maybe if you kept him chained in the garage, it would have been safer, but he wouldn't have liked that, and it wouldn't have been good for him either. It's not your fault he got hurt. But it's not God's fault either. When we give those we love freedom, they get hurt sometimes."

Eric looked thoughtful. "Then I'm going to ask God to help me feel better about losing Rascal," he decided.

His dad squeezed his shoulder. "That's a wise prayer. I'm sure God will do that," he said. *KEC*

HOW ABOUT YOU?

Do you blame God when things go wrong in your life, or do you remember that his love includes your freedom to grow? God does not keep all pain out of life. He does offer comfort when you are hurting, and he loves you always!

MEMORIZE:

"I [God], even I, am the one who comforts you." *Isaiah 51:12*

 Let God Comfort You

Katie's Problem (Read Proverbs 8:6-9)

3

Katie sat quietly on the way home. She had a decision to make. "You're awful quiet," said her friend Jill. Katie just smiled.

At home, Katie hurried to her room to change her clothes. She opened her notebook and again read the note from her friend Jennifer inviting her to sleep over Friday night. Katie really wanted to go. The problem was that she had already promised to go shopping with Jill on Friday night.

Maybe I could tell Jill I'm not feeling well, Katie thought.

Katie bounded down the stairs and into the kitchen. "Mom, I have a problem," she said. "I promised Jill I'd go to the shopping mall with her Friday evening, but today Jennifer asked me to sleep over on the same night!"

"Well, since you already had plans with Jill, didn't you tell Jennifer you couldn't come?" asked Mother.

Katie shook her head. "I would rather go to Jennifer's house," she said. Mother frowned. Katie hurried on. "And Jill wouldn't even have to know. I could tell her I don't feel well or something."

"That would be a lie," said Mom.

"But it wouldn't be *so* bad, would it?" persisted Katie. "Just one little lie?"

Mom pointed to the sink. "Do you see these dirty dishes in the sink?" she asked. Katie nodded. "I'm going to run some nice clean water and wash them," said Mom. "When I'm finished, would you care to drink the water?"

"Of course not," said Katie, puzzled.

"How about a drink after I wash just one small plate?" asked Mom.

"No!" said Katie. "What are you getting at?"

"Well," said Mom, "telling a lie is a little like washing dirty dishes in clean water. You may think one lie won't make a difference, but it does." *VRG*

HOW ABOUT YOU?

Do you think telling a lie just one time won't hurt anything? Remember, each time you tell a lie it makes a difference to you spiritually. God hates lying. Strive to be truthful.

MEMORIZE:

"For I speak the truth and hate every kind of deception."

Proverbs 8:7

 *Tell the Truth*

Gift Happy (Read 1 Corinthians 12:7-11)

4

NOVEMBER

"OK, boys!" called Coach Jensen. "If you want a chance to be goalie, form a line near the goal box." Brad ran to the end of the soccer field and joined the line forming there. He counted nine other players wanting to try out for goalie. "Brad!" Coach Jensen yelled. "It's your turn. See what you can do."

Brad waited while two players kicked the ball back and forth as they neared the goal box. Suddenly one of them sent off a powerful kick. Brad swooped down and grabbed the ball. He saved two out of three goal attempts.

When all of the boys had tried out for the position, Coach Jensen announced the three boys who would practice as goalies. Brad's name was not called.

Coach Jensen put his hand on Brad's shoulder as they headed for midfield. "Brad, why do you think you weren't chosen to be a goalie?" he asked.

"Guess I can't do it," Brad said quietly.

The coach shook his head. "You did a good job," he said. "But running and moving the ball is really your thing. We need you too much at midfield. We can't afford to lose you to being a goalie. Can you understand that?"

"Yeah, I guess," Brad said, his face brightening a little.

That evening Brad told his father what the coach had said. "You know, Brad," he said, "God gives each of us special gifts or talents. One of your soccer talents is running and moving the ball. When you use your gifts at your current position, you do the most good for your team. That's not to say that you will never be a goalie. Just not right now. It's the same in the church. God has given people different gifts. God is pleased and honored when each person uses his or her gift to help others."

"Well, I guess you're right," answered Brad. "I'll try to do my best right where the coach has me." *BMR*

HOW ABOUT YOU?

Are you happy with the talents you have? Would you rather have a gift God has given to someone else? Remember that God in his wisdom gives you the gifts that he knows are best for you. Learn to be thankful for those gifts and put them to good use.

MEMORIZE:

"It is the one and only Holy Spirit who distributes these gifts. He alone decides which gift each person should have."

1 Corinthians 12:11

 **Use Your Gifts**

No Bird Words (Read Hebrews 1:1-2; 2:1-4)

As the Martin family listened to the evening TV news, the reporter told about the oil spill on the West Coast, where many miles of beautiful sandy beaches were smeared with thick, black goo. "It looks as if Mother Nature may have to do the final cleanup job here," stated the reporter.

"Mother Nature!" Dad exclaimed. "Why don't they admit that this is in God's hands? Only he can overrule the weather and oceans to solve a problem of this size."

5

NOVEMBER

On the screen several forlorn seabirds stared into the camera. Unable to move, they were the picture of dejection, and fourteen-year-old Joe's eyes were full of pity. "People who don't know the Lord are a lot like those seabirds," observed Dad. "Can you guess what I mean?"

"Well . . ." Joe was thoughtful. "The birds have to be cleaned up if they're going to live. And someone who doesn't have Jesus as Savior needs to be cleaned up, too, to have eternal life." Joe had recently trusted Jesus as his Savior and had thought a lot about his new relationship with the Lord. The words were spoken with deep sincerity. Now he watched as an oil-soaked seabird struggled to free itself from the hands of a rescuer. "Poor thing!" murmured Joe. "If he doesn't let that lady help him, he'll die. Too bad she can't talk bird language and tell him that she'll help him."

"True," agreed Dad. Then he added, "I'm glad God speaks our language, aren't you? He tells us in the Bible that he has provided a way of cleaning up sin's mess. But people need to quit struggling against God and simply trust Jesus, his Son, to do for them what they can't do for themselves." *PIK*

HOW ABOUT YOU?

Are you struggling to clean up your heart and life? Stop trying. You can't do it by yourself. But God speaks your language—listen to him and let him take care of the "cleanup job." Trust him today.

MEMORIZE:

"How shall we escape, if we neglect so great salvation?"

Hebrews 2:3, KJV

 Trust God for Salvation

Leash That Lion (Read Proverbs 26:12-16)

6

NOVEMBER

All week Melissa had been very busy—so busy that she couldn't seem to find time to study for her regular Friday spelling test. She intended to study, but there was always something more interesting to do—read a book, go to gymnastics, play basketball with her brothers, watch a favorite TV show. The list went on. "I'll study tomorrow," she murmured as she climbed the stairs to her room each night.

After school on Friday, Melissa took her time walking home. She wasn't eager to hear Mom's usual question: "How was your spelling test?" Sure enough, when Melissa finally strolled into the house, the question came. "Well . . . I got a D," admitted Melissa. "I just never had time to study." Mom looked disappointed, but she didn't say anything.

After dinner Dad turned on the news. "Listen to this," he called. "I think you'll find it interesting." Melissa and Mom joined him to listen to a report about a lion that had escaped from a zoo. Those who lived near the zoo locked themselves in their homes when they heard about the lion on the loose. Children were not allowed to go outdoors to play.

Melissa shivered. "I'm glad I don't live there," she said.

Mom nodded. "A lion on the loose can really interfere with the things we want and need to do," she agreed. She looked at Melissa. "Are you sure you haven't met any lions lately?" she asked. At Melissa's puzzled expression, Mom explained, "I once read about a lion named Procrastinate. I thought maybe you had come across him. You see, to procrastinate means to postpone, or put things off. When Procrastinate runs loose in our life, he prevents us from doing what we should be doing—like studying."

Dad added, "The book of Proverbs says the lazy man uses the excuse that there's a lion loose in the streets to not do what needs to be done. It's important that we 'leash that lion' and get busy with what we need to do." *KAB*

 **Don't Put Things Off**

The Soapbox Racer (Read Deuteronomy 10:12-13, 20-21)

Denzel wanted a soapbox car exactly like the one his dad had when he won the Soapbox Derby as a boy, so he and Dad went to the attic to look for the blueprint of the winning car. Dad opened an old chest and took out a yellowed paper. "Ah! Here it is!" he said.

7

NOVEMBER

Denzel looked at the blueprint. "All right!" he exclaimed. "That's gonna show us how to build the best soapbox racer in town! What do we do first?"

He watched as Dad put the old blueprint back in the chest. "Hey! Why are you putting that back?" asked Denzel.

"We can just build the racer according to what we think is right," replied Dad.

Denzel stared at his dad. "Dad, this is a big project," he objected. "We need that blueprint. There's no way we can build a race car like yours without it."

Dad looked thoughtful. "Building a soapbox car is a small project compared to building our life," he said slowly. "But you don't seem to think you need a blueprint for your life."

Denzel frowned. "What do you mean?" he asked.

"Well," said Dad, "a few weeks ago you told us that one of your teachers said reading the Bible is not necessary—that people should believe and live according to what they thought was right. I've noticed that since then you've been complaining about having to go to church and Sunday school. And you've not been interested in our family devotion time. If you don't need the Bible to learn about God and his plan for your life, why should you need a blueprint to build a wooden race car?"

Denzel didn't know what to say. After an uncomfortable silence, he nodded. "I guess you're right," he admitted. "Without the blueprint, we can't build the racer, and without reading the Bible, we can't know God and his plan for our life." *PCS*

HOW ABOUT YOU?

Do you realize that you need God's help and direction in building your life? You find that in the Bible—your "blueprint" from God. Build your life by God's plan.

MEMORIZE:

"Be careful to obey all my commands so that all will go well with you and your children, because you will be doing what pleases the Lord your God." *Deuteronomy 12:28*

 Follow God's Blueprint

Take Your Medicine (Read Deuteronomy 10:12-13, 20-21)

8

NOVEMBER

Brad groaned. "It makes me so mad to be feeling sick on Saturday!"

Mother smiled sympathetically. "I know, but take these pills—they should bring down your fever," she said. While she adjusted the drapes, Brad dropped the pills into the wastebasket beside his bed.

Later, Mother came in with the phone. "Justin wants to talk to you," she said.

When Mother returned to the room later that afternoon, she found Brad tossing and turning from the fever. "Justin's folks are getting a divorce," Brad said wearily. "He's pretty upset, Mom, and I don't know how to help him."

Mother sat down on the edge of the bed. "I'm so sorry, Brad."

"Why doesn't God do something about it?" asked Brad. "He could make them love each other. In fact, God could stop all the fighting in the whole world. Why doesn't he?"

Mother sighed and shook her head sadly. "I know he could, but . . ." She stopped as she stared at the wastepaper basket. "Your pills!" she exclaimed. "No wonder your fever is going up! You haven't been taking your medicine!"

"I don't like it," Brad whined. "I hate swallowing pills!"

"You don't like being sick," said Mother, "and you know how to get well—but you refuse to take your medicine." She sighed, then continued. "In a sense, the world is sick, too, and God has provided a remedy. If men would follow his instructions, there wouldn't be family fights or divorce. There wouldn't be any war. But men have chosen to ignore God's laws. They have thrown the 'medicine' in the trash, so to speak." She stood up. "God doesn't force anyone to take the cure he offers, but I do. I'm going to get you a couple more pills, and this time you are going to take them, like it or not!" *BJW*

HOW ABOUT YOU?

Do you need to take a "dose of repentance"? Do you need to ask someone to forgive you? Are you uptight and unhappy because you've been refusing to obey God's Word? The only cure for sin-sickness is obedience to God's instructions. So . . . take your "medicine." You'll feel better immediately.

MEMORIZE:

"You must fear the Lord your God and worship him and cling to him. Your oaths must be in his name alone."

Deuteronomy 10:20

 *Obey God*

Cleaning Up (Read 1 John 1:8-10; 2:1-2)

"It's time for your baths, kids," said Mom. "Josh, you go first."

"Is it bedtime already? We just started this game," moaned Josh.

"That's OK. We can play tomorrow," his sister, Brianna, suggested. "Don't you remember, Josh? Tomorrow is the teachers' planning day . . . no school!"

"All right!" exclaimed Josh, giving Brianna a high five.

9
NOVEMBER

Brianna and Josh woke the next day to warm, golden sunshine. It was a perfect day for playing in the tree house Dad had built for them.

At eight-thirty that night, Mom announced bath time again.

"But I took a bath last night," Josh grumbled as he came into the house. "Why do I need one again tonight?"

"You need a bath tonight because you got dirty again by playing in the tree house," answered Mom.

"Not a tree house, Mom. A three-masted schooner!" Josh told her as he looked down at his dirty hands and legs and clothes. "I guess I don't look so good, do I?"

"Nope—and a dirty body is not attractive or healthy," said Mom.

"Do you know what my Sunday school teacher said last week?" asked Brianna. "She said sin is like dirt on our heart."

"Good thought," agreed Mother. "Aren't you glad that God says he'll forgive and wash our sins away when we confess them? We can be clean on the outside *and* on the inside. Remember that when you pray before you go to sleep tonight."

"OK," said Josh, giving each of his parents a hug. "Good night, Mom. Night, Dad."

"And don't forget your bath," added Mom as Joshua started to climb the stairs.

"Oh . . . right." Josh sighed. "My bath." *ECK*

HOW ABOUT YOU?

Do you know of any sin in your life—some wrong thing you've done? Have you told God about it and asked his forgiveness? His forgiveness is the best cleanser for every "spot" of sin!

MEMORIZE:

"But if we confess our sins to him, he is faithful and just to forgive us and to cleanse us from every wrong." *1 John 1:9*

 God's Forgiveness Cleanses You

A Snack before Supper

(Read 2 Corinthians 4:16-18; 5:1)

10

NOVEMBER

Jordan and his friend Mike stopped for a snack at an outdoor concession stand. Jordan ordered a hot dog with mustard and relish, but when he got it, he was disappointed. It was cold, the bun was stale, and there was too much mustard on it. "This is the worst hot dog I ever had," Jordan complained.

"Yeah," agreed Mike, "but you know what? I really don't care that much. Today's my birthday, and Mom and Dad are taking me out for supper. That's when I'm really going to eat! I'm gettin' a big, thick burger and fries and a coke and cake and ice cream. . . ."

"Hey! You're making me hungry," protested Jordan. He looked at the hot dog in his hand and took a bite.

As Jordan's father was reading the paper that evening, he found an article announcing the death of one of Jordan's former Sunday school teachers. "Mr. Jarvis never had much money," said Dad, "but now he's gone on to his real reward." He smiled at Jordan. "Sometimes Christians are tempted to envy the people of the world, wishing for some of the material things they have. But you know, Son, it doesn't really matter how much money or how much pleasure we have, because we know we'll enjoy our life in heaven."

Jordan nodded. "Hey, that reminds me of something Mike said!" he exclaimed. Then he told his dad about the poor food and Mike's comment. "Mike didn't even care about the awful hot dog because he was looking forward to going out for dinner," said Jordan.

Dad smiled, then said, "Although this life is a gift from God, I guess it is like a snack before supper. Heaven will be the big feast."

SLK

HOW ABOUT YOU?

Do you ever wish you were more popular or had more nice things? The happiness of the world—as well as the suffering—is only temporary and is nothing compared to what Christ gives to those who love him. Don't complain if life seems rough. For Christians, the real reward comes later!

MEMORIZE:

"Yet what we suffer now is nothing compared to the glory he will give us later." *Romans 8:18*

 The Best Is Yet to Come

Flowers and Thorns (Read Galatians 5:22-26)

Lori stood in front of the mirror and straightened her shirt. She carefully arranged her hair and stepped back to see herself. It was picture day at school, and Lori wanted the picture to be perfect.

Lori's little sister, Jodi, looked up with a smile. "You look pretty," she said. "Will you help me pick out something to wear? I want to look pretty, too."

"I don't have time to help you," replied Lori crossly. "I still have to find a necklace to go with this shirt."

Jodi looked disappointed. "Can I borrow a necklace?" she asked.

Lori shook her head. "You'd just lose it."

Jodi's eyes filled with tears. "No, I wouldn't," she said.

Lori frowned. "I don't have time for this," she snapped. "Quit pestering me!"

When Lori went to the kitchen, she saw a vase of flowers standing on the table. "Ohhh! Roses!" exclaimed Lori. "Where did they come from, Mom?"

"Mrs. Green brought them over," said Mother.

"They're so pretty!" Lori exclaimed. But when she reached for a flower, she pricked her finger on a sharp thorn. "Ouch!" she cried. Tears came to her eyes, and a bright drop of blood appeared on her finger. "The roses are pretty, but the thorns are too sharp," she complained as she held a tissue to her finger.

Mother looked thoughtful. "I wonder if that's what God thinks about people now and then," she murmured.

"People?" asked Lori. "What are you talking about?"

"Actually, I was thinking of you," Mother replied.

Lori was surprised. "Me?" she asked. "Why me?"

"Like the roses, you look very pretty this morning. But I overheard you talking to your sister—you were very sharp with her," explained Mother. "You hurt her feelings much like that thorn hurt your finger."

"You're right," Lori admitted. "I didn't act pretty. I'll go tell Jodi I'm sorry." *KEC*

11
NOVEMBER

HOW ABOUT YOU?

Do you worry about how you look on the outside? It is important to keep a good appearance, but it's even more important to be Christlike in your actions. Remember to treat others the way you wish to be treated.

MEMORIZE:

"Do for others as you would like them to do for you."

Luke 6:31

 Follow the Golden Rule

Benny the Boxcar (Read John 15:1-8)

12

NOVEMBER

Alex snuggled down to listen as Mother began reading a story at nap time. "Benny, a shiny new boxcar, awoke one day to find himself sitting on the tracks in a busy train yard," read Mother. "He thought himself quite handsome in his bright yellow coat of paint with *New York* printed on his side. He practically exploded with pride when he was filled with crates of fresh, juicy fruit. 'Why, I'm the finest boxcar in the yard!' he exclaimed as he looked around.

"'Hey, where are you going?' called a little red boxcar.

"Benny sniffed. 'Can't you read?' he asked. 'I'm going to New York. I'm a very important boxcar.'

"'I'm sure you are,' agreed the red car. 'But how are you going to get to New York?'

"Benny asked, 'Will you push me?'

"'Not I,' answered the other boxcar. 'I can't move by myself, either. But a big engine is coming here tonight, and he can pull us both.'

"All that afternoon Benny thought about the big engine, and he grew angry. 'Who does that engine think he is? After all, I'm important, too. I shouldn't have to sit here waiting for him to come and pull me.' So at nightfall, when the big engine chugged into the yard, Benny just yawned and looked the other way.

"'Hey, yellow car!' called the red car. 'We're leaving now. Are you ready to go?'

"Benny thought about what a fine boxcar he was. He felt like he should be able to go to New York on his own power. He tried to move, but he knew he really couldn't. Then he thought about having to sit in this noisy, dusty train yard for a long time—perhaps forever—with his load of fruit spoiling inside him. 'Hey, wait!' he called to the engine, who was just starting to pull away. 'I'm sorry I was so proud. I do need you. Please pull me to New York!'" Mother closed the book, tucked the blankets around Alex, and tiptoed out of the room. *SLK*

HOW ABOUT YOU?

Are you something like Benny the boxcar? You may think you can make yourself grow as a Christian without God's help. But you can't. You need him to help you grow and to do what's right.

MEMORIZE:

"Yes, I am the vine; you are the branches. Those who remain in me, and I in them, will produce much fruit. For apart from me you can do nothing." *John 15:5*

 You Need God's Help

The Messengers (Read Matthew 21:33-42)

"I'm tired of being preached at all the time!" complained Matt. "I get preached at in school, in church, and even at home: 'Love your brother.' 'Obey your mother.' 'Pray every day.' 'Watch what you say.'"

Dad raised his eyebrows. "Son, God gives us teachers, pastors, and parents to help us," he said.

Matt shrugged. "Maybe so. But it gets to me the way everyone is trying to tell me how to live. They're not perfect. Who are they to lay down laws?"

13

NOVEMBER

"They don't lay down the laws," answered Dad. "They simply bring God's laws to us. They're his messengers."

Matt answered, "Well, I don't like messengers!"

When Matt came in from helping Mr. Bentley at the grocery store the next evening, he was angry. "I made a delivery today to old Mrs. Carrington. Mr. Bentley told me to tell her she wouldn't be able to charge anything else to her account until she paid her bill. And would you believe that old lady bawled me out? She called me a 'smart-aleck teenager.' Why should she yell at me? Why doesn't she yell at Mr. Bentley? I'm just the delivery boy. I just took her the message."

A funny look crossed Matt's face when his dad smiled and said, "I guess she doesn't like messengers. I seem to remember that you don't like them, either." Dad paused, then added, "If you don't like the message your pastor and teacher are giving you, Matt, you should tell God, not the messengers. Right?"

Matt ran his fingers through his hair. "I guess I'm just like old Mrs. Carrington," he admitted thoughtfully.

Dad nodded. "I'm afraid it's not the message or the messengers that are wrong," he said. "It's you."

"Well, I don't know if Mrs. Carrington will ever change, but I'm going to—starting right now!" declared Matt. *BJW*

HOW ABOUT YOU?

Do you gripe and grumble when a message from the Bible applies to you? When others bring you God's message, you had better listen. Don't get mad and grumble at them. They are simply the messengers. Listen to them.

MEMORIZE:

"Obey your spiritual leaders and do what they say. Their work is to watch over your souls, and they know they are accountable to God."

Hebrews 13:17

 Listen to God's Messengers

A Wish Book (Read Psalm 34:8-10)

14

"Here comes the mailman," called Joyce. She had been watching at the window, hoping for a letter from a friend. She hurried out to get the mail. As she pulled letters and pamphlets from the mailbox, a small catalog caught her eye. She began to leaf through it as she went back into the house.

"A wish book," said Mother, glancing at the catalog Joyce was holding.

"A wish book?" Joyce repeated. "Why do you call it that?"

Mother smiled. "Because you look at the pictures and you wish you had this or you wish you had that," she replied. "There are lots of things you'd like to have, but usually you don't really need them."

Joyce sat down on the couch, and Mother came and sat beside her. For a few minutes they turned the pages of the catalog in silence. Then Mother spoke up. "Sometimes we get things all mixed up and think our wishes are really needs," she said thoughtfully. "God has promised to supply all of our needs, but he hasn't promised to supply all our wants and wishes."

Joyce thought about that. There were lots of things in the catalog she'd like to have, but she didn't really need them. Maybe there wasn't anything wrong with wishing for things like that, but Joyce knew her mother was right. She could trust God to supply everything she really needed. And she knew that sometimes he would give her her wants and wishes, too, as one way to show his love. *SLK*

HOW ABOUT YOU?

Do you sometimes get wishes and needs mixed up? Do you wish for a bike? a new toy? more money? Ask God to help you know which are selfish wishes and which are things you really need. He may give you some of the things you want, too, but you can always count on him to supply all your needs.

MEMORIZE:

"And this same God who takes care of me will supply all your needs from his glorious riches, which have been given to us in Christ Jesus." *Philippians 4:19*

 God Supplies Your Needs

Answer the Knock (Read Ecclesiastes 11:9-10; 12:1, 13-14)

"Cindy, I'm going to the store, so I'll be gone an hour or so," said Mother one afternoon. "While I'm gone, I'd like you to clean your room."

"OK," agreed Cindy. She sat down on the edge of her bed and looked around. *It shouldn't take too long to get this done,* she thought. *First I'll straighten my closet.*

15

NOVEMBER

As she worked, Cindy heard a knock on the back door, but she was standing on a chair, straightening her closet shelves, so she didn't bother to answer it. A little later there was another knock, but this time Cindy was dusting her dresser, so she continued to ignore it. *It's probably the little kids next door,* she thought. *I wish they wouldn't always bother me.*

When Mother returned from the store, she seemed surprised to see Cindy. "Didn't Aunt Nel stop by for you?" she asked. "I saw her in the grocery store. She was on the way to Grandpa's farm. She asked if it would be all right if she took you along. I was sure you would want to go. I told her it would be OK."

"Aunt Nel!" cried Cindy. "That's who I heard knocking! Oh, I do want to go with her! I love to play on the farm!"

"Why didn't you answer her knock?" asked Mother.

"I . . . I thought it was the neighbor kids," said Cindy. "Oh, if only I had gone to the door!"

"I'm sorry you didn't," said Mother, "but it's too late to do anything about it now. Come have some milk and a cookie—maybe that will make you feel a little better."

As Cindy ate her snack, Mother smiled at her. "Remember the verse about Jesus knocking at your heart's door asking to come in and be your Savior?" asked Mother.

Cindy nodded. "I'm glad I didn't ignore his knocking," she said.

RIJ

HOW ABOUT YOU?

Jesus is knocking at your heart's door too. He wants to come in to be your Savior. If you want to find out more, ask a trusted adult.

MEMORIZE:

"'Look! Here I stand at the door and knock. If you hear me calling and open the door, I will come in, and we will share a meal as friends.'" *Revelation 3:20*

 *Let Jesus In*

The Pruning (Read John 15:1-5)

16

"Mom, what are you doing?" cried Melissa in dismay as she saw her mother clipping away branch after branch from each of the rose bushes. "These roses were so pretty, and they had grown so much! Why are you cutting their branches all off?" asked Melissa.

Mom looked up from where she was kneeling in the rose garden. "Why, Melissa, don't you remember?" she asked in surprise. "I do this every year. It's called 'pruning.' Roses have to be pruned, or the flowers won't be as large and pretty when spring comes."

"It doesn't hurt the plants?" Melissa asked as she reached out to touch one of the branches.

Mom smiled. "No." She paused. "Did you know that God prunes us? When he does that, it may hurt a little right when it happens, but it helps us grow." Melissa's eyes widened. "Sometimes," Mom added, "hard things happen in our life, and we hurt a great deal, but . . ."

"Like when Grandma got sick?" interrupted Melissa. "And when our dog got run over?"

"Yes," Mom answered. "Hard things in life can cause us to go to God or to run from him. If we choose to go to him, we find out how good he is at giving peace and comfort. We learn that we can trust him even when things look dark. Going through those experiences teaches us to depend on Jesus more than ever."

Melissa was thoughtful. "Then I guess it's worth it to be pruned, right?"

"More than worth it!" Mom said as she continued snipping away. *KRL*

HOW ABOUT YOU?

Everyone has times when life seems especially hard. But if you have given your life to Jesus, he may want to use those hard times to draw you closer to himself and to make you stronger spiritually. So even though you don't like the hard times, remember that Jesus is working out something beautiful in you.

MEMORIZE:

"He cuts off every branch that doesn't produce fruit, and he prunes the branches that do bear fruit so they will produce even more." *John 15:2*

 God "Prunes" You

Keep on Practicing (Read Ephesians 6:10-17)

Tim was excited as he skated out onto the ice for his first hockey practice. Some kids fell as soon as their skates touched the ice. Not Tim. He had started skating when he was three.

"We're going to practice hitting the puck," said Coach.

Smack! Tim's stick hit the ice hard. Then his feet went out from under him.

"Try again, Tim," called Coach as he skated over to help Tim up. "Put your hands on the stick like this, and try again." Tim followed the coach's directions, and this time he hit the puck!

17

NOVEMBER

By the end of practice, though, he was discouraged. "I thought it would be easier," he told his dad.

"You're a good skater, Tim," said Dad, "and with practice, you can learn to play hockey, too. You just need to learn to handle that hockey stick." So Tim practiced each day after school.

"Dad, can I go practice hockey with the guys tonight?" asked Tim after dinner a few days later. "I'm getting pretty good with my hockey stick!"

"Great!" said Dad. "I knew you could learn how to do that. By the way, how are you doing with your 'sword'?"

"My sword?" asked Tim. "What sword?"

Dad smiled and held up a Bible. "This one," he said. "God's Word is called the 'sword of the Spirit.' It's even more important to practice using God's equipment than it is to practice using your hockey equipment." He handed the Bible to Tim. "Have you learned your verses for Bible Club?" he asked.

"I'll get right on it, Dad," answered Tim with a smile. *SLR*

HOW ABOUT YOU?

Do you play any kind of sport or a musical instrument? You need to practice using your equipment! And don't neglect the equipment God offers. Your Bible is your "sword" to fight against the devil. The more you study it, the better you'll be in battle.

MEMORIZE:

"Put on salvation as your helmet, and take the sword of the Spirit, which is the word of God." *Ephesians 6:17*

 Practice Using Your Sword

The Appointment Book (Read Romans 5:12, 17-21)

18

NOVEMBER

Miranda hung up the phone. "Either I'm getting forgetful, or Jennifer is," she told her mother. "I thought I was supposed to meet her at four o'clock, but she says we agreed on three o'clock. This is the second time I've kept her waiting."

"Sounds like you ought to write things down," suggested Mother. "I have something that might help you." She took a small book from a shelf and handed it to Miranda.

"An appointment book—this is perfect," said Miranda. After that, she carefully recorded her appointments, and she didn't fail to keep any of them.

"Pastor's sermon today was interesting," said Miranda on the way home from church one Sunday. "You know—the things he said about heaven."

"Yes, it was," replied Dad. "Miranda, have you trusted Jesus as your Savior so you can go to heaven? You've never really told us that you have."

Miranda shrugged. "Well, I'm real young yet," she said. "I have plenty of time."

"How do you know?" asked Mother. "I was just thinking about your appointment book—you set appointments and you keep them. Do you know that God sets appointments too? The Bible says it's destined that each person dies only once and after that comes judgment.' For some people, this appointment comes late in life. For others it comes early."

"That's right. Your appointment to meet God may come at any time," agreed Dad. "Here's another thing to think about: God has set a time for Jesus to come again and take believers to heaven to live with him forever. But only God knows his time schedule. He simply tells us to be ready."

"Well, perhaps we could talk about it some more at home," answered Miranda. "I have some questions." *MRP*

HOW ABOUT YOU?

Are you a Christian? Or are you interested in becoming a Christian? If so, find a trusted Christian adult or friend you can talk to.

MEMORIZE:

"There are many rooms in my Father's home, and I am going to prepare a place for you."

John 14:2

 Be Ready to Meet God

Stair Steps (Read Psalm 37:23-31)

19

NOVEMBER

"Oh, boy! Fried chicken!" exclaimed Jim. "I'm glad you invited me to dinner."

His grandparents smiled. "I noticed you went forward at the end of the service this morning, Jim," said Grandpa as he passed the chicken. "Was there a special reason?"

"Yes, sir," said Jim. "You know how I've always wanted to be a doctor?" Grandpa nodded, and Jim continued, "Well, even though I'm just a kid, I really feel the Lord wants me to be a missionary doctor someday. Today I said yes." Grandma's eyes filled with happy tears, but Jim frowned slightly as he helped himself to a biscuit. "I just don't know how I can ever do it, though. Mom says it costs a lot of money to go to medical school, and we're pretty poor since Dad died," he said.

"With God everything is possible," quoted Grandma softly.

After dinner Grandpa asked Jim to run upstairs and get a book for him. "And let's see you leap up there in one bound."

Jim laughed. "I can't do that," he said. "There are seventeen steps to the top."

"You have to take one step at a time, don't you—or maybe two steps since your legs are getting so long," said Grandpa. "Now it seems to me that reaching your goal of being a doctor is like reaching the top of the stairs. God doesn't expect you to get there all at once. He expects you to take one step at a time."

"That's where faith comes in," said Grandma. "If the Lord says to step, you lift your foot, trusting him to make your way possible."

"I guess I took my first step today when I said yes," said Jim. "What do you suppose the next one will be?"

"Probably to study hard," suggested Grandpa.

Jim grinned. "I guess I better go home and start on my second step," he said. "I've got a test tomorrow." *MRP*

HOW ABOUT YOU?

Do you feel God wants you to do something that seems impossible to you? He can help you study, witness, be kind, find a job, obey. Be sensitive to what he wants you to do both now and in the future. Don't be afraid to say yes to God. If he wants you to do something, it's not impossible.

MEMORIZE:

"Jesus looked at them intently and said, 'Humanly speaking, it is impossible. But with God everything is possible.'"

Matthew 19:26

 You Can Do What God Asks

The Oyster and the Pearl

(Read James 1:2-4; 1 Peter 1:6-7)

20

NOVEMBER

"It's just not fair," complained Kimberly, pointing to the cast on her leg. "Why do bad things always happen to me?"

"Trials come to all of us," answered her mother. "We all need help in developing Christian character."

"Well, couldn't I get more help for my character at school and church than lying here?" asked Kimberly.

"We have to leave that sort of thing in God's hands," replied Mother. "He knows what you need." She stood up. "I want to show you something," she said. She left the room but soon returned with a small box. She opened the lid, and Kimberly peered inside.

"Oh, the pin Grandma used to wear!" exclaimed Kimberly. "It's so pretty. Is that a real pearl?"

Mother nodded. "Do you know how this pearl was formed?" she asked.

"Sure," said Kimberly. "Something—maybe a grain of sand—got inside an oyster's shell and hurt him. So he made some stuff to cover the sand. And after a long time, it was a pearl."

"That's right," said Mother. "An oyster makes something beautiful out of things that irritate it. Don't you think we should follow that principle?"

"Whew!" said Kimberly with a frown. "My leg really hurts! How can I make anything beautiful from that?"

"Maybe this is a good time to learn patience," suggested Mother.

Kimberly sighed. "Yeah, I guess I do get upset when things don't go my way," she admitted. "OK, I'll work on doing better. But how long am I going to have to wear this stupid cast? It's so . . ." Kimberly stopped. Then she grinned. "There I go again! Maybe I have to wear it just long enough to grow the pearl of patience."

MRP

HOW ABOUT YOU?

Do troubles make you cross and upset? Everything in a Christian's life is there for a purpose. God may use trials to teach you patience and endurance or to teach you to trust him. Learn to trust him as he develops beautiful pearls of Christian character from your troubles.

MEMORIZE:

"Dear brothers and sisters, whenever trouble comes your way, let it be an opportunity for joy." *James 1:2*

 Trials Can Beautify Your Life

The Root of the Matter (Read Ephesians 4:26-27, 30-32)

Jennifer plopped down at the kitchen table. "I'm never going to speak to Melody and Stacie again!" she declared. Mother tried to talk with her about the problem, but Jennifer just grumbled about Melody and Stacie. All evening she was restless and unhappy. She skipped devotions because she was angry, and it took her a long time to go to sleep.

21

NOVEMBER

The next morning she had a dreadful stomachache. "Ohhhh!" she moaned. "It hurts! I can't go to school."

Mother felt Jennifer's forehead. "You don't have a fever, but I'll let you stay home this morning," she decided. "We'll see how you feel by noon."

Again Jennifer was restless. She got up, put on her robe, and went to the kitchen. "What are you doing?" she asked. Her mother was lifting a drooping plant from a small pot to the newspaper-covered counter. "Is that plant dead?"

"No," Mother replied, "it's root-bound and needs more room to grow." As Mother worked, she talked with her daughter. "I suspect you and this plant both have a root problem," she said. Jennifer looked puzzled, and Mother continued. "I don't think your stomachache is really your problem. I think the root of your problem is the anger that has tightened up the muscles of your stomach. Staying home from school and taking medicine won't cure that. The cure is forgiving Melody and Stacie. You need to get rid of the bitterness inside you."

Jennifer stared at her hands. "How can I?" she asked.

Mother put her arm around Jennifer's shoulders. "Ask God to forgive you," she suggested, "and ask him to help you forgive the other girls. Then talk with them. Admit your part in the quarrel and forgive their faults."

Jennifer nodded. "I'll get ready for school." *BJW*

HOW ABOUT YOU?

Bitterness and anger can cause headaches, stomachaches, and many other aches. Confess your anger to the Lord. Ask him to give you a forgiving spirit. He forgives you. Will you not do the same for others? You'll soon be feeling much better.

MEMORIZE:

"Get rid of all bitterness, rage, anger, harsh words, and slander, as well as all types of malicious behavior."

Ephesians 4:31

 Get Rid of Bitterness

Grandma Redwood (Read Psalm 92:1-2, 12-15)

22

NOVEMBER

"Isn't Grandma too old to be teaching Sunday school?" Ryan asked one day. "I mean, she's almost seventy."

"Why, no, she's not too old!" Mother replied. "Her first graders are crazy about her. And she tells me she's learning and growing as much as the kids are."

Some weeks later, Ryan and his parents were enjoying a vacation in the redwood and sequoia forests in California. There they saw majestic old trees. "These are living skyscrapers," one of the guides told them. "They are the tallest and among the oldest living things on earth. And they grew from a tiny seed. Some of these trees were probably already two thousand years old when Jesus was a boy."

"Wow! What makes them live so long?" asked Ryan.

"The bark is sometimes two feet thick," the guide answered. "That helps the tree resist attacks from forest fires, insects, and diseases."

Ryan looked up to the top of the giants. "Is this one still growing?" he asked.

"It sure is," the guide replied. "They grow very slowly, but they never stop growing as long as they live."

"Old, but still growing," Mother said softly to Ryan. He looked puzzled. "Like Grandma," she reminded him. Mother smiled as they walked along the path. "It was God's creative power that put life into a tiny seed and caused it to grow up into a monarch of the forest," said Mother. "That same power put a seed of faith in your grandma's heart when she was very small. That tiny seed grew into a strong, mature Christian. Like the thick bark on the redwood tree, the unfailing love of God protected her from the fires of temptation and the attacks of disappointment and sorrow."

"And now, even though she's getting old, she's still growing and learning," Ryan concluded. *TVV*

HOW ABOUT YOU?

Do you know Christians who are serving the Lord in their old age? Thank God for them. How about you? Are you beginning to grow into a mature Christian? Do you trust in the love of God to surround you and keep you from sin? Begin preparing now for a long life of growth and service to Jesus.

MEMORIZE:

"Even in old age they will still produce fruit; they will remain vital and green." *Psalm 92:14*

 To Live Is to Grow

The No-Feed Horse (Read 1 Peter 1:22-23; 2:1-3)

Jay's Uncle Bill was a rough but kindhearted rancher, and Jay liked listening to the many interesting stories his uncle told. "Did I ever tell you about the no-feed horse?" asked Uncle Bill when Jay was visiting him one day.

"No. What about him?" asked Jay eagerly.

"Well, a fella I heard about once figured out how to raise a horse that didn't need to eat," said Uncle Bill. "Just imagine the money that would save us ranchers!"

23
NOVEMBER

"How did he do it?" asked Jay.

"He started out by reducing the horse's feed by an ounce a day," said Uncle Bill. "Then he reduced it by two ounces, and then three ounces, and so on. He did that until the horse was getting on by almost no food at all."

"Wow!" exclaimed Jay. "Then what happened?"

"That's the sad part," said Uncle Bill. "Just when he thought he was going to make it, the horse up and died."

For a moment Jay sat openmouthed. Then he noticed his uncle's grin, and he realized he'd been had! "Uncle Bill! You're joshing me!" he accused.

Uncle Bill laughed out loud. "Yep, I reckon I am," he admitted. "But I've known some fellas in real life almost as foolish as that farmer. Always seem to think they can get something for nothing." He chewed thoughtfully on a piece of straw. "I've known some Christians like that too," he added. "They start off reading their Bibles and praying and going to church regularly. Then they taper off, and if they don't see any bad results right away, they assume they can get by without nourishing their souls at all. But whether they realize it or not, their spiritual life is suffering."

"Boy," said Jay, "I hope I'm never that foolish." *SLK*

HOW ABOUT YOU?

Do you think you can get by day after day without nourishing your soul? Do you feel you can live your life successfully without God? Watch out! The Bible contains many warnings against trying to live without God's Word, prayer, and fellowship with other believers. Don't let your spirit go hungry. Let God nourish your soul.

MEMORIZE:

"But Jesus told him, 'No! The Scriptures say, "People need more than bread for their life."'" *Luke 4:4*

 Don't Neglect Your Spiritual Life

Some for the Lord (Read 2 Corinthians 9:5-11)

24

NOVEMBER

Matt and Mike had spent an interesting week with their grandparents. They spent a lot of time helping Grandpa chop wood and clean out the barn. Because they had worked hard, Grandpa had given them each twenty-five dollars. "This sure will help my bike fund," Matt said as Dad drove them back home.

"And it'll be enough for me to buy that new game I've been wanting," added Mike.

Dad nodded. "But don't forget that part of the money goes into your savings account," he reminded them.

"Right, and some goes to church," said Mike, but he didn't say it happily. In fact, he sounded rather upset.

"Why are you giving money to the Lord?" Dad asked.

Mike looked at his dad in surprise. "Because I'm supposed to."

"Do you really know what the Bible says about giving?" asked Dad.

"Not exactly," Mike admitted.

"Well," said Dad, "it says we should not only give but that we should do it cheerfully. In fact . . ."

"Oh, I remember when the pastor was talking about that," interrupted Matt. "He said the Greek meaning of the word *cheerful* is 'hilarious.' That's how excited we should be about giving to the Lord."

Mike was thoughtful. Since the Lord had done so much for him, he realized he should be happy about being able to give some of his money in return! *LMW*

HOW ABOUT YOU?

Do you give some of your allowance or some of the money you earn to the Lord? Do you do it grudgingly, wishing you could keep it for yourself? The Lord not only desires that we give our money to him, but he also wants us to do it with a proper attitude.

MEMORIZE:

"You must each make up your own mind as to how much you should give. Don't give reluctantly or in response to pressure. For God loves the person who gives cheerfully."

2 Corinthians 9:7

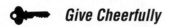 *Give Cheerfully*

All Things, Big and Small (Read Psalm 107:1-2, 21-22)

Tami stepped into the hospital room where her twin brother, Terry, was recovering from foot surgery. In her hands she carried a large poster with the word *thanksgiving* printed on it. "It's part of our Sunday school lesson," she explained. "We have to fill in things that make us thankful—one thing for each letter in the word *thanksgiving.*"

25
NOVEMBER

They decided to do it together, taking turns at suggesting words, and Tami started it off with *turkey* for *T.*

As they worked, Tami noticed that her brother was putting down things like *hospital, nurse,* and *salvation.* "You're always so serious," complained Tami. "I'm putting down fun things!"

When they were finished, their list looked like this:

T —turkey
H —hospital
A —apples
N —nurse
K —kids
S —salvation
G —giblet gravy
I —instruction
V —video games
I —improvement
N —nuts
G —God

The children looked over the complete list. "I'm glad now that you were serious," said Tami. "My words seem a bit silly compared to yours."

"No, they don't," replied Terry. "I'm glad you put those down. It gives us a good balance. Dad says we need to thank God for everything—big or small." *RIJ*

HOW ABOUT YOU?

Do you give thanks for toys but forget to give thanks for parents? Or maybe you give thanks for health but forget to give thanks for sunshine? All things come from the hand of God. Thank him for everything.

MEMORIZE:

"Thank God for his Son—a gift too wonderful for words!"

2 Corinthians 9:15

 Give Thanks for Big and Small Things

The "Fearbreak" (Read Psalm 112)

26

NOVEMBER

"That's enough of that!" Dad said, taking one hand off the steering wheel and clicking off the radio. "The old saying 'No news is good news' is sure true," he commented.

"Who 'napped that little girl?" Jennifer asked fearfully.

"Are those escaped convicts still in this area?" Allan asked.

Mother sighed. "I don't know, but don't be afraid. We're God's children, and he has promised to be with us everywhere we go."

"But I'm scared . . . ," began Jennifer.

"Look! Look! There's a fire over there!" Allan pointed at the horizon. "What a lot of excitement we're having—escaped convicts, and now a prairie fire!"

As they neared the fire, Dad said, "That's a controlled fire. It looks like the farmer has set it to make a firebreak."

"What's a firebreak?" Allan asked.

"It's a wide strip of plowed or burned-off ground around the buildings," explained Dad. "When a fire that's raging across the prairie reaches the firebreak, it dies because there is nothing to feed it. I don't know why this farmer is making one now. Perhaps because it's a dry season, and he just wants to be prepared. If a fire should come, his property will be safe."

"Just as he fights fire with fire, we can overcome fear with fear," Mother put in. "Fear of the Lord drives other fear out of the heart."

Dad nodded. "Our fear of God builds a 'fearbreak' around us," he said.

"But I'm not scared of God," Allan said. "He loves me."

"The kind of fear we're talking about is a kind of respect and honor," explained Mother.

Jennifer wrinkled her brow, then smiled. "Well, I 'spect God's gonna take care of us, so I'm not scared now." *BJW*

HOW ABOUT YOU?

Are you afraid of the dark? of being kidnapped? of losing someone you love? Try fighting fear with fear. Fear (or respect) God. Trust and obey him as your heavenly Father. Build a "fearbreak" around your heart now.

MEMORIZE:

"Those who fear the Lord are secure; he will be a place of refuge." *Proverbs 14:26*

 *Trust God*

Best Friends (Read John 15:9-15)

Andy played all afternoon with his best friend, Joe, who lived down the street. When Mom called him home for supper, Andy came in smiling and whistling a happy tune. "My," said Mother, "you're in a good mood. Did you enjoy your day?"

"Boy, did I!" exclaimed Andy. "I just spent the whole afternoon with my very best friend in the whole wide world."

27

NOVEMBER

"I see," said Mother. "How do you know he's your very best friend?"

Andy thought a moment and then replied, "Well, we spend a lot of time together. We always have fun playing games or talking or just hanging around. We help each other, and we cheer each other up when we're feeling bad."

"You know," said Mother in a quiet, gentle voice, "you just described my best friend, too—except for one thing. My best friend did something extra special for me a long time ago. Something that no other best friend could ever do."

"Really? What did your best friend do for you?" wondered Andy.

Mother smiled. "My best friend loved me so much that he gave his life for me so that I could have eternal life with him."

"Oh, you're talking about Jesus, aren't you?" asked Andy. "I never really thought about him as a best friend."

"Well, he will be if you let him," Mother said. "You can do some of the same kinds of things with Jesus that you like to do with Joe. You can include him in everything you do. He's always there for you, just like a best friend."

"Yeah, he is, isn't he?" said Andy thoughtfully. He grinned. "I guess Joe won't mind much if he's only my second-best friend, especially after I tell him who my very best friend in the whole wide world really is," he said. "And I'll tell him I don't mind if he makes Jesus *his* best friend, too." *DVG*

HOW ABOUT YOU?

Do you have a best friend? Friends are special blessings—especially Christian friends. They have wonderful times together. Even more special is the friendship you may have with Jesus. He wants to be your friend, and he's the most faithful friend you can ever have.

MEMORIZE:

"There are 'friends' who destroy each other, but a real friend sticks closer than a brother." *Proverbs 18:24*

 Make Jesus Your Best Friend

Water of Life (Read John 4:5-14)

28

NOVEMBER

"Hey!" said Penny. "What's going on here?" She had turned the kitchen faucet as far open as she could, but all she got was a sputtering sound. Penny thumped her glass on the counter with disgust. "I'm so thirsty I could croak!"

"Sorry," replied Mother. "When I got home from town, I found a notice on the door saying the water department would be working on our street today. If I had known it earlier, I would have filled some containers. But you won't die of thirst. There's some orange juice in the fridge."

Soon Penny's thirst was satisfied, but her brother, Mike, was not so fortunate. When he came in and reached for the juice jar, it was empty. "Do we have some milk?" he asked hopefully.

"Sorry. I emptied the carton this morning," said Mother.

Mike swallowed hard and staggered to a chair. "Water! Water!" he cried.

Penny laughed as she went to answer a tap at the door.

It was Molly, their next-door neighbor. She walked in with a gallon jug of water. "I thought you might be needing this," she said, pouring some into a glass.

Mike reached out and eagerly drank the whole glassful of water. Then with an ecstatic sigh, he said, "Oh, thank you, Molly. You saved my life!"

During dinner the family talked about how grateful they were for their restored water supply. "It must be terrible to be without water," observed Mike.

Dad nodded. "But there's a thirst even more terrible," he said. "It's the thirst for love, for forgiveness, for God. Just as a drink of water can save us from physical death, Jesus, the Living Water, can save us from spiritual death." *TVV*

HOW ABOUT YOU?

Do you feel unsatisfied even though you have many good things in your life? Then you have a thirsty soul. Jesus can satisfy that thirst. Will you reach out in faith and take from him the salvation that he offers?

MEMORIZE:

"But the water I give them takes away thirst altogether. It becomes a perpetual spring within them, giving them eternal life." *John 4:14*

 Jesus Satisfies Thirsty Souls

All Better (Read Psalm 103:1-5)

29

NOVEMBER

Tessa put her baby doll in its cradle. "Night-night," she said and covered the doll with a blanket. She set her Raggedy Ann and Andy dolls on a rocking chair and pushed them gently back and forth. "One, two, three dolls," she counted. "That's how many old I am—one, two, three."

Tessa's new puppy, Darby, bounded into the room. Quick as a wink, he snatched Raggedy Andy in his mouth and ran away. "No! No!" yelled Tessa, and she ran after Darby. "Bad puppy!" She caught hold of one of Raggedy Andy's arms. Darby thought it was a game. He held on tightly to the doll and shook his head back and forth. He pulled one way, and Tessa pulled the other way. There was a loud ripping sound. Andy's arm came off, and the stuffing started to come out.

Tessa finally got the doll away from Darby and ran to Mother. "Mommy," said Tessa, "my dolly got hurt, and I want a Band-Aid to make it all better."

Mother looked at the doll. "A Band-Aid won't make Andy's arm better," she said. "I'll have to sew it back on."

"A Band-Aid made *my* finger better," said Tessa.

Mother shook her head. "Band-Aids keep your sores clean," she said, "but they don't make injuries heal."

"Then how did I get better?" asked Tessa.

"God makes us better because he created us in a wonderful way. When we are sick or hurt, our antibodies fight the germs and infections so we can heal," said Mother as she threaded a needle.

Tessa watched as Mother began to push the needle back and forth through Raggedy Andy's arm and body. "I'm glad God makes me better," said Tessa, "and you don't have to sew me!" *PLR*

HOW ABOUT YOU?

Do you thank God for giving you a wonderful body? Thank God for doctors and medicines, too. But always remember that it's God who has the power to heal. When you're sick or hurt, ask him to heal you. Ask him to heal others who are ill also. And be sure to thank him when you feel better again.

MEMORIZE:

"Praise the Lord, I tell myself, and never forget the good things he does for me. He forgives all my sins and heals all my diseases." Psalm 103:2-3

 **God Heals**

Tasting the Turkey (Read Psalm 84:10-12)

30

"Yum!" murmured Bryan softly. It was Thanksgiving Day, and he was in the kitchen, sneaking bits of turkey.

"Bryan!" exclaimed Mother. "What are you doing?" She shooed him out to take his place at the table. Soon dinner was served, and it was all delicious!

The following Sunday, Bryan attended his Sunday school class. "Hey, Bryan, did you hear that Joe Neilson died?" asked Aaron, one of his classmates.

"Really?" asked Bryan. "Wow! That guy spent his whole life doing bad stuff!"

Aaron nodded. "Yeah. He drank, gambled, and lived a wild life," he said.

Mr. Harper, the boys' teacher, spoke up. "That's true," he agreed, "but here's the good news. When Joe Neilson became sick, he knew he was dying and sent for Pastor Smith. Pastor said Joe decided to trust in Jesus and asked God's forgiveness. So when he died, he went to heaven to be with the Lord."

"The same as if he had loved and served God all his life?" asked Aaron. Mr. Harper nodded.

"Hey, that's not fair!" exclaimed Bryan.

"No, it's not fair," agreed Mr. Harper. "It's not fair, because Joe missed the greatest joys in life."

"What do you mean?" asked Bryan.

Mr. Harper smiled. "Tell me, Bryan," he said, "have you ever sneaked into the kitchen to taste a little bit of turkey before the Thanksgiving meal?"

Bryan nodded as he remembered his time in the kitchen just three days before. He grinned. "It's the best part of Thanksgiving," he said.

"Well," said Mr. Harper, "the time we spend with other Christians and serving God is a little like sneaking into the kitchen to taste the turkey. It's almost like getting a little taste of heaven. Joe didn't get to 'taste the turkey' in this life."

"Wow," whispered Bryan. "I never thought of that." *MMS*

HOW ABOUT YOU?

Do you take time to be with other Christians? Do you make time to serve the Lord? Those are the most pleasant and rewarding things you can do. Thank God for each day he gives you to spend in service for him.

MEMORIZE:

"I would rather be a gatekeeper in the house of my God than live the good life in the homes of the wicked."

Psalm 84:10

 Serving God Brings Joy

Martha, Martha (Read Luke 10:38-42)

Pete looked up from his homework as his father came into the house. "Hi, Dad," said Pete.

"Hi, Son," said Dad. They talked for a little while, and then Dad turned to Mom. "Are you getting as much as I am out of that devotional book we both decided to read?" he asked. "Today's Scripture reading helped me make a decision about that problem I was having at work."

"That's great!" replied Mom. "Actually, I haven't gotten around to reading it today," she admitted. "I've just been so busy!"

1

DECEMBER

"Oh, Martha, Martha," Dad reproved lovingly.

"I know, I know," said Mom.

"Why did you call mom Martha?" Pete asked his father.

Mom and Dad both laughed. "Martha is the name I use for Mother when she gets too busy and starts acting too much like the Martha in the Bible," explained Dad. "Remember the story? Martha was so busy that she didn't take time to sit and learn at Jesus' feet."

"That's right, and that's what's been happening to me lately," added Mom. "I've allowed things to keep me from what is really important. You know, I bet it wouldn't be the end of the world if I bought pies for the school bake sale tomorrow. And if I let this floor stay dirty a little longer, maybe I could just go into the other room and catch up a bit on my Bible reading."

Jennie came bursting into the room. "Where's my Bible?" she demanded. "I'm in charge of devotions tonight at youth group, and I haven't had a minute to prepare all week."

"Oh, Martha, Martha," said Mom as Pete and Dad burst out laughing. *LFW*

HOW ABOUT YOU?

Do you let distractions keep you from the study of God's Word or from prayer? Maybe the mystery you want to read can wait. Maybe you could skip a TV show. Or maybe you could play with your friends later. When something has to be left out, don't let it be your time with the Lord.

MEMORIZE:

"But the Lord said to her, 'My dear Martha, you are so upset over all these details! There is really only one thing worth being concerned about.'"

Luke 10:41-42

 Remove Distractions

Prized Antique (Read Leviticus 19:32; Proverbs 16:31; 20:29)

2

DECEMBER

Marcy enjoyed looking at old things, so she decided to visit the antique store that had just opened up. When she got to the store, she saw all sorts of old bottles and jars in the window. Just inside the front door there were several antique oil lamps on a table and some boxes filled with old dishes. The walls were lined with shelves, which held old books, knickknacks, and some dolls.

All of the dolls looked quite old, but one in particular looked quite ancient. It had tin eyes that were scratched, the paint on its wooden body was peeling, and it wore old tattered clothing. Marcy looked at the price tag on the old doll. She gasped when she saw the price. "Why would anyone pay such a high price for an old doll like this?" she said in a near whisper.

The owner of the store heard her question. "That doll may not look so good to you," he said, "but because she is old she is valuable to a doll collector."

When Marcy went home, she told her mom about the old doll she had seen. "An old doll like that reminds me of the people we visit at the nursing home," said Mom.

"What do you mean?" asked Marcy.

"Well," said Mom, "the people we visit are old and getting worn out too, but they are still special and valuable."

"That's right," Marcy agreed. "I learn a lot from the stories they tell me. I'm sure they are very special to God." *WEB*

HOW ABOUT YOU?

Do you see the value and worth in the elderly people you come in contact with? Do you honor and respect them as you should? Remember to thank God for the elderly people you know. They are more valuable than a prized antique.

MEMORIZE:

"**You are more valuable to him than a whole flock of sparrows.**" *Matthew 10:31*

 **Honor the Elderly**

A Good Pressing (Read 1 Peter 1:3-9)

Sandy bounded into the kitchen and slammed her books on the table. She stuck her head in the fridge, emerged with an apple, and took an angry chomp. "Hi, Sandy," said Mom.

"Hi." Sandy almost snarled the word.

"How was school?" Mom asked as she picked up a shirt and began ironing it.

"Rotten!" growled Sandy. "Mr. Loukens makes me so mad!"

3

DECEMBER

"Mr. Loukens!" exclaimed Mom. "I thought you liked your basketball coach!"

"I did, at first," Sandy replied. "But now it's always, 'Hold the ball like this. . . . Come on, run . . . you're lazy. . . . Work on those shots!' Honestly, Mom, sometimes I think he hates me!" Sandy sighed and picked up a blouse from the pile. She stared at it. "Mom," she wailed. "My blouse looks terrible! What happened to it?"

Mom laughed. "It always looks like that when I've washed it," she said. "It just needs a good pressing." She took the blouse and ironed it while Sandy finished her apple. "There. See how pretty it looks?" Mom asked with a smile. "I needed to put a little heat and pressure on it, just like Coach Loukens has to put a little heat and pressure on you to help you become a good basketball player. You may not like it, but it will help you."

"Well, you're right about my not liking it," agreed Sandy. "But you have a good point," she admitted. "When the coach puts the heat on, I know he's just trying to make me a better player, and that's what I want too."

Mom smiled. "We tend to forget that the valuable things in life take patience and discipline," said Mom. "If you can learn to see hard times as a chance to grow and improve, God will be able to use them to make something beautiful out of your life." *JKB*

HOW ABOUT YOU?
Do you sometimes feel life is treating you harshly? Do you feel hurt or angry when someone points out an error? Don't resent criticism and correction; rather, look on them as a chance to grow.

MEMORIZE:

"For when your faith is tested, your endurance has a chance to grow. So let it grow, for when your endurance is fully developed, you will be strong in character and ready for anything." *James 1:3-4*

 *Grow Through Trials*

The Ugly Stain (Read Psalm 51:1-12)

4

DECEMBER

"I think my friends all had fun at my slumber party," said Sally after everyone had left. "I did, too!"

"Good," said Mother. "Everyone seemed to get along. I didn't hear one cross word from anybody! And you were a perfect hostess. I'd say it was a perfect party."

"Well, not quite," said Sally with a sigh. "Cathy spilled Coke on my new bedspread, and it left an ugly stain. She felt so bad, but I told her I was sure it would come out and not to worry about it. It *will* come out, won't it, Mom?"

"Oh, I think so," replied Mom. "Let's go take a look at it."

Sally's little sister, Julie, trailed along as they went to check the spread. "Julie behaved very nicely with your friends too," said Mother.

"That's a miracle," said Sally, "considering she's a pest."

"Sally!" said Mom.

"Well," Sally said. "Look at the paint she spilled on my new jeans."

"Sally, you need to show Julie the same kindness you show your friends," said Mother sternly as they entered Sally's room.

"My friends aren't a nuisance," retorted Sally. She pointed to the stain on her bedspread. "Will that come out?" she asked.

"I know what you can do," said Julie. "You can put this pillow over it." She picked up a pink pillow from Sally's bed and placed it over the stain. "There! That fixes it!"

"That doesn't fix anything," grumbled Sally. "That just covers it up."

"True . . . but you *could* just cover it up when you have company—like you cover up the stain in your heart," murmured Mother.

"What?" asked Sally. "What are you talking about?"

"Well, when your friends are not around, you're impatient and unkind toward your sister. But when they're around, you're kind and forgiving. It's like covering up a stain." Sally blushed. Deep down, she knew Mother was right. *PCS*

HOW ABOUT YOU?

Are you as kind and gracious when you're with only your family as you are when other people are around? If that's a problem to you, give that ugly "stain" to God.

MEMORIZE:

"I will lead a life of integrity in my own home." *Psalm 101:2*

 *Be Kind at Home*

Hungry Mouths (Read Psalm 107:8-15)

5

"Why did Pastor Cummings have to preach so long?" grumbled Chuck on the way home from church.

"I wished Pastor Cummings had not quit so soon," said Dad. "He helped me understand some Scriptures that had been hard for me to figure out before."

Chuck added, "Our Sunday school class was really boring, too."

"I didn't think so," said his sister, Melissa. "Mr. Kline was telling us some neat stuff, Chuck. He's so good at explaining the Bible."

When they arrived home, Chuck filled his cat's dish with food. "Come here, Mac. Time to eat," he called. Mac, the cat, walked to the dish, sniffed the food, and walked away, his tail held high. "That dumb old cat. He doesn't know what's good," Chuck declared.

Just then Melissa called, "Come here to the window and see the baby birds in their nest." She laughed out loud. "The mama bird brought food for them. Just look at those wide-open mouths!" she squealed.

Chuck went to look. "Well, they're smarter than Mac is," he decided. "Mac wouldn't even taste the good food I offered him, but those little birds pop open their mouths as soon as their mother comes around. They take anything she gives them."

"Hmmm," murmured Mother. "So that's why you were bored at church while the rest of us got a lot of good from the services."

"Huh?" said Chuck. "What do you mean?"

"Well, we were hungry for God's Word, and we opened our heart to be filled," Mother told him. "But you're like Mac, who figured the food was no good without even trying it. You expect to be bored. Next time, how about going with an appetite for some spiritual food?" *MRP*

HOW ABOUT YOU?

When you go to Sunday school and church, are you eager to see what you can learn about God? God's Word feeds both your mind and your soul. It helps you become a strong Christian. It is sweeter than honey. Take a good appetite to church, for God always satisfies a hungry soul.

MEMORIZE:

"When you [God] open your hand, you satisfy the hunger and thirst of every living thing."
Psalm 145:16

 Be Hungry for God's Word

Pretty Inside (Read 2 Corinthians 5:14-21; 6:1)

6

DECEMBER

For two weeks Debbie worked on her ink drawing for the poster contest. Finally she was satisfied. "Wow! That's beautiful!" said her father.

The next morning a loud wail came from the family room. "Just look at my poster," moaned Debbie. "I was signing my name, and I accidentally knocked over the ink bottle. My poster is ruined." She was in tears.

Mother shook her head as she looked at the poster. "I'm so sorry," she said. "You draw so beautifully, and . . ."

"Doesn't look very beautiful to me," interrupted Debbie's brother.

"Jack, your sister spilled ink on her poster," explained Mother. "The picture underneath that black ink is beautiful."

"Yeah? Well, maybe you can have it cleaned," suggested Jack. "I've read that they do that to famous paintings."

Debbie smiled faintly. "This one isn't famous," she said. "It's hopeless." Now Debbie would have to go to school with no poster to enter in the contest.

That evening Jack reported on a new student in his class. "He's going to be a pain!" declared Jack. "He's brand-new in school, but he acts like he owns the place!"

"Well, maybe he's really scared and nervous," suggested Mother. "Maybe he's just putting on a brave act."

"That's right," agreed Dad. "Don't judge him too quickly. Maybe deep down inside he's a pretty nice fellow."

"Yeah—maybe he's like my poster," added Debbie. "A little messy on the outside, but really nice underneath."

"Maybe," said Jack doubtfully. "But your poster was hopeless, remember?"

"Ah!" said Mother. "But a person would be more like that famous painting you talked about. He may be covered with problems, but God can see his potential beauty and wipe away the mess so that the beauty can shine through." *DSM*

HOW ABOUT YOU?

Do you know someone who is ugly in the way he or she acts? Someone who isn't very nice? Does that person know about Jesus, who can change a mean, unhappy, grumbling attitude into something beautiful?

MEMORIZE:

"If anyone is in Christ, he is a new creation; old things have passed away; behold, all things have become new."

2 Corinthians 5:17, NKJV

 God Can Change People

Turtle on a Post (Read Psalm 18:31-36, 46)

"I knew I'd win a prize. I just knew it!" exclaimed Corey as he and his father drove home from the horse show. He stroked the ribbon he was holding. "This is the *first place* ribbon," he added. "That means *I* had the best horse shown at halter. Blaze squared up fast and gave me his ears right away." Corey thought about how quickly his horse had stood straight and still with his ears flicked forward. "Blaze was the best because he had the best trainer, me!" Corey bragged.

7

DECEMBER

"You certainly did a good job training your horse," Dad agreed, "but remember, you didn't train him alone."

"Sure I did," said Corey. "No one helped me—at least not much."

Dad suddenly slowed down and stopped at the side of the road. Then he backed up. "Aha!" he exclaimed. "I thought I saw something odd."

"What?" asked Corey. Curious, he peered out the window.

"Come and see," said Dad, opening the car door. Corey followed Dad to the fence that ran beside the road. "Look." Dad pointed to one of the thick, round fence posts. A big old turtle sat on top of the post, sleeping in the sun.

Corey laughed. "How did he climb up there?" he asked.

"Well, I'd say someone must have put him up there," Dad said, "but he probably thinks he got there all by himself. I'll bet he never even saw the hands that picked him up." He lifted the turtle and set him on the ground. "Nor the hands that put him down," he added. Corey had a feeling that Dad was talking about more than just the turtle. "Invisible hands," said Dad quietly. "And I'd say that's what you had to help you train Blaze. God's invisible hands."

"You mean God helped me?" asked Corey. "God helped me train a horse?"

Dad nodded. "God gave you a brain and arms and legs and the ability to train Blaze, right?" he said.

"Right," added Corey thoughtfully. *JKC*

HOW ABOUT YOU?

Do you sometimes get so excited about your good grades or winning a game that you forget about God? Are you proud that *you* did it? It's OK to feel good about your accomplishments. Just remember to thank God for your success.

MEMORIZE:

"The person who wishes to boast should boast only of what the Lord has done."

2 Corinthians 10:17

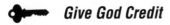 *Give God Credit*

Worthwhile Journey (Read 2 Corinthians 5:1-10)

8

DECEMBER

Less than halfway up the mountain, Bryan struggled to keep up with his dad. He wondered why he'd ever thought it would be fun to climb Squaw Peak. Of course, he hadn't been in a happy mood when the day began. Last night's visit with Grandpa in the nursing home had upset him. "Why does Grandpa have to suffer so much?" Bryan had asked Dad.

"I don't know, Son," Dad had answered. "I know it hurts to see Grandpa the way he is now, but it helps me to know that he'll soon be in the wonderful place Jesus has prepared for him."

Bryan nodded, but the thought that Grandpa would go to heaven didn't seem to make much difference in the way Bryan felt now. His thoughts were interrupted by Dad's voice suggesting that they stop for a break.

After they rested awhile, Dad got up. "Ready to go?" he asked.

Bryan hesitated. "Maybe we should just go back down," he suggested.

Dad rumpled Bryan's hair. "You're not going to quit on me, are you, Buddy?" he asked. "When we get to the top, you'll see it was worth the effort."

Bryan wasn't so sure about that, but he trudged along. Finally they reached the top. Dad found a nice spot and spread out their lunch. As they ate, they could see the city below, surrounded by hills and desert. It was awesome! A sense of wonder came over Bryan. "You were right, Dad!" he exclaimed. "This was worth the struggle."

Dad nodded. "I've been thinking," he said as he replaced the empty soft drink cans in the picnic container. "What's happening to Grandpa is a lot like climbing this mountain."

Bryan had to think only for a moment before he caught on. "You mean Grandpa has a tough journey, but it'll have a happy ending." That was really what Dad had said the night before, but now Bryan understood. *EMB*

HOW ABOUT YOU?

Is someone you love fighting a battle with death? It will be hard to say good-bye, but if you're both Christians, you will meet again. In the meantime, your friend or loved one will go to a far better place.

MEMORIZE:

"For to me, living is for Christ, and dying is even better."

Philippians 1:21

 Heaven Wipes Away Pain

Doggy Kisses (Read Psalm 118:1-3)

Dad had given Ken and Larry a new puppy! Bucky, the pup, wriggled and bounced. It was difficult for Ken to hold him. "Don't, Bucky!" said Ken as he wiped his cheek, wet from the puppy's tongue.

"He's giving you doggy kisses," said Mom with a smile.

Larry laughed. "Let me have him, Ken," he said. Larry reached for the puppy as he spoke.

The boys enjoyed playing with Bucky and training him. "Look, Mom," Larry called as he threw a squeaky toy. Bucky was off in a flash to fetch and return it. When he reached Ken, Bucky held tightly to the toy. Larry pulled it away and threw it again. Bucky went to retrieve it.

9

DECEMBER

"Come, Bucky," Ken called. The pup instantly obeyed him. Ken looked at Mom. "See how good he obeys? He likes us."

When it was time to feed the puppy, Larry filled his dish. "Bucky, come and eat your dinner," he called.

Bucky made a dash for the dog dish and began to eat. He paused to see if the boys were still there, then quickly devoured his food.

The boys watched silently. "Hey!" said Larry suddenly. "Bucky just gulps his food like it's going to disappear. He didn't thank God for it."

Ken laughed. "He's just a puppy, silly," he said. Bucky ran over to Ken, jumped up, and tried to lick Ken's face. "But he's thankful and he loves us. This is his way of showing that," added Ken.

Mom had come back out on the porch. "You know, there's another way Bucky shows you that he loves you," she said. "Ken, you mentioned it before."

"What is it, Ken?" asked Larry.

"Well," said Ken, "he obeys us when we tell him to do something."

"That's it," said Mom. "Bucky is a good example to us. He shows how he feels by giving doggy kisses and by obeying. We can—and should—both *say* that we love God and *show* that we love him by obeying him." *BEL*

HOW ABOUT YOU?

Do you tell God you love him? Do you also obey God's Word? That's how Jesus said he can tell if we mean what we say.

MEMORIZE:

"Jesus replied, 'All those who love me will do what I say.'"

John 14:23

 Let God Know You Love Him

The Transplants (Read Acts 12:1-10)

10
DECEMBER

Cammie moved a flower to a new location and carefully packed dirt around it. She remembered how careful she and Mom had been when they had transplanted some flowers earlier. Even so, only a few of the flowers had lived. Now they were trying again.

"It sure would have helped a lot if Ricky hadn't pulled up some of the flowers right along with the weeds," Cammie remarked glumly. Ricky and his brother, Travis, had recently been adopted by Cammie's family.

"It wasn't just Ricky," said Mom. "Some of them would have died anyway. Some plants are harder to transplant than others."

Cammie sat down beside her mom. "They've got so many problems," she said.

"These flowers?" asked Mom as she lifted an eyebrow.

"No!" Cammie laughed. "I mean Ricky and Travis."

"They actually are a lot like these transplants," Mom said thoughtfully. "It's hard for kids to be moved out of their own home into someone else's. Sometimes it works, and sometimes it doesn't. They need a lot of special care. You can help, Cammie."

"Me?" Cammie asked in surprise. "How?"

"For one thing, show them love whenever you can," Mom answered. "And pray every day for them. God is the only one who can make our transplants bloom—kids or flowers!" *KRL*

HOW ABOUT YOU?

Do you know someone who seems to have a lot of problems? Do you wish you could help? You can! When you pray, God listens and helps. Maybe you have problems of your own. Pray about them, and ask others to pray for you also. God acts when his children pray.

MEMORIZE:

"But while Peter was in prison, the church prayed very earnestly for him." *Acts 12:5*

 Pray for Each Other

Secret Mission (Read Matthew 6:1-4)

11

DECEMBER

"Mom, may I have an advance on my allowance?" Katie asked.

"What do you need it for?" asked Mom.

Katie took a deep breath. "I can't tell you," she said. "It's a secret."

Mom looked at Katie thoughtfully. Then she asked how much Katie needed. She got her purse and gave Katie the money. "Remember. This comes out of your allowance," said Mom.

Katie nodded and tried not to think about all the things she'd be giving up. She thought about her friend Sarah as she placed the money in an envelope and put it into her school backpack. Her class had been studying sea life, and their teacher had made arrangements for them to visit an aquarium in a nearby town. Signed permission slips and money for tickets had been coming in for several days now. But not for Sarah. Sarah was the oldest of several children. Her dad had just been laid off at the factory, and there was no extra money in Sarah's house.

The next morning Katie arrived at school early. Her classroom was empty. Heart racing, she crept quietly to Sarah's desk and slid the envelope into Sarah's math book. *Sarah will find it soon*, she thought. *We almost always have math first thing in the morning.* Earlier that morning Katie had written on the envelope, "Field trip money."

The bell rang, and Katie went quickly to her desk. She pulled out her spelling words. She kept one eye on the door. Soon Sarah came in. She went to her desk and pulled out her math book. Finding Katie's envelope, she opened it. Her eyes grew wide. Katie giggled and put her attention to her spelling words. *Please, God,* she prayed, *please don't let her ever find out it was from me. CMG*

HOW ABOUT YOU?

Have you ever done something good for someone else in total secret—without telling *anybody?* This week ask God to show you someone who needs your help, and then give it in a way that only you and he will ever know who it was. It's fun!

MEMORIZE:

"But when you give to someone, don't tell your left hand what your right hand is doing." *Matthew 6:3*

 **Give Secretly**

The Good Samaritan (Read Luke 10:30-37)

12

DECEMBER

One day Jeff's dad, who was a pastor, wrote letters to all the people in his church. He asked Jeff to take the letters to the post office. So Jeff got on his bike and took off down the road. "Whoa!" he yelled as he hit a bump, and the envelopes flew everywhere!

Jeff got off his bike. There he stood in the middle of the road with envelopes scattered all around him. To make it worse, as Jeff began to pick them up, a boy came by and stared at him. Then the boy laughed and called his friend over, and they both laughed at Jeff and called him silly names. Jeff felt very foolish.

Soon a third boy came along. When he saw Jeff scurrying to pick up the envelopes before they blew away, he stopped and helped. "It's hard to carry a lot of things when you're riding a bike," he said with a smile. "I know, because I've tried. I could help you carry them the rest of the way."

"Oh, thanks," Jeff said, feeling much better. It was good to have a new friend at his side and to leave the laughing boys behind.

When Jeff got home and told his family what had happened, his sister grinned. "It sounds like you met a good Samaritan," she said.

Jeff smiled. "Oh, I didn't think about that, but you're right. That boy acted just the way Jesus taught we should in that parable. I'm glad to know that there are still good, helpful people just like that Good Samaritan!" *LMW*

HOW ABOUT YOU?

Next time you see an older person struggling with a load of groceries or a younger one being picked on by others, help that person. Next time you see a teacher or a classmate with too many books to carry, help that person.

MEMORIZE:

"Whenever we have the opportunity, we should do good to everyone, especially to our Christian brothers and sisters."

Galatians 6:10

 Help Those in Trouble

A Latchkey Kid (Read Psalm 27:1-6)

"It's estimated that there are over 6 million latchkey kids in the United States," said Mrs. Rich, Brandon's teacher. "A latchkey kid is one who is home a certain period each day without adults."

Brandon sighed. He knew what a latchkey kid was—he was one. Each day after school he was alone for an hour, and knowing that there were 6 million other kids in the same situation didn't make him feel any less lonely or afraid!

13

DECEMBER

Mrs. Rich went on. "Many of these children are afraid but don't want to tell their parents. They feel it's babyish to be afraid."

Brandon agreed with that. It was exactly the way he felt! After all, at twelve you should be able to stay home without jumping at every little noise.

"Don't hesitate to talk to your parents or another adult if you are in this situation," Mrs. Rich concluded as the bell rang.

I guess I should tell someone I'm afraid, Brandon thought as he headed home. He dreaded going into the empty house. So that evening he told his mother what Mrs. Rich had said about latchkey kids who are afraid to be home alone.

"Is that the way you feel, Brandon?" asked Mother. Brandon nodded. "Well, I'm glad you brought it up. I've been thinking about it, too. I'm sorry it's necessary for me to get home later than you do. Would it help if I called or if you occasionally went to Aunt Ruth's house?"

Brandon brightened. "I'd like that," he said.

Mother hung up the dish towel and hugged Brandon. "Always remember that I love you but that the Lord loves you even more," she said. "He promises to be with you, and he's there when you feel lonely and frightened. You can talk to him about your fears, too."

LMW

HOW ABOUT YOU?

Are you sometimes frightened when you're alone? The Lord is always willing to listen to you. Talk to him about your problem. He can help you. If you're a Christian, remember that God has promised to be with you all the time.

MEMORIZE:

"Then David continued, 'Be strong and courageous, and do the work. Don't be afraid or discouraged by the size of the task, for the Lord God, my God, is with you. He will not fail you or forsake you.'" *1 Chronicles 28:20*

 **God Is with You**

The Bird Feeder (Read Psalm 119:41-48)

14

DECEMBER

Alicia sat at the window of her grandmother's house, watching the birds fly to the feeder in the backyard. "Hey, look!" she called out. "That squirrel is taking the food you put out for the birds."

Alicia's grandmother nodded. "I know," she said. "It almost seems like it's a 'first come, first served' event." Grandma didn't seem to mind, but Alicia wanted the birds to get the food, especially the beautiful red cardinals.

The squirrel sat on the top of the feeder for a long time. Mourning doves came to eat, but the squirrel sat erect and made a loud noise that frightened the doves away. A little later some blue jays flitted around the feeder. They, too, tried to get the seeds that had been put out for them, but once again the squirrel refused to move. Although they scolded the squirrel, it seemed to make little or no difference. Then, as Alicia watched, some woodpeckers approached the area. One perched on a branch just above the feeder; another sat on top of the birdbath. For some time nothing happened. Then, without notice, the woodpeckers flew to the feeder and began to eat. The squirrel seemed stunned and moved slightly to one side. The woodpeckers began to make loud sounds, working closer and closer to the squirrel. In a few minutes, the bird feeder was cleared and available to all the other birds.

"Wow!" exclaimed Alicia. "That squirrel sat right there and wasn't going to let any birds get to the food, but those woodpeckers chased him away."

Alicia's grandmother nodded. "Reminds me of some of Satan's tricks. He doesn't want Christians to get to their spiritual food—the Bible. So he encourages us to put all sorts of things in the way. Sometimes it's school activities; sometimes it's friends. But the Lord in us is stronger. If we watch for it, we'll see that he makes a way for us to spend time in his Word. Then it's up to us to eat and grow as we obey." *RIJ*

HOW ABOUT YOU?

Do you fill your time with things that keep you from reading God's Word? "Things" will always be in the way if you allow them. Let God lead you in planning your day, so that you will get to his Word. It's your spiritual food.

MEMORIZE:

"I will delight in your principles and not forget your word." *Psalm 119:16*

 Persist in Reading the Bible

The Expired Coupons (Read 2 Corinthians 5:14-21; 6:1)

15

"Won't you accept Jesus tonight?" asked Mr. Anderson, the teacher at Josh's Bible club. "If you'd like to learn more about being saved, raise your hand and let me know. I'd like to pray for you and talk with you about it. You don't want to wait until it's too late." Josh squirmed in his seat. He certainly intended to be saved someday, but not yet! *What would the kids think if I raised my hand?* he thought. *Besides, I'll have plenty of time to get saved when I'm older.*

When he got home, Josh poured a glass of milk for himself. His mother had been to the grocery store and was putting away the groceries. Then she took some coupons from her purse, sorted through them, and threw several away. "Don't you want to use those?" asked Josh.

"I would, but I goofed," replied Mother. "I was going to use them tonight, but when I got them out, I noticed they had expired a few days ago." She sighed. "They were good for about five dollars' worth of groceries, too. I should have used them last week. Now it's too late!"

Josh took his milk and walked out to the porch. He sat down on the top step. There were those words again—"too late"—the same words Mr. Anderson had used. As Josh thought about it, he made a decision. He jumped up and went back to the kitchen.

"Mom!" he exclaimed. "Mr. Anderson said that someday it will be too late to accept Jesus as Savior. You missed the chance to use your coupons, but I don't want to miss the chance to be saved. Will you help me?"

Mother hugged him close. "I sure will!" she said. *LMW*

HOW ABOUT YOU?

How often have you heard a teacher, pastor, or parent give the plan of salvation, but you decided to put it off until later? Why not talk to a trusted adult now to find out more?

MEMORIZE:

"Seek the Lord while you can find him. Call on him now while he is near." *Isaiah 55:6*

 *Accept Jesus*

Let's Have a Party! (Read Matthew 1:18-25)

16

DECEMBER

"We're starting to sing Christmas songs at school," Jason told his mother as he took off his coat. "Just songs like 'Deck the Halls,' though. No Christmas carols."

"That's too bad," replied Mother. "Teachers may be afraid to use anything considered 'religious,' including Christmas carols. People who don't believe in God sometimes make a big fuss about mentioning God in school."

As Jason and his friend Mark were walking home from school a couple of days later, they talked about their plans for the Christmas season. "Grandpa and Grandma are coming for Christmas this year," said Mark. "They're coming for a whole week, and on Christmas Eve we're all going to go see a special Santa Claus movie! Wanna come with us? I'm sure Mom will say it's OK."

Jason shook his head. "Our family always goes to church on Christmas Eve," he said. "We're having a candlelight service with a special program about the real Christmas story. And then we'll have refreshments and stuff afterwards, too."

Mark looked puzzled. "What's the real Christmas story?" he asked. "Something about angels and stars and shepherds—stuff like that, right?"

Jason was surprised. "It's about when Jesus was born," he said. He could hardly believe that Mark didn't know the real meaning of Christmas!

When Jason told his mother about it later, she had a suggestion. "Since the teachers don't talk about Jesus at school, would you like to have a party for your friends?" she asked. "You could play games and have prizes. Then I'll help with singing Christmas carols and telling the Christmas story before serving refreshments."

"That'd be fun," agreed Jason. So he sent invitations to seven friends. He felt good that he was giving them the opportunity to hear about Christ. *LMW*

HOW ABOUT YOU?

Do your friends know the real story of Christmas? Perhaps you, too, could have a party to share Christ with others. This year find some way to make sure your friends know the real meaning of Christmas.

MEMORIZE:

"God did not send his Son into the world to condemn it, but to save it." *John 3:17*

 Share Christ at Christmas

The Right Reason (Part 1) (Read Ephesians 6:5-10)

The church storeroom was packed with cans and boxes that had been collected during the food drive for needy families. After the food was sorted so that each family would have a variety, the next step was to deliver the supplies to the homes.

17

DECEMBER

"I have to take food to the Connells," Shane's dad said.

"Oh, I know Ray Connell," Shane told his father. "He's in my class at school."

"Why not come along then?" suggested Dad. "You can invite Ray to the church Christmas program."

After supper Shane and his dad loaded the car and drove to the Connell home. Mrs. Connell met them at the door and ushered them through the living room, where Mr. Connell was watching TV, and into the kitchen. Shane and his dad put the bags on the table and went to get the rest of the groceries. When they came back, Mr. Connell was complaining because there wasn't enough room for the groceries in the refrigerator. Ray was there, too, complaining because the church had sent peanut butter cookies. "Yuk! I hate peanut butter. Why didn't you bring chocolate cookies?" he grumbled as he stormed out of the room.

Shane felt uncomfortable and couldn't wait to leave the Connells' home.

"How can people act that way?" he blurted when they were back in the car. "We're trying to be nice, but they didn't even say thank you."

"It's hard to understand people sometimes, Son," Shane's dad said gently. "You must remember, though, that we're doing this for the Lord. We didn't do it so the Connells would like us—or thank us. We did it because they needed it and because God wanted us to show his love." *LMW*

HOW ABOUT YOU?

Have you been hurt when trying to be kind. Have you smiled at someone, only to be ignored? Have you offered to help someone, only to have that offer rejected? Remember, the reason for being kind should not be to impress others but to glorify the Lord. God knows your thoughts. That's what is important.

MEMORIZE:

"**Work hard, but not just to please your masters when they are watching. As slaves of Christ, do the will of God with all your heart.**" *Ephesians 6:6*

 **Do All for God**

The Right Reason (Part 2) (Read 1 Timothy 6:6-11)

18

DECEMBER

"Oh no!" exclaimed Shane as he and Dad drove home after delivering groceries to the Connells. "It's thawing again. We need snow for our ski trip."

"Well," said Dad, "the weatherman said to expect above-average temperatures all week." Shane groaned. "But maybe it will snow," encouraged Dad.

When they arrived home, Mother had hot chocolate and crackers and cheese waiting for them. Shane frowned. "I wanted popcorn and a soda tonight," he said.

"It hits the spot with me!" declared Dad, sipping his chocolate.

Shane munched a cracker. "Can I get some new cross-country skis?" he asked. "And a new jacket, too?"

Dad shook his head. "No new skis this year," he said. "I don't know about the jacket—that's more Mom's department."

"Your old jacket will make it through the winter," said Mom, "or at least until they go on sale again. If you get a new one now, it probably wouldn't fit again next year, at the rate you're growing."

Shane frowned. "All my friends have ski jackets," he grumbled. "You and Dad never let me get as much stuff as they have."

Dad looked at Shane. "Is your last name Connell?" asked Dad. Shane looked startled; then he shook his head and looked down. "You complained because Roy and his dad didn't seem thankful for the groceries we brought," said Dad. "Now you're acting the same way."

"I'm sorry," said Shane. "I'll do better." He glanced at his mother. "This chocolate is really good—the crackers are, too."

Mother smiled. "And . . . ?" she prompted.

Shane grinned. "And I just love my old coat and skis."

"And . . . ?" prompted Dad.

"And, oh, yeah!" said Shane. "And the weather—I just *love* warm winter weather!" They all laughed. *HWM*

 Be Content with God's Provision

Best Friends (Read Ephesians 4:29-32)

19

Marcy really wanted to win the ten-dollar prize that would be given for the best costume in the Christmas parade. She had decided to go as a giant gift, so she had decorated a huge box. When she got inside, it covered all but her feet. Two peepholes allowed her to see. "How will Jill be dressed?" Marcy wondered as she joined the other costumed students. "She never would tell me, even though I let her see my costume."

"Hi! Is that you in there, Marcy?" Recognizing Jill's voice, Marcy slowly turned around to look through her peepholes. She almost bumped into . . . another box! Jill had a costume almost identical to her own. "I decided to surprise you so we could be the Boxy Twins," said Jill. "Aren't we magnificent?"

Marcy was furious! How dare Jill copy her idea! But the parade was beginning, so they marched off together. They awkwardly bowed before the judges. They laughed, and the audience cheered.

When the winner was announced, a judge said, "We all agreed that the boxes were the best, but there is only one prize. So we're going to divide it between the two. Each will get five dollars." Marcy forced a smile on her face, but she was fuming inside as she walked up and accepted her money.

"Mom, I'll never speak to Jill again," declared Marcy when she told her mother what had happened. "Can you believe what she did?"

"Easy, honey," cautioned Mother. "You've been best friends for years. Think about Jesus, your very best friend, for a moment," she suggested.

"What about him?" asked Marcy. "He's not like Jill. He's never done anything wrong to me."

"But *you* wronged *him*, Marcy," said Mother, "and still he forgave you and saved you. That's the way he wants us to treat others."

"That's hard to do, Mom," Marcy answered. "But I will try it."

MRP

HOW ABOUT YOU?

Is it hard to forgive someone who has wronged you? You'd usually rather get even, wouldn't you? But aren't you glad Jesus doesn't treat you like that? Being true friends means forgiving when you've been wronged— and loving just the same.

MEMORIZE:

"A friend is always loyal, and a brother is born to help in time of need." *Proverbs 17:17*

 True Friends Love and Forgive

Which Path? (Read Proverbs 4:10-19)

20 DECEMBER

"Isn't this fun?" said Tracie as she tramped along through the snow with other juniors from her church.

"Yeah," answered Sarah. "It's neat. Mr. Bailey is a good camp director."

Soon they came to a fork in the path. The kids ahead of them took the path to the left. "Wait!" called Tracie. "Mr. Bailey said to turn right at each fork, and then we'll end up back at camp."

The other campers hesitated. "Yeah, but look—this path on the left is full of footprints, and there are none in the right-hand path," argued one of them. "I think we should take the one everybody else has used." The others agreed and started down the well-trodden path again.

Tracie and Sarah didn't know what to do, but they finally decided to take the path on the right for a little way. "If we don't get back to camp soon, we'll turn around," they agreed, and they started off. To their delight, it wasn't long before they did, indeed, arrive back at the camp.

When Mr. Bailey heard that the other campers had taken the wrong path, he shook his head. "They'll come to a dead end and have to turn around," he said. "But I'll send someone out on a snowmobile just to make sure they're all right. I guess I should have sent a guide along, after all."

That evening Mr. Bailey conducted devotional time. "We have some tired campers tonight," he said. "Most of you took a longer hike than you planned." He opened his Bible. "I believe there's a lesson in this experience," he told them. "Most of you failed to heed the directions you were given and chose to follow where others had gone. Those you followed probably didn't know where they were going, either. Fortunately, they just led you out of your way and not into any danger. But I want you to remember that when you're tempted to forsake the teachings of God's Book in favor of following the crowd, the well-worn path may lead to disaster. Choose God's way. The crowd could be wrong, but he's always right." *MRP*

HOW ABOUT YOU?

Is it hard for you to go a different way from others around you? Do you hate to be called "chicken"? Sometimes it's easier to go along with the crowd than to stand up for what is right. But it pays to go God's way.

MEMORIZE:

"Do not do as the wicked do or follow the path of evildoers."

Proverbs 4:14

 Follow God, Not the Crowd

Spare Attitude (Read Leviticus 19:15-18)

Haylie's mother was in the midst of a Tupperware party in which neither Haylie nor her dad found any interest, so they decided to go out for a Coke. As they drove along, they passed a couple of girls about Haylie's age. "I can't stand those girls!" said Haylie. "Well, at least not the short, chubby one. Alicia says she's a pain."

"But you don't know her personally?" Dad asked.

"No way," Haylie answered, "and I don't want to know her, either."

21

DECEMBER

Bang! The car unexpectedly veered to the right. "Oh no," groaned Dad. "Flat tire."

Haylie chatted while Dad changed the tire. "You know that girl we saw?" she said. "She's the one who beat me out of a place on the volleyball team."

"Haylie," said Dad, "you're not being a very good sport about that, are you? That's not a reason to dislike her."

Haylie's eyes fell. "Maybe not," she replied, "but Alicia knows her, and she doesn't like her, either."

"Don't you think your attitude toward this girl needs to be changed?" asked Dad as he removed the flat tire and put the spare in its place. "A person can't go around driving a car with a flat tire," he continued, "but it's even worse to go through life with a 'flat attitude.' Maybe it's time for you to reach inside yourself and find a spare attitude to replace your flat one."

"I guess I did sound pretty hateful, didn't I?" admitted Haylie slowly.

"I'd say so," agreed Dad as he finished the job. "Shall we drive by those girls again and invite them to join us for a Coke?"

Haylie hesitated a moment, then said, "Why not!" *VLR*

HOW ABOUT YOU?

Do you have a hateful attitude toward someone? Has that person really given you a good reason to not like him or her? Is any reason good enough to hate someone God loves? Reevaluate your attitude toward that person. Perhaps you need to reach inside yourself and pull out that spare attitude!

MEMORIZE:

"**Never seek revenge or bear a grudge against anyone, but love your neighbor as yourself.**" *Leviticus 19:18*

 Don't Hold Grudges

Microwave Popcorn (Read Psalm 133:1-3)

22

DECEMBER

Lynne put a paper packet in the microwave oven, set the timer, and waited. Four minutes later she took a plump red sack filled with steamy hot popcorn out of the oven. "That's not how we used to make popcorn," Dad told her, reaching for a few kernels. "We had to put oil in a pan, set it on the stove, wait till the pan was hot, pour in the kernels, cover it, and shake it like everything."

Mother added, "And then get out a big bowl to put the popped corn in, melt the butter, sprinkle on the salt . . ."

"I didn't have to do any of that," Lynne said, "and I eat it right out of the bag. No mess and nothing to clean up."

"It tastes good too," Dad said as Lynne's brother came in, slamming the door behind him. "Something wrong, Tony?" asked Dad.

"It's Bob," Tony complained. "He's got a new idea for our service project. The guys in our club always raked leaves and picked up trash for the senior citizens before. It's a lot of work, but we always made them real happy."

"So," Mother said, "what is Bob's idea?"

"He wants us to pick up a bunch of boys from an inner-city church where his dad works and have them help us," said Tony with a frown. "And then our Boys' Club would take those kids and the senior citizens to the park for a picnic."

"And you don't want to do that?" Mother asked quietly.

"We were just talking, Tony," Dad said, "about the old way and the new way to make popcorn. It tastes great either way."

"And you think a new project might be just as good as the old?" Tony asked.

Dad nodded. "Your way of doing the service project worked fine, but I think Bob's way will, too—and it will also help those boys. Besides, you won't have to work nearly as hard. There was nothing wrong with your old way, but when someone offers a better way, be willing to cooperate." *TVV*

HOW ABOUT YOU?

Do you feel rejected or jealous when someone has a better idea than yours? Don't take the attitude that you always know best. God has given people many different ideas of ways to serve him. Cooperate and serve him together.

MEMORIZE:

"Finally, all of you should be of one mind, full of sympathy toward each other, loving one another with tender hearts and humble minds." *1 Peter 3:8*

 **Be Cooperative**

Deadly Dialogue (Read Proverbs 18:19-21; 21:23)

23

DECEMBER

"Liar!" Tabitha yelled into the phone. "I don't ever want to talk to you again!"

"Oh, Tab, I didn't know . . ." But Tabitha slammed down the receiver before Janella could say another word.

"What was that all about?" asked Mom.

"Janella said she wasn't going to enter the Christmas art contest this year, but she did," Tabitha said angrily. "I would have won if she hadn't entered."

"But, honey, Janella has as much right to enter the contest as you do," Mother reminded her. "I'm sure she enjoys winning, too."

"But she knows how much I need the prize money to help pay for Christmas presents," wailed Tabitha. "She doesn't need it."

"That doesn't excuse the way you talked to her," said Mother.

"I don't care," Tabitha insisted stubbornly.

While Tabitha helped her mother prepare supper that evening, her little sister, Lori, was playing with a tube of biscuits. Suddenly . . . pop! A doughy mess oozed through the split in the tube. "Lori, what have you done?" Mom asked as Lori's pudgy little fingers tried to push the dough back into the tube.

"You can't put the dough back, Lori, once it's come out!" Tabitha said, smiling.

Mom turned to Tabitha. "You're right, Tabitha," she said solemnly, "and I'm reminded that it's the same with hurtful words."

Just then the back door opened, and Tabitha's brother, Rob, came in. "I just saw Kirsten, Janella's sister," he said. "She told me you were mad at Janella about the contest. But Kirsten said *she* was the one who entered Janella's drawing in the contest without Janella knowing it. Janella was shocked when her name was announced."

Tabitha bit her lip. *Oh no!* she thought. *I wish I hadn't said those mean things to Janella.* She felt awful. *Boy, am I glad for Jesus,* she thought. *He'll forgive me. And I hope Janella will, too, when I apologize. LJR*

HOW ABOUT YOU?

Do unkind words or names pop out of your mouth? Have you been sorry about what you said and wanted to stuff the words back in? You can't, but you can apologize. And be thankful that Jesus gives second chances.

MEMORIZE:

"Those who love to talk will experience the consequences, for the tongue can kill or nourish life." Proverbs 18:21

 Don't Say Things in Anger

Waiting to Live (Read Luke 2:1-20)

24

DECEMBER

The weatherman had said a big snowstorm was coming, so all morning Katie and Will watched for it. By noon the wind was howling and snow was falling fast. Katie was so excited she could barely stand still. "Do you think the storm will be here soon?" she asked her brother.

Will shrugged. "I guess so," he said,

When Mom came into the room to say lunch was ready, Katie and Will were patiently watching the scene in front of them. "Will said the snowstorm should be here soon," Katie told Mom.

"It looks to me like it's already here," said Mom.

Katie jumped up. "It's here!" she squealed, jumping up and down.

Mom laughed. "While you were waiting for the storm to come, you were actually watching it happen and you didn't even know it," said Mom. "That makes me think of a message I heard on the radio about how the Jewish people were waiting for the Messiah to come but missed it when he did come. Do you know when that was?"

"When Jesus was born," said Will promptly.

Mom nodded. "Can you think of other times we don't even notice that what we're waiting for is happening?" she asked. No one said anything. "How about answers to prayers?" suggested Mom.

Will nodded. "Sometimes I wait so hard for Jesus to answer a prayer that I can't think of anything else," he said slowly. "Maybe I'm looking so hard for an answer that I'm missing it."

"And I'm waiting for Christmas," said Katie.

Mom smiled. "Just don't be so busy waiting that you don't enjoy today," she said. "Enjoy each day God gives." *NMS*

HOW ABOUT YOU?

Does it seem as if you're constantly waiting for something—are you waiting to live? God has given you this day. Thank him for it. Enjoy it. Use it to serve him. Make every minute count right now.

MEMORIZE:

"This is the day the Lord has made. We will rejoice and be glad in it." *Psalm 118:24*

 Enjoy and Use Each Day

Two Baby Boys (Read Luke 4:1-13)

Hannah scrunched her nose against the viewing window in the nursery. Her baby brother was just five hours old. He lay snuggled in a blue flannel blanket with a tiny cap on his fuzzy head.

Dad walked up behind her and squeezed her shoulders gently. "So, Big Sister, how does it feel?" he asked.

Hannah answered by doing a twirl on her tiptoes. "It feels great!" she said.

25
DECEMBER

A little later Hannah and her dad were walking hand in hand out into the crisp December air. The stars twinkled overhead like millions of Christmas lights. "Dad," Hannah said, "when Jesus was born, was he really as little as our baby?"

"Yes, he was," Dad answered. "But Jesus didn't have a nice clean hospital to stay in like our Jeff. He was born in a stable, far away from home. Of course, God gave him Mary and Joseph's love, and his own love and care, too."

Hannah shivered and pulled her scarf tighter. "Mrs. Johnson told us in church that Jesus came as a baby so he would know what it's like to be a person. When we pray to him we can be sure he understands the problems and troubles we have."

"That's true," answered Dad. "Isn't that wonderful to think about?"

Hannah nodded. "I'm glad," she said. "And I'm glad we have our very own baby now, too. I'm going to make sure he knows about the baby Jesus." *REB*

HOW ABOUT YOU?

Jesus grew up on earth with all the problems you have—hunger, tiredness, temptations, and all the rest. You can go to him and know he understands your problems and troubles. Do you think of him as a little baby in a manger? Or do you see him as he is today—a wonderful High Priest who understands you perfectly?

MEMORIZE:

"This High Priest of ours understands our weaknesses, for he faced all of the same temptations we do, yet he did not sin." *Hebrews 4:15*

 Jesus Understands You

The Right Part (Read Ecclesiastes 8:5-7)

26

DECEMBER

Susan waited at church until her friends started home. She didn't want to walk with them. She didn't want anyone to know how disappointed she felt.

As she climbed the back steps to her house, she tripped and fell, skinning her knee. Opening the door, she began to cry. "What's wrong, Sue?" Mother asked. Sue pointed to her knee. "Let's get some medicine and a bandage," Mother said, picking up Susan's baby sister, Angie.

Sue followed her mom to the bathroom. As her mom fixed her knee, she asked, "Is this all that's bothering you?"

Susan shook her head. "I didn't get the part in the Christmas play that I wanted," she said. "I'm singing in the choir again. And don't tell me to pray about it. I have prayed about it for two years now, and I never get the part I want. I don't think God is listening to me."

Mother knelt beside her. "Did you notice how Angie kept reaching for the things I keep in the medicine cabinet?" Sue nodded. "I knew she wanted them," continued Mother, "but I didn't let her have them. Why not?"

"Because they're not good for her right now."

"That's right," Mom said.

With a sigh Sue said, "And I know what you're going to say next: that we sometimes ask for things that aren't meant for us, or perhaps the time is just not right. Do you think the right place for me is in the choir?"

"It seems that way," said Mom. "It doesn't mean you will always be in the choir. But for now you need to trust that God is listening to your prayers. Even though he may not answer them the way you would like. Perhaps next year will be your time for a role. But for now . . ."

"I'll be the best singer in the choir!" said Susan with a smile.

KEC

HOW ABOUT YOU?

Do you get discouraged when God doesn't give you what you asked for in prayer? Remember, he hears every prayer and he knows what is best for you. Trust him.

MEMORIZE:

"You can make many plans, but the Lord's purpose will prevail." *Proverbs 19:21*

 **Trust God's Answers**

Snowflakes and People (Read Psalm 139:13-16)

"Mom, may I have plastic surgery and get my nose shortened?" asked Erika. "It's so ugly."

"I like your nose just fine," said Mother. "You're a beautiful girl."

"Oh, you have to say that," answered Erika. "You're my mother."

27

DECEMBER

Mother smiled. "I think anyone would say that you are very nice looking. Besides, the Bible says real beauty comes from within." She gave Erika a hug. "Now I need to take some groceries to Mrs. Baxter. She's not feeling well. How about watching Ricky while I'm gone?"

"Sure," agreed Erika. "I'll get my boots and take him outside. It's snowing again."

Soon Erika and Ricky were playing in the snow. "What big snowflakes!" shouted Ricky. "Let's catch them." So they reached out their dark-colored mittens and sleeves.

"Want to see them even better?" asked Erika. "Wait here." She dashed into the house and returned with a magnifying glass. As she showed Ricky what the snowflakes looked like up close, he squealed with delight. "God made each one different and special," she told him. "Did you know that in the whole world there have never been two snowflakes that were alike?"

"Mommy says there is no one like me in the whole world either," said Ricky smiling. "And there's nobody like you. God made us special too," he added. Erika thought about what Ricky had said and smiled to herself.

"Maybe my nose isn't as bad as I thought," she said to herself.

BRE

HOW ABOUT YOU?

Are you happy with the way you look? The Bible says that God made each of us special. He loves you. And he never makes mistakes. You're wonderful just like you are.

MEMORIZE:

"For we are God's masterpiece." *Ephesians 2:10*

 You Are God's Masterpiece

What's the Catch? (Read Romans 5:12, 17-21)

28

DECEMBER

"Oh, wow!" yelled Michael. "Look at the neat offer on this cereal box! A race car that's so big you can sit in it! Best of all, it's free!"

"Free?" asked Dad. "I doubt it!"

"It is!" insisted Michael. "It says so right here. Listen! 'Send for your life-sized race car absolutely free.' Can I do it, Dad? Can I?"

Dad picked up the box and read the instructions to himself. "It may be free—but there's a catch. You need $2.50 for postage and handling," he said.

"That's still a great price, Dad," said Michael. "Two-fifty for a race car is terrific! Wait until my friends see it."

"I still don't like the idea," said Dad, "but if you use your own money, I'll let you send for it. I may be wrong, but I think there's a lesson here for you."

Excitedly, Michael filled out the form and sent the money on its way. Then he waited eagerly for the mail each day. Finally, a package arrived for him. It was surprisingly small for a race car. He read the instructions and wrestled with the pieces of cardboard, trying to get the car together.

When everything was finally in place, Michael didn't know whether to laugh or cry. "If this is life-sized, it must be for a two-year-old!" he told his dad. Cautiously he sat down, and with one *kerplop*, the car collapsed. Michael sighed. "So much for the race car," he said. "You were right, Dad. There was a catch."

"There often is," said Dad. "I can think of an exception, though. The Lord offers us the gift of salvation without any catches. He loves us so much, he gives it to us outright—really free."

"Yeah," said Michael thoughtfully, "and God's gift of salvation will never disappoint us either, will it, Dad?" *LMW*

HOW ABOUT YOU?

Have you ever been disappointed by an offer that sounded super? That will never happen when you're dealing with God. He offers you a gift so valuable that a price tag could not even be placed on it. It is eternal life through a personal relationship with Jesus Christ.

MEMORIZE:

"For the wages of sin is death, but the free gift of God is eternal life through Christ Jesus our Lord." *Romans 6:23*

 Salvation Is a Free Gift

Glasses and Goblets (Read 2 Timothy 2:19-22)

"Mom, I told Mrs. Adams I'd help in the nursery Christmas Sunday, but I really don't want to. I want to wear my new dress and be in church," Kristy complained.

"I know, but I'm pleased that you agreed to help," said Mom as she turned from the kitchen counter toward her daughter. In her hand she held a beautiful, long-stemmed, crystal goblet. "Isn't this lovely?" she said as she set it on the table with some other pieces of crystal. They sparkled in the sunlight. They were antique pieces that had once belonged to Kristy's great-grand-mother.

29

DECEMBER

"Wow! They look like they're made of diamonds!" Kristy exclaimed. "I wish we could use them at every meal instead of just on holidays."

Mom smiled. "If we did that, they'd soon be broken," she said, touching them gently. She placed the fragile objects in a cabinet, closing the glass doors. "C'mon, honey," she said. "Let's have lunch."

While her mother made sandwiches, Kristy filled two glasses with milk. She took a big swallow from one and then poured it full again. "I guess I like these glasses best after all," she said with a smile. "At least I don't worry about chipping an edge or breaking a stem."

Mom set a plate of sandwiches on the table. "You know, the Bible compares us to different kinds of containers," she said. "We use fine goblets for company so everyone can see them, and plain glasses when no one else is around. But we can be like the beautiful goblets even when we're serving in a place where no one will see us. Second Timothy says that if we keep our life clean and pure, God can use us for his purpose." Mom smiled at Kristy.

Kristy laughed. She knew what her mom was saying. "OK, OK," she said. "I'll do my best to be a 'goblet' in the nursery even though I feel like a 'water glass.'" *PIK*

HOW ABOUT YOU?

Are you willing to do work that isn't always to your liking? Do you walk away or pretend you don't hear when you're asked to help in "ordinary" jobs? Jesus spent his life doing good whenever he could. Follow his example.

MEMORIZE:

"And if you give even a cup of cold water to one of the least of my followers, you will surely be rewarded." *Matthew 10:42*

 Be Willing to Serve

Uprooted (Read Ecclesiastes 3:1-8)

30

Unopened boxes were stacked against the wall in Jesse's room. He sighed and turned away from the one he was unpacking. "Tired of opening boxes?" his mother asked, stepping back from the picture she'd just hung up.

"No, it's just that I wish we hadn't moved," said Jesse glumly.

Mom put down the hammer. "This is a tough time for you, isn't it?" she said.

"Yeah, I don't know anyone here. I'm a stranger at school and at church and everywhere," said Jesse.

Mother lifted a plant down from a shelf. "Look at this," she said. The leaves of the plant were droopy.

"That plant doesn't look very happy, either," mumbled Jesse.

"It isn't," said Mom. "It's an African violet, and I repotted it two days ago. It needs to send its roots into the new dirt to get the nourishment it needs to survive. Right now, it's in a state of shock. But it has me to take care of it," said Mom, smiling. "It will soon begin to take root in the new dirt."

"Are you saying that I just need more time too?" asked Jesse.

"I'm trying to say that making a new start is difficult. But also that you have someone looking after you," said Mom. "Jesus can give you the courage and strength you need to get used to new places and to get to know new people."

"I guess I'm still in the shock stage," said Jesse. He stood up and stretched. "Think I'll take the dog out for a run."

As they walked, Bailey's long velvety ears flapped with every step. He seemed as happy to be outdoors as Jesse was. At a corner a boy about Jesse's age was waiting for the traffic light to turn. "Hi," said Jesse. "Is there a park around here?"

"Just a couple of blocks away. I'll show you," answered the boy.

Hmmm, thought Jesse. *Perhaps this will turn into a friendship.*

CLK

HOW ABOUT YOU?

How do you feel when you find yourself in a new school, sports club, church, or neighborhood? Do you sometimes feel like not even trying to get to know the new people around you? You may have to ask the Lord to give you the courage to be friendly. Ask him to help you adjust to your new surroundings.

MEMORIZE:

"God has made everything beautiful for its own time."

Ecclesiastes 3:11

 God Helps in Times of Change

Added Inches (Read 1 Peter 2:1-5)

31
DECEMBER

"Mark, you're growing like a weed!" Mark's mother said as she stood with tape measure in hand. She was checking to see how much Mark had grown in six months. "Almost two inches," she announced.

"Mom, what makes kids grow?" Mark wanted to know.

Mom smiled. "I don't know exactly," she answered. "Scientists can measure growth, and they can slow it down or help speed it up sometimes. They know that a good diet and proper exercise and rest help you grow properly But I'm not sure they can fully explain what makes you grow. Of course, we know that it's really God who gives life and has made our bodies so that they will grow."

"I wish I were as tall as Dad," said Mark.

"Someday you may be," said Mother with a smile. "Often children grow as tall or taller than their parents. But no matter how often you wish, or how hard you try, you can't do anything about it. In fact, the Bible says that we can't add an inch to our height by our own efforts."

"Billy says he hangs by his hands from a bar every day, hoping he'll get taller," said Mark.

"Well, all he'll get is sore arms for that," commented Mother. "There is one kind of growth you can do something about, though."

"There is?" asked Mark eagerly. "What is it?"

"It's your spiritual growth. Just as you eat food to help you grow physically, so you need to 'feed' on the Word of God to grow spiritually," explained Mother. "In 1 Peter 2:2 we are told that we should 'crave pure spiritual milk.' We can grow as we obey and use God's Word in our life." *CV*

HOW ABOUT YOU?

Are you a growing Christian? Do you love Jesus more now than you did a year ago? When God speaks through his Word, accept it and obey it. He will use it to help you grow spiritually! Make the new year one in which you will grow strong in Jesus.

MEMORIZE:

"You must crave pure spiritual milk so that you can grow into the fullness of your salvation."

1 Peter 2:2

 Grow Spiritually

Index of Topics

Index of Scripture Readings

Index of Memory Verses